Panchayati Raj Experience in India

Panchayati Raj Experience in India

Professor (Dr) K. Raman Pillai
Dr R. K. Suresh Kumar
Dr P. Sukumaran Nair

KALPAZ

ISBN: 978-93-5128-191-7

Price: ₹ 1125

First Published, 2016

Published by

Kalpaz Publications
C-30, Satyawati Nagar,
Delhi – 110052
E-mail: kalpaz@hotmail.com
Ph.: 9212142040

Printed at: G. Print Process, Delhi

Cataloging in Publication Data—DK
Courtesy: D.K. Agencies (P) Ltd. <docinfo@dkagencies.com>

Panchayati raj experience in India / [editors], Prof. (Dr) K. Raman Pillai, Dr R.K. Suresh Kumar, Dr P. Sukumaran Nair.
pages cm
Contributed articles.
ISBN 9789351281917

1. Panchayat—India. 2. Panchayat—India—Kerala. 3. Decentralization in government—India. 4. Decentralization in government—India—Kerala. I. Pillai, K. Raman (Kesavakurup Raman), 1929- editor. II. Suresh Kumar, 1957- editor. III. Sukumaran Nair, P., 1955- editor.

JS7009.P36 2016 DDC 320.840954 23

Contents

List of Contributors

Professor (Dr) N.R. Madhava Menon - Former Director, National Judicial Academy, Bhopal, Member, Advisory Committee, National Mission on Justice Delivery and Legal Reforms, Government of India, New Delhi.

Shri.V. Ramachandran IAS (Retd) - Former Chief Secretary, Kerala.

Professor (Dr) M.A. Oommen - Emeritus Professor of Economics, Formerly Professor of Economics, John Mathai Centre, University of Calicut, Kerala.

Professor (Dr) K.P. Kannan - Former Director, Centre for Development Studies, Thiruvananthapuram, Kerala.

Shri. S.M.Vijayanand IAS - Former Secretary, Local Self Government Department, Government of Kerala.

Dr M. Kuttappan - Member, Kerala State Statistical Commission and Former Director, Dept. of Economics and Statistics, Government of Kerala.

Professor (Dr) P. Suresh Kumar - Former Head, Dept. of Economics, Govt. College, Attingal, Thiruvananthapuram, Kerala.

Advocate, Kollam

Dr P.P. Rajasekharan Pillai - Former, Head, Department of Economics, N.S.S.College, Pandalam, Kerala.

Dr P. Rajendran Nair - Principal, University Institute of Technology, Mavelikkara, Alappuzha Dist.

Dr N. Madhava Menon - Associate Professor of Economics, N.S.S. College, Cherthala, Kerala

Professor (Dr) B.S. Bhargava - Senior Fellow, Institute for Social and Economic Change, Nagarbhavi, Bangalore.

Professor (Dr) Midatala Rani - Professor of Political Science, Department of Studies in Social Science, University of Mysore, Karnataka.

Professor (Dr) G. Palanithurai - Chairman, Rajiv Gandhi Chair for Panchayat Raj Studies, Gandhi Gram Rural University, Madurai.

Professor (Dr) M.A. Hussain - Former Professor, Dept. of Political Science, S.V. University, Tirupati (AP).

Professor A.R. Reddy - Professor, Dept. of Political Science, S.V. University, Tirupati (AP).

Dr P. Krishna Kumar - Former Head, Dept. of Economics, Mahatma Gandhi College, Thiruvananthapuram. Now working Monitoring and Evaluation specialist, Kerala Local Government Service Delivery Project in a World Bank Aided Project.

Dr Manjula Bharathy - Associate Professor, Tata Institute of Social Science, Mumbai.

Dr R. Sreekantan Nair - Head, Dept. of Political Science, VT NSS College, Dhanuvachapuram.

Ashitha - Research Scholar, Mahatma Gandhi University, Kottayam.

Dr S.S. Sreekumar - Associate Professor and Head, Dept. of Political Science, JNRM College, Port Blair, Andaman.

Dr T. Rajan - Head, Dept. of Political Science, University College, Thiruvananthapuram, Kerala.

Acknowledgement

We are grateful to all the contributors for their scholarly articles. Thanks are also due to the Executive Committe and Staff of the C.Achutha Menon Foundation for their support in bringing out this volume. We are indebted to N.Shanmughom Pillai, Secretary, C.Achutha Menon Foundation for his unfailing interest in publishing this book. Sincere thanks are also due to Ms.Bindu.N, for typing the manuscript. We are grateful to our publisher, Gyan Publishing House, New Delhi for publishing the book in stipulated time.

K. Raman Pillai
R.K. Suresh Kumar
P. Sukumaran Nair

Introduction

Independence must begin at the bottom. Thus every village will be a Republic or Panchayat having full powers. It follows therefore that every village has to be self-sustained and capable of managing its own affairs.

—Mahatma Gandhi

A cursory glance through the history of local bodies in India which dates back to the resolution of Lord Rippon in 1882 will show that decentralisation of power was paid only lip service. Contrary to the concept of democratic decentralisation, the process of bureaucratisation, politicisation, criminalisation and casteism has been strengthened in rural India. The system of Panchayati Raj has failed to realise the dreams of its architects.

The genesis of rural local self-government institutions is linked with the launching of the Community Development and National Extension Service Programmes immediately after the initiation of planned economic development in India. These programmes were viewed basically as "people's programmes with government participation." However, people's participation was not forthcoming in them.

Ultimately, the National Development Council (NDC) constituted a committee on plan projects under the chairmanship of Balwantrai Mehta and its report was submitted in 1957 with the main suggestion of instituting Democratic Decentralisation in rural areas with the help of a three-tier system – the village panchayat as the basic grassroots institution, panchayat samiti at the block level and zilla parishad at the District level.

However, all these years since 1957, the Panchayati Raj institutions remained moribund except in a few states like Gujarat, Maharashtra, West Bengal and Karnataka. The inertness and inertia afflicting them became so pervasive that the grassroots institutions came to be known as "grass without a root." Interestingly enough, another committee known as Ashok Mehta Committee looked into the functioning of democratic decentralisation. It calls the period of 1959 to 1964 as the period when the grassroots institutions took root, the period from 1964-69 as one of corrosion of those institutions and the period 1969-73 as the period of non-performance. The committee found that it suffered a serious set-back in the absence of regular elections and due to perfunctory audit. What is more, there has been an allergy to sharing authority with those nascent institutions both at official and political levels. Therefore, it was suggested that the PRIs should be reconstructed, reinforced and revitalised as an organic integral part of our democratic process and that they should be accorded appropriate constitutional status and recognition. The committee also said that the dynamics of development require that a high level of technical expertise be made available at the district level, where planning of a more comprehensive and sophisticated kind can be undertaken, and concomitant administrative functions can be discharged more fruitfully. Recommendations along the same lines were made by the G.V.K. Rao Committee in 1985 and the L.M. Singhvi Committee in 1987, as also the Chief Minister's conference on Panchayats held in May 1989.

The committee under the chairmanship of L.M. Singhvi formed in 1987 reviewed the functioning of PRIs in order to suggest measures for their revitalisation. The committee recommended reorganisation of villages to make village Panchayats more viable. It suggested that they should have more financial resources. The committee wanted to vest Panchayati Raj with a constitutional status, saying that a separate chapter should be added in the constitution so as to make the identity and integrity of PRIs reasonably and substantially inviolate.

In 1989, Rajiv Gandhi took up the cause of democratic decentralisation in right earnest and proposed to provide constitutional status to local bodies with the object of securing for them continued existence, coupled with the empowerment of the weaker sections of the rural society as well as women. The provision of finances to the local bodies was proposed to be taken out of the absolute discretion of the state governments by the appointment of a state level Finance Commission.

The union government introduced in Parliament on September 16, 1991 a Bill to amend the constitution. Ultimately Parliament approved the 73rd Amendment to the constitution along with the Nagarpalika 74th Amendment Bill. The constitution (73rd Amendment) Act of 1992 added a new part relating to Panchayats in the constitution under Articile 243 to provide for the following among other things.

1. A Gram Sabha in a village or group of villages.
2. Direct elections to all seats in Panchayats at the village and intermediate level.
3. Reservation of seats for Scheduled Castes and Scheduled Tribes in proportion to their population for membership and office of chairpersons.
4. Reservation of not less than one-third of the seats for women.

5. Fixing a term of five years for Panchayats and holding elections within a period of six months in the event of supersession of any panchayats.
6. Devolution of powers and responsibilities, by the state legislature upon the Panchayats with respect to the preparation of plans for economic development and social justice, as also for the implementation of development schemes and
7. Setting up of a Finance Commission within one year of the Amendment and thereafter every five years to review the financial position of panchayats and powers of state legislature to make provisions with respect to election to Panchayats under the supervision, direction and control of the chief electoral officer of the state.

The amendment came into force on April 24, 1993. All the states were required to legislate afresh or amend their existing Panchayat laws to bring them in conformity with the provisions of the constitutional Amendment within a year.

The lack of enthusiasm on the part of the state governments including those run by the Congress in implementing the law is evident from the fact that some of them adopted the Panchayat law on the last day prescribed viz 23rd April 1994, that too under persuation and mild threats. The statutory requirement that elections to Panchayats have to be conducted within six months of the legislation coming into effect was also ignored by several of the states under some pretext or other. The union government directed the erring states to conduct elections latest by February 1995. Warnings were issued to nine of the states under Article 257 of the constitution with a threat of withholding of grant. States like Gujarat, Bihar, Andhra Pradesh and Karnataka have cited Assembly elections as an excuse, while Kerala and Tamil Nadu have ignored the warning.

The assumption was that democratic decentralisation can minimise corruption and ensure transparency. Besides it can accelerate the process of development and ensure peoples' participation at the grass roots level. Potentialities of thousands of unemployed men and women in villages can be harnessed for socially useful projects. If they can be mobilised and put to work by way of developing agriculture, fisheries, social forestry that would give reasonable dividends by way of creating assets for the country and solve to some extent the problem of lack of resources. Assistance of NGOs can also be mobilised.

It is notable that the PRIs are the primary institutions of democracy where people from village, block and district can participate. The PRIs especially the 'Gram Sabhas' make the concept of direct democracy like that of the Greek city-states. The Gram Sabha has been designed to be the place where development issues should be discussed, development programmes initiated and beneficiaries of the development schemes selected.

It can be observed that the democratisation of our pluralist society cannot be ensured merely through legislative and administrative actions of the states. The enabling provision will require massive mobilisational support and more governmental organisations, academies and professional bodies, political parties and other groups should involve themselves in exerting pressure to restore power to the place where it belongs. Above all, the PRIs elected representatives should also be trained in rising over their electoral rivalry and work together for the welfare of the people.

Unless there is a strong political will to back the decentralisation process at the grassroots level and unless a certain degree of financial autonomy is guaranteed to village panchayats, no development worth the name can take place in the Panchayati Raj institutions.

Panchayat legislation adopted in different states confer wide powers on the state bureaucracy. These processes conferred through statutory rules makes it clear that it is neither the state level politicians nor the panchayats but the bureaucracy which gains the upper hand in the scheme of democratic decentralisation. Consequently, decentralisation as a measure of debureaucratisation has utterly failed in the present set up.

Do we seriously believe in democratic decentralisation or is it a mere paper exercise? It can be said that if the problems both at macro and micro levels are not solved; if 'vested interests' and 'power brokers' are not knocked out of the system; if a half-hearted, uncooked and unplanned exercise is not abandoned; if the financial autonomy conferred with accountability is not improved, we may land up in a difficult situation. If the policy of the government in giving impetus to the Panchayati Raj movement is implemented faithfully and fully it will surely bring about the political, social and economic revolution which will not only strengthen the democratic character of our society, but will also provide a perennial source of throwing up energetic leadership which may change the entire face of the country and guide the destinies of the people most efficiently and effectively.

It is more than fifteen years since the PRIs have come to stay in India. Time has come to take stock of the experiences gained so far in the working of the PRIs in various states. Have we really achieved the goals set up by the 73rd Constitutional Amendment while implementing the programme of 'democratic decentralisation'? If not, what are the impediments in achieving the goals? How best can we remove them based on our experience during the last fifteen years? What corrective steps can we take to put the programme on the right track? Accordingly, we requested leading experts on Panchayati Raj in various states to contribute articles highlighting the achievements and failures in the working of the PRIs during the past fifteen years. They were also requested to make concrete suggestions for making the PRIs vibrant institutions for bringing about democratic decentralisation in the true-sense of the term. The response to our appeal was highly rewarding. We have received a number of scholarly papers on the 'state of art' of the PRIs in different states in India. The articles broadly bring out the fascinating story of the working of PRIs in different states of India. We thought it most appropriate to publish a book compiling the scholarly articles for the benefit of planners, administrators and general public and hence this book. Those who have contributed articles include Professor (Dr) N.R.Madhava Menon, Shri.V. Ramachandran IAS (Retd), Professor (Dr) M. A. Oommen, Professor (Dr) K. P. Kannan, Shri. S. M.Vijayanand IAS, Dr M. Kuttappan, Dr P. Suresh Kumar, Professor P. P. Rajasekharan Pillai, Dr P. Rajendran Nair and Dr N. Madhava Menon, Professor (Dr) B. S. Bhargava, Professor (Dr) Midatala Rani, Professor (Dr) G. Palanithurai, Professor (Dr) M. A. Hussain and Dr A. R. Reddy, Dr P. Krishna Kumar, Dr Manjula Bharathi, Dr R. Sreekantan Nair and Smt. Ashitha, Dr S. S. Sreekumar and Dr T. Rajan. We profusely thank them for their valuable articles.

Editors
—Thiruvananthapuram

1

Inter-Governmental Relations and Constitutional Governance

—*N.R. Madhava Menon*

India is variously described as a soft State, a country with more of government and less of governance and a place having more and more laws but less and less justice. Of late, it is said that India is on the path of becoming a "failed State" because of a variety of governance issues which it is unable to resolve under existing structures and procedures. Assuming there is an element of truth in these views, one has also to acknowledge the fact that India is a fast growing economic giant, a functioning democracy under rule of law and a country with a demographic advantage, the potential of which is yet to be assessed in the knowledge society of tomorrow. If the systems of governance can be galvanised to let them function in synergy under the constitutional scheme, we would be able to achieve the constitutional promise set out in the Preamble in the very near future. It is in this context we need to have a fresh look at inter-governmental relations, not only between the Union and the States but also between the States on the one hand and the panchayats and municipalities on the other.

Centralisation is Changing Due to Political Compulsions and Globalisation

Whether one looks at legislative powers or administrative authority or taxation and economic powers, the Indian Constitution is biased in favour of the Centre and over the years it has tended to increase in favour of the Central Government through the centralised planning, use of emergency powers by the Centre and long period of single party rule in Union and States. The rise of regional parties in States and national parties being compelled to have coalition with them at the Centre have changed equations and sought a different balance of power. Markets, technology and civil society involvement in governance further raised different set of problems to be addressed in the changing scenario of public administration.

Though Constitution assigned economic and social planning as a subject in the Concurrent List, no institutional mechanism was provided for in the Constitution itself. By an Executive Order the Planning Commission was set up in 1950 with Prime Minister himself as the Chairman. There is no representation for the States. The National Development Council set up again by an executive order in 1952 with membership of all Chief Ministers came to discuss and approve the Five Year Plans delineating investment parameters. The States thus get participation in the national planning process and have a say in allocation of resources in development programmes. However, because of the short time available for the meetings, interaction on plan items are more of a formality than real consensus. Therefore, there is dissatisfaction among States particularly because of the large funds commanded by the Planning Commission which is far greater than what States get through the Finance Commission.

Another contentious issue on financial relations is about Centrally Sponsored Schemes which are projects initiated by Union Ministries to be implemented by States for which Central Government allocates funds. These are formulated with or without conditionalities such as contribution from states. If states opt out of these schemes they lose central funds. If they adopt them, then substantial state funds are to be assigned to these schemes which leave little flexibility in state budgets. The states complain that these schemes are formulated without adequate consultation with the result the priorities based on local conditions get distorted. Furthermore, because of increase in the number of Centrally Sponsored Schemes, the powers on subjects in the States' exclusive domain get curtailed which is considered an unjust interference of the Centre on the States.

Coalition politics have impacted the system of resource transfers complicating the process still further. The importance of the principle of equal and equitable distribution of resources in a federal system is strained as a result. With states lobbying for special funds coupled with pressure from coalition partners, the scheme of devolution of funds has become contentious which the Finance Commission has been addressing every five years.

Implementation of nationally significant mega projects across states has been a thorny issue which strained Centre-State-local body relations on many fronts. Of late, maintenance of internal security which is supposed to be entirely a State subject has thrown up difficulties which threaten national security as well. The constitutional promise of establishing a unified and integrated domestic market is an unfinished dream affecting the development of the country as well as possible trade advantages in the global market. Finally, the goal of decentralised governance through panchayat raj institutions attempted through Constitutional Amendments fifteen years ago is not being realised because of the reluctance of States to devolve functions and finances to the local bodies. It was these stalemates in constitutional governance which persuaded the first UPA Government at the Centre to appoint a Commission on Centre-State Relations in 2007. The seven volume report of the Commission was recently submitted to the government which contain many recommendations on re-structuring legislative, administrative and financial relations in such a manner so as to advance sustainable development, good governance and better quality of life to the people.

Re-organising Centre-State Relations for Better Governance

(i) Need to increase institutional mechanisms for inter-governmental consultation

In any scheme of division of powers, there could be conflicts around the division if there is ambiguity or overlapping. It is possible that while exercising functions assigned to one's own domain, it might impinge on the responsibilities of others leading to conflicts. Or power may gravitate to one or other partner due to various developments upsetting the original balance conceived by the Constitution. When these things happen tension develops in relations often leading to conflicts and sometimes paralysis in governance.

In a federal polity consultation and consensus building through transparent and participatory processes are key to better implementation. There is need for more institutional mechanisms to accomplish this goal. Given the joint yet separate responsibility on matters in the Concurrent List it is imperative to have continuing consultations on organised basis through the Inter-State Council and outside for better development and implementation of policies. The Inter-State Council should be made a vibrant mechanism for Centre-State co-ordination and dispute resolution. Art. 263(a) should be fully implemented to build its capacity. It is to be staffed with technical personnel drawn from states and given authority to function independently.

(ii) Treaty making to be more participatory

Entering into treaties and agreements with foreign countries is part of the function of the Union Executive (Entry 14 of List I). Parliament has power to make law for implementing treaty obligations (Art. 253). This is not withstanding the division of powers between Centre and States. Some treaties on defence and foreign relations have no direct impact on State's powers. Others which directly impinge on State subjects, State involvement is desirable. Initially, the concerned Union Ministry may prepare a note and seek the views of States. Further, if implementation of treaty obligations affect financial capacity of States, the Centre should underwrite additional liability of States according to a negotiated formula. Furthermore, all such cases should be a permanent term of reference to the Finance Commission for recommending compensatory formulae to neutralise additional financial burden of States arising out of treaties and international agreements.

(iii) **Centre to have more active role in internal security**

Given the obligation of the Union to protect States from external aggression and internal disturbance (Art. 355), when security situation worsens Union intervention in States is a constitutional necessity. Union can advise the State, augment state efforts, deploy Union forces and, if required, take over the state administration (Art. 352 to 356). It is possible to avoid the extreme step under Art. 356 by interpreting the provisions in such a way as to read into them what may be called "localised emergency" (Art. 355 read with Entry 2A of List I and Entry I of List II). However, to keep such intervention within constitutional limits and to achieve administrative co-ordination, it is desirable to have a Parliamentary statute on the model of the Disaster Management Act or the Prevention of Communal Violence and Rehabilitation Bill, 2006.

(iv) **Rajya Sabha to be true custodian of State's interests at Centre**

Rajya Sabha in a federal set up can function as the agent of the States in the Central legislature monitoring, co-ordinating and influencing policy developments, resource allocation and effective governance. Unfortunately it is not structured to assume that role. Rajya Sabha should provide equal representation for all States and should protect States' rights in Centre. Whenever Central policies are formulated which affect States' rights, they must be discussed in an empowered committee of Rajya Sabha which must come out with acceptable solutions for adoption in law making.

(v) **On Centre-State fiscal relations a lot of changes are necessary**

Firstly, there is need to minimise discretionary transfers, particularly those channelled through centrally-sponsored schemes. Where State Courts funded by States are implementing a large number of Central laws, the Centre is not meeting the costs of maintaining State Courts. As such Centre should underwrite part of the budget of subordinate judiciary.

The experience of the empowered committee of State Finance Ministers in evolving the VAT and GST schemes is an excellent initiative in evolving harmonious fiscal relations between Centre and States. This should be institutionalised and extended to other areas affecting the States.

There is an immediate need to set up an Inter-State Trade and Commerce Commission as envisaged under Article 307 read with Entry 42 of List I. As a constitutional body its decisions should be final binding both the Centre and States with a provision for appeal to the Supreme Court. It is essential for the economic integration of the country and to make Indian economy globally competitive.

(vi) Local self-government and decentralised governance cannot be delayed anymore

The three-tier panchayat structure need to be simplified by a two-tier structure by abolition of the intermediate level panchayats. By 2015 all the constitutionally stipulated functions should be devolved for which if necessary a separate commission be set up involving state representatives. For resolving disputes or smoothening relations a body comparable to the Inter-State Council needs to be set up at the State level.

(vii) Natural resources management and infrastructure development should receive specialised attention

Environment, ecology and climate change are too big and complex subjects affecting the livelihood of common people to be left to the bureaucrats and politicians. They require collective effort of experts from many fields and the government should set up appropriate agencies to make co-ordinated efforts to manage natural resources for public good. A national policy to compensate forest-rich and mineral bearing states should be evolved through consultation and consensus.

As land is becoming scarce, states should try to identify in advance lands which could be made available for infrastructure development. All such identified lands can be pooled together and offered to prospective project developers for infrastructure development. The creation of such land pools would significantly reduce the cost of acquisition and also lead to faster implementation of the projects.

(viii) Citizen involvement in policy-making and delivery of public services

It is imperative that more and more avenues of involvement of people and NGOs in policy-making are developed at all levels of government. The National Advisory Council is a welcome development. Similar bodies at the State and local levels outside political parties will inject greater social relevance and acceptance in public policy matters. Article 350 provides a window for citizens petitioning the government on policies as well.

Similarly there is need for social audit of government functioning particularly in respect of implementation of Directive Principles of State Policy which are declared fundamental in governance. There is no oversight mechanisms in this regard outside Parliament and State Assemblies. An example is provided under the Mahatma Gandhi Rural Employment Guarantee Act for social audit of implementation. We need more of it across social and economic sectors to promote good governance. For this government itself should develop measurement parameters through a National Standards Organisation for the social sector on the lines of the Bureau of Indian Standards.

Pubic-private partnership is good not only in economy but also in other sectors of governance. Private sector participation can help in introducing innovative ideas, technological upgradation and generation of additional resources and good corporate management practices in the delivery of public services. All these may lead to greater efficiency and accountability to users.

Obviously a system of multi-level government operations under a federal democratic framework cannot deliver good governance unless there is continuing interaction between the various levels of government. The Constitution has provided a good framework for the same. Unfortunately, corruption and politics based on narrow loyalties and sectoral identities have fragmented the polity and weakened the government's capacity to fulfil the constitutional obligations. What is required is a realisation of the complimentality of constitutional institutions and better co-ordination across parties and governments if economic growth is to be sustained for welfare of all sections of people in the country.

2

Decentralisation in Kerala: Opportunities and Challenges

—V. Ramachandran

The attempts at decentralisation in Kerala prior to 1988 were described in my "Report of the measures to be taken for Democratic Decentralisation at the District and Lower Levels." The formation of District Councils as recommended in that Report, for a short period in 1990-91, and the efforts at decentralisation since the Constitution 73rd and 74th Amendments in 1992 have been covered extensively in several reports and papers. There is no need to repeat them in any form. What is needed is to look ahead at the opportunities and challenges facing decentralisation in Kerala in the coming years and to examine how the objective of the Constitution in Art. 243 G (regarding Panchayats) and Art. 243 W (regarding urban local bodies) - that the legislature of the State may endow such powers and authority as may be necessary to enable them to function as **institutions of self-government** - can be achieved atleast by the year 2017. That year will mark the completion of twenty five years since constitutional status was given to local governments.

Kerala has taken many steps towards decentralisation since 1994 and has been ranked first among the States for several years now. These initial steps provide a great opportunity but there are major challenges facing further progress.

In 2002, on completion of ten years of the relevant constitutional amendments, Sri S.M. Vijayanand and myself had prepared a 'Plan of Action' consisting of "Dos and Don'ts" for the Government of India, State Governments, donors and local governments. That Plan of Action was widely circulated by the Government of India, but there has been very limited progress in the country as a whole. The subject is so vast that it cannot be dealt with adequately in an article. Some of the most important points alone are briefly dealt with here.

Decentralisation is generally discussed as State Government – Local Government relations. The role of the Government of India is equally vital for decentralisation. There are several reasons for this. Firstly, the fundamental principle of decentralisation is 'subsidiarity' – that a matter should be dealt with at as low a level at which it can be attended to efficiently. There is also the constitutional division of responsibility between the Union and the States. It is the view of some States and those of left or regional parties in particular, that the principle of 'subsidiarity' should be applied not only within a State but also between the Centre and the States, and that the role of States has been whittled down considerably since liberalisation in early 1990s. Hence, their demand has been to revisit the relations. This has been done by the second Centre-State Relations Commission (2005-10), but its Reports have not yet been published or acted upon. Whatever be the decisions regarding this, the issue will continue to cast its shadow on devolution of powers and functions from the State to local levels in Kerala. One already hears such voices.

Secondly, in the interests of national minimum attainments and standards in human development, especially in the context of millennium goals, the Government of India have initiated a large number of centrally sponsored schemes in subject areas which fall within the domain of States and local governments. Some examples are the Mahatma Gandhi National Rural Employment Guarantee Scheme, Sampoorna Gramin Rojgar Yojana, Sarva Siksha Abhiyan, National Rural Health Mission, Integrated Child Development Services, Mid-Day Meal Programme, Drinking Water Mission, Total Sanitation Campaign, Indira Awas Yojana, Swarna Jayanti Gram Swarojgar Yojana, Pradhanmantri Gram Sadak Yojana, Rajiv Gandhi Grameen Vidyutikaran Yojana, Adult Literacy and the Remote Village Electrification Programme - in rural areas - and the Jawaharlal Nehru National Urban Renewal Mission for cities in addition to the programmes for small towns. Out of this long list, nine major programmes provide for nearly Rs 1,30,000 crore, during the year 2010-11. Since a large quantum of resources flows through these schemes to the States, efficient implementation of these programmes is critical. The schemes taken up under such programmes also need to find place in the overall development plan of the local body. It is, accordingly, essential that the centrality of local governments is recognised in fulfilling the objectives of these programmes. While some of the schemes do give a crucial role to the local governments in implementation, some bypass them and create separate structures. Even the schemes which allow participation, often do not give the local governments enough flexibility in decision making.

It appears that in a modern nation – State, that is large and has regions with widely different levels of development, the principle of 'subsidiarity' cannot be applied in an absolute sense. At the same time, an approach of 'one size fits all' is equally inappropriate. The challenge is to find a balance, by providing flexibility to lower levels.

The large allocation of funds for these schemes provides an opportunity for leveraging to empower the local governments. In due course, the present system of release of funds for CSSs should be substituted by a system where most of the transfer is in the form of untied grants, with the responsibility for State and local governments to achieve the stipulated outputs and outcomes.

As regards the State Government, as in most other fields, the challenge is that of second generation issues in the case of decentralisation also. As already stated considerable progress has been made in providing a quantum of untied funds (though it is going down as a percentage of the State Plan, since the content of the State Plan has changed) and in devolution of functions. The challenge lies in bringing about the institutional and personnel changes. The political will shown in going in for establishment of local governments, in the elections to them and for formal devolution (including amendments of subject matter laws) does not seem to extend to personnel issues. In Kerala, interest groups have always been able to stand in the way of larger objectives and this is the case in this matter also. There is excessive 'departmentalism' and functionaries belonging to departments are generally reluctant to work under or even with local governments. The societies and parastatal organisations that have been set up over the years and are still being set up, are reluctant to give up any of their roles. In my Report of 1988, I had observed that "the ship of decentralisation may well founder on the rock of service problems!" It was not a cynical prognosis, but was based on the then prevailing situation. It is unfortunate that departments and agencies, instead of going down in number, have proliferated. One or two agencies like the DRDA have been merged with the local government system, but the process has to go a long way. An opportunity lies here for the officers and other employees, whose conditions of service will in any case be protected, to demonstrate their spirit of public service and participate in the efficient functioning of local governments.

While the redeployment of staff to local governments has not been to the desirable extent - and not even as ordered by government from time to time - there has been reluctance to agree to enhance the staff strength of local governments - urban and rural. Since large amounts of funds are being channelled through them and the agency function of local governments has increased manifold, a major challenge has been to enhance their very weak organisational capacity. It is urgently necessary to break through the stale-mate, so that utilisation of funds will be much better than at present. The maintenance of accounts will also improve. While the weakness of organisational capacity is common to all local governments, it is particularly so in the case of municipal corporations (which are unable to take on major projects under JNNURM). A certain percentage of funds needs to be earmarked for improving organisational capacity.

Another important aspect is 'training'. It is a major challenge as the numbers involved are truly large. The elections to local governments are now on and it is expected that there will be 21682 elected representatives in all, of which 11209 will be women:

	Number	*Total No. of Members*	*Women Members*
Village Panchayats	978	16680	8631
Block Panchayats	152	2095	1107
District Panchayats	14	332	169
Municipal Corporations	5	359	181
Municipalities	60	2216	1121
Total	**1209**	**21682**	**11209**

Since this is the first election after reservation for women was increased to 50 per cent, the number of fresh entrants among women can be expected to be high. Kerala Institute of Local Administration (KILA), has been conducting a number of programmes in association with other Institutes to train elected and appointed functionaries or urban and rural local governments. But the challenge this time is much greater. Firstly, the number of 'freshers' will be large. Secondly, in addition to training in rules, projects and implementation, emphasis needs to be given to training in leadership qualities, conflict resolution and integrated local area development. Since the largest number of persons will be at the village panchayat level, innovative methods of in-situ training, using folk arts and drama, for example will have to be adopted. The State Government and KILA will have to work out a detailed plan of action within the next two months for a wide-ranging training programme.

For their part, the local governments - the Mayors, Presidents, Councillors and Members - have to strive hard to earn the confidence of the public. The sad fact is that at present there is no 'lobby' for local governments. Despite institutions like Ombudsman, one hears of growing corruption and partisan behaviour. The extent and quality of public participation, as for example, through Gram Sabhas, is very low. There is a perception that office in local government is viewed as one for exercise of power and not for rendering service for common good and that local governments behave like 'clones' of State Government. Instead of attempting convergence of schemes, filling up of gaps to ensure better public services and integrated planning of resources - financial, material and human - there is emphasis on member-wise schemes (especially works) and plans turn out to be a mere collection of isolated schemes. It is also pointed out by certain studies that since the availability of funds through national schemes has vastly increased, the incentive to raise own resources has gone down. There are always exceptions to these weaknesses, as seen from the participating local governments in Doordarshan's Green Kerala Express. Innovative programmes of local relevance, a non-partisan inclusive approach under proper leadership with emphasis on common good has been able to achieve commendable results, despite other constraints. Their experience shows the opportunities that are open. It is a challenge to other local governments.

3

Local Democracy in Kerala: Retrospects and Prospects

—*M.A. Oommen*

Local Democracy in India and Kerala: A Brief Narrative

It is useful to begin with a brief narrative of India's local democracy. In real democracy, supreme power vests in the people and is best exercised directly as in the case of old village panchayats in India or city states in Athens. As population expanded and organisation of governance became complex, practice of direct democracy was difficult and representative democracy became the ubiquitous pattern. But representative democracy can gain legitimacy only when social choices reflect the will of the people. This can be ensured only with the participation of the people in governance. Local democracy offers great opportunities for participation, and in facilitating a government of the people by the people for the people. Looking back, I have no hesitation in saying that the framers of the Indian Constitution committed a grave mistake in neglecting local democracy and wasted more than four decades to give it constitutional recognition. Long before Independence, Gandhi envisaged a decentralised polity based on governance by the village panchayat with tremendous autonomy. This was not something within a representative democracy, but based on a new way of organising human life. Of course, one can say that Gandhi was a visionary and his idealism difficult to be practised. Even so I think his concern for the helplessness of the poor individual in the context of a centralised power was a vital social value that ought to have been recognised in the constitution instead of borrowing its philosophical foundations and institutional models from the west. The concern for the people was shared by several of Gandhi's contemporaries like Rabindranath Tagore and M N Roy. Roy believed that a democratic society might emerge only if it were based on the foundations of a 'local republic' which could "combine all functions of the state as they affect the local life" [Roy (1960):72]. It appears somewhat strange that the Constitution makers neglected local democracy. Panchayat was accommodated in Article 40 under the Directive Principles of State Policy to "organise village panchayats and endow them with such power and authority as may be necessary to function as units of self-government." Evidently the founding fathers of the Constitution never entertained any lofty goals about the prospects of the 'units of self-government' because in item 5 in the state list of the Seventh Schedule of the Constitution, "local authorities for the purpose of local self-government" have been equated with 'Improvement Trust', mining settlement and so on. In the words of B D Ghosh:

> "Leave aside Gandhi who might be dismissed as an impractical visionary. But how can the framers of the Indian Constitution avoid the blame that they were reluctant to accept even those principles of local self-government that were enunciated in the Ripon Resolution dating back to 1882" [B D Ghosh (2000):13].

The move to recognize local democracy as a vital and viable component of Indian democracy was a slow and dialectical process, predicated upon two major committee reports viz., the Balwantrai Mehta Committee Report (1957), and the Asoka Mehta Committee Report (1978) besides several debates and state level experiments. As Partha Nath Mukherji puts it:

> "The period between the passing of the Indian Constitution by the Constituent Assembly in 1950 and *passing* of the Constitution (Seventy-third) Amendment Act has been marked by a tortuous dialectic in the form of contestations between the forces of participatory and parliamentary representative democracy" [Mukherji Partha Nath (2007):6].

The 73rd Amendment took off from Article 40, precisely because of the failure of the Government of India to create institutions of self-government at the village level and build a vibrant rural India. The Balwantrai Mehta Committee (1957) constituted to review community development projects and recommend systems of local self-government brought home the need for "democratic decentralisation" without radically altering the district administration arrangements of the British times. The function of the district administration was differentiated into regulatory and developmental with the district collector handling the former and a three tier panchayat institutions the latter. Under the Balwantrai Mehta model, the district panchayat was advisory; the intermediate level had developmental functions and the village panchayat with elected representatives had only limited civic functions. The years from 1959 to 1964 saw the creation of Panchayati Raj Institutions (PRIs) in several states with the Collector Raj remaining very much in the saddle. Balwantrai Mehta Committee model which enjoyed strong support from Jawaharlal Nehru fell into disrepute after his death in 1964. An era of centralisation followed which reached its peak with the emergency in 1975.

The Ashok Mehta Committee (1978) appointed by the Janata Dal Government gave a new lease of life to the process of decentralisation. It sought to "devolve" more planning and development functions to the Panchayati Raj Institutions (PRIs). The Ashok Mehta model welcomed elections to all tiers and gave more powers and responsibilities to the district tier. However, it kept the Collector Raj almost untouched. The dissenting note by E M S Namboodiripad, a member of the Committee and a known Marxist attracted considerable attention and debate. He argued for democratising the sub-state level governance. In his own words:

> "Democracy at the Central and State levels, but bureaucracy at all lower levels – this is the essence of Indian polity as spelt out in the Constitution" (Government of India (1978):160). It is clear from his note that EMS Namboodiripad was talking of a 'four-pillar democracy' comprising the centre, the states the district and the lower levels of administration which would remain decentralised.

The aftermath of this dissenting note as well as subsequent events stepped up the momentum of the decentralisation process. To begin with West Bengal, Karnataka, Andhra Pradesh and Kerala took measures for democratic decentralisation at the panchayat and municipal corporation levels. Rajeev Gandhi's initiatives for Constitutional Amendment in 1989 made democratic decentralisation a serious political agenda and the 73rd/74th Constitutional Amendments were but a natural consummation. The process of enacting conformity legislations was completed by April 24, 1994. Eighteen years have passed since then.

The fiscal significance of local governments (LGs) in a federal system may be measured by four parameters: (1) the share of local government expenditure to total public sector expenditure (the centre, states and local governments), (2) the share of LG expenditure to gross domestic product (GDP), (3) the share of local governments' own source revenue (OSR) to total public sector OSR and (4) the LG share of OSR to GDP. Table 1 attempts to capture the share of LGs with reference to public sector expenditure and OSR for six years from 2002-03 through 2007-08.

It is significant that the share of local governments' expenditure in the total public sector expenditure has increased almost steadily from 5.5 per cent in 2002-03 to 6.7 per cent in 2007-08. Equally important is the visible stepping up of the share of PRIs which increased from 2.5 per cent to 3.7 per cent during this period. Actually, the share of urban local governments (ULGs) stagnated around 3 per cent and even declined in some years. However, the LG share in public sector expenditure in India is small compared to the OECD countries where it broadly ranges from 20–35 per cent. Although as a share of GDP also, the LG share of expenditure demonstrates an increasing trend from 2.13 per cent in 2002-03 to 2.42 per cent in 2007-08, it falls way below the corresponding share of nearly 14 per cent of GDP for OECD countries and over 10.8 per cent for China during the same period.

Table 1: Trend in the percentage Share of LGs in the public sector expenditure, public sector OSR (2002-03 – 2007-08)

Items	*2002-03*	*2003-04*	*2004-05*	*2005-06*	*2006-07*	*2007-08*
			PRIs			
Share of Public Sector Expenditure	2.5	2.9	3.1	3.7	3.9	3.7
Share of Public Sector OSR	0.4	0.4	0.4	0.4	0.3	0.3
			ULGs			
Share of Public Sector Expenditure	3.0	2.2	2.5	2.7	2.8	3.0
Share of Public Sector OSR	3.2	3.1	2.9	2.9	2.7	2.5
			LGs			
Share of Public Sector Expenditure	5.5	5.1	5.6	6.4	6.7	6.7
Share of Public Sector OSR	3.6	3.5	3.3	3.3	3.0	2.8

Note: Calculations based on FC-XIII website data; Government of India, *Economic Survey* for relevant years and Reserve Bank of India, *State Finances: A study of Budgets* for relevant years [see Oommen (2010)].

This increasing trend of local governments' share in India has to be understood subject to two important qualifications: one is that this increase in many cases are due to the step up in agency functions such as the centrally-sponsored schemes and several state-sponsored programmes routed through PRIs and ULGs in recent years. Indeed this goes counter to the avowed mandate of the Constitution to create 'institutions of self-government' at the local level. A study of the FC-XIII data shows that the all-states' average of central transfers including that of eleventh and twelfth finance commissions to total revenue and total expenditure have increased during the six year period from 2002-03 through 2007-08. The percentage of central transfers to total LG expenditure goes as high as 31.1 per cent in 2007-08 while it was only 19.5 per cent in 2002-03. The magnitude and trend of the percentage of central transfers to expenditure shows a disturbing picture in 2007-08 for it was as high as 90.7 per cent for Bihar, 87 per cent for Assam, 71.6 per cent for Odisha, 51.81 per cent for Andhra Pradesh and so on. Actually it was only 24.7 per cent for Kerala. What autonomous space can you expect of a state like Bihar where nearly 91 per cent of the expenditure of rural local governments is met by transfers from central government.[1] The second is the poor level of the own revenue and its declining trend and in some cases even zero revenue collection. This indicates the fragile autonomous space of the LGs notably that of the PRIs. The share of local governments in the total public sector OSR has declined from 3.6 per cent in 2002-03 to 2.8 per cent in 2007-08 (See Table 1). Nearly 90 per cent of the OSR share is accounted for by the ULGs. The most striking aspect is the extremely poor own revenue share of the PRIs in the total own revenue base of the public sector. It declined from 0.4 per cent in 2002-03 to 0.3 per cent in 2007-08. That this works out only to a negligible percentage of 0.08 per cent of GDP in 2002-03 and a still lower number of 0.06 per cent in 2007-08 is surely not something to write home about. The declining own revenue and growing expenditure trend indicates a clear dependency syndrome. Figure 1 graphically illustrates this yawning gap, the y-axis represents both the expenditure and own source revenue (OSR) of LGs as percentage of public sector and the x-axis the six year period from 2002-03. While the expenditure share of local governments in the total public sector has improved, the share of own revenue has posted a decline signalling the narrowing of the autonomous space of these institutions. However, it is to be noted that the relative decline in the revenue share of the local governments

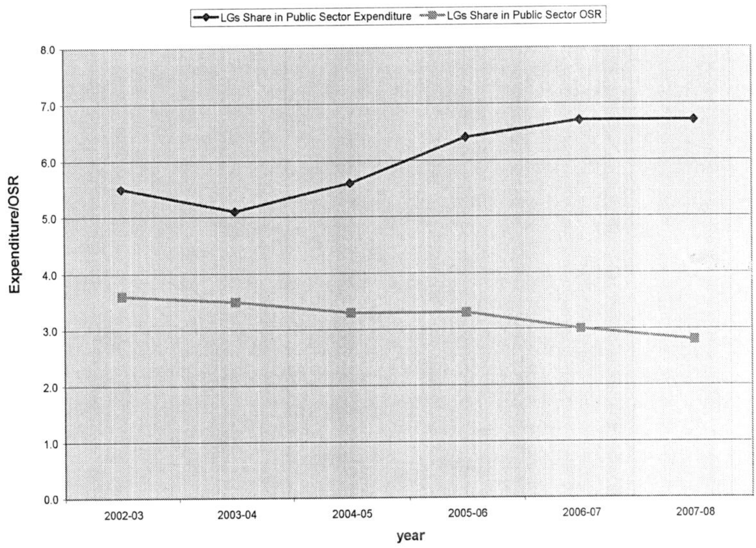

Figure 1. Trend in LGs' share of public sector expenditure and public sector OSR.

may also is the obverse of the very buoyant and faster growth of both central and state revenues in recent years *vis-à-vis* local revenues. The unfortunate part of the fiscal reform processes of the last two decades has been that they were concentrated only at central and state level.

The Kerala Story

The story of local democracy in Kerala during the pre-Independence period is not far different from the rest of India during the pre-Independence period. Kerala had an antiquity of village collectivities in which all people irrespective of caste or wealth differentiation assembled to make common decisions. But by the eighth century onwards village society came to be organised on firm caste basis with caste-based locations and habitats. The Brahmins or priestly class organised themselves into sectarian habitats (*bramhodayom*) with assemblies of their own (*Sabha*). Other castes also developed their own exclusive gatherings. They paved the way for a more stratified society. Subject to the overall discipline of caste hierarchy within each group there was some democratic governance although generally only the voice of the elders prevailed. The age-old traditions of Kerala significantly changed with the advent of the British rule in India.

The evolution of local bodies in the different parts of Kerala which comprise the princely states of Travancore, and Cochin as well as the Malabar district of the erstwhile British Indian province of Madras presidency came to be considerably influenced by Viceroy Lord Ripon's resolution of 1882, establishing local bodies called "little republics" in urban centres. Later it was extended to rural areas. Following the report of the Royal Commission on Decentralisation (1909) a two-tier system was introduced in Malabar- the Malabar District Board at the district level and panchayat board at the village level. The recommendations of the Royal Commission (1909) and the Government of India Act (1919) influenced the formation of Panchayat Acts in the princely states of Cochin and Travancore which considerably modified the traditional village system of these regions.

After the native state of Cochin came under British supremacy the Cochin Village Panchayat Act was enacted which divided the state into five taluks, with five government-nominated local prominent persons to take care of villages. Only those who paid Rs 50 or above as taxes, or government officials and retired officials and graduates alone could be members of the governing body of villages. Slowly powers of gram panchayats (GPs) increased and in 1919 panchayats were allowed to run Ayurvedic hospitals. It was too early in history to expect a more democratic base.

In 1925, a Village Panchayat Act was enacted in Travancore and seven panchayats were formed. The assigned functions (viz. construction, maintenance and improvement of wells and tanks, maintenance and improvement of communications and drains, primary education, lighting of public ways and places, improvement of minor irrigation works and public health and sanitation) and taxes (land cess, profession tax, vehicle tax etc) were way ahead of the times [For details see Velu Pillai T.K. (1940): p. 244]. The financial needs of panchayats were mostly met by a system of grants [G.K. Pillai (1986)]. A special feature of the 1925 Act was that it delegated certain judicial functions to the panchayats. [Government of Kerala (GoK) (1986):2].

In 1940, a new form of panchayats called Village Unions was constituted in several villages of Travancore in order to promote rural development. They however had the same functions as that of the early panchayats. The government gave a matching grant equal to the own collection of local revenue, subject to a maximum of Rs 1000 per panchayat. [G.K. Pillai (1986)]. After the formation of the Travancore-Cochin state in 1949 the term village union was changed to panchayat.

Although Travancore started with only five panchayats, by 1934, the number of panchayats rose to 87 covering the entire state. The major functions of the panchayats were construction and maintenance of minor irrigation works, village roads, control over vaccination and supervision of elementary education. There was no taxing powers and the primary source of income was the liberal grants from state government.

In the Malabar district, which was part of erstwhile Madras province before it was integrated with Travancore-Cochin, village panchayats were functioning under the Madras Village Panchayat Act, 1950, which came into force from 1st April 1951. Under this Act every village or hamlet with a population of 500 and above will have a panchayat. Villages with a population of less than 500 were made part of an adjoining panchayat or grouped with other contiguous villages and a single panchayat formed for the group. Panchayats having a population above 5000 and with income exceeding Rs 10,000 were classified under Class I and all the others under Class II. The duties and functions of the panchayats under this Act were almost similar to those contained in the Travancore Cochin Act 1950. The main sources of revenue of the panchayats were share of land cess and duty on transfer of property. Further, house tax, profession tax and vehicle tax were compulsorily levied. Under the Madras Act, panchayats were not eligible for any statutory grants. But government paid ex-gratia grant to panchayats. The entire Malabar area was not covered by panchayats. Such areas which were not covered by Panchayats were under the administrative jurisdiction of Malabar District Board. This District Board carried out all the statutory functions of panchayats in respect of the non-panchayat area. They derived their income from profession tax, entertainment tax, education cess, land cess, surcharge on stamp duty, license fees and grant-in-aid from government. The District Boards continued to exist even after the States reorganisation in 1956 till Kerala Panchayat Act, 1960 was brought into effect from 1st January 1962.

In 1956 when Malabar was integrated with Travancore-Cochin state to form the present day Kerala, there were 892 panchayats. Their major sources of revenue were land cess, building tax, profession tax, vehicle and entertainment tax. The history of panchayati raj system in Kerala from the first Kerala Ministry (1957) till date has been a chequered one and has been influenced by the ups and downs of coalition politics in the state.

Long before Namboodiripad made his historic dissenting note in 1978, the first Ministry of Kerala state appointed an Administrative Reform Committee with the Chief Minister (E.M.S. Namboodiripad) as chairperson to suggest measures for the democratisation of the organs of government at various levels. The Committee recommended the strengthening of panchayats in the state as viable and basic units of administration and development in the state. Following the recommendations of the Committee, the Kerala Panchayat Bill (1958) and the District Council Bill (1959) were placed in the state assembly. The functions of the district council designed to become an autonomous executive body envisaged mostly development matters. Certainly these legislations were way ahead of the times. The bills could not be enacted into law as the ministry was dismissed by the Central Government and the Assembly dissolved. The new government that was formed after the general elections, passed the Kerala Panchayat Act, 1960 incorporating several recommendations of the Balwantrai Mehta Study Team (1957). This came into force from January 1, 1962. The Act, besides unifying the laws existing in Malabar and the Travancore-Cochin state, sought to enlarge the functional domain and financial resources base of the panchayats. Despite the legal expansion of functions, for all practical purposes, the operational domain of village panchayat was confined to traditional civic functions only. Based on the new Kerala Panchayat Act the first panchayat election in Kerala state was held by the end of 1963 and the new panchayats came into existence on January 1, 1964. There were 922 village panchayats in the state on that date.

In 1964, the next government which came to power introduced the Kerala Panchayat Union Councils and Zilla Parishad Bill largely modelled on the recommendations of Balwantray Mehta Study Team (1957) and incorporating an intermediate tier at the block level to do planning and rural development called Union Council and an advisory council called Zilla Parishad at the district level. This bill proved to be an abortive effort as the Ministry fell and an era of President's rule followed. After a long spell of central administration, following a general election a new ministry was formed in 1967 with E.M.S. Namboodiripad as Chief Minister. A fresh bill called the Kerala Panchayat Bill, 1967, was introduced in the state legislature. This bill envisaged a two-tier system at the village and district levels. The Zilla Parishad was to have executive functions and some sources of revenue with powers of supervision and control over the gram panchayat. The bill was referred to a select committee which made drastic revisions. This too did not become law as the Legislative Assembly was dissolved in August 1970. But it was revived as Kerala District Administration Bill in 1971 by the Ministry under C. Achutha Menon. Actually due to a variety of reasons it was left to the next government under A.K. Antony to enact a slightly modified legislation called Kerala District Administration Act, 1979. This Act however was kept in cold storage for long due to several contradictions and problems in the law. The E.K. Nayanar Ministry that came to power in 1986 wanted to renew the process of decentralisation. They appointed a committee under the former Chief Secretary and Vice Chairman, State Planning Board, (V. Ramachandran) to study the defects of the existing legislations and make suggestions. This Report (1988) entitled "Report on the measures to be taken for democratic decentralisation at the District and lower level", recommended drastic amendments. The state government however made only minimum amendments. Elections were held for District Councils at the eve of 1990 and the District Councils came into existence in February 1991. The government that came to power in May 1991 under K. Karunakaran in the state wanted to reverse the decentralisation initiatives taken. While the Annual Plan outlay for 1991-92 for district councils was Rs 250 crore, the Karunakaran government reduced it to a paltry sum of Rs 1.97 crore in the next year's budget. Not only that the District Councils were dissolved but took various measures which put the clock back. It was at this point that the historic 73rd and 74th Constitutional Amendments happened.

Having briefly traced the history, it is important to reiterate some of the features of the pre-amendment panchayat regime of Kerala. First, Kerala except for a very brief abortive period of District Council in the early 1990s, had only a Gram Panchayat system. The several Bills introduced by the various governments since the first Kerala Ministry (1957-59) recommended only a two-tier panchayat system. Second, the village panchayats had a fairly good revenue base with power to levy property tax, profession tax, entertainment tax, show tax etc. Third, expenditures were confined largely to traditional civic functions. Fourth, statutorily every panchayat was required to formulate annual budget of receipts and expenditure and had to maintain a five per cent budgetary balance. In fact it has gone as high as 10 per cent during 1991-92 to 1993-94. Fifth, Kerala has had a tradition of raising own revenue and has generally raised large amounts by comparison with other states. As far back as 1960-61 the average own revenue of Kerala Panchayats was the highest among the Indian States with Rs 10902 per panchayat as against an all-India average of Rs 1798 [Government of India (1963):55]. Own tax revenue as a percentage of total receipts was 33 per cent in 1990-91 and 38 per cent in 1991-92 and including non-tax revenue, and assigned revenue, own source revenue was over two-thirds of the total income of gram panchayats. [See Government of Kerala (1996): Table 4.2].

Table 2: Trend in the percentage Share of Kerala State LGs in the public sector expenditure and public sector OSR (2002-03 – 2008-09)

Items	*2002*	*2003*	*2004*	*2005*	*2006*	*2007*	*2008*
	03	04	05	06	07	08	09
Share of LGs in Public Sector Expenditure	7.3	9.5	10.4	10.8	10.5	9.4	11.9
Share of LGs in Public Sector OSR	4.6	4.1	4.7	4.9	4.2	3.6	2.9

To complete the picture, let us have a snap shot picture of the economic place of local governments following the 73rd/74th Constitutional Amendments and the initiatives of the LDF government towards devolution. Table 2 shows the trend in the share of LGs of Kerala in the total state public sector (only state expenditure + LG expenditure) and the corresponding OSR share. Evidently the share of LGs in the public sector expenditure in Kerala is generally around ten per cent and that of OSR a little over four per cent. Reckoned in terms of total expenditure of the state, the LGs still do not command a respectable share. In what follows only certain issues are singled out to facilitate discussion.

Local Democracy and Decentralised Planning

The 73rd and 74th Constitutional Amendments opened a golden opportunity to bring about decentralisation in the state and the Left Democratic Front (LDF) which came to power in May 1996 seized the opportunity and launched what they called People's Plan Campaign (PPC) or *Janakeeyaso-othranam* to carry forward the process of decentralised governance. LDF made the 'big bang' pronouncement announcement to devolve 35-40 per cent of plan fund to local governments. In order to streamline and institutionalise the process, the LDF government appointed a committee under Dr S.B. Sen to suggest changes in the Panchayat and Municipality Acts of 1994. The given task of the committee was to create a new legal and institutional framework that will make functional, financial and administrative autonomy of the local governments a reality. This committee did yeoman service to the cause of local democracy in the state. It rightly realised that without simultaneous transfer of functions supported by activity mapping with role clarity for each tier matched by adequate flow of funds and deployment of functionaries, the constitutional mandate to create institutions of self-government will be a failure. The scheme of functional devolution to the various local government tiers was done on the basis of the principle of subsidiarity and the proposal of deployment of functionaries on the basis of detailed work studies and discussions. Another unique aspect of the Sen Committee was that almost all of the Acts which were directly related to the functional domain of LGs under the Constitution and the State Acts (e.g. water supply, electricity, education, land development etc.) were recommended to be suitably modified to enhance the effective functioning of local governments. The recommendations regarding the appointment of the quasi-judicial body of the Ombudsman to redress the grievances of citizens and local government was a great step forward to safeguard the sustained working of local democracy. The actual amendments incorporating the various recommendations of the Committee were passed in February 1999.

As already noted the prime objective of the constitutional amendments was to create 'institutions of local government' with focus on local area planning to deliver 'economic development and social justice'. The LDF Government launched the People's Plan Campaign (PPC) keeping this mandate very much in view. It also used it as a tool of social mobilisation.[2] The campaign mode was considered to be in the best tradition of public action and social capital of Kerala. Not only that, E.M.S. Namboodiripad in his several writings and speeches had been alerting his party cadres as well as the people of Kerala about the desparate need to build the material base of the state and improve the quality of public services. He even wanted the gram panchayats (GPs) to be self-reliant in vegetables, fruits, fish, meat and eggs besides reducing dependence on other states for rice. [See Nambooripad's *Preface* to Isaac (1997)]. It is in this setting that one of the prominent campaign managers made the significant observation that bottom up planning and decentralisation is to be seen as "an important political response to Kerala's development crisis." [Isaac (2000):4]. Unlike in the rest of India where decentralisation largely focused around anti-poverty programmes, panchayats playing only an agency role, Kerala has endeavoured to deepen democracy and expand development without compromising on social welfare and poverty reduction. No wonder some scholars have chosen to call this a 'new' Kerala model. Unlike the 'old' Kerala model the emphasis of state policies has to a certain extent been shifting from welfare to participatory growth and from top down intervention to bottom up planning. [Veron (2001):607]. Looking back, one can say that the multi-stage decentralised planning methodology from the convening of the gram sabha to identifying the felt needs of the people, the projectisation of these through working groups, the discussions at the development seminars to the final vetting by the voluntary technical advisory groups and sanction by the District Planning Committee and so on could be considered as one of the remarkable experiments in participatory democracy anywhere in the world. It was evolved and shaped through a participatory exercise of learning by doing spread over several months. This methodology itself has undergone several alterations under different regimes during the last fifteen years. Although the decentralised planning triggered several innovative initiatives, I think in the interest of democratic decentralisation and governance, the project needs continued support and fostering by the state and the wider society. Not only that, several vital institutions like the

State Development Council were allowed to sink into atrophy by both the LDF and UDF. An official Committee for Evaluation of Decentralised Planning and Development that assessed the working of decentralisation and made several recommendations to put the local planning process on a stable and sustained basis. Although the Report of the Committee attracted some discussions at the national level as also at the state level, political parties in the state took no notice of it although copies were distributed to all MLAs and MPs. Today, although more than 50 per cent of elected representatives in local governments in the state are women, they do not seem to have made any critical impact. Women empowerment depends on how you define women's autonomy and foster their functionings. Instead of preparing silly projects as part of the so-called women component plan every village panchayat ought to have prepared a women status report and should have initiated a strategic planning for women based on those reports.

District planning remains an unfinished agenda not only in Kerala, but also in the county. The trifurcation of local governance and local development may be politically convenient but from the perspective of providing an integrated vision keeping people's well-being above partisan politics is woefully missed in the game. It is unfortunate that the Technical Advisory Group (TAG) stands abolished. True, the Technical Advisory Groups (were dominated by non-experts, they failed to work as a team, they were routinely regulatory instead of being a source of technical support and indeed became an inane agency. But to abolish TAGs instead of suitably reforming them is like cutting pockets for fear of pick-pockets. Although as per Article 243ZD, local governments are entrusted with the task of conservation of natural resource, they remain by and large silent spectators to the ecological over kill of paddy lands, hillocks, river systems, backwaters, forest reserves and the like. It appears Kerala is in a King Lear like fury to 'Smite flat the thick rotundity of the world!'. Although the guidelines issued by the state government in June 2012 in the context of the Twelfth Plan have some positive aspects, such as the introduction of watershed planning in the stages of local planning process and did give some measure of autonomy, no one can miss the fact that there is a conscious effort towards a process of bureaucratic recapture of the decentralised planning process. This is a serious democratic deficit Kerala encounters at the moment.

I also wish to raise the ugly episode of one local government fighting another (the reference here is to the long standing struggle between Thiruvananthapuram city Corporation and the Vilappilsala gram panchayat where the waste processing plant of the Corporation is located) for protecting the right to have a clean environment for its citizens. As per Kerala Panchayat and Municipality Acts, "collection and disposal of solid waste and regulation of liquid waste disposal" is a mandatory function of the local governments, viz., the panchayats, municipalities and corporations. The Corporation of

Thiruvananthapuram and the Vilappilsala gram panchayats are on a war path risking court disapproval. The capital city which attracts a regular flow of people including frequent protest march and even patients from other parts of the state adding to the waste heaps need a collective approach from all concerned if you think in terms of people's health, pollution of ground water and air and certainly holding high the goal of collective good. The residents as well as the visitors to the city including those coming from Vilappilsala are spared from fatal epidemic episodes because of the lack of continuous rains. This phenomenon is not confined to Thiruvananthapuram Corporation. Trichur Corporation versus Laloor panchayat was a long standing problem although now settled. The waste disposal problem is alive in the Corporations of Kochi and Kollam and the municipalities of Mancheri, Kannur, Thalasserry, Alappuzha, Kottayam, Guruvayoor and many others who are confronting their panchayat neighbours often with aggressive confrontationist postures. This is a systemic failure which makes a mockery of local participatory governance.

Here it is pertinent to raise a few questions keeping the future of democracy in general and of local politics in particular. Do we have time for cool reasoning and honest solutions? Why is it that given the pertinent reality that this consumerist state has been producing growing mountains of wastes and need to be managed comes out only as a crisis management issue? We failed to make a perspective plan for a clean environment on a sustained basis. Who is to be blamed - the local government, state government, bureaucrats, political parties or the media or the general public? Why have public reason failed in Kerala on this and similar such issues? Quoting a discerning scholar on the question of peoples participation may not be wide of the mark here...

> "Exclusive residential zones of international standards that come up in otherwise backward localities make the problem of apathy towards participation still worse. The residents of such luxury islands are averse to local politics and social life and restrict local contact. They regulate horizontal transactions by maintaining private security, private roads, etc., and sport a 'local people and dogs not allowed' attitude. Such exclusive colonies of the elite disrupt local public life in various ways, break the contiguous nature of public space, and render local people inferior citizens', and demean their existence" [K N Harilal (2012):12].

My question is whether such upper and middle class posturing render public sphere and local democracy a redundant exercise? Seeking answers to these and similar such questions is an important first step towards building local democracy on a stable footing in Kerala.

Kerala proverbially described as a rural-urban continuum with a scattered settlement pattern has been witnessing an explosive urban population growth from 8.27 million in 2001 to 15.93 million in 2011, a 93 per cent growth making urban population size 48 per cent of the total population. If the rate of per capita income is increasing at a higher rate than that of urbanisation which itself is very high, you encounter problems of urban service delivery unless you plan for meeting them. We are heading to the global rate of urbanisation. This is happening in a state known for its aggressive consumerism that has been generating per capita solid, liquid and medical wastes of an unprecedented dimension. It is high time we examine whether the citizen charter which every local government has to publish and ensure service quality has succeeded. But before that we have passed the Right to Services Act in 2012. Commendable indeed. A legal Act at best is only a necessary condition. Without sufficient conditions being fulfilled much progress could not be achieved in practice. Local politics (which itself is a subject of independent research) and macro bipolar Front politics have failed to help the citizens of the state through perspective and strategic planning. Visual media is filled with meaningless saber-rattling and ego clashes. Why not our political leadership discusses the various issues such as the state urbanisation report (SUR of the Town Planning Department) that recommends various planned interventions for selective concentration of urban and rural economic activities, streamlined through balancing spatial order of the settlements! To conclude, the focus of my article was to put the evolution of local democracy in Kerala in some perspective. Local governance like state governance clearly lacks a vision as to where it is going. The biggest endowment of Kerala is its public space, public action tradition and its capability to debate. The great political philosopher John Stuart Mill famously said that democracy is governance by discussion. That means governance by public reason, a thesis several contemporary political philosophers have been projecting as significant. Kerala society is deeply divided on caste, communal, religious and political lines. Its politics as I said at the outset is annoyingly individualised and interest based. To see a Malayalee you probably may have to go to Gulf or USA or North India. Truth is as important to public life as oxygen is to human existence. I have an uneasy feeling that truth is a major causality in the public sphere of Kerala. This makes valid public reason difficult. With probably the highest density of print and visual media per unit of population in the world and an active political class alive and kicking the scope for public reason and justice is very high and could act as an effective mediator between state and society. Can we debate on the prospects of improving local democracy in Kerala and make it a new Kerala model. The constitutional status accorded to gram sabha and the local government, the elaborate institutional and legal framework created to enable it to function as local self-government, the 50 per cent reservation to women and above all a decentralised planning methodology that remains in place against severe odds holds out tremendous potential for democratic reforms. But local governance and local politics may require radical rethinking, refashioning and considerable fostering. Can we use this occasion for such a rethinking?

References

1. Ghosh B D (2000): 'Panchayati Raj- Evolution of the Concept', *ISS Occasional Paper Series 25*, Kalpana Printing House, New Delhi.
2. Government of India (1957): *Report of the Team for the Study of Community Projects and National Extension Service*, National Development Council, Committee on Plan Projects, New Delhi.
3. Government of India (1963): *Report of the Study Team on Panchayatai Raj Finances,* Ministry of Country Development and Corporation, New Delhi.
4. Government of India (1978): *Report of the Committee on Panchayatai Raj Institutions,* Ministry of Agriculture and Irrigation, New Delhi.
5. Government of Kerala (1986): *Report of the Panchayat Finance Commission,* Government of Kerala, Thiruvananthapuram.
6. Government of Kerala (1996): *Report of the First State Finance Commission,* Government of Kerala, Thiruvananthapuram.
7. Isaac Thomas T.M (1997): *People's Planning: Theory and Practice* (Malayalam), State Planning Board, Thiruvananthapuram.
8. Isaac Thomas T M. (with R Franke) (2000): *Local Democracy and Development: People's Campaign for Decentralised Planning in Kerala*, Left word, New Delhi.
9. Harilal K N (2012): 'Planning as an Instrument of Politics? Rethinking the Methodology of Local Level Participatory Planning in Kerala', *RULSG Occasional Papers 2012:1*, Centre for Development Studies, Trivandrum.
10. Mukherji Partha Nath (2007): 'Participatory Democratisation: Panchayati Raj and the Deepening of Indian Democracy', *ISS Occasional Paper Series 34*, Kalpana Printing House, New Delhi.
11. Oommen M A (2010): 'The 13th Finance Commission and the Third Tier' *Economic & Political Weekly,* Vol. xlv No. 48.
12. Pillai G K (1986): *Local Finance in a Developing Economy,* B R Publishing Corporation, New Delhi.
13. Pillai Velu T K (1940): *The Travancore State Manual,* The Government of Travancore, Trivandrum.
14. Roy M N (1960): *Politics, Power and Parties,* Renaissance Publishers, Calcutta.
15. Veron R (2001): "The 'New' Kerala Model: Lessons for Sustainable Development", *World Development,* Vol. 29, No. 4.

Footnotes

1. Because the term 'central transfers' is not defined, there can be serious omissions. This definitely includes all direct transfers to local governments by central government and may not include all centrally sponsored schemes by different ministries. Even so, the data are good enough to highlight the poor autonomous space.
2. It was fondly hoped that the various class and mass organisations the left parties helped to build up would spearhead the process. [See Isaac (2000)]. More over genuine participation is much more than social mobilisation.

4

Institutionalising Panchayati Raj in Kerala: Some Reflections

—*K.P. Kannan*

Introduction

But for the bold initiative by the late Prime Minister Rajiv Gandhi in proposing two constitutional amendments to establish a third tier of government in the Indian federal set up, the agenda of Panchayati Raj would have remained as a regional agenda dictated by socio political circumstances in a few states. Having said that, one must also acknowledge the revival of this agenda by a combination of political parties in the aftermath of the revocation of the state of Emergency in the late nineteen seventies. In that sense, a new political consensus emerged once again in favour of reviving the Panchayati Raj with constitutional protection. However, the actual implementation of the Panchayati Raj has so far not lived up to the expectations raised by this broad political consensus. In fact, many state governments remain so lukewarm to the transfer of power, not to speak of the required finances and personnel, for the effective functioning of Panchayati Raj. Even states that started with such great expectations - Karnataka and West Bengal, for example - have either gone back from their earlier enthusiasm and commitment or have allowed letting the Panchayati Raj remain with a minimum of functions, functionaries and finance.

In such a context, the track record of Kerala is something that calls for celebration, despite the very many challenges and the presence of petty politics arising out of a fragmented party-political system and its unending lust for all forms of rent-seeking. In terms of the actual functioning of the decentralised system of development planning and administration as well as some form of local level governance, Kerala seems to have on the track of what one would like to call progressive realisation of the full potential of the Panchayati Raj.

Laying the Foundations

Although Kerala started with a 'Big Bang' approach (something antithetical to the very idea of planning) with devolution of functions and finance in the mid-nineteen nineties, it took a while for the deployment of functionaries. The opposition to such deployment came from the very functionaries called the state government employees; a highly organised group that has, over time, become overtly self-serving rather than serving the society. The inability of the two political coalitions to implement the 'will of the people' by deploying functionaries seemed, for a while, irredeemable. Fortunately, such hurdles have now been overcome. The result is the availability of a critical number of functionaries in the Village, Block and District Panchayats. For example, the Village Panchayats in Kerala today have, on an average, ten to twelve employees that should be the envy of such Panchayats outside the state. Moreover, most of them have their own buildings with reasonable office facilities with the necessary accessories including the availability of computers and internet connectivity. But the mere presence of physical infrastructure is not a sufficient condition for the effective functioning of the Panchayats. It is here that Kerala scores much higher points compared to its other sister-states in the country. Successive state governments in Kerala have provided critical institutional support for enhancing the governance capability of Panchayats. The role of two institutions needs to be specially mentioned in this context.

The first is the functioning of the Kerala Institute of Local Administration (located in Thrissur district) which has been engaged in the training of both elected representatives as well as officials of the Panchayat institutions. Besides training, they have also documented the various activities for discussion, dissemination and further improvement. While the infrastructural facilities in this institution seem to be of a reasonable standard, there is still a critical gap in the form of inadequacy of the existing faculty as well as its quality. The institute has the potential to contribute more effectively to the quality of its training and documentation and move to research, analysis and critical support in formulating plans and projects. The situation today calls for bolder initiatives in these areas.

The other critical support has come from the establishment of an Information Kerala Mission in 1999 with a view to introducing e-governance in Panchayat institutions at the district, block and village levels. While the initial five years or so have been marked by undue delays in developing appropriate software and the establishment of Information and Communication Technology (ICT)-based systems of functioning, considerable progress seems to have been achieved during the last five years or so. Mention should be made of the availability of computers in almost all Panchayats including the Village Panchayats and the use of specially developed software (called Sulekha) for plan formulation. Many Panchayats have also linked up with hospitals for internet-based services for issue of birth certificates. Computerised documentation systems are also now becoming common with regard to such schemes as the disbursement of social security benefits (state pensions for the poor old aged, widows, destitute, etc.). What is significant to note is the fact that ICT-based system of governance has emerged as an ongoing activity and a realisation that the time has come to move towards a system of e-governance. While most elected representatives and officials are neither proficient nor comfortable with the ICT systems, they have realised its emergence as a necessary and powerful tool for governance. The required manpower is currently taken care of by the Panchayats themselves by recruiting specially trained youth. There is also an increasing tendency among the younger officials to acquire such proficiency, if they have not already done so. What is now called for is a programme of periodic training to the officials to expand and strengthen the emerging e-governance system.

Socio-Political Context

Despite their overt differences in matters of detail, the two political coalitions - the Left Democratic Front led by the Communist Party of India (Marxist) and the United Democratic Front led by the Indian National Congress - have accepted the Panchayati Raj as an integral part of the governance structure. Although there are elements and groups within each political formation that are either not comfortable with the idea of sharing power (and hence privilege) or opposed to the very concept of decentralisation from an ideological point of view, I think the social reality in Kerala today is overwhelming in favour of a decentralised system of governance if one goes by the enthusiasm with which the new experiment has been received by the people at large. I think it is this ground reality that has been singularly responsible for advances that Kerala has so far registered. This was borne by an innovative 'social reality show' (called Green Kerala Express) that was telecast in Kerala from March 6 to July 27, 2010 about which we shall discuss later.

In this context it is also important to underline that the social, economic and political terrain in Kerala has been quite conducive to the functioning of Panchayati Raj. Among these, I would like to single out the density of associational organisations in the civil society. The three important such organisations that have, in my opinion, contributed to strengthening and effectiveness of the Panchayati Raj are (a) the organisation of women from relatively poor households called the *Kudumbasree*, (b) the Parent-Teacher Associations in schools, and (c) organisations of farmers. In certain situations and places, cooperative credit societies/banks have also played a positive role especially with regard to the revival of agriculture. In the same vein, one may also speak of the youth organisations that often manifest in the form of Youth Clubs, Village Reading Rooms and so on in every village in Kerala.

However, it is a matter for serious investigation and research as to why the all powerful trade unions that are omnipresent in Kerala have not been seen as an enthusiastic supporter, let alone facilitator, of the Panchayati Raj. Whether it has to do with their 'insider' character (concerned with the protection of the interests of members) and their progressive delinking with the larger emancipatory project are questions that will have to be probed into.

I must also mention here that the experience so far gained in the functioning of Panchayati Raj in Kerala has also disapproved an earlier and quite widespread notion that women representatives would not be able to function effectively and that they are likely to be mere 'puppets' in the hands of their controlling forces whether from the male members of the family or that of their political parties. I think this myth has now been belied as was revealed by their stage performance in the GKE show. If there are any drawbacks in their functioning, they were no more than what their male counterparts experienced in their respective roles and their being subject to some kind of remote control in a party-political system by their political bosses was hardly due to their gender identity. We shall come back to this issue later.

In the rest of the paper I would like to reflect on the experience gained through my participation in the GKE show since that opened up a new reality often far removed from what was being reported in much of the print media.

The Green Kerala Express

At the outset, let me say that this is perhaps the first time in India that a 'social reality show' on the performance of Panchayat Raj Institutions (PRIs) was conceived and implemented.[1] With the successful conclusion of the show called Green Kerala Express (GKE), I think it constitutes an innovative initiative in the field of development communication. Given the digital technology revolution that has spread to the media in a short span of time in this country, there has been a proliferation of TV Channels whose contents are often dominated by what may loosely be called 'entertainment' programmes. Moreover, much of what comes out of both the print and electronic media in the name of 'news' are of a negative kind - often based on isolated events rather than representative of a group behaviour - that often dampens ordinary people's hopes and expectations for a better life. The show named Green Kerala Express belongs to the class of 'positive news' that projects what ordinary people think and do in their collective space at the local level.

As a developmental activist since the mid-nineteen seventies, I have had the opportunity to interact with people at the village level on issues relating to local level development. I distinctly recall the exhortations of late Sri P.T. Bhaskara Panicker who was a social activist in multiple spheres and who took the lead in propagating the idea of *Grama Sastra Samitis* through the Kerala

Sastra Sahitya Parishad in the nineteen seventies. Although there were several isolated experiments in village development in Kerala, this idea was later expanded into 'planning for development at the village level' in which the Kerala Sastra Sahitya Parishad played a leading role. The revival of this agenda by the political parties in the eighties added a political dimension to hastening the process of setting up decentralised governance institutions. From an intellectual point of view, I was inspired by the late Professor. K.N. Raj, an internationally well known development economist (and founder of the Centre for Development Studies in Trivandrum) who, among others, argued for a systematic push in the area of decentralised development planning for the country as a whole.

It is in this background I responded enthusiastically to the invitation to join the Jury constituted to 'interrogate' the Panchayats participating in the GKE Social Reality Show.

Enthusiastic Participation

As of 2009 there were 999 Grama Panchayats (GPs) and 58 Municipalities in Kerala; out of this, 140 GPs, 12 Municipalities participated in the GKE show. Although neither the organisers nor the participating Panchayats had any prior idea about how the programme would evolve, I could see the enthusiasm and energy of all participating Panchayat Presidents and Members. As many of the Panchayat Presidents later opined in the show, they welcomed this opportunity to showcase their performances as well as discuss their challenges at a time when there was an impression that the PRIs were not performing so well. In the print media, Panchayats were often portrayed as centres where 'chickens and goats' are distributed or made fun of when some members in some Panchayats switched their party loyalties to gain positions of power forgetting that such 'dramas' were more often enacted at state and national levels with a greater degree of alacrity. Although the focus of the show was on developmental activities the Panchayats took this opportunity, rightly so in my view, to project their primary responsibilities as laid down in the 73rd and 74th amendments to the Indian Constitution and the consequent state level Kerala Panchayat Raj Act.

Two areas need to be mentioned here. One, the Panchayat institutions in general contributed to the development of infrastructure of the schools as well as healthcare centres under their supervision. Many of them have further contributed to the quality of teaching as well as healthcare delivery by special efforts. Some of the examples are: initiatives in creating special facilities for children who had problems in catching up with the rest of the students in their class rooms; recruiting reserve teachers when appointed school teachers were on leave; creating in-patient facilities in Primary Health Centres (though such centres were not meant for such care facilities); and, extending financial assistance for purchase of additional medicines. The improvement in school facilities as well as teaching quality has stemmed, to some extent the increasing tendency for parents to send their children to unaided schools with high school fees in the hope that such schools would ensure not only the success of the children but also help them gain a measure of proficiency in English language.

While management of waste has emerged as a major concern in Kerala, a number of Panchayats seem to have earnestly tackled this problem. However, it was evident that many GPs and Municipalities are yet to tackle this problem in a satisfactory manner. Lack of awareness of technological solutions is only one side of the problem; the bigger challenge seems to be recognising the need to differentiate waste (degradable and non-degradable solids, and the latter in terms of plastics, electronic, toxic and so on) and create organisational and management systems for their efficient and timely collection, processing and disposal. This is an area where the Panchayats need a 'hand-holding approach' from the State Government and its agencies that should go beyond issuing 'sanctions' and 'guidelines'. Unless tackled on a priority basis, the problem of waste management is likely to emerge as a source of social conflict in a densely populated region as Kerala. In fact, such conflicts are already in evidence in a number of places where local residents have objected to the dumping of wastes in their areas.

Innovative Initiatives

One could see several innovative initiatives especially by the GPs in the fields of agriculture, dairying and fish culture, healthcare, education and so on. Several GPs have come up with the idea of creating Labour Banks meant to provide labourers for various agricultural operations while providing them a regular income and some social security. Use of agricultural machinery especially for rice cultivation was seen to be catching up rapidly with a view to reduce the cost of cultivation while increasing labour productivity that would enable payment of competitive wages. All these organisational-cum-technological initiatives are in tune with the rising expectations of workers in Kerala's rapidly transforming labour market. What the new generation of workers - majority of whom have at least secondary level of school education - expect is employment with dignity, regularity and social security. In sum, they are seeking 'jobs' not just work even if such casual work would give them high wages for the tasks performed.

Emergence of institutions for special education and care for the physically and mentally challenged children is another innovative initiative that was showcased by the Green Kerala Express. Then there were 'Group Farming' by groups of Kudumbasree women workers by 'leasing in' land for cultivation of mainly rice and vegetables. Such new initiatives have been facilitated by Panchayats by securing uncultivated land and providing technical and financial assistance. The revival of rice cultivation has assumed a serious situation since the area under rice has declined to just 239 thousand hectares in 2009 accounting for a mere nine per cent of the gross cropped area from a peak of 885 thousand hectares in 1975 accounting for 30 per cent of the gross cropped area. Of course, agriculture in Kerala is undergoing a complex process of transformation with periods of stagnation and growth along with changes in cropping intensity biased towards less labour-absorbing and high-valued cash crops. This has raised a set of new challenges for agricultural development in a fast emerging non-agrarian Kerala economy (for a discussion of the issues see, Kannan, 2010).

As I mentioned in the beginning, the existence of associational forms of organisations were critical to the success of many of these initiatives. The *Kudumbasree* played a remarkable role in facilitating the implementation of several schemes such as the National Rural Employment Guarantee and National Rural Health Mission. In fact, the state government's decision to implement the NREG through the agency of Kudumbasree has not only ensured a very high participation of women but also given them the autonomy to execute such programmes and strengthen their capacity for undertaking similar poverty alleviation schemes. Mention should also be made of *Ashraya* Scheme of the Government of Kerala under which destitute persons identified by the Village Panchayats are taken care of by *Kudumbasree* groups. Such a humane and socially sensitive programme as *Ashraya* is worthy of emulation in other parts of this country. The Parent Teacher Associations in schools were instrumental in collaborating with the Panchayats in improving the infrastructural facilities in schools such as toilets for the children, additional buildings, purchases of vehicles for transporting children, building of kitchens for mid-day meal preparation and so on.

Governance of Panchayats consisting of elected members from a large number of political parties could have led to conflictual and disharmonious decision-making process given the fact that every issue is contested on a party-political basis in Kerala; some times, I must say, to the detriment of the overall interests of the state. However, and in the words of almost all Panchayat representatives, there has been a basic consensus with regard to decision making. This is not because the members do not hold divergent views but because of a conscious approach to arrive at a consensual decision-making at the end. This has been a pleasant and surprising revelation that the GKE Show has brought out to the public domain.

It was a remarkable experience to see that a majority of Panchayat Presidents and the Members belong to relatively young age group of 30 to 45 years. Women Members and Presidents demonstrated their extraordinary capacity for leadership and decision-making as well as articulation of the collective views of the Panchayats in the programme. The initial doubt in certain circles about women's capability to function effectively in the PRIs now stands belied. Kerala is fortunate in having a largely educated population especially those of below 45 years of age group. Most Presidents and Members belong to an educational level of not less than ten years of school education; a number of them who participated in the GKE Show were graduates and post-graduates. This has, in my view, been a favourable factor in the ability of Panchayat institutions in Kerala to function effectively.

During the interaction in the GKE Show some of the weaknesses of existing Panchayat system were also evident. First and foremost was the absence of a consciousness on the need to document quantitative data relating to the implementation of many schemes and benefits arising therefrom in a systematic manner. Consequently, the same weakness was reflected in the way the accounting system was maintained. This is an area which needs to be strengthened through posting of competent persons for accounting and training of personnel especially in the GPs.

Second, although computer facilities are now available the capability for using them is quite limited. Consequently the advantages of e-mail and internet facilities remain largely, if not fully, unexplored. Nevertheless, the efforts of the Information Kerala Mission in computing accounts of the Plan Funds through the installation of specially designed software was seen to be working in most of the participating Panchayats. Ideally, such a system should be extended to all revenue and expenditure items.

Response to the GKE Show

Response to the GKE Show from a wide range of common people as well as from the print media was quite positive. I have often been told by a number of viewers that they did not often know what was happening in their own neighbourhood GPs and this show has opened up their eyes as to what could be done in their own villages. Viewers from outside Kerala as well as India wrote to some of us in the Jury saying as to how pleased they were to see such programmes. Some of them said they got nostalgic while viewing such programmes and wanted to have CDs with English sub-titles so that they could show it to their non-Malayali friends. I think such responses were not only genuine but also were intended to convey their 'sense of pride' in what was happening in their own land. Development, after all, is not just a matter of material well-being but also feeling and sharing a sense of pride in the achievement of one's own people.

Concluding Remarks

The fact that 14 per cent of the GPs and 20 per cent of the Municipalities participated in the GKE provides us some credible basis for evaluating the overall functioning of the Panchayat institutions. However, it may also be argued that this sample size probably represents the relatively well performing Panchayats and generalisations based on this sample may not necessarily reflect the overall picture. While I tend to agree with this, the fact that around 15 to

16 per cent of Panchayat institutions (including Municipalities) were prepared to voluntarily submit themselves to public scrutiny in a TV programme should be welcomed as a positive sign. Documentation of the performance of a larger number of Panchayats by the Kerala Institute of Local Administration suggests that the percentage of Panchayats with a creditable record of achievement is indeed much higher than that revealed in the GKE Show. However, the important message is that these well-performing Panchayats have now emerged as 'role models' for other Panchayats that could have a positive cascading effect in strengthening the emerging decentralised system of governance. The journey is long and need not be smooth but it has begun.

Reference

Kannan, K.P. (2010), *Agricultural Development in an Emerging Non-Agrarian Regional Economy: Kerala's Challenges*, Dr K.N. Shyamasundaran Nair Memorial Lecture delivered on 13 August, Kerala Agricultural University, Vellanikkara.

Notes

1. The idea of producing a TV Show on the performance of Panchayats, especially Village Panchayats, was first conceived by Sajan Gopalan of the Trivandrum Station of the Door Darshan and K. Mohan Kumar of the Centre for Development of Imaging Technology, an institution that now serves as a centre for ICT-based information dissemination for the Government of Kerala as well as training of youth in ICT-based media. This idea was accepted and implemented by the Government of Kerala through its Local Self Government Department, the State Sanitation Mission, Kerala Institute of Local Administration in collaboration with the Trivandrum Station of the Door Darshan.

5

Local Governments* and Socially Disadvantaged Groups -Learning from the Kerala Experience

—*S.M. Vijayanand*

Introduction

The Constitution of India has created Local Governments with the explicit and sharp objective of planning and implementing programmes for economic development and social justice and it can be deduced that economic development is for social justice. Accordingly the Constitution has indicated several functions to be discharged by them and a good number of them relate to social justice. Thus, the Constitution envisages Local Governments to proactively strive to bring the socially disadvantaged groups into the mainstream.

Yet from the days of the freedom struggle there has been a continuing dialectic and even contestation between the Gandhian faith in Local Governments as community-based trustees for common good and the Ambedkarite fear of Local Governments especially Panchayats as institutions reflecting the inequalities and exploitative power relations among social and economic groups and becoming potential resistance points against the constitutional ideals of liberty, equality and fraternity.

But it took a long time to realise that the two need not be adversarial but can at least in the realm of plausibility, be complementary and synergetic. While the Ambedkarite fear is more than justified by the objective conditions in the society, polity and the economy, it should not be forgotten that the

* The word 'Local Government' is used instead of PRI as appropriate to the Kerala context.

antidote to the ills poignantly depicted by Ambedkar lies in the Gandhian vision of vibrant inclusive local democracy.

Local Governments widen participation and deepen democracy. Whatever be the initial conditions, if the entitlements are properly defined and access to them made clear and easy through a transparent and participatory process, democracy by itself can enhance the capabilities of hitherto excluded to use progressively the processes and institutions to their advantage. It may not be all of a sudden and it may not be even automatic but it would appear that even with severe initial handicaps the only feasible means of empowering the socially disadvantaged groups is to experimentally educate them through participation in local democracy to become capable of autonomous rights-oriented public action.

From a Freirian sense, democracy at the door steps offers the highest potential for analysis of one's situation, reflection of the causes and effects of being in such a situation and working out strategies and actions for liberation. Local Governments offer the best chance of peaceful social transformation as the focus would be more on local development issues and challenges which more often than not can transcend social and political divisions and even economic differences.

Theoretically once Local Governments mature, the authoritarian and feudal concept of "power over" can only decline and in the process stimulate "power with" or the democratic strength of collective action. In such a scenario a fair and legitimate "power to" situation can be attained in which the socially disadvantaged groups can negotiate on equal terms. Unfortunately there seems to be no natural course of action – no "per se" or "ipso facto" factors for the potential of local democracy to include socially disadvantaged groups. There is need for proactive public policy which can be shaped by political enlightenment and/or civil society advocacy and public action. The Kerala experience illustrates this thesis.

Initiatives of Kerala for Socially Disadvantaged Groups through the Panchayat Raj System

(A) General initiatives

1. For Local Governments to exercise their powers for the betterment of socially disadvantaged groups it is necessary for the State to transfer responsibilities related to this broad function very clearly, for in the Indian context Local Governments can exercise only powers specifically delegated by the State Government. In this respect Kerala is far ahead of other States in delineating the responsibilities of Local Governments in general and, particularly, in respect of socially disadvantaged groups. Broadly two-third of

new development investment for SCs and half of new development investment for STs is the responsibility of Local Governments. Women and Child Development and development of the other-abled groups are a Local Government responsibility to the tune of about 90 per cent. Care of the destitutes and identification of eligible beneficiaries for social security assistance are again vested with the Local Governments. Further, direct poverty reduction initiatives are mostly operationalised through Local Governments.

2. The second important tenet of decentralisation is that functionaries required for discharging the transferred functions have to be placed at the disposal of Local Governments, Kerala followed the principle of "the work and worker going together." All the staff in Government carrying out the responsibilities transferred to Local Governments have been placed under the control of Local Governments with control being interpreted as right to assign work, review work, call for reports, carry out inspections and, if required, take disciplinary action and impose any minor penalty. Thus, cutting edge level officials up to the district level from the departments of SC Development, ST Development, Social Welfare and Rural Development have all been transferred to Local Governments. They work as "implementing officers" of programmes and projects prepared by Local Governments and funded by them.

3. The critical *sine qua non* of decentralisation is provision of sufficient funds to match the expenditure responsibilities along with the necessary autonomy for their application according to local priorities and needs. In this respect Kerala is the acknowledged leader in the country transferring about 25 per cent of its plan budget in a practically untied manner to its Local Governments to prepare the highly participatory People's Plan. An important feature of the devolution is that it is totally formula-based with zero discretion and the formula is equity oriented with the result that backward Local Governments with a naturally higher proportion of socially disadvantaged groups get larger allocations irrespective of their location or clout. Further the funds are fully predictable over the five-year period coinciding with the award of a Finance Commission and are properly ring-fenced through a separate Budget document which shows even Village Panchayat-wise allocation of funds.

4. An interesting feature of Kerala's fiscal decentralisation is the balance struck between local fiscal autonomy and the needs of social justice through reservation of funds and presumption of mandatory spending requirements and fiscal responsibility features. To illustrate, 10 per cent of the devolved development funds have to be set apart for women to be spent on practical and strategic gender

needs. Five per cent of the funds have to be spent on children, aged and the other-abled. Similarly two-third of the funds under Special Component Plan and half the funds under Tribal Sub Plan (which are totally investible and do not include any salary component or notional expenditure) are devolved to Local Governments purely on the basis of SC/ST population. To ensure fiscal responsibility if the funds are not spent in a particular year funds from other sectors have to be compulsorily diverted to these social justice sectors during the succeeding year.

5. Kerala is the pioneer in participatory budgeting with plans being prepared by following an elaborate methodology which itself ensures transparency, visibility, inclusiveness and accountability. The methodology in respect of Panchayats is summed up below:

   Needs identification: Through a meeting of Gram Sabha covering the ward or the electoral constituency of a Village Panchayat Member, the felt needs of the community are identified. There is a period of environment creation to mobilise maximum participation in the Gram Sabha/Ward Sabha. Statistics reveal that about 10-12 per cent of the rural population participate. The meetings are held in a semi-structured manner with plenary sessions and sub-group sessions and dealing with specific developmental issues. The decisions are minuted and forwarded to the Village Panchayat. Each meeting is chaired by the elected member and has an official as its Co-ordinator.

   Situation analysis: Based on the demands emanating from the first special Gram Sabha and based on developmental data, both primary and secondary, exhaustive Development Reports are prepared and printed in the case of every Village Panchayat in the State. These reports describe the status in each sector of development with reference to available data, analyse the problems and point out the directions for further development. This is an one-time exercise for a Plan Period and the Reports are revised Five years.

   Strategy setting: Based on the Gram Sabha feed back and the Development Report, a one day Development Seminar is held at the level of each Panchayat in which participation of experts, elected members, representatives nominated by the Grama Sabhas, practitioners from among the public is ensured. The Development Seminars suggest the broad priorities and general strategies of developmental projects to be taken up for a particular year.

   Projectisation: The ideas thrown up by the above three stages are translated in the form of projects by Working Groups at the Local Government level. For each Local Government there are about eight to twelve Working Groups dealing with different sectors of development. Each Working Group is headed by an elected member and is convened by the government official concerned. The Vice Chairman of the Working Group is normally a non-government expert in the sector, the other members are activists, experts, academics and stakeholders. The projects are prepared in the suggested format outlining the objectives, describing the benefits, explaining the funding and detailing the mode of execution and phasing of the project.

Plan finalisation: From among the projects, based on the allocation communicated, the concerned Panchayat finalises its plan for the year and this plan is submitted to the District Planning Committees (DPCs) through the Technical Advisory Group which again is a multi-stakeholder group. The Panchayat is free to take up any project, irrespective of its cost, subject of course to the resources actually available and within the sectoral limits.

Plan vetting: The Technical Advisory Groups at the Block or the District level consisting of official and non-official experts vet the projects for their technical viability and conformity with the mandatory government guidelines on planning and costing and forward them to the DPC. They cannot change priorities or projects; they can only ask for rectification.

Plan approval: The DPC gives the formal approval to the plans after which the panchayat can start implementation. It is to be noted that the DPC also cannot change the priority of a Panchayat. It can only ensure that government guidelines are followed. Administrative approval for implementation is given project-wise by the panchayat. Every Panchayat has unlimited powers of administrative sanctions subject only to the limits of its financial resources.

The same methodology is followed in Municipalities and Corporations also.

6. Special features have been built into the planning process in respect of sectors related to social justice. These include community consultations over and above the Gram Sabha, mandatory inclusion of representative of socially disadvantaged groups in the Working Groups constituted for the purpose of situation analysis, plan identification and project preparation. Another special feature worth mentioning is compulsory preparation of social maps for infrastructure schemes under SCP and TSP showing distinctly the benefited SC or ST families and other families to prevent possibilities of spending such funds surreptitiously for the benefit of more powerful social groups.

7. A range of support systems which are particularly sensitive to the issues related to socially disadvantaged groups has been put in place for the planning process. They include:-
   - (i) 1183 social animators from among SCs and 1000 social animators from among STs for extension and feedback.
   - (ii) NHG network of women covering the bottom half of the population.
   - (iii) Working Groups consisting of officials, professionals, stakeholders and activists for assisting local governments in situation analysis, to generate development ideas and develop detailed projects.
   - (iv) Hand books for different sectors with focus on sectors relating to socially disadvantaged groups.
   - (v) Massive capacity building efforts through the Kerala Institute of Local Administration (KILA) giving special importance to functions related to social justice.
8. Selection of beneficiaries for different schemes is generally an area of patronage reflecting local power relations and militating against social justice and Antyodaya, which almost go together. Here Kerala has elaborated a process ensuring absolute transparency and equity. For each scheme the Local Government has to state clearly the basic eligibility criteria and the prioritisation criteria for the eligible applicants. To ensure objectivity each prioritisation criterion should be assigned definite marks so that the total would come to 100. Applications are invited for each scheme, marks assigned according to eligibility by verification teams consisting of officials and elected representatives, and then read out in the Gram Sabha and the selection finalised. The marking sheets are available for public scrutiny. This has improved the targeting of benefits considerably though it must be admitted that it has not eliminate patronage completely proving the adage that things can be made foolproof but not crook-proof.

(B) Specific Initiatives

In order to ensure that the processes related to planning for socially disadvantaged groups are fully adhered to and the funds reserved for them are properly spent, certain innovative safeguards have been put in place. They include:

- (i) Cutting edge Local Governments have been requested to prepare locally a study on the Status of Women. In order to guide the Panchayats, detailed instructions on the manner of preparing the status report have been issued. This activity enhances gender awareness and provides a clear understanding of gender issues prevalent in the Local Government so that the funds reserved for women are properly spent.

(ii) A special planning methodology has been prescribed in the case of Tribal Sub-Plan where ST hamlets are given the full power to decide what they want in the full assembly of all adults of a hamlet called "Ooru Koottam (Ooru = hamlet; Koottam = assembly). If a Panchayat cannot implement the suggestion of a Ooru Koottam it has to get back to it and seek prior consent for modification of the plan or scheme.

(iii) There is a close liaison at the State level by the Department of Local Self-Government with the Women's Commission and the SC/ST Commission and the Commissioner for People with Disabilities to discuss issues related to the socially disadvantaged groups concerned.

(iv) Jagratha Samithis have been set up in all cutting edge Local Governments as a forum to discuss issues related to gender discrimination and even atrocities against women.

(v) Among the special initiatives, Kudumbashree deserves elaboration. It is essentially a networked organisation of women with focus on the poor. At the local level Neighbourhood Groups (NHGs) of 15 to 20 families are organised in which every family below poverty line is mandatorily included. NHGs within a Ward of a Village Panchayat/ Municipality are networked into an Area Development Society (ADS) and all ADSs with the Village Panchayat are federated into a Registered Society called Community Development Society (CDS). The special features of Kudumbashree which make it distinct from the SHG set up in rest of India are:

(1) Kudumbashree is conceptualised as the community wing of PRIs and as such it is not a "parallel body" competing for space and power with elected Local Governments. At the same time the independence and freedom of functioning of the NHG network is protected; the elected Local Government cannot interfere in the decision-making processes of Kudumbashree but it has the right to information.

(2) Each NHG has five volunteers looking after education, health micro enterprise, micro planning and general administration of the Group. This enables the Kudumbashree Neighbourhood Groups to grow beyond thrift and credit based self-help groups and become genuine community-based organisations creating the developing capacities and demand for development.

(3) Kudumbashree has a wide coverage including in its fold more than 50 per cent of the families of the State. Since every family

below poverty line is automatically included it lends powerful voice to the poor.

(4) The existence of development volunteers ensures quick and effective outreach and genuine real time feedback.

Thus, Kudumbashree has contributed to the effectiveness of decentralisation in Kerala, by generating the social capital needed for influencing the course of local development.

(vi) To top up, Kerala has set up unique autonomous institution of accountability exclusively for citizen complaints against local government acts of commission or omission. In matters relating to maladministration including corruption, partisanship, inactions etc., citizens can approach the Ombudsman who is a High Court Judge, serving or retired; in the case of appeals against decisions taken by Local Governments in their regulatory or administrative capacity there is an Appellate Tribunal who is a District Judge.

(C) New Initiatives

Certain new initiatives are being introduced in respect of socially disadvantaged groups. They include:-

(i) An extraordinary programme for rehabilitation of destitutes called 'Asraya' has been developed by Kudumbashree and implemented in two-thirds of Village Panchayats and a few Municipalities. It targets absolute destitutes covering about one or two per cent of the population who need continuous handholding for their very survival. This is an interesting experiment in community, based social security under the leadership of Local Governments, to explore the possibility of introducing care and compassion in governance by local democratic institutions.

(ii) A detailed survey of tribal families and Scheduled Caste habitats is nearing completion. This will provide a robust data base for micro-level planning for these communities.

(iii) Kudumbashree is all set to launch focused programmes targeting SCs and STs and differently-abled people.

(iv) Experimentation has begun on developing programmes to include aged and children on specific target groups while preparing local development programmes.

(v) A methodology for inclusive, convergent, anti-poverty sub-plan has been developed under the leadership of Kudumbashree touching different facets of poverty as illustrated below:

Poverty features Anti-poverty Sub-Plan	***Component of***
Income poverty	NREGS
Lack of skills and capabilities	Capacity building programmes of PRIs and Kudumbashree
Human Development (a) Health (b) Education	 NRHM SSA
Food security Mid-day meals PDS	ICDS
Social Security	Health Insurance Life Insurance Pensions Asraya
Basic minimum needs like shelter access to water and power	People's Plan for Local Governments

(vi) Community based monitoring utilising the Kudumbashree network is being developed.

(D) Assessment of Performance

Thus, a conscious and comprehensive set of policies, processes and procedures have been developed by Kerala for the proper inclusion of socially disadvantaged groups in local level development efforts under the leadership of Local Governments. A quick qualitative assessment is summed up below:

(1) There has been equitable flow of funds and a high level of pro-poor expenditure with focus on minimum needs infrastructure i.e., housing, sanitation, water supply, power and connectivity.

(2) Infrastructure in public institutions servicing the poor like Anganwadis, Schools and Hospitals has improved considerably leading to improved service delivery.

(3) Kudumbashree has become a powerful means of strengthening the people's side – especially of socially disadvantaged groups – democratic decentralisation.

(4) Economic development of the socially disadvantaged groups has not been as pronounced as achievements in other aspects of development.

(5) Tribal development does not seem to have improved and empowerment process does not seem to have worked so far in their

case. This is probably attributable to the tiny and scattered nature of tribal population constituting only a little more than one per cent of the population.

(E) Issues to be addressed

It is necessary to flag issues emerging out of the decentralisation process in relation to empowerment of socially disadvantaged groups and they are indicated below:

(a) The five year rotation of reserved constituencies has affected the empowerment of women, SCs and STs considerably.

(b) There is always a tension among the different roles of elected representatives – as representative of socially disadvantaged groups, representative of political parties, and representative of the full constituency. Balancing these roles requires a lot of maturity as well as sensitivity.

(c) Unless consciously targeted the invisible poor or the destitutes get left out.

(d) There is competition among the ultra poor, the poor and those marginally above the poverty line for benefits. PRIs face difficulties in identifying the groups especially at the margin.

(e) Surprisingly the potentially radical experiment in democratic decentralisation has been largely ignored by the intelligentsia, academics, activists, the media and even the mainstream and local political entities.

Conclusion

The discussion of the Kerala experience reveals the need for proactive government policy which is translated into action through multiple points covering processes, procedures, fund flows, capacity building mechanisms etc. In such a scenario Local Governments can achieve the goal of inclusive development and reduce disparities and disadvantages in a phased manner utilising the strength of proximity to people and their problems. Even if they do not succeed in the initial stages stumbling at the hurdles created by existing power relations there is need for patience. Even if the socially disadvantaged groups remain as passive observers, in a short period of time they will understand and internalise the art of gaining power in a democratic set up. Therefore, it is necessary to widen the scope for participation for, in addition to learning by doing; there is also a process of learning by observing and learning by knowing the basic entitlement – both of which can lead to effective public action.

Of course, not all States may be proactive in grooming Local Governments into democratic and egalitarian institutions promoting sound justice. In such cases there is adequate space for civil society groups to step in to fill the vacuum. Of course, this process will take a longer time and may not be smooth.

Thus, it can be boldly concluded that Local Governments are potential vehicles for gradual but sustainable empowerment and inclusion of socially disadvantaged groups. Once again it has to be clarified that this cannot be natural and automatic but needs to be catalysed and nurtured, at least in the initial years either through enlightened State intervention and/or Civil Society-sponsored public action.

6

Data Base for Decentralised Planning in Kerala

—*M. Kuttappan*

Introduction

In the Constitution of India, which is federal in nature, part XI has clearly specified the division of powers and functions between the Union and the States. There was no constitutional status for administrative units below the State government. Rural and urban local governments of panchayats and municipalities, though extant for a long period, had very limited powers and functions. The 73rd and 74th Constitutional Amendments (CAs), giving constitutional status to local governments, were envisaged to endow the local governments with such powers and functions so as to make them self-reliant and vibrant institutions for local development. With these amendments the structure of governance in India has changed from a two tier to a three tier of Union, States, and Panchayats/Nagarapalikas.

The Constitutional Amendments envisage planning for economic development and social justice by Panchayati Raj Institutions (PRIs) and Urban Local Bodies (ULBs) and their consolidation by the District Planning Committees (DPCs) after consideration of matters of common interest between panchayats and municipalities. Here planning has to be carried out by the panchayats and urban local bodies at the grassroots level, Intermediate panchayat at the Block level and District panchayat at the District level. This is also known as multi-level planning. In this context it is important to note that while the Planning Commission of India was constituted by an executive order of the Union government, the District Planning Committee is a constitutional body (Article 243ZD) with specific powers.

Decentralised Planning

According to Conyers Diana, "Decentralisation means reassigning responsibility, authority and resources from higher level government organisation to local government bodies along with sufficient autonomy and accountability so as to enable them to provide efficient and adequate services to the people."[1] Planning is defined as an attempt by the society to consciously regulate the economic process through collective decisions so that equitable and sustainable economic development is achieved. It is a 'technical process that involves assessment of needs and resources, fixing of priorities, preparation of projects and formulation of plans.'[2] Decentralised planning meant the setting up of objectives and priorities and to transform them into concrete actions in the context of local economies.

Historically the concept of planning is centralised in nature and advocated as a cure for the defects of market mechanism. It may also be remembered that the erstwhile Soviet Union, the pioneer in planning, initiated it within a centralised frame work. Therefore, the planning techniques available were based on centralised macro models. Influenced by the Soviet Union experience, planning in India has also been a highly centralised proposition where the objectives, priorities and programmes have been formulated at the national level by the Planning Commission. At the same time there has been a growing realisation that, India being a vast country with the size of almost a continent, it is difficult to ensure that the results of centralised planning reaches all areas and sections of the population. Till the 73rd and 74th CAs there was a general belief among the people that planning can be done only by the top level bureaucrats and technocrats at the Central and State Government levels.[3] The CA's were the result of the growing realisation that the top down planning has not addressed the felt needs of the people but has removed them away from governance and participation in development. Decentralised planning is a system through which planning process is brought close to the people who are the ultimate target of development.

Relevance of Local Level Data

As Local Self-government Institutions (LSGIs) and decentralised planning are experienced reality, collection and maintenance of adequate, timely and relevant data in the manner required by policy-makers and other decision-makers at disaggregated levels is essential for effective planning. Data are required not only for planning but also for monitoring and assessing the impacts of various projects or programmes. Dependable statistics are also an indispensable element in the information system of a democratic society especially when the Right to Information is accepted as a fundamental right of every citizen in India. The CAs ushering a third strata of local governments and the conformity Kerala Panchayat Raj and Municipalities Acts of 1994 created a compelling need for a new set of data to help the formulation, monitoring and evaluation of local level planning and development in the State. Therefore, the task of building, monitoring and managing a set of reliable data is the essential prerequisite for good governance.

National Initiatives

Efforts to develop data bases required for planning and decision-making at lower than the State level were initiated way back in 1982, when the Planning Commission constituted a "Working Group on District Planning" under the chairmanship of Prof. C. H. Hanumantha Rao, then Member, Planning Commission. On the basis of the suggestion of this Working Group a lot of data were collected, processed and published for the country as a whole and for individual states, but not much disaggregation of the data for sub-state level was done. The issue of development of local level database became a subject of serious discussion after the 73rd and 74th CAs. The Department of Statistics constituted an Expert Committee on Small Area Statistics in 1996 to analyse the data implications of the CAs and the capability of the existing system to cope with the emerging requirements. The Committee in its report made useful suggestions on the collection and compilation of panchayat/ municipality level information, which could be computerised by National Information Centre (NIC) and transmitted from District to State and National levels.

The National Statistical Commission chaired by C. Rangarajan in its report pointed out that though the importance of local level statistical information for decentralised planning has been emphasised by various committees and study groups, even today there is no standardised system for the collection, compilation and maintenance of local level data and their aggregation at block, district, state and national levels.[4] In keeping with the recommendation of the Rangarajan Commission, the Ministry of Statistics and Programme Implementation constituted a "High Level Expert Committee on Basic Statistics for Local Level Development." The Committee, based on the experiences of the pilot studies carried out in many states, made a number of recommendations, the important among them are the following.[5]

(1) The Gram Panchayat should consolidate, maintain and own village level data.

(2) The village level information may be collected uniformly by using a village schedule containing following details:

- (a) Availability of basic facilities and information on assets in the village.
- (b) Demographic and socio-economic status of villagers.
- (c) Land utilisation statistics.
- (d) Data on livestock and poultry.

(2) There will be periodic data sets which may be collected once in a year such as demographic and socio-economic details and dynamic data sets to be collected every month such as birth, death, marriage etc.

(3) Directorate of Economics and Statistics in respective states should play an important role in ensuring the quality and standards by providing necessary guidelines and training to panchayat staff in the consolidation and maintenance of local level statistics.

(4) Compilation of local statistics at the panchayat level being an annual work, no additional staff would be employed for this purpose. The existing staff in coordination with Anganwadi workers will have to take up this work.

(5) A Steering Committee under the chairmanship of Director General of Central Statistical Organisation (CSO) involving Ministry of Panchayati Raj, Health, Education and Registrar General of India at the Centre and corresponding committees in the states may be set-up to look into the operation of village level statistics and data contents.

Initiatives of Kerala Government

Following the CAs the Kerala Government followed a big-bang approach in the devolution of 3 Fs – Functions, Functionaries and Funds- to LSGIs and is now considered as the leader in the decentralisation process in India. In fact, the Kerala Panchayat Raj and Municipalities Acts of 1994 and their amendments effected in 1999 'provides the statutory framework for creating functional, financial and administrative autonomy at the level of the third stratum of the Government.'[6] Realising the compelling need for statistical details at LSG level for formulating local level development schemes, the Department of Economics and Statistics (DES) made an attempt to conduct a comprehensive census type socio-economic survey in 1995. In the Interview Schedule designed for this survey some questions to elicit certain information required by the State Backward Commission were also included. These questions invited resistance from some social groups and on this basis the survey was abandoned. However, considering the suggestions from the then Vice-Chairman of the State Planning Board, Sri. V. Ramachandran, the DES compiled various secondary sources of data relating to each rural and urban LSGIs and prepared the Panchayat Level Statistics for all the 14 districts. Some of them were published during 1995-96 and others in 1996-97.

After the landmark decision of the State government to earmark 35 to 40 per cent of the State's plan fund to LSGIs to Implement Projects formulated by them, the government also launched a People's Campaign for Decentralised Planning in August 1996 to enable the LSGIs to prepare their Ninth Five Year Plan (1997-2002) projects in a scientific manner with people's participation.

During the campaign year 1996-97, rural and urban LSGs were directed by the State Planning Board to Prepare Development Reports based on data collected and compiled through a participatory process. Almost all the LSGs had prepared and published the report based on secondary sources of data and primary data collected by the volunteers recruited locally for the purpose. The Development Reports were found to be a very useful document which seeks to spell out the vision of the local governments in relation to their material, human and financial resources. But from a professional point of view the data can be used only with considerable review and scrutiny. Unfortunately after preparing the report in most of the LSG's, no attempt was made either by the elected representatives or the local bureaucracy to preserve, to improve the quality and to update them. The collected data sets unless updated and used cannot be retrieved easily. Any information which cannot be retrieved easily is as good as non-existent.

As in 1996, in 2001 and 2006 also panchayat level statistics for all the districts were prepared and published by the DES. These attempts were largely to compile secondary data from various sources and bulk of it was from census reports. The DES made its first attempt to generate data sets based on primary data in 2004 in the Malapattam panchayat of Irikkur Block of Kannur District. Here primary data on variables considered important for the identification and prioritisation of projects and programmes for the development of the panchayat were collected. This panchayat was chosen on consideration of size, existence of definite boundaries and the dedication and keen interest of the President and other elected members of the panchayat. The primary data relating to infrastructure, agriculture, demographic and socio-economic condition of households was collected on a mission mode after dividing wards into well identifiable boundaries.

Considering the need for dependable and timely data in the context of the importance for decentralised planning, the Kerala Government initiated a study "Action Research on Local Level Statistics – a UNDP Project on Improving Kerala Statistical System." The project is aimed at critically evaluating the type and quality of data in different sectors, to identify the data gaps and to suggest necessary modification. The study was entrusted to five agencies, each agency focusing on a particular sector. The agencies reviewed the existing data availability at LSG level and found that the statistical information contained in various registers and documents are neither up-to-date nor easily retrievable. There is no mechanism to check the reliability of data and to consolidate them at LSG level. All the agencies in their reports recommended the restructuring of the state statistical system to meet the data requirements for decentralised governance and planning.[7] The Committee for the Evaluation of Decentralised Planning and Development chaired by Professor M. A. Oommen in its report (Government of Kerala, 2009) critically reviewed the data sources at LSG level and observed. "The sources of data relating various aspects of the day-to-day functioning of the panchayat and municipal offices are numerous and are of good, bad and indifferent categories." The Committee further felt "that government departments, parastatal agencies and LSGs have a poor track records in data compilation, documentation, analysis and application and in keeping data records."[8] The committee emphasised the need for appointing statistical personnel at the rate of one person per panchayat and an appropriate number of persons for each of the municipalities and city corporations, after a detailed assessment of the work load. The committee also recommended the State Planning Board to constitute a study group consisting of persons with experience in statistical work to conduct a work study of the Department of Economics and Statistics and the statistical units in the different departments of government to assess the work load and the number of persons required for that work so that surplus staff, if any, already existing can be identified and redeployed suitably in the local bodies against the newly proposed posts.

Recently, the Union Ministry of Panchayati Raj sanctioned a project to Kerala Statistical Institute (KSI) to conduct a Methodological Study to "Design a System for Collection, Compilation Updating and Maintenance of Statistics for Decentralised Planning in Kerala." The Report of the Study (KSI, 2012)[9] critically evaluated the existing data availability at LSG level and found that most of the data required for local level planning are either available or can be made available without much difficulty except in the case of agricultural sector. Agricultural statistics in the state since 1975-76 are estimated on the basis of sample survey under the centrally sponsored scheme of "Establishment of an Agency for Reporting Agricultural Statistics (EARAS). Nearly 50 per cent of the statistical personnel of the DES, including 811 investigators are engaged in this scheme. When the scheme was introduced in 1975-76, agricultural sector contributed nearly 50 per cent of the State Domestic Product and seasonal and annual crops accounted for 52 per cent of the gross cropped area of the state. Bulk of the work under this scheme is for the collection of data relating to seasonal and annual crops like rice, tapioca, vegetables, and plantain. Now agricultural sector's contribution to the State Domestic Product is only around 11 per cent and the area under seasonal and annual crops is only 18 per cent of the gross cropped area of the state (i.e., decreased from 14.3 lakh hectares in 1975-76 to 4.9 lakh hectares in 2009-10). As such the work load of investigators has been reduced considerably. Since year to year changes in the area under perennial crops, which now account for 82 per cent of the total cropped area, is only marginal area estimation of perennial crops needs to be conducted only once in five years preferably along with the quinquennial Agricultural Census. The area under seasonal and annual crops can be estimated by local enquiry if a statistical person is posted in the LSG. Therefore, if the EARAS scheme is restructured in accordance with the changes in the cropping pattern it would be possible not only to generate LSG level data but also to improve the quality of data. Now only district level data are published and as such it is not possible to verify the quality of data. Once LSG level data are generated it would be easy to verify the reliability of data as the area covered is small. Further the 811 investigators of this scheme can be posted in 811 panchayats and for the remaining 167 panchayats and 65 urban local bodies the required persons can be identified through a proper work study of the DES and the statistical units functioning in various departments. Once the investigators are posted in panchayats and urban local bodies complete enumeration of all households and agricultural operational holdings have to be carried out once in five years using the services of Anganwadi workers and the staff of other local offices of line departments under the close supervision of the investigators of DES. If staff of line departments can not be mobilised, locally available experienced persons from Kudumbhashree or other self-help groups can be employed for the enumeration of agricultural plots and households.

Meanwhile the Government of India with World Bank assistance launched the National Strategic Statistical Plan (NSSP) to strengthen the statistical system in the country. As part of this, State governments were given full freedom to design and implement their own strategic plan to strengthen their statistical system. On this basis, the DES of the State Government with the assistance of two consultants prepared the Kerala State Strategic Statistical Plan (KLSSSP) [10] and signed a Memorandum of understanding with the Union Ministry of Statistics and Programme Implementation for the Implementation of the Strategic Plan. This is now a centrally sponsored scheme with a budget of Rs 52.72 crore to be implemented during the five year period of 2011-2016. Even though the stated objective of the Plan is to equip the State Statistical system for the timely dissemination of adequate reliable and credible statistics to the planners and decision-makers from the LSG level to the State level, in the long list of summary of findings and recommendations, more emphasis is given for the creation and upgradation of posts and the constitution of Committees and Commissions. A disturbing component of the State Strategic Plan (KLSSSP) is the provision of large amount of fund for the construction of own buildings for Taluk Statistical Offices and for additional physical infrastructure facilities in the 61 Taluk statistical offices. With the emergence of three-tier Panchayati Raj system in the State, there is no need for Taluk Statistical offices. The amount earmarked for this need to be provided for improving the quality of data generated at grassroot level of panchayats and municipalities. Once rural and urban LSG level data of good quality are generated, their aggregation at higher levels is easy as it involves only additions.

Conclusion

Even though the importance of Local Self-government level data for decentralised planning has been emphasised by various committees and study groups constituted by the Central and State governments, the implementation of these recommendations has not been taken up seriously by the Kerala government. As such even today no standardised system exists for the collection, compilation and maintenance of LSG level data and for their aggregation at block, district and state levels. In this connection it is important to note that the Draft Approach Paper of 12th Five Year Plan of Kerala (2012-17) clearly stated that there would be a thorough revamping of all ongoing schemes and public institutions. The paper also stated that PRIs will be strengthened to make them capable to take the 'Next Step' issues in decentralisation. Therefore, the State Planning Board and the State Government have to re-examine the recommendations of various Committees and Study Groups and also the KLSSSP to find out a proper strategy to build up a statistical system from the LSG level to the State level.

References

1. Quoted from Jain, S. P. (2003): 'Decentralisation in India: An Appraisal' in S. N. Mishra, Anil Mishra and Sweta Mishra (eds): *Public Governance and Decentralisation*, Mittal Publications, New Delhi.
2. Thomas Issac, T. M. with Richard W. Franke (2000): *Local Democracy and Development: People's Campaign for Decentralised Planning in Kerala*, Leftword Books, New Delhi.
3. Palanithurai, G. (2007): 'Planning for Development at Grassroots in India; Tamil Nadu Experience' in Sundar Ram (ed): *Panchayati Raj Reforms in India: Power to the people at the Grassroots*, Kanishka Publishers, New Delhi.
4. Government of India (2001): *National Statistical Commission.*
5. Government of India (2006): *Report of the High Level Expert Committee on Basic Statistics for Local Development*, Ministry of Statistics and Programme Implementation.
6. Oommen, M. A. (2004): 'Deepening Decentralised Governance in Rural India: Lessons from the People's Plan Initiatives of Kerala', *Working Paper No. 11*, Centre for Socio-economic & Environmental Studies, Kochi.
7. Government of Kerala (2005): *Action Research on Local Level Statistics – a UNDP assisted project for Improving Kerala Statistical System*, Institute of Management in Government.
8. Government of Kerala (2009): *Report of the Committee for Evaluation of Decentralised Planning and Development.*
9. Kerala Statistical Institute (2012): *Report on the Methodological Study to Design a System for Collection, Compilation Updating and Maintenance of Statistics for Decentralised Planning*, Thiruvananthapuram.
10. Government of Kerala (2011): *Kerala State Strategic Statistical Plan*, Department of Economics and Statistics.

7

Decentralised Planning in Kerala : Some Reflections

—P. Sureshkumar

Good economics requires efficient allocation and good politics requires equitable distribution of resources. Can good economics and good politics exist together? The whole spectrum of social science is concerned with this. Economists speak about two powerful institutional mechanisms available with them to settle this issue. These are the market mechanism and the concept of planning.

The market mechanism has been proved as the most powerful entity to secure efficiency. However, in the context of globalisation it became clear that absence of an 'equal level playing' ground deprive its efficiency. The competitive spirit involved in the market mechanism is the stimulant to trigger efficiency and equity. Alternatively, state intervention and complementarity involved therein create efficiency and equity in the planning process. Thus, it is true that both mechanisms are capable of producing both efficiency and equity. There is no trade off involved between market mechanism and planning process. But the issue is that in which context that these mechanisms can be appropriately used? What is the right blend one has to choose?

In a democratic society both efficiency and equity are prime motives. In a dynamic framework efficiency enhances equity realms and in turn equity enhance efficiency. It implies that both efficiency and equity should be vigorously pursued for the betterment of a society. If efficiency and equity is to be simultaneously achieved, both market forces and planning process should be judiciously balanced. India's development experience shows that the two entities have been widely used for its progress. In India, its resource allocation has been pursued by planning to maximise the social objectives set out by the Planning Commission. However, the planning process missed its, comprehensive character and efficiency when it failed to ensure equality particularly among the lower rungs of the society. This shortcoming of Indian planning required to be rectified with more effective planning process. It was the decentralised planning that has been suggested as a strategy to overcome the weaknesses of the centralised plan.

From an economic perspective, the need for decentralised planning arises basically from four angles.

1. To have an idea about the local level resources available and the spacially specific economic activities pursued at household and village levels.
2. To formulate programmes to bring the marginalised and poor within the ambit of mainstream economic process.
3. To formulate stable and dependable arrangements for the provision of relief and supply of minimum needs on an adequate scale.
4. To evolve participatory mechanisms in the planning for resources and needs with a view to promoting among people motivation, habits of self-help, local level leadership and active role in strategic and planning decisions. (Ramayan Prasad, 1991)

These aspects justify the necessity of decentralised planning. Also, it reveals its potential, scope and limitations as it is to be used for development purposes.

For example, the information about the resource availability and the dominant economic activities prevailing in a community enable individuals residing there to relate it with their private resources such as the entrepreneurial capital and ability. This will enable, them to realise the opportunities so that more productive activities will be ventured into by them. Simultaneously, the possibilities of collective or cooperative use of the resource will also be reckoned and identified. Secondly, the importance of empowerment of the weaker sections is vigorously taken at policy levels in the decentralised planning. In a globalised economy, the empowerment measures need to be taken beyond the conventional approach of ensuring minimum needs. Drastic socio-economic changes necessitates new approaches towards empowerment. Decentralisation enable the community to find out adequate and proper empowerment mechanisms. The decentralisation process further enable the community to make appropriate organisational choices to make effective decisions including that of project selections. They may go for collective efforts or individual efforts and in both cases the outcome will be maximisation of societal benefits.

Though the necessity and importance of decentralised planning was recognised much earlier its implementation was not so smooth. Finally, it was the 73rd and 74th Constitutional amendments that led to the effective implementation of decentralisation planning in India.

Obviously the state of Kerala responded to this mandatory requirement with its own legal enactments. It had passed the Kerala Panchayat Raj Act in 1994. This Act envisaged the transfer of powers and functions of various departments of the state governments to the three-tier of Panchayat and Municipal Councils and Corporations.

How far this has helped to improve the socio-economic conditions of the people of the state? By and large, we may say that the Kerala economy has ventured into this planning process more vigorously. However, later the concern with the new change has waned, and now it seems that it has become another area of polemics among the politicians in the state.[1] Broadly speaking, the decentralisation process has not delivered the much needed growth and development of the state.[2] Why, decentralisation has not produced desired changes in the state? How far decentralisation became effective in affecting the transitions of the Kerala economy particularly in the context of globalisation. Some of these issues are discussed in this paper.

At the socio-economic and political level, Kerala is a typical state in comparison with other states in India. Its remarkability of development process is much reflected in its fame as Kerala model of development. The model beams the fact that substantial achievement in social sectors can be secured even with a modest growth. Though much debate is there around the Kerala model of development, it became an increasing concern that its growth level is insufficient to sustain the social development it has secured over time. Another, aspect relating to its growth is that inspite of the potential growth possibility stemming from improved social sector performance such as good health, better education, skilled manpower and the like, it has not materialised in higher growth rate. In fact, the state's economic indices such as state domestic income and per capita income are often found to be falling behind the national averages:

The following tables reveal this:

Table 1: Growth Rates (per cent) in Net Domestic Product (at 1993-94 Constant Prices). Kerala and All India

Period	*Kerala*		*All India*	
	Annual Average	*Exponential*	*Annual Average*	*Exponential*
1971 - 72 To 1980 - 81	2.34	1.91	3.24	3.45
1981 - 82 To 1990 - 91	3.85	3.53	5.55	5.38

Source: Rajasenan D (2005).

Table 2: Growth Rates (per cent) in Per Capita Net Domestic Product (at 1993-94 Constant Prices) Kerala and All India

Period	*Kerala*		*All India*	
	Annual Average	*Exponential*	*Annual Average*	*Exponential*
1971 - 72 To 1980 - 81	0.56	0.17	0.93	1.19
1981 - 82 To 1990 - 91	2.47	2.15	3.32	3.24

Source: Rajasenan.D (2005).

Why the growth rate decelerated inspite of many unique favourable conditions.

It should be remembered that Indian economy is poised for a planned economic growth since its independence. The planning process, as suggested earlier, rely much on the complementarity among the different sectors coming under its span. The plan success in triggering growth depends on appropriating the complementarities. The national plan envisaged such a complementarily to exist and it is expected to be replicated at the state level also. The national plan always with the state plans co-ordinated by the planning commission became instrumental in putting the economy on a fair growth rate upto the mid-1980s.[3] The economy has also allowed the market mechanism within the regulated framework of the national plan. The growth stimulants that have sprouted and strengthened in the economy enabled it to achieve many of the plan objectives. While many of the states pursued development perceptions on the national line, the approach of Kerala was different owing to the influential dominance of the left parties. Though the state has to function with the constitutional limit, it was always critical of the national economic policies.[4] It was difficult to design and implement any alternations to the national schemes. However, the state focused on people-centred empowerment programmes, particularly beneficial to the marginalised and downtrodden communities. Broadly speaking, though such an approach was important and much needed, it was insufficient for enhancing the economic momentum of the state.[5] Further, in an incipient economy, the assertion of class division and polarisation in policy-making deprive prioritation in favour of growth for more of welfare measures. The maximisation and appropriation of complementarities involved among different sectors, the formulation of policies for creation of backward and forward linkages and strengthening of the market principles for boosting the productive stimulants among the economic agents and similar institutionalisations were not consciously nurtured to raise the productive powers of the economy.[6] The antagonistic relation with the national policy-makers further fuelled the political differences feeding one up on another resulting in missing the much needed growth inevitable for further strengthening of further growth and distribution. Thus, the state economy has worked without any remarkable achievement in its growth rate. The economic structure evolved in the state economy is a testimony to the missing elements of growth in Kerala economy. The following table indicate the type of economic structure that emerged in Kerala.

Table 3: Growth Rate (Exponential) by Conventional Sectors in Kerala

Period	*Primary*	*Secondary*	*Tertiary*
1971 - 72 to 1980 - 81	-0.27	3.89	2.16
1980 - 81 to 1990 - 91	2.72	3.36	4.36
1991 - 92 to 2000 - 2001	1.66	6.01	8.13

Source: Rajasenan D. (2005).

A reading of the Table 3 reveals that the tertiary sector was surging fast ahead of other real sectors. In terms of the sectoral contribution, the major sectors share in the state's income is shown in Table 4.

Table 4: Sectors shares (per cent) in Kerala's NSDP

Year	*Primary*	*Secondary*	*Tertiary*	*Total*
1971	50.40	16.64	32.96	100
1981	39.46	25.20	35.34	100
1991	36.45	23,85	39.70	100
2001	32,69	22.63	44.69	100

Source: Rajasenan D. (2005).

The table reveals that the shares of the primary and secondary sector is falling and that of the tertiary sector is rising.

Again, we may look at the different sectors contribution to the net state domestic product growth rate which is shown in Table. 5.

Table 5: Sector's Contribution (%) to NSDP growth rate

Year	*Primary*	*Secondary*	*Tertiary*	*Total NSDP*
1971-81	39.78	22,19	38.03	100
1981-91	28.93	27.36	43.71	100
1991-01	28.35	20.21	51.43	100

Source: Rajasenan D. (2005).

All these tables reveals that the tertiary sector leads the economy at the cost of the real sectors. It indicate structural pattern of growth which is not maintaining an inevitable conventional balance. As such an important issue the Kerala economy has to face is about the sustainability of this pattern.[7]

In the post-globalised scenario drastic changes has happened in the Indian economy. Under the liberalised regime it has secured tremendous growth. The average growth rate since the inception of the New Economic Policy has more than doubled in comparison with the pre-globalised period. Many of the Indian states also became enthusiastic in making use of the new opportunities opened under globalisation. The Kerala economy has also showed signs of improvement. It has been pointed out that a turn around has started in its sluggish growth. However, it is to be seen whether the imbalance that has crept into the growth pattern of Kerala would change under the new strategy? Indications are that no such possibility is spawning in Kerala's growth pattern. In fact, the imbalance is getting worsened to develop into a sort of lopsided growth. Ideological positions does not allow it to go for an open acceptance of globalisation process as is freely done by other states. As such the real sectors remain slow in their growth and the service sector happen to be an area where capital can be invested without adhering to competition through seeking political patronage. The monopoly and duopoly forces flourish with their investment occurring in undesirable directions seeking quick profits.

The prospects of real sector growth has been sidelined blocking potential economic forces embedded in globalisation polices. Further, it was claimed that growth is possible with an alternative strategy of decentralised planning.

The potential growth and development stimulation that is expected from the concept of decentralisation seems to be beyond any economic rationality under the new situation of the global reality. The decentralised planning has been taken more on its political rhetoric rather than its economic potential. It was taken for granted that the market mechanism cannot achieve socio-economic development with social justice and equity. It was pointed out that investment decision stimulated by profitability criterion is not socially desirable and against long-term interest and sustainable progress of the state (B.A. Prakash, 2005). Hence, it was argued that a decentralised planning process by delegating more administrative and financial powers to local bodies will safeguard the interest of the poor and weaker sections and ensure social justice.

The decentralisation process in the state based on the above perception had the following objectives:-

1. Transferring 35 to 40 per cent of total plan outlay to the local bodies.
2. Ensure people's participation in plan formulation and implementation and mobilisation of local resources both manpower and physical resources for local investment.
3. Strengthen the local bodies in their decision-making powers.
4. Expand the plan outlay and activities through effective mobilisation of local resources.

While these objectives will strengthen the decentralisation process can it be considered as a substitute for alternative policies to stimulate growth? The concept of decentralised planning should not be interpreted as an alternative to the much needed economic reforms. Rather it should be viewed as a complementary mechanism to ensure effective empowerment of the people and to enhance their potential productive economic powers. The empowerment mechanism evolved under the decentralised policies should enable the people to appropriate the opportunities available from the interdependence and interconnection that is coming up with the new reforms. As such the empowerment should bypass the conventional approach of ensuring minimum needs of a community. Much more than that it should be related with their productive potential enabling them to release their latent powers to make use of their private resource and the market mechanism.

The implementation of decentralisation in Kerala simply involved a transfer of resources with an element of control. In order to ensure the overall thrust of the state plan, broad guidelines were issued as norms for allocation of the resource.[5] Accordingly the percentage share of allocation was fixed for three broad sectors such as 40 to 50 per cent for general sector plan, 30 to 40 per cent on service sector and 10 to 30 per cent on infrastructure for local bodies. The organisational set up made under the decentralised arrangements was also not popularly accepted, though massive cadre participation was successfully managed in the name of people's plan. Since the implementation of decentralisation was done under an ideological base by mobilising a sectarian segment, the decentralisation process could not emerge as a viable empowerment system. Rather, the development plans were turned simply as outlet, for distribution of favours to individuals. Though 30-40 per cent of the plan allocation is earmarked for developmental schemes, it could not generate substantial sustainable productive units.

In this context, it should be realised that the decentralised planning as a concept of development has a scope limited to the level of a complementary role to the strengthening of market mechanism. The efficient working of market mechanism requires an equal level playing field. The decentralised planning should ensure that the community is empowered with adequate level of minimum needs including the socio-economic infrastructure. The success of the decentralised planning depends on how effectively the productive impulses latent in a community can be released and linked with the market system. The spirit in Kerala under the peoples plan programme deprived such a link. The whole planning process happened to be an exercise with a political agenda. Such an exercise could not become sustainable either in the popular mind or in the economic sphere.

Notes

1. In the initial years of implementation of decentralised planning in Kerala as 'People's Plan', the participation of people was large. However, at present, the Grama Sabhas, are poorly attended.
2. It has been pointed out that more local roads were constructed and maintained and many beneficiaries were empowered at individual levels. However, what is required for growth is spin off effects and sustainability feautures of the schemes implemented. Such outcomes were glaringly absent.
3. Between 1950-51 and 1984-85 the average growth rate of the economy was 3.5 per cent.
4. The communist party believed that nothing substantial could be achieved for the people if it required to be worked within the limits of the constitution.
5. A general feature of the governance of the state was that it prioritise much for distribution of favours to different segments of the people. However, such prioritisation is an outcome of competitive politics of the two fronts (LDF and UDF) to capture power alternatively.
6. The reasons for low growth are elaborated in the work of Suresh Kumar R.K. and P. Sureshkumar (2008).
7. Many writers have related the service sector growth of Kerala with the migrants remittances from abroad.

References

1. Ramayan Prasad (1991): *Decentralised Planning*, Deep and Deep, New Delhi.
2. Suresh Kumar R.K. and P. Suresh Kumar (2008) : *Development, Politics and Society : Left Politics in Kerala*, APH, New Delhi.
3. Rajasenan D. and G. Groot (2005): *Kerala Economy: Trajectories Challenges and Implications*, Directorate of Publications and Public Relations, CUSAT.
4. Joseph Tharamangalam (2006): *Kerala the Paradoxes of Public Action and Development.*
5. Frons J. Schraman (2004): *Globalisation and Development Studies: Challenges for the 21st Century*, Vistaar Publications, New Delhi.

8

Kerala's Decentralisation Experience and Women

—*P. P. Rajasekharan Pillai*

World over, the twentieth century has witnessed the emergence of decentralisation in the development system. The decades of 1950's and 1960's saw the demands (Kueck, 1998) coming from the people and a number of civil society groups for a variety of development needs ranging from health to poverty alleviation to marketing of agricultural produces to civic amenities. The central governments in several countries felt the pressure for addressing these problems. Thus, it was a period that was marked with the setting up of local governments in a number of countries. The decade of 70's saw the emergence of decentralisation as a development alternative and got the focused attention when the debate picked up momentum in 1980's. Many countries in Asia and Africa emphasised the role of decentralisation as a means of national development and for achieving a variety of development objectives ranging from people's participation to meeting their aspirations to political stability. This period saw a paradigm shift in the approach for development and led to shift in orientation from structured development planning to planning from below and from growth to redistribution of income with the objectives of equality, improved quality of life and reduction in poverty.

The causes that have led to decentralisation differ substantially from country to country. The decentralisation has been adopted by a number of countries irrespective of their political thinking - left, right and centre; economic condition, rich or poor or under debt-trap; and practising autocracies and democracies. It makes it clear that a diversity of influences has been at work, and that decentralisation has been undertaken for a variety of reasons and with a variety of objectives in mind.

Considerations underlying decentralisation

Against the widespread notion that centralised governance has not succeeded, many countries facing a variety of problems- political, social or economic- have adopted the path of decentralisation. It also provided opportunity to political leadership with diverse considerations and compulsions to have a decentralised form of governance. Also, there is little or no empirical evidence to indicate what decentralisation could and could not achieve or how specific types of decentralisation would produce specific results (Manor, 1998). Though the unease with commandism was very perceptible in East European, African and other developing countries, yet it offered few clear and specific indicators to help leaders choose particular form of decentralisation. Countries like Nepal, India, Bangladesh, Nigeria, China, Sri Lanka, Brazil and Chile, which had adopted decentralisation more vigorously in the last two decades, do not have any similarity of either the cause or the objective or the form. It has emerged due to their socio-economic and politico-cultural factors that are more country specific than represent any general trend.

Notwithstanding the above, some evidence (Smith, 1985 and Sundaram, 1997) suggest that the development concern has its share in adopting the course of decentralisation as it would facilitate in addressing local problems, in improving administrative efficiency and in meeting needs of diverse groups.

Decentralisation for Welfare and Development Concerns

Most countries have gone for decentralisation with a variety of goals in mind. Some of them have often proceeded on the basis of genuine considerations of empowering the people at the grass root level.

- Providing opportunities to people for their socio-economic development;
- Enhancing people's participation at lower level by providing them opportunities in the decision making;
- Utilising the local knowledge in the development planning;
- Raising the competence level of development functionaries and the capacity of local institutions for more sustained development;
- Equitable distribution of resources;
- Empowering the weaker sections through improvement in their capabilities and by giving them voice in the decision making;
- Facilitating socio-economic development including alleviation of poverty by way of tapping individual potential and the services of social groups at local levels;
- Enhancing the transparency of functioning and responsiveness as well as accountability of departments, elected representatives and political institutions to people, and thus improving the efficiency of functioning; and

- Also providing opportunities to people at the lower level for future political role.

Decentralisation with Narrow Focus and Political Gains

Similarly there have been considerations having more inclination towards narrow or partisan political advantage such as;

- Providing a feeling of democratisation without giving adequate functions and responsibilities;
- Giving responsibility to local institutions of raising resources, but giving no financial and institutional support;
- Providing patronage to the inconvenient political figures by way of giving some powers;
- Entrusting tasks which the central government finds costly or inconvenient, or both on to lower level authorities;
- Providing funds and powers at the lower levels and facilitating the ruling party in building its political base at the local level, and thus to get votes through this strategy;
- Diverting the attention of country men and out side observers from other coercive action of the central government and;
- Appealing donor agencies who favour decentralisation (Manor, 1998).

Objectives of Decentralisation

Decentralisation refers to a process of assigning the public functions and responsibilities of planning and implementation from central government to sub-district level in order to carry out specific tasks at the local level. As indicated by this definition the public affairs are to be managed at the local level and there are certainly specific objectives for the need to choose the path of decentralisation. The prominent among them are:

- Firstly, to handle promptly the local specific development needs.
- Secondly, to improve the efficiency of programme implementation.
- Thirdly to reach the distant locations effectively.
- Fourthly, to increase the responsiveness of local administration to people's needs.

Decentralisation Initiatives in Kerala

Government of Kerala thought of democratic decentralisation immediately after the state was formed in 1956. The Administrative Reforms Committee appointed by the government made detailed recommendations in 1958. Despite enactment of laws, nothing significant in decentralised development was done for over three decades. There was a short lived attempt to form District Councils in 1990, following a comprehensive Report on Decentralisation. However, with the 73rd and 74th amendments to the Constitution of India in 1992, Kerala carried out pioneering reforms and embarked up on a path of comprehensive decentralisation since 1995.

By April 1994, the government of Kerala passed conformity legislation for the 73rd and 74th amendments to the Constitution of India. In March 1994, the Kerala Panchayati Raj Act was passed and elections were held to the three-tier panchayat in 1995. The decentralisation process as a meaningfull march towards participatory democracy was launched in August 1996 with the introduction of People's Plan Campaign (PPC). Under the PPC, the government announced the earmarking of 35-40 per cent of the outlay of the ninth five year plan towards projects and programmes to be drawn by LSGs. The government insisted on mass participation and transparency in the utilisation of the devolved fund. A comprehensive plan has to be democratically prepared by each local body before it can claim the grant-in-aid. The planning process starts below the ward members with maximum involvement of the masses. Mass participation is not limited to elected representatives or voluntary agencies, but includes ordinary people assembling in Grama Sabhas with non-official experts and volunteers participating in preparing reports, for making projects and drafting plans. Officials have to work along side non-officials. The PPC was launched to empower the elected bodies with department officials, experts, volunteers and the people rallying around them.

A Profile of Women in Kerala

Kerala's human development indices are not only high when compared to those of the rest of the country but are also comparable to the advanced countries of the world. This is applicable almost equally for both men and women. It is widely acknowledged that women in Kerala fare much better than their counter-parts elsewhere in India. Historically, Kerala has been quite different from the rest of country in terms of the indicators of women development. The provisional data of Census 2011 put the overall sex ratio (the number of women against 1000 men) one of the most important social parameters indicating the balance between males and females in the society, at 1084 (1058 in 2001), which should be compared to the all-India figure of 940. Kerala has a very unique position with regard to sex ratio by dint of the fact that in all the censuses, the number of females outnumbered the number of males contrary to the pattern shown at the all-India level. Details of sex ratio for India and Kerala during the period 1951 to 2011 are given in Table 1.

Table: 1: Sex Ratio – India and Kerala (1951 to 2011) Year

	India	*Kerala*
1951	946	1028
1961	941	1022
1971	930	1016
1981	934	1032
1991	927	1036
2001	933	1058
2011	940	1084

Source: Census of India 2011.

The profile of literacy in the state throws up interesting trends. Of course, male literacy has been quite high, it being as high as 97.90 per cent in 2011 Census. But unlike in many other states, literacy among women has also been quite high, as much as 91.98 per cent as per Census 2011. Whereas the overall literacy rate of the state nearly doubled from 47.18 per cent in 1951 to 93.91 per cent in 2011, the female literacy rate during the same period has more than doubled – it increased from 36.43 per cent to 91.98 per cent. See Table 2.

Table 2: Kerala's Literacy rate 1951 to 2011

Year	*Persons*	*Males*	*Females*
1951	47.18	58.35	36.43
1961	55.08	64.89	45.56
1971	69.75	77.13	62.53
1981	78.85	84.56	73.36
1991	89.81	93.62	86.17
2001	90.86	94.24	87.12
2011	93.91	96.02	91.98

Source: Census of India 2011.

Other indicators of development like life expectancy, mean age at marriage, the infant mortality rate for girl child (only 13 in 2009 as against the corresponding all-India figure of 52), declining reproductive rate (1.7 in 2009 as against 1.5 for western Europe) also establish the distinctive status of women in Kerala.

The state's excellent gender development indicators are also clouded with contrasts. The gender paradox is more visible when we take into account the work participation of women which is lower than the national average and it has also tended to decline. An important reason for this decline is the severe unemployment rate in the state (Issac Thomas: 1999). The level of unemployment is higher among women and men in both rural and urban areas.

The social status of women in this state is considered to be high as a consequence of matrilineal practice existed among some communities and due to the higher educational level. Yet this is not reflected in the political participation as one would expect and here Kerala reflects the trend in the country with the participation rate of women in the state legislature less than 10 per cent. Women's representation is also low in the various decision-making bodies of the political parties and trade unions.

Violence against women in Kerala shows increasing trends. According to Crime Records Bureau data, reported cases of violence in the state were 1867 in 1991 and it multiplied almost four fold in 2002 and total of 7298 cases were reported that year. The data also indicate that crimes against women have actually doubled between 1995 and 2010. Kerala with 2.96 per cent share of population has accounted for 3.9 per cent of the total crime against women in India in 2009. Among the states, Kerala stood at Seventh rank as per the rate of total cognisable crimes (23.2 per cent) and at the tenth rank as per percentage share in total offences against women. In the total incidence in Kerala, seven per cent of the total cases where those in which the offenders were known to the victims, like parents/close family friends, relatives, neighbours and other known persons. Nearly half of the total offences were reported as cruelty by husband and relatives.

A matter of great concern is the declining child sex ratio (the number of girls against 1000 boys in the age group of 0 to 6); it declined from 963 in 2001 to 959 in 2011. This indicates male preference which clouds the state's claim of a high level of gender status. Kerala has also the dubious distinction of having the highest suicidal rate among Indian states as reported in several studies.

Women and Decentralisation Efforts of Kerala

Among other things one of the main objectives of People's Plan Campaign was raising the social and economic status of women and converting them in to active and meaningful participants in the process of development. From the very outset of the PPC, organisers and activists realised that the campaign needed women's participation to make decentralisation democratic and effective. Women's participation in turn, could create conditions for altering the relations between women and men in Kerala "The campaign's philosophy and interventions have been to institutionalise gender equity in planning by the following:

1. Raised numerical inclusion or greater numbers of women participating in each stage of the plan exercise through the constitution

and activation of poor women's self-help groups, neighbourhood groups etc.

2. Giving substance to their nominal presence by devolving powers and resources as well as institutionalising gendered planning procedures and exercise. Ensuring the participation of women in planning, implementation and execution, monitoring and audit. building accountability and transparency into the system.
3. Massive supportive capacity building measures.
4. Demystification of planning and governance so that the myth of their inaccessibility can be broken.

These should lead to greater gender equity (Issac Thomas, *Women Elected Representatives in Kerala (1995-2000): From Symbolism to Empowerment)*

While employment of women outside home could itself be one of the factors altering social attitude, a few women acting individually may not produce as much impact in challenging gender-conservative biases as would women acting in groups. It is in this context that economic activities of women's groups assume added importance. Collective action of people including women having similar economic status was highlighted throughout the campaign. Such thinking has led to the formation of neighbourhood groups (NHGs) and self-help groups (SHGs) for the emancipation and empowerment of women as part of the people's campaign.

Kudumbasree- the state poverty eradication mission- started functioning on April 1, 1999. By March 2002, it covered the whole state of Kerala and aims at the eradication of absolute poverty in ten years through concerted community action under the leadership of Local Self-Governments by facilitating organisation of the women from BPL families, combining self-help with demand led convergence of available services and resources to tackle the multiple dimensions and manifestations of poverty holistically.

Kudumbasree, a new venture for generating employment and income to women drawn from BPL families, operates through a three tier Community Based Organisation (CBO); the Neighbourhood Group (NHG) at the grass-root level, the ADS (Area Development Society) at the middle level and CDS (Community Development Society) at the apex level. The NHGs are an association of 15-40 adjoining poor families represented by one woman each from every family.

With the launching of Kudumbasree, the LSGs began to earmark plan fund both for the training of office bearers and members and for the income generating projects of NHGs under WCP. Besides, self-help credit groups which are formed within the NHGs are also given credit facilities as well as subsidies from LSGs as well as directly from Kudumbasree. In short, the Kudumbasree aims at eradicating absolute poverty through the social and economic empowerment of women. But it also leads to the political empowerment of women from BPL families through their involvement in the decentralised planning and development process. Thus, the process of decentralised and participatory development aims at the empowerment of women. At the same time active involvement of women can contribute substantially to the process of decentralised and participatory development.

Guidelines were issued to ensure active participation of women at every stage of the planning process. Although a gender perspective was integrated into each of the various phases of the planning process, it soon became clear to the campaign organisers that the formal integration of women into the structures and process of decentralisation, while increasing their visibility did not automatically ensure their participation. For that a conscious policy of activation was required. A special subject group on women and development was made mandatory in the Grama Sabha meetings. A separate chapter in the development report drawn up by each LSGs is devoted to women and a strategy for women's development is discussed and adopted at every development seminar. This includes a review of the status of women in the locality, their unemployment situation, problems of working women and the social status of women (ranging from issues such as their involvement in public activities to the many forms of violence against them). Among the task forces set up to implement the recommendations of the development seminar there is one on women which prepares a gender impact assessment.

Development plans were to pay attention to the special requirements of women and most importantly special women targeted projects for which at least 10 per cent of the budgeted outlay was to be earmarked. Considering the shortfall in the allocation of funds for Women Component Plan (WCP) during the first year, 10 per cent allocation was made mandatory from the second year onwards.

A Critique of Women Development Initiatives Under Decentralisation

Kerala is one of the few states in the Indian union that has made an earnest attempt in implementing the provisions of 73rd and 74th constitutional amendments in letter and spirit. The Ninth Plan Period coterminous with the 'People's plan campaign' started with an experimental phase, followed by a corrective phase. With the advent of the Tenth Five Year Plan the institutional phase has begun through the Kerala Development Plan. In the Eleventh Plan, government revamped the entire process giving stress to the concept of 'People's Planning' focusing on completion of the process of institutionalisation of decentralisation. There are several features of Kerala model of decentralisation which makes it unique. Among other things, introduction of women component plan and several other initiatives towards gender mainstreaming through ensuring better participation of women in the various stages of decentralised planning, a gender impact statement in project assessment and so on need special mention. Fifteen years have passed since the launching of the decentralisation process and hence an attempt is made here to evaluate what happened to the women development initiatives under PPC, which is an important plank of democratic decentralisation in Kerala.

A section upon whom the process of decentralisation has had a significant impact is women. The development planning at the local level aims at resolving or at least trying to resolve the social paradox that is distinct to contemporary Kerala society today. Women in Kerala, even as they have made several impressive gains in the areas of education, life expectancy and health, have remained relatively "invisible" in the public domain with falling work participation rates and a conspicuous absence from leadership roles in trade unions and other mass movements. With the introduction of 33 per cent reservation for women in local bodies since 1995 elections and 50 per cent reservation since 2010 elections and opening up of multiple avenues of people's participation like Grama Sabha meetings, Development seminars, Working groups/Technical Advisory Groups created an environment to break traditional barriers and to strive, not without difficulties or setbacks, of course, to become equal partners with men in the planning for development process that the PPC has envisaged. For example in 2005-06 out of a total number of 15470 citizens who participated in the various ward sabha meetings in the Thiruvananthapuram corporation, 67 per cent were women and more or less the same pattern continued (Report of the Committee for Evaluation of Decentralised Planning and Development, Govt. of Kerala).

"The participation of women in development seminar and working groups shows a mixed picture. Continuous and consistent involvement of women in these bodies was seen missing. While women participation in development seminars was reportedly strong in some Grama panchayats and in most urban local bodies studied, the representation in the working groups that should translate demands and resolutions in to action performed poorly in all the local governments. The share of the women participants which was low in the Kalamassery Municipality in 1997-98, progressively increased to more than 60 per cent largely thanks to the Kudumbasree units. But in the Koothattukulam Grama panchayat during the eleven years from 1996-97 through 2006-07, only in four years, women participation was above 33 per cent. In the Karimkulam panchayat 11 working groups were functioning and women representation was less than 50 per cent in all of them. It is definitely disturbing that in the working group on women, eight out of nine members in the Grama panchayat were men. In the Thiruvananthapuram Corporation also men dominated all working groups including the one for women. Under such a situation the role of women is but marginal and ineffective. Participation is to be understood as equal participation of women and men in the decision-making process, in policy-making, planning, implementation and so on." (The Committee for Evaluation of Decentralised Planning and Development, Govt. of Kerala)

In the initial stages women, including elected representatives struggled to establish their own identities. Obstructive social attitudes were for them the major impediment for empowerment. Participation by itself, in the exercise of power by the people is the soul of democracy. In this sense, it can be said that the achievement of the women community in the state is indeed remarkable but a long way has to go for a quality participation so that they will be the beneficiaries and participants of decentralised development in a real sense which is expected to be one of the major and lasting contributions of the PPC.

The Women Component Plan (WCP)

Introduction of Women Component Plan is one of the salient features in Kerala's decentralisation. As per guidelines, the LSGs should earmark a minimum of 10 per cent of their total plan outlay exclusively for projects which address the special problems of women. All the LSGs fulfilled this mandate in all annual plans of the 11th Plan. It was 13 per cent, 15 per cent, 13 per cent and 17 per cent for the years 2007-08, 2008-09, 2009-10, and 2010-11 respectively. The detailed figures of allocation and expenditure under WCP from 2007-08 to 2010-11 are given in Table 3.

Table: 3: Women Component Plan – Allocation and Expenditure (Rs iIn Lakhs)

Sl No.	*Types of LSGs*	*Women Component Plan*					
		2007-08			*2008-09*		
		Allocation	*Expenditure*	*Per cent*	*Allocation*	*Expenditure*	*Per cent*
1.	Grama Panchayat	11937.96	9144.52	76.6	16492.28	11202.20	67.92
2.	Block Panchayat	4761.35	4209.40	88.41	5591.27	4690.44	83.89
3.	District Panchayat	3085.37	2418.50	78.39	3799.72	2083.29	57.46
4.	Municipality	1400.04	1019.03	72.79	2164.86	1335.05	61.67
5.	Corporation	904.99	711.79	78.65	1749.58	874.72	50.00
	TOTAL	**22089.71**	**17503.24**	**79.24**	**29797.71**	**20285.70**	**68.08**

Sl No.	*Types of LSGs*	*Women Component Plan*					
		2009-10			*2010-11*		
		Allocation	*Expenditure*	*Per cent*	*Allocation*	*Expenditure*	*Per cent*
1.	Grama Panchayat	16629.81	11407.09	68.59	20651.10	12477.34	60.42
2.	Block Panchayat	6477.40	5704.56	88.07	6744.08	5289.13	78.43
3.	District Panchayat	4219.91	3160.46	74.89	5213.27	2182.22	41.86
4.	Municipality	2319.03	1505.81	64.93	3200.12	1750.32	54.70
5.	Corporation	1373.61	555.78	40.46	2875.66	659.51	22.93
	TOTAL	**31019.76**	**22333.70**	**72.00**	**38684.23**	**22358.52**	**57.80**

Source: Information Kerala Mission.

It deserves special mention that all local bodies adhered to the mandatory allocation of plan outlay for WCP (on an average 15 per cent). But the enthusiasm shown in earmarking fund has not been reflected in fund utilisation. The expenditure as a percentage of the fund allocated declined from 79.24 per cent in 2007-08 to 68.08 per cent in 2008-09. The year 2009-10 witnessed a marginal increase (72 per cent) but declined substantially to 57.8 per cent in 2010-11 (Table 3).

A comparison of the utilisation of general category fund with that of WCP shows that the percentage of expenditure under general category is much higher than that of WCP (Table 4). Despite a high level of women participation at all levels of plan formulation and implementation, this trend can be attributed mainly to the non-viability and non-feasibility of the projects along with the negligent attitude towards WCP.

Table 4: Grant-in-Aid to LSGs- Outlay and Expenditure under general category during 2007-08

Types of LSGs	*Budgeted Outlay*	*Fund Available*	*Expenditure*	*Per cent w.r.t col. 3*
1	*2*	*3*	*4*	*5*
Grama Panchayat	12825.37	12144.36	9780.89	80.54
Block Panchayat	12775.37	12533.04	10850.84	86.58
District Panchayat	59616.71	59584.59	50003.79	83.92
Municipalities	9707.46	10056.39	8594.20	85.46
Corporations	7755.09	7885.48	7186.34	91.13
TOTAL	**102680.00**	**102203.86**	**864616.06**	**84.55**

Grant-in-Aid to LSGs- Outlay and Expenditure under general category during 2008-09 Types of LSGs

	Budgeted Outlay	*Fund Available*	*Expenditure*	*Per cent w.r.t col. 3*
1	*2*	*3*	*4*	*5*
Grama Panchayat	65601.98	74092.86	58976.39	79.60
Block Panchayat	14058.01	15202.91	12469.59	82.02
District Panchayat	14108.01	13794.71	9346.44	67.75
Municipalities	10683.30	11961.13	9860.42	82.44
Corporations	8530.70	7425.00	4827.20	65.01
TOTAL	**112982.00**	**122476.61**	**95480.04**	**77.96**

Grant-in-Aid to LSGs- Outlay and Expenditure under general category during 2009-10 TYPES OF LSGs

	Budgeted Outlay	*Fund Available*	*Expenditure*	*Per cent w.r.t col. 3*
1	*2*	*3*	*4*	*5*
Grama Panchayat	71951.38	85817.13	68395.28	79.70
Block Panchayat	15350.99	17635.16	14407.56	81.70
District Panchayat	14939.85	18429.22	13129.47	71.24
Municipalities	11550.87	13394.93	10649.31	79.50
Corporations	9383.88	11500.37	8490.56	73.83
TOTAL	**122176.97**	**14677.81**	**115072.18**	**78.40**

Grant-in-Aid to LSGs- Outlay and Expenditure under general category during 2010-11 TYPES OF LSGs

	Budgeted Outlay	*Fund Available*	*Expenditure*	*Per cent w.r.t col. 3*
1	*2*	*3*	*4*	*5*
Grama Panchayat	112880.21	148018.83	104685.18	70.72
Block Panchayat	37662.37	42351.53	28782.24	67.96
District Panchayat	43611.99	54348.23	29415.18	54.12
Municipalities	18551.09	23092.34	16194.90	70.32
Corporations	14884.55	20502.65	12626.80	61.59
TOTAL	**227590.21**	**288250.58**	**191704.30**	**66.51**

Source: Information Kerala Mission and Appendix IV of the Budget for the respective year.

Compared to the WCP, though the LSGs exhibited a better performance in general category, it is to be noted that the percentage of expenditure has steadily declined from 84.55 per cent in 2007-08 to 66.51 per cent in 2010-11 (Table 4). This points out to some inherent weaknesses of the present system of plan formulation and implementation as a whole which is applicable to WCP as well. Such weaknesses include the lack of a clear cut perspective on the part of many of those associated with the planning process, including elected representatives and officials, lack of good quality projects and the bunching of plan projects and expending a lion's share of the fund at the fag end of the financial year which results in large number of spill over projects and derailing the execution of projects in subsequent years.

Further WCP is seen as a fully subsidised programme. There is not much of beneficiary contribution or loan from financial institutions depriving the beneficiaries of having any direct stake in the project. Moreover, in the case of group projects, absence of group cohesion adversely affects sustainability.

Lastly, projects are conceived and formulated in isolation and integration is always absent.

A bird's eye view of the pattern of the programmes and projects shows that the WCP was not properly designed and the projects did not address the strategic needs of women. Many projects were of a short-term nature with poor impact. In several cases, WCP expenditures have gone to support the anganvadis. Allocation of funds for female-headed households account for another large chunk of the WCP. Although money has been spent on training, they were mostly for making soaps, umbrellas, mushroom farming and tailoring, mostly stereo typical cases. Despite all these, there are several noteworthy exceptions, some of them utilising the expertise of NGO and academic institutions, training to women in heavy vehicle driving, masonry, servicing of household appliances and other non-conventional programmes like observance of human rights day, setting up of women resource centre, skill training for deaf and dumb children and the like. Further the WCP of many of the LSGs were not based on any gender status report although the idea was very much there from the beginning of the PPC.

Kudumbasree

The Kudumbasree now functioning as a subsystem of local governments must be refashioned to function as a viable women empowerment programme. Started in mid-1998, the Kudumbasree (KDS) is the largest network of women's organisation (covering 38.31 lakh families as on 30/09/2011) in the state for poverty eradication, self-employment and microfinancial services. "This outfit has performed well as an integral associate of the Local Government system for nearly a decade with remarkable resilience. It has gone much beyond its immediate microfinance mandate towards empowering women, both poor and non-poor and made some progress in gender mainstreaming." (The Committee for Evaluation of Decentralised Planning and Development, Govt. of Kerala).

"While we acknowledge the creative role the KDS has played in the decentralised governing process in this state, we may spell out certain shortcomings that need corrections to enable the institution to function as a stable and well performing agency that works hand in hand with local governments. First the KDS is no longer an organisation of the poor as it was originally meant to be. There is a clear mixture of the poor and the non-poor, the latter enjoying the commanding heights. The so-called nine-point criteria used to identify the poor women families are no longer operationally valid. Second, there is need to evolve a poverty line measurement that will take note of the emerging ground realities of Kerala. The Planning Commission's measure of poverty based on calorific norms is at best only a macro measure and is operationally irrelevant for identifying the poor from the non-poor by the local governments. Third, in view of the clear mixing up of APL (Above

Poverty Line) and BPL (Below Poverty Line), the KDS may do well to consider the question of introducing a sort of auxiliary membership to those who consider themselves as APL (or they could be identified on the basis of clear cut norms). It is important to note that poverty is a multi-dimensional deprivation and the KDS has to continue to play a crucial role in the future. Fourth, the micro enterprises programme of KDS be strengthened along with a definite agenda to escort the non-poor into better fields. Fifth, members borrow from multiple agencies with KDS being only one among many and land themselves in debt. This is a dangerous trend. Sixth, the multiplication of microfinance agencies possess a great threat to the KDS.... The answer lies in strengthening the KDS organisations making it more transparent and efficient. Seventh, overloading the NHGs can break the back of women and the organisation itself. The CDS should not function as a handmaid of the panchayat or even of the KDS bureaucracy. In short, now that KDS has travelled a long way during the last decade, its goals and roles should be redefined vis-a-vis that of decentralised governance, (Committee for Evaluation of Decentralised Planning and Development – Govt. of Kerala).

The Jagratha Samithi (JS)

When we consider the women development initiatives of the local bodies, it is essential to mention about Jagratha Samithis (JS). Built on the basic principles of gender equity and gender justice, the Jagratha Samithi (JS) is an initiative of the State Women's Commission at the Panchayat ward level upwards to the district level to protect the rights of women and children. The Samithi aims at mainstreaming gender in the decentralisation process in Kerala, leading to qualitative strengthening of status of women in society under the programme for capacity building for decentralisation.

Jagratha Samithis were constituted in two Corporations and 832 Grama Panchayats due to the initiatives and co-operation of the State Women's Commission, Social Welfare Department and Kerala Institute of Local Administration (KILA). Reportedly only very few Samithis are active. This is indeed disgraceful.

Achievements of WCP

In spite of the various weaknesses and limitations mentioned already due attention has to be given to the positive impact of WCP. For the first time the development of women was brought on the agenda of all civic bodies in the state and thereby gender dimensions were brought to the planning and development process. Over the years, the WCP helped the local governments to understand the specific issues of women through studies on status of women and reflected some of these needs in the planning process. By and large, the mandatory allocation for women addressed their economic empowerment through income generating programmes under the poverty eradication mission for Kerala Government – the Kudumbasree. Further the statutory requirement of setting apart funds for WCP helped the women to occupy sufficient space to intervene into the development process. As a result new forms of women organisations such as NHGs and SHGs were successfully promoted in local bodies under WCP. Moreover, the involvement of women in plan formulation and implementation in general and capacity development initiatives under WCP in particular has created a positive impact in women empowerment such as leadership qualities, communication skills, group dynamics, confidence in decision-making capacity etc. Though the extent and sustainability of achievement of WCP in economic empowerment may be far from satisfactory, the involvement of thousands of women in the process of planning and development as well as in anti-poverty programmes under Kudumbasree by itself is definitely a milestone on the way to gender justice and gender equity.

Suggestions

1. Local Government-wise gender status study is a pre-requisite for any gender based planning and hence it should be made mandatory.
2. Micro enterprises have to be identified on the basis of proper feasibility study and must be taken up with preparations.
3. "A clear perspective on what constitutes women development is lacking and hence the whole approach to WCP was opportunistic and adhoc" (Sakhi Resource Centre for Women). All those associated with the planning process at the local level - elected representatives, officials, social workers and resource persons – irrespective of whether men or women should be sensitised to women issues through gender sensitisation training.
4. Ensure expertise during the process of plan formulation and implementation.
5. An effective mechanism for periodic review, monitoring and co-ordination of all gender related empowerment initiatives is to be evolved both at the district and state level. The monitoring system needs to be revamped and strengthened on the basis of well-defined parameters.
6. The individual beneficiary approach must be discouraged and emphasis shall be on group initiatives.
7. As far as possible, the projects under WCP should be credit linked and the possibility of beneficiary contribution shall also be utilised in order to ensure viability and sustainability via active involvement of beneficiaries.
8. Ensure better co-ordination among the three-tier local governments in plan formulation and implementation.

9. Jagratha Samithis should be made active by giving proper guidance and training so as to convert them into an effective community-based mechanism against all kinds of gender based discrimination and violence by upholding women's right.
10. Though rare, allegations of fraudulent and politically partisan practices have been reported which, if true, may vitiate the entire process of decentralisation in due course. Hence, be very cautious in this regard.
11. The possibility of involving non-governmental organisations of repute shall be explored.
12. For the success of decentralisation process as a whole, there is a need for infusing financial discipline and streamlining the project preparation and implementation procedures in a time bound manner. A clear time table should be laid for implementing the projects and spending the funds in a meaningful and systematic manner and it should be strictly adhered to. A mandatory public accountability system shall also be introduced. The financial decentralisation shall be accompanied by autonomy, accountability, transparency and people participation so that the civic representatives would be obliged to improve their overall performance.

Conclusion

"In 1931 itself, Gandhiji emphasised that the reconstruction and development of the nation would not be possible without full participation of women as equal partners" (L.C. Jain, 2005). "Women's empowerment and their full participation on the basis of equality in all spheres of society including participation in the decision-making process and access to power are fundamental for the achievement of equality, development and peace" (Paragraph 13, Beijing Declaration). The strong emphasis on gender mainstreaming in Kerala's decentralisation efforts can be thought of as a genuine and sincere attempt to create such a state of affairs. There is no doubt that fifteen years of decentralisation experience of the state has tremendously improved the social and political awareness of women. Moreover, their self-confidence and self-image have also shown an upward graph. They have also become increasingly aware of their capabilities, problems and limitations. There has also been much improvement in their financial status. On the other hand the involvement of women has positively contributed to the quality of planning and development process. In short, there has been substantial empowerment of women in Kerala following their participation and involvement in decentralisation efforts but we have to travel a long way to ensure their empowerment in the full sense of the term which means expansion of the capacity and freedom to choose and act to shape one's life as well as that of the community to which she belongs.

References

1. Dayal, Rajeshwar, (1965): *Community Development, Panchayati Raj and Sahakari Samaj,* Metropolitan Book Co. Pvt Ltd, Delhi.
2. Dube, S. C. (1958) : *India's changing villages,* Cornell University Press, Ihaca. N.Y.
3. *Economic Review,* SPB, Kerala, 2008-2011.
4. Issac, Thomas T M (2005): *Women Elected Representatives in Kerala (1995-2000) From Symbolism to Empowerment: Decentralisation and Local Governance*, edited by L.C. Jain, Orient Longman.
5. Issac, Thomas T.M. and Franke, Richard (2000): *Local Democracy And Development,* Leftword, New Delhi 2000.
6. Jain, L C (2005): *Decentralisation And Local Governance*, Orient Longman.
7. Kueck, Gret W, Mathur S C and Sachindler Klaus (1998): *Federalism Democratisation,* Konard Adenauer Foundation, New Delhi.
8. Maddick, H (1970): *Panchayati Raj- A Study of Rural Local Government in India*, Longman Group Ltd., London.
9. Manor Games (1999): *The Political Economy of Democratic Decentralisation,* The World Bank, Washington.
10. *Report of the Committee for Evaluation of Decentralised Planning and Development, Government of Kerala,* (2009).
11. *Report of Sakthi Resource Centre For Women,* Thiruvananthapuram.
12. Smith, B C (1985): *Decentralisation, The Territorial Dimensions of the State,* London, Allen and Unwin.
13. Sundaram, K V (1997) : *Decentralised Multi Level Planning*, Concept Publishing Company, New Delhi.

9

Mahatma Gandhi National Rural Employment Guarantee Scheme - Problems and Prospects

—P. Rajendran Nair and N. Madhava Menon

NREGA, renamed as Mahatma Gandhi National Rural Employment Guarantee Act (MGNREGA), is one of the largest rights based social protection initiatives in the world. NREGA is the first ever law, internationally, that guarantees wage employment at an unprece dented scale. It is the largest financial inclusive measure for providing poor people access to the formal banking system. Therefore, NREGA is different from the earlier government employment schemes, since it treats employment as a right and is intended to be demand driven.[1]

Launched in February 2006, NREGA covers all the 614 districts across the country. The objective of the Act is to provide to every rural household a guarantee of at least 100 days of employment during a financial year by providing unskilled manual work in rural areas to those members of the rural household who volunteer to do such work.

Since its inception the programme has benefited over 10 crore rural households. It is also increasingly recognised that the NREGA has the potential to transform rural economic and social relations at many levels. The huge potential of the NREGA has already been evident particularly in the enthusiastic response of the local people, landless, the marginal farmers and women workers in particular, wherever information about the programme has been properly disseminated.[2]

NREGA has also initiated the world's largest financial inclusive measure by providing poor people access to the formal banking system. Near to five crore saving bank accounts have been opened with post office and banks across the country just for the payment of wages under NREGA. States like Andhra Pradesh, Karnataka, Uttarakhand, Kerala, Himachal Pradesh have opened saving bank accounts for all the NREGA workers while others like Odisha, Jharkhand, Chattisgarh, Madhya Pradesh, and Rajasthan have made substantial progress in providing banking services to poor rural folks.

The NREG Act was notified on September 7, 2005. The objective of the Act is to enhance livelihood security in rural areas by providing at least 100 days of guaranteed wage employment in a financial year to every household whose adult members volunteer to do unskilled manual work. The Act aims at (a) a strong social safety net for the vulnerable groups by providing an employment source, when other employment alternatives are scarce or inadequate. (b) it seeks to strengthen the natural resource base of rural livelihood and create durable assets in rural areas (c) Employment of rural poor through the processes of a rights based Law. It fosters conditions for inclusive growth from basic wage security and recharging rural economy to a transformative empowerment process of democracy.[3]

The Act was notified in 200 districts in the first phase with effect from 2nd February 2006 and then extended to additional 130 districts in the financial year 2007-08. The remaining districts have been notified under the NREGA with effect from April 1, 2008. It covers the entire country with the exception of districts that have a hundred per cent urban population.[4]

Salient Features of the Act[5]

(1) Adult members of a rural household, willing to do unskilled manual work, may apply for registration in writing or orally to the local Grama Panchayat.

(2) The Grama Panchayat after due verification will issue a job card.

(3) The Job Card should be issued within 15 days of application.

(4) A job card holder may submit a written application for employment to the Grama Panchayat, stating the time and duration for which work is sought. The minimum days of employment have to be at least fourteen.

(5) The Grama Panchayat will issue a dated receipt of the written application for employment, which guarantee employment with-in 15 days.

(6) Employment will be given within 15 days of application for work, if not then daily unemployment allowance as per the Act has to be paid by the state.

(7) Work should ordinarily be provided within 5 km radius of the village. In case work is provided beyond 5 km, extra wages of 10 per cent are payable to meet additional transportation and living expenses.

(8) Wages are to be paid according to the Minimum Wages Act 1948 for agricultural labourers in the state. Equal wages will be provided to both men and women.

(9) Wages are to be paid according to piece rate or daily rate. Disbursement of wages has to be done on weekly basis and not beyond a fortnight in any case.

(10) At least one-third beneficiaries shall be women who have registered and requested work under the scheme.

(11) Work site facilities such as crèche, drinking water, shade have to be provided.

(12) The projects for a village will be recommended by the Grama Sabha and approved by the Zilla Panchayat.

(13) At least 50 per cent of works will be allotted to Grama Panchayat for execution.

(14) Permissible works predominantly include water and soil conservation, afforestation and land development works.

(15) A 60:40 wage and material ratio has to be maintained. No contractors and machinery is allowed.

(16) The Central Govt. bears 100 per cent wage cost of unskilled manual labour and 75 per cent of the material cost including the wages of skilled and semi-skilled workers.

(17) Social Audit has to be done by the Grama Sabha.

(18) Grievance redressal at mechanism have to be put in place for ensuring a responsive implementation process.

(19) All accounts and records relating to the scheme should be available for public scrutiny.

The Key stake holders include[6], Wage seekers, Grama Sabha, PRIs, especially the Grama Panchayat, Programme Officers at the block level, District programme co-ordinator, State Government and Ministry of Rural Development.

The wage seekers are the primary stake holders of the Act. The rights of the wage seekers are - application for registration, obtaining a job card, application for work, choice of time and duration of the work applied for, provision of work within fifteen days of application, provision of creche, drinking water, first aid facilities on work site, the right to check their Muster Rolls and to get information regarding their employment entered in their Job Cards, payment of wages within fifteen days of work done and the right to get unemployment allowance in case employment is not provided within fifteen days of submitting the application.[7]

The Grama Sabha has been given the following rights and responsibilities under the Act. It will recommend works to be taken up under NREGs. It will conduct social audits on implementation of the scheme. Moreover, Grama Sabha will be used extensively as a forum for sharing information about the scheme.

The Grama Panchayat is the pivotal body for implementation at the village level. It is responsible for the following activities such as (a) planning of work (b) receiving applications for registration, (c) registering households (d) issuing job cards; (e) allotting employment within fifteen days of application, (f) executing works, (g) maintaining records, (h) convening the Grama Sabha for social audit and monitoring the scheme at the village level.

At the block level, the intermediate panchayat will be responsible for the consolidation of the Grama Panchayat plans into a Block plan and for monitoring and supervision. The programme officer essentially acts as a co-ordinator for NREGS at the Block level. His chief responsibility is to ensure that anyone who applies for work gets employment within 15 days. His other duties include (a) scrutinising the annual development plan proposed by the Grama Panchayats, (b) Consolidating all proposals into the Block Plan and submitting it to the Intermediate panchayat, (c) Matching employment opportunities with the demand for work at the Block level, (d) Monitoring and Supervising implementation, (e) Disposal of complaints, (f) Ensuring that social audits are conducted by the Grama Sabha and following up on them and (g) Payment of unemployment allowance in case employment is not provided on time.

At District level, District Panchayats will be responsible for finalising the District plans and the Labour Budget and for monitoring and supervising the Employment Guarantee scheme in the District.

The State Government will designate a District Programme Co-ordinator, who can be either the chief Executive Officer of the District panchayat or the District Collector or any other District level Officer of approximate rank. His primary duties are (a) Information dissemination, (b) Training, (c) Consolidating block plans into a district plan, (d) Release and utilisation of funds, (e) Ensuring 100 per cent monitoring of works, Muster Roll verification and (f) submission of monthly Progress Report.

At the State level, a State Employment Guarantee Council (SEGC) is to be set up by every State Government under section 12 of NREGA. The SEGC shall advice the state government on the implementation of the scheme and evaluate and monitor it. The State Council will prepare an annual report on the implementation of the NREGS in the state to be presented to the state legislature.

The state government will be responsible for wide communication of the scheme, setting up of the SEGC, ensuring that the state share of the NREGS budget is released on time, delegation of financial and administrative powers to the district programme co-ordinator and the programme officer, training, establishing a network of professional agencies for technical support and for quality-control measures, regular review, monitoring and evaluation of NRGS processes and outcomes and ensuring accountability and transperancy in the scheme at all levels.

At the Center level a Central Employment Guarantee Council (SEGC) has been set up under the Chairmanship of the Minister of Rural Development. The Central Council is responsible for advising the Central Govt. on NREGA-related matters and for monitoring and evaluating the implementation of the Act. Ministry of Rural Development is the nodal ministry for the implementation of NREGA.

The Potentialities and Possibilities of the Scheme[8]

NREGA strengthens the democratic decentralisation processes at the grass-root level by incorporating Grama Sabha the entire planning and decision- making process. It visualises the massive involvement of local people especially women in all aspects such as selection of work and work sites, project implementation and social audit.

It focusses on strengthening natural resource management such as afforestation, drought proofing, flood proofing and water conservation. In fact, the Act has become a kingpin for regeneration of depleting natural resources. By securing livelihood and creating employment opportunities at the home village itself, NREGA reduces migration of rural people to industrial areas.

By reducing poverty and unemployment, NREGA mitigates social issues such as farmers suicides, prostitution and thus reduces the spread of HIV/ AIDS and other sexually transmitted diseases. It is recognised that the NREGA has the potential to transform rural economic and social relations at many levels. The legislation is having a positive impact on the socio-economic empowerment of woman.

Health status of villagers is likely to improve through proper implementation of NREGA due to (a) regular availability of potable drinking water, (b) construction of drainage that will improve the cleanliness in the village and reduce the chances of water-borne diseases, (c) improvement of public health status and (d) construction of child care centres will improve the general health status of children.

Most of the employment is in agriculture and allied activities. Wages are rising, migration is slowing down, productive assets are being created and the power equations are changing too. In Rajasthan, where public awareness of the programme is high, 77 days of employment per rural household were provided in 2006-2007. In Tamil Nadu, the participation of women was as high as 81 per cent. In Uttar Pradesh and Jharkhand, the NREGA has created positive changes in the implementation of public work programmes.

Financing the NREGS[9]

The Central Government will bear the entire cost of wages for unskilled manual workers and 75 per cent of the cost of material and wages for skilled and semi-skilled workers. The rest 25 per cent will be supported by the State Government. The Administrative expenses, which include salary and allowances of programme officers and their support staff, will be sustained by the Central Government. Administrative expenses of the central employment guarantee council will be taken care of Central Government and the State Government will bear the expenses of the state employment guarantee council.

Participation Rate[10]

An attempt was made to estimate the NREGS household participation rate. It was based on employment demanded by rural household in 18 states as a proportion of the total number of rural households in districts in which the NREGS was being implemented (phase I and II). Result is shown in the following table:

Table I: NREGS Participation rate

States	*No. of Rural HHs in NREGS Phase 1 and 2 districts (in Lakhs)*	*Employment Demanded by HHs (in Lakhs)*	*Participation Rate (in per cent) (Column 3/ column 2) 100*
(1)	(2)	(3)	(4)
Andhra Pradesh	105.92	48.04	45.36
Assam	19.88	14.48	72.86
Bihar	124.07	38.63	31.13
Chhattisgarh	29.43	22.97	78.05
Gujarat	19.88	2.91	14.62
Haryana	5.07	0.71	13.99
Jharkhand	37.37	16.80	44.96
Karnataka	29.39	8.64	29.39
Kerala	10.50	2.59	24.69
Madhya Pradesh	53.26	43.47	51.62
Maharashtra	53.50	4.75	8.87
Orissa	51.98	11.35	21.83
Punjab	8.18	0.50	6.03
Rajasthan	24.64	21.73	58.19

(Contd...)

Tamil Nadu	31.35	12.35	39.38
Uttar Pradesh	120.95	41.04	33.93
Uttarakhand	5.05	1.89	37.45
West Bengal	108.69	39.20	36.07

It is clear from the table that 13 out of the 18 major states have reported less than 50 average person days of employment. The government attributes this to lack of funds, lack of mobilisation and awareness, delay in institutional set up, poor delivery structure and nature of job provided. During 2006-2007 Rajasthan was the only state, which was able to generate more than 50 person days of employment on average. The corresponding figure for May 2008 show a marked improvement with a number of key states like Chhattisgarh, Haryana, Madhya Pradesh, Rajasthan and Tamil Nadu reporting greater than or equal to 50 average person days of employment. This is shown in the table given below.

Table II: Estimates of Employment Demanded and Generated under NREGS

States	*Employment Demanded by HHs*	*Employment Provided to HHs (in Lakhs)*	*Person Days of Employment Provided (in Lakhs)*	*Employment Provided as a per cent of Employment Demanded (Col 3/Col 2)*	*Average Person Days Generated per HH (Col 4/Col 3)*
(1)	(2)	(3)	(4)	(5)	(6)
Andhra Pradesh	48.04	48.04	2010.28	100.00	42
Assam	14.48	14.03	487.61	96.87	35
Bihar	38.63	38.60	855.10	99.92	22
	22.97	22.85	1316.10	99.47	58
Gujarat	2.91	2.91	90.06	100.00	31
Haryana	0.71	0.71	35.76	100.00	50
Jharkhand	16.80	16.80	747. 56	99 .99	45
Karnataka	8 .64	8 .60	320. 91	99. 51	37
Kerala	2. 59	1. 85	60. 75	71. 50	33
Madhya Pradesh	43. 47	43. 47	2753. 02	100. 00	63
Maharashtra	4. 75	4. 75	184. 86	100 .00	39
Orissa	11. 35	10. 97	405. 23	96. 65	37
Punjab	0. 50	0. 50	19. 15	100. 00	39
Rajasthan	21. 73	21. 70	1678. 38	99. 88	77
Tamil Nadu	12. 35	12. 35	645. 23	100. 00	52
Uttar Pradesh	41. 04	40. 96	1363. 06	99. 81	33
Uttarakhand	1. 89	1. 89	80. 34	100. 00	42
West Bengal	39. 20	38. 43	968. 80	98. 04	25

Official records show that demand for employment was fully met in Madhya Pradesh, Andhra Pradesh, Gujarat, Haryana, Maharashtra, Punjab, Tamil Nadu and Uttarakhand. Except for Kerala with a proportion of 71.50 per cent, the estimates for other states are above 96 per cent.

NREGS in Kerala[11]

In Kerala, the scheme was introduced in Palakkad and Wayanad districts initially on 5th February 2006 and it was extended to all the 14 districts in the state on Ist April 2008. The scheme now provides Rs 125 per person for a stipulated quantity of manual labour offered as registered worker in the local Government in Kerala.

In Kerala local government are given a central role in planning and implementation of NREGA. Engineering support is also given to the programme. In addition to one diploma/degree holder working on contract at the level of the village panchayat, there is a system of accredited engineers. These engineers are paid for their work at rates fixed by government. Technical sanction of the work is given by a technical committee consisting of government engineers, accredited engineer, agriculture officer and officers and other technical staff. An appellate system has been put in place at the district level to facilitate speedy sorting out of dispute. To mobilise the workers and the public and to assist the local government in carrying out its duties, grama panchayat has been given the freedom to appoint one public servant from the local body as NREGS co-ordinator.

Kudumbasree plays an important role in the implementation of the NREGS. The NHGs (Neighbourhood Group) are federated into an ADS at the ward level. ADSs in a grama panchayat are federated into registered body called the CDS. The ADS has been entrusted with the task of organising public work under NREGS. Muster rolls are maintained by the ADS. Since ADS, is an organisation of the poor and is basically women's group, there has been greater sensitivity and community participations in the implementation process.

Since Kerala has limited public land, the eco-restoration works are selected. The road works has been limited to 10 per cent of the total expenditure and to give special priority to integrated watershed development works. Compared to the earlier wage employment programmes such as IRDP, RLEGP, JRY, SGRY, SGSY, there are significant achievements under NREGS due to the combination of transparent processes and procedures, local action and constant vigilance. The implementation of NREGA has been comparatively corruption-free, because of the following factors:

(a) A clear political decision was conveyed to the panchayat that the scheme has to be implemented strictly as per the laws in force.

(b) The work is organised through the Kudumbasree system and the poor have a stake in the work right from the beginning.

(c) Technocratic power to accord technical sanction measure works and recommended payments has been made more spread out and accountable through the committee system.

(d) Special emphasis has been given to the rights of workers and they have been made fully aware of their entitlements.

(e) All the payments are made only through the individual bank accounts of workers.

(f) **Social Audit.** An innovative feature of the NREGS is that it gives a central role to Social audit as a means of continuous public vigilance. The basic objective of Social audit is to ensure public accountability in the implementation of projects, laws and policies.

Implementation of NREGA has contributed much to the empowerment of women. It is reflected in the following aspects:

(a) as the work is organised by women's group, the gender perspective gets built in automatically.

(b) Since 80 per cent of workers are women they feel more comfortable.

(c) Equal wages are paid and this has boosted the earnings of women.

(d) Since the wages are paid in to bank accounts the habit of thrift is generated.

(e) As the Bank deposits are increasing, the intra-household status of the women has also been improving and she controls the cash resources and withdrawal can be only on her decision.

It is clear from the Table that in Kerala the total number of Household who received job card till the reporting month amounted to 25,76,944. Out of it Scheduled Caste households are 3,48,325, Scheduled Tribes 91,286 and others 21,37,333. The cumulative number of households demanded employment till the reporting month amounted to 4,56,005 and the cumulative household provided employment till the reporting month amounted to 4,35,803. The cumulative person days generated till the reporting month is as follows. SCs 12,46,015, STs 2,14,336, others 52,28,664 and total 66,89,015. Out of this no. of women amounted to 61,27,618.

Empowerment Effects of NREG

Women's empowerment was not among the original intentions of the NREGA. However, provisions like priority for women in the ratio of one-third of total workers, equal wages for men and women workers and creches for the children of women workers were made in the Act with the view of ensuring that rural women will get benefit from the scheme in a certain manner.

TABLE III: Employment generated during the financial year 2010-11 through NREGS in Kerala[10]

Employment Generated During the financial Year 2010-2011																		
1	2	3				4	5	6	7	8	9					10	11	12
		a	b	c	d						a	b	c	d	e			
		Cumulative No. Of HH issued jobcards (Till the reporting month)				*Cumulative No. Of HH demanded employment (Till the reporting month)*	*Cumulative Labour Budget estimation of employment of employment provided*	*Cumulative No. Of HH provided employment (Till the reporting month)*	*No. Of HH working under NREGA during the reporting month*	*Cumulative Labour Budget estimation of personday*	*Cumulative Persondays generated (Till the reporting month)*					*Cumulative No. Of HH completed 100 days (Till the reporting month*	*No. Of HH which are beneficiary of land reform/IAY*	*No. Of Disabled beneficialy individuals*
S. No	District	SCs	STs	Others	Total						SCs	STs	Others	Total	Women			
Phase I																		
1.	Palakkad	47766	13873	167898	229537	51922	49996	50326	9582	1699014	224483	68980	565064	858527	801777	7	2365	95
2.	Wayanad	7603	33715	90722	132040	20614	27129	19029	6809	448429	15968	54906	101450	265324	222703	2	955	22
	Total Phase I	**55369**	**47588**	**258620**	**361577**	**72536**	**77125**	**69355**	**16391**	**2147443**	**240451**	**123886**	**759514**	**1123851**	**1024480**	**9**	**3320**	**117**
Phase II																		
3.	Iqukki	26888	12940	159678	199506	32141	23000	30775	21893	83500	47410	27533	322395	397338	296090	3	1131	75
4.	Kasargod	6256	6318	98323	110897	19912	8000	19723	6370	148800	19624	18074	288889	326587	780590	23	339	70
	Total Phase II	**33144**	**19258**	**258001**	**310403**	**52053**	**31000**	**50498**	**28263**	**983800**	**67034**	**45607**	**611286**	**723925**	**576680**	**26**	**1470**	**145**
Phase III																		
5.	Alappuzha	30452	1141	713736	245329	51794	20695	49070	20170	724325	116811	3526	634347	754684	713827	5	3223	159
6.	Ernakulam	25829	1594	147482	174905	24749	10933	23781	11909	567434	55055	1301	233260	289616	273703	0	1329	43
7.	Kannur	6466	6700	141404	154570	22922	14226	22379	5393	330706	9923	7942	306955	324820	309825	5	974	44
8.	Kollam	21211	977	171166	193354	36187	26687	34269	13089	698328	63979	3428	455155	522562	454770	20	767	90
9.	Kottayam	15556	2824	112865	131245	21252	15340	20274	5966	368160	39070	8193	250864	298127	283996	7	1072	55
10.	Kozhikode	24215	1911	204244	230370	26962	22200	25995	8864	490100	62658	3595	307417	373670	352649	0	1111	58
11.	Malappuram	22033	1365	68104	91502	10309	10889	8656	3526	275548	35083	724	64201	100008	95797	0	419	32
12.	Pathanamihitta	22033	1365	68104	91502	10309	10889	8656	3526	275548	35083	724	64201	100008	95797	0	419	32
13.	Jhiruvananthapuram	36042	3380	229554	268976	52583	45000	48317	17638	900000	107639	9707	564887	680433	621884	2	2715	112
14.	Thrissur	40392	1615	159434	201441	50122	23728	49611	26410	1040969	267724	3951	668166	9398441	902344	17	1450	85
	Total Phase III	**259812**	**24440**	**1620712**	**1904964**	**331416**	**224193**	**31590**	**119904**	**6640425**	**938530**	**44843**	**3857866**	**48441239**	**4526458**	**70**	**14236**	**846**
	Total	**348325**	**91286**	**2137333**	**2576944**	**456005**	**332318**	**435803**	**164558**	**9771668**	**1246015**	**214336**	**5228664**	**6689015**	**6127618**	**105**	**19026**	**1108**

Provisions like work within a radius of 5 kms from the house, absence of supervisor and contractors and flexibility in terms of choosing period and months of employment were not made exclusively for women but have been conducive for rural women. The share of women in total person-days was relatively high in Kerala, Tamil Nadu, Andhra Pradesh, Karnataka, Rajasthan and Tripura in all the four years i.e. 2006-07, 2007-08, 2008-09, and 2009-2010. The emergence of women workers as independent bread earners with control over their earnings has significant empowerment effect, such as greater decision-making roll in the family, discretion to spend and control the use of their earnings and confidence to earn independent of male family members.

The empowerment effects of NREGA can be analysed in two ways one at the individual level, or Household level and the other at the community level. While individual level effects are income-consumption effects, intra-household effects (decision-making roles) and enhancement of choice and capability, the community level effects include realisation of equal wages, increased participation in community development processes and overall impact on gender relations.[12]

Household-level effects

Women's contributions to household income and to the national economy remains largely unaccounted as they undertake a significant amount of unpaid work. The average number of hours spent by women on unpaid work is high and their contribution to the household income and overall welfare remain unaccounted. The NREGS has helped women in converting some unpaid hours of work in to paid work with significant effects, especially for those women for whom NREGS is a primary work opportunity outside the home.

Paid work under NREGS has helped rural women in realising income-consumption effects through monetised earnings. This results in greater consumption effects. A study on women worker's earning in four districts shows that NREGS constitute 14 per cent of the total annual income of the household on an average. It is 21 per cent in Dungarpur, 15 per cent in Kangra, 11 per cent in Ranchi and eight per cent in Gaya. It appears that account payments leads to greater incidence of self-collection and control over wages.

Decision Making

The dominance of males in intra-household decisions in rural areas is unmistakable. As per the National Health Survey III (2005-06), only 29 per cent of married women in rural areas take decisions about the purchase of daily household needs, 26 per cent decide about their personal healthcare, 7.6 per cent take decisions about purchasing major household items and only 10 per cent decide on visits to relatives. If we compare this with observed changes in the case of NREGS women workers, the impact is remarkable. A large number of women who retained either part or whole of their NREGS wages also retained choice over their use. Thus, NREGS reduce the dependence of women on male members for their personal needs. Now 71 per cent women are able to do so.

The NREGS has broadened choices for rural women in two ways. One, it has opened for them an entirely new avenue for paid employment. Second, it has broadened their choices and capability.

Community level effects

Women's participation at grassroot level of community development processes and decision-making remain weak inspite of their increased representation, following the 73rd constitutional amendment. NREGS enhances the role of women in NHGs activities. Their participation in selection of work, social monitoring, auditing, management of assets created it has enhanced. Before NREGs only 16 per cent of women worker's households had an account in a bank or post office. Now 100 per cent NREGS households have access to a bank or post office account.

Shortcomings[14]

Various reports and surveys conducted by different organisations, researchers and institutions have pointed out an assortment of flaws in the working of NREGA. In the 2007 Report the Comptroller and Auditor General specified that the guidelines of the NREGA have not been followed effectively. According to the study of the Centre for Environment and Food Security on NREGA in Orissa, out of 733 crores spent under NREGA, good amount was unaccounted. K.S. Gopal, Director of the Centre for Environmental Concerns has mentioned that all the assets being built under the schemes are unproductive. Lack of devoted administrative and technical staff for NREGA is an obstacle responsible for procedural lapses. Implementation irregularities and misappropriation of allotted funds were found out on a large scale. Even if work opportunities were provided, there was no attempt to upgrade the skills of the rural folk. In the present format, NREGS could befall into another subsidy programme which will pose a threat to national exchequer. According to the NREGS website, as on March 2009, out of total 99 million household that demanded employment, the number of households working under NREGS is only 14 million and the cumulative number of households that have completed 100 days work is about four million.

Conclusion

It may be concluded that empowerment of rural women has emerged as the unintended consequence of NREGS. Women have benefited more as workers than as community. Women as individuals have gained because of their ability to earn independently through paid employment opportunity under NREGS. Independent and monetised earnings have increased consumption choices and reduced economic dependeney. This has helped women in accounting their tangible contribution to the household's income. It has sounded a voice to women in family decision making. This is a historic and unique legislation reiterating governemt's commitment towards livelihood security of people of rural areas.

References

1. *Kurukshetra*, December 2009, p. 2.
2. *Op cit* p. 3.
3. *NREG Act 2005.*
4. *Ibid.*
5. *Ibid.*
6. *Ibid.*
7. *Ibid.*
8. *Ibid.*
9. *NREG Act 2009.*
10. *Ibid.*
11. *NREGS in Keala.com*
12. Ashok Pankg and Rukmini Thanka, *EPW*, UA 24, 2010, p. 45.
13. Anupam Hazra "Transforming Rural India", *Kurukshetra,* p. 13.
14. Dr MS.Tomar and Dr BS Yadav: "Need to Sharpen NREGA", *Kurukshetra*, December, 2009, p. 11.

10

Decentralised Rural Local Governance: Trends and Direction in Karnataka

—B.S. Bhargava

The focus on rural development started with the realisation that the rural sector was underdeveloped economically, socially, politically and needed social attention from the government. Hence, the Community Development Programme (CDP) was launched in 1952 covering the entire nation. Unfortunately, this programme could not deliver much. According to the observations of the Balwant Rai Mehta Committee (1957), the main factor that caused the failure of the CDP was the absence of people's participation. The committee recommended the creation of a three-tier institutional arrangement to make people's participation meaningful and effective. Necessary, legislation was to be enacted by every state to implement the Panchayat Raj (PR) system as a form of rural local self-government to perform developmental, administrative and political tasks. Rajasthan and Andhra Pradesh were the first states to adopt this system in 1959, followed by Karnataka and Orissa. Since then Karnataka has been at the forefront of decentralisation.

However, with exceptions, the Panchayati Raj system had not received a fair deal since its inception (1959/1960). The Panchayati Raj Institutions (PRIs) had not been assigned specific and sufficient powers, responsibilities as well as resources to carry out even the routine functions. Besides, elections to this institutions had not been held for years on one pretext or the other. This, among other compelling internal and external factors, necessitated the need to include Panchayati Raj as a mandatory provision in the Constitution of India. Conferring constitutional status on this institution of grassroots governance reaffirmed the nation's faith in the philosophy of 'demo cratic decentralisation'. Accordingly, provisions were made for a mandatory three-two-tier setup of Panchayati Raj, conferring legal status to Grama Sabhas, regular five-year term elections, and reservations for the weaker sections and women, an independent finance commission and state election commission. The Amendment, therefore, was intended to lay a strong foundation for 'democratic decentralisation', thereby paving the way for planning from below, a concept which had eluded the people ever since the beginning of the era of planned development.

The Constitutional (Seventy-third) Amendment Act of 1993, which was brought into force from 24 April 1993, established India's PRIs on a sound footing. The Amendment gave the much-needed impetus to the concept of local self-government, which till then suffered from lack of constitutional protection.

Looking Back

Before the reorganisation of the state on 1 November 1956, five different legislations (Acts) on Panchayats were in operation in different regions of the state. The Mysore Village Panchayats and Local Boards Act 1959, which was brought into force in December 1960, replaced all these acts. Elections to the PRIs were held in 1960, 1968 and 1978 under this Act.

Basically the evolution and performance of PRIs can be divided into two phases: the first phase (1959-87) and the second phase (1987-93). The various acts and amendments therein were introduced between the two phases from 1959 to 1993. The third phase is the current one (since 1993).

Mysore Village Panchayats and Local Boards Act 1959

In Karnataka, the panchayati raj system started as early as 1959. The legislation aimed at ensuring people's participation in rural development and transferring power to them through the institutions of local governance.[1]

The Act followed partly the recommendations of the Balwant Rai Mehta Committee, which recommended a three-tier PR system. They were the village panchayat/town panchayat (VP/TP), taluk development board (TDB) and district development council (DDC), the last being an ex-officio body headed by the deputy commissioner, with the presidents of the TDBs, also MLAs, Members of the Legislative Council (MLCs) and MPs as members. The indirectly elected chairpersons headed the VP/TP and TDB. The PRIs were assigned a large number of functions grouped as obligatory and discretionary. The DDC was essentially a coordinating and supervisory institution. Under this Act, about 8,411 village panchayats and 96 town panchayats, 175 TDBs and 19 DDCs were established.

The report of Asoka Mehta Committee submitted in 1978, recommended a two-tier system of PR, and emphasised the need for constitutional sanction to it. Karnataka's panchayati raj legislation, drafted by the Janata Government of Rama Krishna Hegde was enacted in 1983. It recognised the principle of party-based elections to the two-tier of elected office- the mandal panchayats and zilla parishads. The panchayati raj experiment in Karnataka was hailed all over the country as a 'major' and 'bold step' in the direction of democratic decentralisation for development.

Karnataka Zilla Parishads, Taluk Panchayat Samitis, Mandal Panchayat and Nyaya Panchayat Act, 1983

Most of the principles enunciated in the report of the National Committee on PRIs, headed by Asoka Mehta, became the basis of this radical change. It was implemented to prioritise rural development as a means of eradicating poverty and improving the rural economy through people's participation.

In additional to the zilla parishad at the district level followed by the mandal panchayat comprising a group of villages, the Act provided for two other statutory institutions – the taluk panchayat samiti at the taluk/block level, which was an advisory and coordinating body with no executive function and the gram sabha (village assembly) below the mandal panchayat.[2] The grama sabha was vested with the right to prepare and approve the development programmes of the village. The grama sabha, the foundation of the structure, consisted of all those registered in the electoral rolls in a revenue village. It met twice a year and was enjoined with the review of the accounts and the performance of the grama panchayat. It had the responsibility of considering the development programmes proposed by the latter. In addition, it identified beneficiaries under poverty alleviation and the development programmes. The mandal panchayat was the first elected tier located between the village and the taluk while the zilla parishad, the second directly elected tier, was a powerful body which administered schemes and programmes developed by it. Cadres were maintained for manning the zilla and mandal parishad. Election processes started in 1986 and ended in January 1987. For the first time the elections were conducted on party lines.

Another significant feature of the Act was that it realised women were inadequately represented in the political system and an effort was made to do justice to them. Reservation of upto 25 per cent was provided in the local bodies. Women's participation in the political process took a different turn in the history of Karnataka. The lowering of the voting age to 18 years and the extension of anti-defection bill to the PRIs constitute other important aspects of the PR system.

After the first five-year tenure of the panchayats in 1992, the 1983 Act was repealed by a new act of the state- the Karnataka Panchayati Raj Act 1993, which incorporated the essential features of the Seventy-third Constitutional Amendment and established elected bodies at the three levels- the village, taluk and district so that there is 'greater participation of the people'.

The Act now provides for 33 per cent reservation to women unlike the 25 per cent under the 1983 Act. The first elections to the three-tiers were conducted under the 1993 Act in December 1993 for grama panchayats, and for taluk panchayats and zilla panchayats in March 1995.[3]

The three-tier PR system with the elected bodies at grama, taluk and district levels for increased participation of the people and more effective implementation of rural development programmes are shown in Table 1.

Table 1: PRIs in Karnataka, 2000

Tiers	*Number of Panchayats*	*Number of Seats (Members)*
Zilla Panchayat	27	890
Taluk Panchayat	175	3255
Grama Panchayat	5659	80114

Present PR System

Grama Panchayat: According to the Act (1993), normally a grama panchayat will be constituted for a population between 3,000 to 5,000 (now ranging from 5000-7000). The area covered by a grama panchayat will consist of a village or a group of villages. There will be one member for every 400 persons.

The adhyaksha and upadhyaksha (president and vice-president) will be elected from among the elected members. There are three standing committees, namely, (i) production committee, (ii) social justice committee and (iii) amenities committee. A secretary is appointed by the government as the administrative head of the grama panchayat. The main functions of the grama panchayat are to promote economic and social welfare, education and health. Financial powers of the grama panchayat are given in the Act itself. It is only the panchayat which has taxation powers in addition to government grants and other sources of income.

Taluk Panchayat: The Act stipulates that for each taluk there shall be a taluk panchayat consisting of local representatives, from the state legislature and parliament, one-fifth of the grama panchayat adhyakshas in the taluk chosen by lots every year (in rotation). Members are directly elected from separate territorial constituencies in the ratio of one member for every 10,000 population.

The elected members of the taluk panchayat have to choose two members from among themselves to be the adhyaksha and upadhyaksha. There are three standing committees, namely, (i) general standing committee, (ii) finance, audit and planning committee and (iii) social justice committee.

A Group - An officer of the state civil services is to be the administrative head of the taluk panchayat. Taluk panchayats are empowered to supervise the activities of grama panchayats in their jurisdiction.

Zilla Panchayat: The Act further stipulates that each district will have a zilla panchayat consisting of the members of parliament and state legislature from within the district, the adhyakshas of taluk panchayats in the district, and elected members in accordance with the scale of one member for 40,000 of the population.

The elected members shall choose two members from amongst them to be adhyaksha and upadhyaksha. There are five standing committees, namely, (i) general standing committee, (ii) finance, audit and planning committee, (iii) social justice committee, (iv) education and health committee and (v) agriculture and industries committee.

As regards finances, both taluk panchayat and zilla panchayat have no taxation powers; they mainly depend on government grants- plan and non-plan.

The grama sabha is the soul of panchayati raj for effective functioning and transparency in decision making; it is accompanied by panchayat *jamabhandi* (social audit mechanism) where audit of accounts and works is carried out with public participation and the report is put forward before the grama sabha for further action.

Election Process: In Karnataka, after the Seventy-third Constitution Amendment Act 1993, a three-tier system was envisaged and a State Election Commission (SEC) was appointed. The SEC is empowered to deal with all major issues connected with elections to the PRIs. The purpose of the provision to appoint SEC was to ensure that the conduct of elections would be entrusted to an impartial authority. A model code of conduct is provided for the peaceful conduct of elections.

Elections to 5,640 grama panchayats were held in December 1993. They consisted of elected members each representing about 400 people. The average population of each grama panchayat was 5,300 according to 1991 census. Of the total number of 80,627 members in all the grama panchayats, 35,305 (43.8 per cent) were women. Elections to grama panchayats were conducted on a non-party basis.

Elections to all the 175 taluk panchayats in the state were held between 13-18 March 1995, on a party basis. The offices of adhyaksha and upadhyaksha of taluk panchayats have also been reserved for different categories. Elections to all the zilla panchayts were held during March 1995 on a party basis. Likewise, the second term elections took place between 23-27 February 2000[4] to grama panchayats and on 2 and 6 June 2000 to taluk and zilla panchayats.

The number of candidates in the fray for zilla panchayat elections in 2000 was 3,071 compared to 3,612 candidates in 1995. In the case of the taluk panchayats, there were 9,860 candidates as against 11,497 candidates in 1995. The number of zilla panchayat constituencies itself had come down from 919 in 1995 to 890 this time. Likewise, the number of taluk panchayat constituencies had come down from 3,340 to 3,255. This was to increase the size of the panchayat.

Comparing the results of the zilla panchayat and taluk panchayat elections, with the elections held in 1995, there appears to be a dip or at least stagnation in the interest of people and political parties in contesting the elections, if the number of contestants and unanimously elected or unopposed members were of any indication.

In the natural course, one would expect the number of contestants to increase and the number of unanimously elected members to come down in view of the keen interest shown by the political parties and rural masses in general in the local body elections. But, in reality there has been a fall in the number of contestants and an increase in the number of unanimously elected candidates in 2000 as compared to the 1995 scenario. On an average there were 3.9 candidates per zilla panchayat seat last time, whereas this time the average worked out to be only 3.4. In case of taluk panchayats also, the average number of candidates per seat had come down from 3.4 to 3.00.

The main reasons for unopposed elections might be: (a) reservations of seats created confusion for the contesting candidates; (b) candidates did not come forward to contest due to lack of awareness; (c) political parties were dormant; (d) conciliation or compromise; and (e) rejection of nomination papers.

The number of contestants had decreased despite the number of parties remaining the same, though some of the parties were different this time. In the last elections, the contesting parties were the Janata Dal (JD), the Congress, the Bharatiya Janata Party (BJP), the Karnataka Congress Party (KCP), the Communist Party of India (CPI), the Communist Party Marxist (CPM), the Karnataka Rajya Raitha Sangha and the Janata Party whereas this time the parties were the Congress, BJP, JD (S), JD (U), Bahujan Samaj Party (BSP), CPI, CPM and National Congress Party (NCP). The number of independents also came down from 784 to 613 in case of zilla parishads and from 2,277 to 1,889 in case of taluk panchayats.

An all-women panchayat came into existence during 1993-98 in Shimoga district, namely, the Mydolalu Gram Panchayat. During the 2000 election, three all-women panchayats came into existence. The case of the Athanur Gram Panchayat (one of the all-women panchayats) in Gulbarga District is quite reflective of the rural power structure scenario. The all-women gram panchayat came into existence in Gulbarga due to the intervention of the local elite. A popular local leader of Athanur village, who was a zilla panchayat member, decided that only women needed to be elected to this panchayat. He convened a meeting of caste leaders and elders and indicated that it would be desirable to have an all-women panchayat, and that they should be elected unopposed. The others in the meeting agreed to this proposal. There were indeed, others who wanted to contest (and one man had even filed his nomination papers) but they yielded to the decision of the local elite at the instigation of the zilla panchayat member. This clearly shows that it was a local leader who decided on such course of action.

It can, therefore, be said that the hold of village elders/traditional village leaders over village social institutions is still prevalent. Though the political parties have made great inroads into the remote villages, they too have to take the opinion and support of these leaders. The two are thus inter-related and together play a significant role in deciding the membership of the panchayat.

A significant factor, however, in the elections is the role of political parties. The Panchayati Raj Act clearly affirms that the grama panchayat elections should not be conducted along party lines. Naturally, political parties should not play any role either in the election or in the functioning of these panchayats. But it is evident that the grama panchayats are influenced or controlled by locally dominant people from different political parties. The gram panchayat election in Karnataka, which was due in December 1998 and was postponed indefinitely, is an instance of the control of local leaders. Although the state government had not made a formal announcement to this effect, it was the natural outcome of a decision taken at the cabinet meeting on 18 January 1999 to incorporate certain changes in the panchayati raj structure of the state. The SEC had taken all steps in connection with the preparation of polls and issuance of notifications, but the elections, nevertheless, were postponed though the Constitution does not allow postponement of elections of PRIs.

The state decision to make toilets mandatory for a candidate in the panchayat elections also led to a stalling of the election process. The presence of a toilet became a prerequisite for any person to contest in the grama panchayats elections and its absence would be a reason to reject (disqualification) the nomination papers. This was contested and the court allowed for a conditional relaxation of this rule on 9 February 2000. All this created a lot of confusion during the grama panchayat elections of 2000.

Thus, although Karnataka was going to conduct the second term elections to the PRIs after the adoption of the Seventy-third Constitutional Amendment Act, various issues came up before the elections, creating confusion and leading to their postponement. The need was to set right these issues so that elections would be conducted on the scheduled dates. Regular and periodic elections are the only solution to ensuring greater participation of the local people. A conducive environment could be created only by ‘political commitment’.

Emerging Institutional Issues and Strategies

The preamble to the Act (1993) expresses its basic tenet by declaring that PRIs should function as units of local self-government. Among other changes, achieving universal enrolment in primary schools, providing sanitary latrines, improving water supply, establishing health and maternity centres and social forestry are to be among the priorities at each level. Though these developmental functions had been transferred to the zilla panchayat it was seen that the zilla panchayats had not been able to give any priority to the stated development matters. Though the new system has provided membership and positions of authority in local bodies to the weaker sections namely, the SCs, STs, OBCs and women, these provisions did not lead to any significant social gains. The intended beneficiaries access to the existing facilities, the methods of access and so on were limited mainly due to their lack of awareness. They were, thus exploited by 'middlemen' and 'political brokers'. Therefore, these schemes should be given wide publicity.

Another major instrument for ensuring people's participation is their organisation into community groups such as the NGOs/CBOs. They have increased substantially in number in the country in recent years and have assumed an important role in rural development. As voluntary agencies, they work with the people and catalyse their development. In this effort, they focus not just on developmental programmes but also on the process of awareness building and community organisations. In Karnataka, there has been some progress in bringing about a working relationship between the various government departments and the voluntary agencies in the areas of social forestry and wasteland development. The goal of such a relationship is to meet more effectively the basic needs of the rural people, such as providing fodder, fuel, timber fruits and raw material for rural artisans.

There is no doubt that the NGOs have come to play an important role in influencing the PRIs in crucial areas of development. But there is no proper 'organic linkage' between NGOs and PRIs. Very few opportunities are there for constructive cooperation between the two due to lack of proper communication and information. The NGOs could play a significant role in strengthening the rural local self-governance. Some activities on which the NGOs could concentrate are: (a) During the panchayati raj elections, they can organise and motivate people for electing only genuine representatives who can work for the people (b) They can train and educate the elected representatives of the PRIs, specially women, SCs, STs and OBCs who have limited access to information and are new entrants relatively to the PR system (c) They can provide technical know-how on different aspects of developmental work and help in the planning and implementation of many of the panchayat programmes to make them more effective.

Reservation plays a crucial role in breaking the stranglehold of traditionally dominant sections of PRIs. Leadership is no longer confined to a particular class, caste or gender. This reflects the strength of our democratic structures and political processes. The amended PR system has been the emergence of a new leadership, increasingly determined by the 'achieved status' of an individual. The distinction of Karnataka is striking in the field of representation of women. The state has been following a progressive 'policy of inclusion'; of the hitherto neglected/weaker sections of rural society in one form or the other from the very beginning (under the Panchayati Raj Act of 1959). Even before Seventy-third and Seventy-fourth Constitutional Amendments, it introduced and practiced 25 per cent reservation for women under the Panchayati Raj Act 1983. The Panchayati Raj Act 1993 (Conformity Act) took it further in the direction of inclusion, by implementing 33 per cent reservation to the backward classes and a rotation system for the positions of president and vice-president (20 months in case of zilla panchayat and taluk panchayat and 30 months for grama panchayats). Vokkaligas and Lingayats have been conventionally known as 'dominant castes' but the state witnessed a 'shifting of dominance' at different levels in the last few years. All these enabled the weaker sections to have access to PRIs in huge members and to broaden the social base of democracy.[5]

However, the skill, knowledge and correct attitude required of panchayat members are often missing in the local leaders. They *lack awareness, and hence, are not able to articulate their rights and demands in an effective manner.* Therefore, the leadership at the grass-roots level has to be strengthened through 'capacity building' programmes. The need for training/orientation is necessary as 'political education' is a prerequisite for their effective participation.

The concept of PRIs grew out of the failure of the community development administration in involving the people in the development process. The normative theory of decentralisation assumes that the grass-roots level elected bodies facilitate people's participation in local governance and are more accountable as they are nearer to the people. But, the term of the president of the zilla panchayat being 20 months has weakened the position of the elected head and strengthened the positions of the administrative heads. Since they lack education and awareness, they are not able to comprehend their roles and discharge their duties effectively. Their role thus tends to be reduced to that of mere overseers who bring the local problems to the notice of the concerned officials.

It has been observed that panchayat elections have been postponed in several states violating the constitutional norms. Though Karnataka is a pioneering state in holding elections to PRIs under the new dispensation, it has not been an exception to the trend of delayed elections. The issue of postponement of elections becomes serious especially in view of the fact that the zilla panchayat is that facilitator and coordinator, responsible for integrating the plans of the taluk panchayat and grama panchayat and overseeing their functioning and allocating finances. This reflects the need for effective inter-institutional relationship. Therefore, postponement of elections should be checked at the earliest in the light of the present 'development paradigm'.

In 2000, elections to many panchayats were postponed due to ballot paper problems such as errors in serial numbers in the ballot paper, confusion over the nomination of candidates and symbol problems. These events clearly indicate that postponements on simple grounds are also taking place. In addition, elections to the different tiers of panchayats are bifurcated by holding one on time and postponing the other. This practice not only creates confusion in the administration but also deprives the development of a proper linkage between and among the three tiers, which is crucial for development. This demands more efforts by the SEC and sincerity on the part of the contesting candidates. The SEC should be strengthened as an independent body. All functions related to the electoral process should be under the supervision and control of the SEC. The present status of the SEC is not enough to conduct free, fair and timely elections (based on events during PR elections in 2000). The state government should intervene less and instead coordinate more with the SEC.

Today 'good governance' is the key word, yet corruption, money and muscle power continue even in the local elections scenario. It is necessary to put a ceiling on canvassing and overall election expenses on the same lines as the general elections. There is also an urgent need to curb practices such as snatching and tampering of ballot boxes, violent incidents, group clashes, booth capturing and rigging in order to have fair and free elections. It becomes even more important when we consider the hitherto disadvantaged sections of the society entering politics and the political process. Moreover, there is a need for effective and timely dissemination of information during elections in order to reduce confusion. Gazette notifications and important decisions should be made clear to the people quite in advance. Website, newspapers, pamphlets, periodic bulletins, press briefings, radio and television can be used to make information readily available for public use. This also leads to transparency in government functioning, which is the need of the hour.

An interesting development in the 2000 grama panchayat election was that more than 26 per cent of the members were elected unopposed all over the state. One reason could be that there were no candidates interested to contest from the category for which the concerned seat was reserved. It could also be said that the traditional power centres of the rich and influential prevailed upon the people not to oppose the candidates selected by them. Also, in some cases, the villagers themselves showed unity to elect their leader unanimously. Another reason could be the role of the local leaders in dissuading aspirants from filing nominations. However, this type of control over local affairs is a blow to the voter's privilege and it lead to an authoritarian polity. Trading leads to gerrymandering and results in certain interests not finding representation at all. This is not desirable and hence, it is more appropriate to have popularly elected members to represent the heterogeneous interests of the village.

When the results were announced after the village panchayat elections in 2000, all the major political parties claimed majority. It is clear that the grama panchayat elections are to be held on a non-party basis. But each party was able to in Identify the number of seats bagged by them. They are engaged in counting the number of winning candidates sponsored by them. It was obvious that many candidates were identified by their party affiliations. In this context, one has to question the feasibility of the system of having non-party elections at the grama panchayat level when that elections confirm the opposite, namely, that political parties are entering the remotest villages and influencing local politics. It is time to rethink the issue of non-party based elections at the gram panchayat level.

On the other hand again, in many constituencies, the winning candidates were selected for contest and their style of campaigning. The parties are pushed to the background when candidates enjoying a good rapport with the villagers contest the election.

Another important phenomenon in the 2000 elections was the emergence of the three 'all-women panchayats'. From the empowerment angle, this is a positive and progressive trend. But a deeper probing revealed that it was the decision of the local political elite to have all women members. It was an unopposed election as no other candidates was allowed to contest. This practice is undemocratic as leadership is forced on certain sections of the society depriving other people of their political rights.

In rural India today, PRIs are evolving institutions and with proper inputs over a period of time they are bound to stabilise as a strong democratic base. With this aim in mind, the Karnataka government decided to conduct training programmes for the newly-elected members of the grama, taluk and zilla panchayats. Taking into effect the problems encountered in the running of these local bodies as well as the new provisions incorporated in the 1993 Act, the following matters/issues[6] need to be considered: (a) The zilla panchayat should be strengthened financially by increasing the untied grants and by giving them powers to levy taxes and mobilise other resources such as the powers of the grama panchayat, (b) A proper coordination mechanism should be developed between the zilla panchayat and the line departments and among the departments in the district. Single line of command, effective communication and strict adherence to the guidelines of the Karnataka

Development Programme can help in developing close coordination, (c) Domination of MPs and MLAs is threat to local decision making. They should be kept outside the PR system. It is, therefore, suggested that the Karnataka Panchayat Raj Act should be amended accordingly/appropriately, (d) Though the bureaucracy provides stable leadership when the elected body is in a state of flux, the administrators have a decisive role in translating various policies and programmes of the government into reality. The efficacy of decentralised planning depends on their commitment. They must, therefore, be oriented towards the local self-governing bodies. This presupposes a drastic and purposive change in their outlook so that they identify themselves with the PR system. Placed in positions of authority and responsibility, they can reactive the political process and create a better climate. The administrative process, therefore, needs to be reformed. This demands trained personnel with the requisite skills and a commitment to developmental goals, (e) The electorate no longer ignores the performance of the local political leaders, which implies that the work of the representatives during their tenure is of great significance. Only when they spend their time resolving the problems of their constituencies, can they rely on the support of the voters, (f) Now that the electronic media has reached most villages, serious thought should be given to developing satellite, radio and TV programmes on panchayati raj. Of late, the government has taken initiatives in this regard, (g) Special programmes to train the presidents and the vice-presidents on their role, responsibilities and limitations should be taken up so that they develop a cordial relationship with the officials. The members should be made aware of their roles and responsibilities so that the standing committees develop as real decision-making bodies and the purpose for which they are formed, is fulfilled, (h) The election procedure seems to be reasonably efficient but a close examination has revealed some weaknesses. Effective methods of election administration have a direct impact on the accuracy and honesty of elections. A start has been made by giving due attention to the election machinery and the election process. The reforming zeal of the government in power can further strengthen this in the interest of honesty and efficiency, (i) The district planning committee should be constituted on time and it should be made functional to be effective. Adequate skill building at the district and sub-district levels on techniques of planning is necessary to develop an effective planning mechanism, (j) The target groups should be empowered to take up the programme themselves. Encouraging user group like water users committee, an education committee for ensuring proper education and a health committee for ensuring health facilities and the like can facilitate community participation in programmes but without by passing PRIs and (k) The grama sabha is the soul of the panchayati raj and the idea is to progressively strengthen its functioning to ensure full participation of the people and assure accountability and transparency. It should become a people's movement. Grama sabhas should meet regularly, failing which it should be construed as a disqualification on the part of the president. The area of the grama sabha should be such that people particularly women, daily-wage earners and the old can reach the venues of meetings conveniently. The grama sabha can be held on shandy (weekly market) days, so that there will be opportunity for meaningful participation of all.

Recent Developments

The Karnataka government, irrespective of political hues, has been generally responsive to the need for the necessary reforms in the PR system since its inception, and especially after the Panchayati Raj Act 1993. This is evident from the fact that it constituted a high-power committee to look into the problems in the PR system and to suggest remedial measures as early as 1995. This committee submitted its report in March 1996 and as a follow-up, necessary amendments were made in the Act. Again, in 2001, a working group on decentralisation was constituted to look into the problems and to suggest ways and means to take panchayati raj further for decentralised governance. Later, the government brought about another comprehensive amendment (The Karnataka Panchayati Raj Amendment Act, 2002) to overcome the institutional and administrative lacunae in the composition and functioning of PRIs.

Keeping in mind the many issues and problems that emerged in course of the elections in 1995 and 2000, several corrective steps (including GOs) were taken by the government to remove some of the drawbacks and dysfunctionalities in the functioning of the system.

Some of the amendments and correctives undertaken by the government are: (a) Establishing ward/vasathi sabhas with sufficient functions such as approval of the panchayat budget, programmes and development projects in ward area, selection of beneficiaries and planning, (b) Provisions have been made to see that SC, ST, BC and women participate in ward sabha and grama sabha in stipulated percentages, (c) By making general body meetings of the panchayats at all the three levels to be held every month (with a quorum of one-half instead of one-third), an opportunity is provided to members to voice their views quite frequently, (d) for ensuring sanctity, transparency and accountability, panchayats have to display the proceedings of the meetings within three days of the meetings, on the notice board of the respective panchayat, along with the details of the names of the members voted respectively for or against the resolutions passed in the meetings, (e) In order to make the electoral process clear, clean, transparent and corruption free, provisions for declaring assets of the candidates, ceiling of expenditure on election and strengthening the SEC by giving it more powers to enable it to function independently and freely for conducting elections, (f) Right to information, social audit and bringing PRIs under the purview of the Lokayukta (ombudsman at the state level) have been introduced, (g) Mapping out of activities for three tiers, to be performed under 29 subjects given in the Eleventh Schedule of the Seventy-third Constitutional Amendment Act followed in the Panchayati Raj Act 1993 under three schedules, have been completed and necessary government orders have been issued (h) The state government's decision to transfer 176 state schemes to the district sector and additional funds for implementing them. (In the 2004-05 budget, there was provision for Rs 40,000 million, an addition of Rs 8000 million over the previous year's budget for the districts sector for strengthening PRIs financially).

Having the reputation of a high-level commitment to democratic decentralisation on the part of the Karnataka elite cutting across party lines, the various governments in the state have considered many serious proposals for strengthening panchayati raj in the state. Some of the proposals may, however, appear to be extraordinary. There is a proposal for establishing ombudsman institution in each district, to contain corruption in its different form at the grass-roots. Passingly, it may be mentioned (as reported in *The Hindu*, 30-7-07) that the Comptroller and Auditor General of India (CAG) has, indicted officials in 23 zilla panchayats in the state for cases of malpractices, misappropriation and defalcation involving Rs 30.4 crores as on March 2006.

Another is rotation of a constituency on the basis of reservation quota should be done after 10 years (two terms). There are other proposals which invite national attention. For instance, considering the problems of local bureaucracy *vis-à-vis* control by political heads, the government is contemplating having a separate panchayati raj cadre for these institutions, thereby avoiding the problems of deputation, transfers and skill development necessary for rural development.

Based on past experience, the Government of Karnataka has gone for capacity-building programmes in a big way for elected members of PRIs and other related functionaries. This programme is conducted by Abdul Nazir Sab State Institute of Rural Development (ANSSIRD), Mysore through satellite. In a short span of time this innovative experiment has become a model for the country and outside in the neighbouring states (Bangladesh, Pakistan and Sri Lanka etc).[7] All these positive steps mentioned so far, are expected to transfer sufficient finances, functions and functionaries to the three-tier Panchayati Raj system.

Being committed to decentralised governance, the government maintained the schedule of the third round of elections, which were conducted in three phases on 25 February, 27 February and 6 March 2005. During this election, some of the grama panchayat polls were postponed because the SEC found that the election process in certain grama panchayats constituencies was 'flawed' and cancelled it. Repoll was held on 20 and 26 March 2005, as ordered by the SEC and 15,189 candidates were elected unopposed. The elections to zilla panchayats and taluk panchayats were conducted in December 2005. The following picture emerged after PRIs elections 2005.

Table 2

Grama Panchayats (Total Number 5653) Total number of Members - 91402	***Taluk Panchayats Total Number 176) Total Number of Members – 3683***	***Zilla Panchayats (Total Number 27) Total Number of Members – 1005***
SC – 19 per cent	SC – 18 per cent	SC – 18 per cent
ST – 11 per cent	ST – 9 per cent	ST – 8 per cent
BC – 33 per cent	BC – 34 per cent	BC – 38 per cent
General Category - 37 per cent	General Category – 39 per cent	General Category – 36 per cent
Women – 43 per cent (From all categories, of the total number of members)	Women – 41 per cent (From all categories, per cent of the total number of members)	Women – 37 per cent (From all categories, per cent of the total number of members)

During the election conducted for grama panchayats, the following had been observed among others, which are worth mentioning.

It should be noted that legally the grama panchayat elections should be held on a non-party basis. However, involvement of political parties in the campaign was visible everywhere as it happened in the past. In almost all places, the legislators were openly supporting their candidates. In some villages, of course, candidates fought the elections without any political support. On the days of voting, most candidates were seen offering meals and *tambula* (gifts) to the voters to woo them. In the camps of some candidates, the festivities matched only those of a marriage ceremony. Enthusiasm and active participation of women in the elections was noticeable. Kodihalli and neighbouring Gopalapura villages are the first two villages in Mandya District in Karnataka to jointly elect an all-women grama panchayat. Women candidates were fielded for all the eight panchayat seats, which include the SC and BC seats. Seven members were elected unopposed. Polling was peaceful barring a few incidents.

Concluding Observations

It is evident that decentralisation has encouraged local participation. However, it is still far from the normative standards and has not led to increased efficiency, effectiveness and efficacy. This means that these institutions should be made much more participatory as involving the beneficiaries will automatically lead to improvement in the works executed. Adequate empowerment of the grama sabha is the crux of effective decentralisation (but not at the cost of the grama panchayat) as that is where people's democracy can be put into practice. It is there that the voice of the people, including the weaker sections and women, can be really heard. The elected grama panchayat must be accountable to the grama sabha, which should be convened according to the statutory requirements and government guidelines. The annual statement of accounts and the 'social audit' report must be formally placed before the grama sabha, as also the development report relating to the preceding year and the programme for the current year, including the annual plan and selection of beneficiaries. The annual plan should be considered against the background of a five-year plan based on the local priorities.

All relevant information should be systematically made available to the grama sabha in accordance with the Transparency Act and the Right to Information Act, which have been enacted in Karnataka. Full use should be made of the grama sabha to create awareness regarding the policies and programmes, which are of great relevance at the grass roots level, so that people's participation can be progressively increased and improved. The grama sabha should be fully representative, especially of the weaker sections and women as mandated by an amendment to the Panchayati Raj Act 1993. Each separate habitation in a grama panchayat should have its own people's committees, which could be like sub-committees of the grama panchayat with suitable links with the grama sabha, to strengthen people's participation. Any user or stakeholders group that is set up should have organic links with the grama panchayat to ensure that it is not sidelined. The media should also work towards bringing about a fundamental change in the development thinking, that is, participatory human development for sustainable growth.

Since one cannot dissociate political parties from panchayati raj, it is essential to have a 'culture of democracy' or unity among the various political parties. This means that they should incorporate groups and individuals, who have been hitherto excluded, under-represented or discriminated against, in local politics, cooperate in the development activities of the villages, take responsibility for their representatives to carry out their tasks and be accountable for their actions. The PRIs should be developed as a medium of community development and not as a power mechanism where they are treated as centres of power.

Democratic decentralisation is a remedial measure to mobilise popular voluntary participation. The PRIs, therefore, have a vital role in rural development being the only institutions to facilitate planning, participation and mobilisation of resources. The emergence of these institutions has brought governance closer to the people. Yet, we have seen that the elective base of the local self-government system is facing various pressures, stresses and strains. Popular enthusiasm and 'collective actions'; should, therefore, emerge to meet the present challenges. In all probability only 'activism' can make any difference in the political orientation of the system.

The entire discussion in this paper reveals quite effectively that Karnataka has till date, quite famously incorporated many progressive ideas and innovative mechanisms for strengthening PRIs. The commitment of the government to decentralised governance is beyond doubt. It is heartening to note that recently, the Ministry of Panchayati Raj, Government of India, adjudged Karnataka as occupying second rank/position in the country after Kerala, based on 'Devolution Index' (broadly devolution of functions, functionaries and finances to PRIs). Again coming to 'empowerment of women'. Karnataka occupies second place in the country after Kerala. The recognition of these achievements may be called two newly added feathers in the cap of 'decentralised governance' in Karnataka.

One can say confidently that the state is moving further in the direction of genuine decentralisation, that is, to make these institutions sustainable as 'institutions of self-government' as envisaged in the provision of 243G in the Seventy-third Constitutional Amendment Act 1992.

Notes

1. For details about the structural and functional aspects of the panchayati raj system under the Act of 1959, see Bhargava et.al. (1982); see also Bhargava (1984).
2. A plethora of literature is available on the panchayati raj system and its functioning under the Act of 1983 conducted by foreign and Indian scholars. Among others, two empirical studies by B.S. Bhargava and N. Sivanna (1990 and 1992) are worth noting.
3. For structural and operational aspects, especially election process and related issues, see Mathew (1994, 2000). See also Subha (1996).
4. For extensive coverage of pre, during and post phases of panchayati raj elections, 2000, See, Subha et al. (2001). Also, see, Subha and Bhargava (2000).
5. For the concept of 'dominant caste', 'shifting of dominance', 'inclusion' and 'exclusion' and their testing at the field level in Karnataka, refer to the unpublished research report of the ISS (2002).
6. In this paper, observations and findings are based on the data (primary and secondary) collected in connection with recent larger research projects/studies on Karnataka's panchayati raj system and election process at the Institute of Social Sciences, Southern Regional Centre, Bangalore. For instance, see, a chapter on PR system in Karnataka: Trends and Issues, in Grass-roots Democracy in India and China (2007).
7. For other related details, see, a chapter on Capacity Building for Panchayati Raj Functionaries in Karnataka through Satellite, in Dynamics of New Panchayati Raj System in India (2008).

References

Bhargava, B.S. (1984): 'Working of Town Panchayats in Karnataka: Problems and Prospects' (mimeo), Institute for Social and Economic Change, Bangalore.

Bhargava, B.S., C.R. Bada and V.N. Torgal (1982): *'Panchayati Raj System* (in Karnataka), Jackson Publications, New Delhi.

Bhargava, B.S. and N. Sivanna (1990): 'Emerging Pattern of Leadership in Panchayati Raj System: Case Study of a Zilla Parishad in Karnataka', *Working Paper*, Institute for Social and Economic Change, Bangalore.

……., (1992): 'Place and Role of Taluk Panchayat Samiti in Panchayati Raj System of Karnataka: A Case Study'. *Working paper*, Institute for Social and Economic Change, Bangalore.

Bhargava, B.S. and K. Subha (2007): 'Panchayati Raj System in Karnataka: Trends and Issues', in *Grass-roots Democracy in India and China: The Right to Participation,* Richard and Baun et.al (ed). Sage Publications, New Dehi.

Mathew, George (ed). (1994): *Status of Panchayati Raj in the States of India*, Concept Publishers, New Delhi.

………, (2000): '*Status of Panchayati Raj in the States and Union Territories of India*', Concept Publishers, New Delhi.

Subha, K. (1996): *Karnataka Panchayat Elections 1995, Process Issues and Membership Profile*, Concept Publishers, New Dehi.

Subha, K. and B.S. Bhargava (2000): 'Feminism and Political Empowerment of Women: The Karnataka Experience', *South Asian Journal of Socio-Political Studies*, Kollam-1 (2).

Subha, K., B.S. Bhargava and Mangala Nayak (2001): 'Women in Panchayati Raj Institutions: Political Empowerment through Capacity Building', *South Asian Journal of Socio-Political Studies*, Kollam, 2(1).

Subha, K, B.S., Bhargava and Mangala Nayak (2008): 'Capacity Building for Panchayati Raj Functionaries in Karnatak, through Satellite' (chapter 8), in *Dynamics of New Panchayti Raj System in India*, G. Palanithuria (ed), Concept Publishers, New Delhi.

Unpublished Research Report (2000): 'An Overview of Panchayati Raj Election in Karnataka 2000', Institute of Social Sciences, Bangalore.

Unpublished Research Report (2002): 'Inclusion of the Excluded Communities, Panchayati Raj System and Social Cohesion: The Case of Karnataka', Institute of Social Sciences, Bangalore.

11

Democratic Decentralisation: The Karnataka Model

— *Midatala Rani*

Introduction

The available literature from 1980's onwards credits Karnataka's first non-Congress government with the major initiative in devolution and ascribes it largely to the then Chief Minister Ramakrishna Hegde and Abdul Nazeer Sab, Minister of Rural Development. Their commitment to Panchayati Raj was never in dispute, the 1983 legislation and its implementation needs to be looked in terms of an historical evolutionary perspective. This will enable us to understand the various factors which have facilitated the development of institutions of democratic decentralisation.

The state of Mysore (renamed Karnataka in 1973) was formed in 1956 by bringing together the erstwhile princely state of Mysore, four districts of Bombay, three districts of Hyderabad, two districts of Madras and the centrally administered territory of Coorg. Prior to the re-organisation of states, development of local government institutions in these five areas had proceeded independently, the devolution of powers and functions having been faster in the British Provinces than in the native states. Each of these areas from states mentioned above brought its own history and legislation relating to local government. After enlargement of the state a new Act came into operation and the inter regional differences at the legislative level ceased to exist.

Historical Evolution

Even before the 5th Century A.D. Local Self governing institutions called Ur (village Assembly), Mahajana (Assembly of Brahmins' Agrahara), Nagara (town Assembly), Nadu (Taluk level Assembly) and Mahanadu (District Level Assembly), had their innings in the Karnataka region. Their golden period was upto the sixteenth century. They were spontaneous local bodies with no central control and almost appearing like "Republics." They started declining under the centralising medieval kingdoms and more so the British colonial rule.

Pre-1956 Period

Modern rural local government began to appear in 1862 with the establishment of the "Local Fund" and more so in 1874 with the establishment of the "Local Fund Committees." In the old state of Mysore a three tier structure of Union Panchayats, taluk boards and district boards was established under the Mysore Local Boards Act, 1902 with a minority of elected members, the rest being either nominated or appointed as ex-officio members. The union panchayat had a nominated chairperson while officials presided over the higher level institutions. Further revision took place in 1918 and 1926 when statutes were enacted for creating village Panchayats and district boards with enlarged elected membership, eliminating the middle tier, i.e. the taluk boards. The franchise for election to these institutions remained limited as also the powers vested in them.

In the Madras Presidency, by virtue of the Madras District Boards Act, 1920 district boards had been allowed to have directly elected presidents and members and were vested with substantial powers relating to education, public health and maintenance of roads. Panchayats had also been established at the village level with wider powers under the 1920 Madras Panchayat Act.

Under the Bombay Act 23 of 1928, district boards with elected presidents and vice-presidents also started functioning in the Bombay Presidency. The Bombay Village Panchayat Act, 1920 underwent a series of changes in 1928, 1933, 1939 and 1947 providing for a gradual enlargement of scope and functions. A unique feature in the Bombay setup was the continued existence of the district school boards to look after primary and secondary education with members elected from rural and urban local bodies. From 1941, local government institutions at the village and district levels had also been established in the state of Hyderabad with elected district boards having come into existence. In Coorg there were only village panchayats established in 1926 under the Coorg Village Panchayats Act.

The attainment of independence introduced an important dimension of democracy namely, adult franchise. The demand for strong local self-government had been voiced during the freedom struggle. This called for substantial changes in the statutes. These changes were made in 1950 in Madras and Bombay and in 1953 and 1956 in Hyderabad. In the old state of Mysore, two committees namely, the V. Venkatappa Committee 1950 and D.H. Chandrasekaraiah Committee 1954 recommended major changes in the structure and functions of local government.

V. Venkatappa Committee (1950) and Mysore Village Panchayats and District Boards Act (1952)

The Committee recommended Group Panchayats and District Boards indirectly elected by members of the former. The 1952 Act was based on this model. There was opposition to the absence of Taluk Boards, abolition of single village panchayats and indirect elections. The Act was never fully implemented.

Local Boards Enquiry (D.H. Chandrashekaraiya) Committee (1954)

This Committee suggested a three tier system with Village Panchayats, Taluk Boards and District Boards. It recommended reservation for SCs, STs and women. The Venkatappa and Chandrashekaraiaya Committees differed from each other in significant ways. The former did not recommend a taluk level institution. It opted for Group Panchayats and district councils. Indirect elections were recommended for the latter. While agreeing with the need for representation for the SCs the method suggested was co-option.

Since 1956

Karnataka State was re-organised in 1956 and the Panchayat Raj movement accelerated in 1957. Under the influence of the Balwant Rai Mehta Report, Karnataka had three Panchayat Raj Legislations. They include "The Mysore Village Panchayats and Local Boards Act 1959", second "The Karnataka Zilla Parishad, Taluk Panchayats, Mandal Panchayats and Nyaya Panchayat Act, 1983" and the third is "The Karnataka Panchayat Raj Act 1993."

The 1959 Act

The formation of the new state synchronised with the release of the Balwant Rai Mehta Committee report which provided a new impetus for Panchayati Raj. Taking note of the recommendations of this committee as well as the historical evolution of local government institutions in the state, a new local self-government setup was introduced covering all parts of the reorganised state. The Mysore Village Panchayats and Local Boards Act, 1959 was enacted and a three-tier structure was introduced with directly elected bodies at the village and taluk level and indirectly constituted body at the district level. A directly elected village panchayat was constituted for every village or group of villages with an average population of 2500. Members of the taluk development board ranging from 11 to 19 were also directly elected. Seats were reserved for the SCs and STs, at both the village and taluk levels according to their population in the area while two seats each at both levels were reserved for women.

At both the levels members elected the office bearers from amongst themselves. Members of the state legislature were members of the taluk development board with the right to vote, but not to hold office. All the presidents of the taluk development boards together with MPs and MLAs from the district and some official members constituted the district development council (DDC), which was headed by the deputy commissioner. There was provision to nominate one SC or one ST member and one woman member to the district development council.

Taluk Development Boards (TDBs)

Primacy was given to the taluk development board from the point of view of devolution of functions and powers. Both administratively and financially the TDBs were regarded as viable instruments for undertaking the responsibility of development in their areas. Besides the usual regulatory functions such as control of fairs and festivals, the TDB were entrusted with construction and maintenance of primary school buildings, minor irrigation work, promotion of industry, agriculture and relief work. The TDBs also took over the Community Development Programme.

The DDC was visualised as a coordinating body its only substantive function being approval of the budgets of the taluk development boards. Village Panchayats performed limited local municipal functions. They had the power to levy some local taxes but these fetched only limited revenue. The taluk development boards were empowered to levy a surcharge on stamp duty. The state government transferred 50 per cent of the land revenue collected in the local area and 10 per cent of the total collection in the state to these boards and village panchayats. But given the low rates of land revenue and concessions of various kinds, this did not amount too much. The TDBs and village panchayats has limited fiscal independence and most of their funds came from the government. These Boards functioned well and made development process more participatory and responsive. In early years they were quite popular. But insufficient transfer of finances and lack of political support hampered the maximum utilisation of potential of Panchayati Raj Institutions.

The decline of interest in Panchayati Raj at the national level after the passing away of Jawaharlal Nehru was reflected in Karnataka also. The elections which were due in 1964 were postponed till 1968 when fresh elections were held. Meanwhile the state government setup the Kondajji Basappa Committee which submitted its report in 1963.

Kondajji Basappa Committee, 1963

Its main recommendations were a three-tier structure consisting of Village Panchayats, Taluk Development Boards and Zilla Parishads, exclusion of MPs and MLAs from Panchayati Raj institutions, reservation for SCs, STs and women, constitution of Gram Sabha, representation of Panchayats in TDBs and for the latter in Zilla Panchayats and the Constitution of Nyaya Panchayats.

Mysore Panchayat Raj Bill, 1964

Accepting the recommendations of the committee the State Government introduced a Bill in 1964 to establish a three-tier structure of rural self-government in the then Mysore State. The select committee headed by the then Rural Development Minister, Ramakrishna Hegde enthusiastically recommended enhanced powers to the Panchayati Raj Institutions but nothing came out of it as neither the ruling party nor the Government was prepared for launching such an experiment then.

The 1983 Act

The Janata Party Government in power at the Centre setup the Asoka Mehta Committee. Its report was made public in 1978. In 1983, when the Janata Party came to power in Karnataka there was a revival of interest in establishing Panchayati Raj with genuine devolution of powers and functions. This was the electoral commitment of the Janata Party in Karnataka. The new Government steered the Karnataka Zilla Parishads, Taluk Panchayat Samitis, Mandal Panchayats and Nyaya Panchayats Bill through the legislature within the first year in office. The President's assent to the Bill was given only on 10th July 1985. Elections under the new law were held in January 1987 and the elected Panchayati Raj Institutions started functioning from April of the same year. Elections to Zilla Parishads and Mandal Panchayats were fought on party lines.

The 1983 Act can be regarded as a landmark in the history of local government in India as it demonstrated for the first time the willingness of a state government to divert itself of substantial powers and functions in favour of sub-state institutions. The 1983 Act brought in a fresh air of democratisation of PRIs and decentralisation of especially the district development administration. The 1983 Act was so progressive that it became a model which led and even shaped the famous 73rd Constitution Amendment Act. The 73rd Amendment is indeed a virtual tribute to the 1993 Act of Karnataka and an attempt to universalise it with some marginal changes. The 1983 Act was modelled on the suggestions made in the Asoka Mehta Committee report, with a two-tier structure – Zilla Parishads at the district level and Mandal Panchayats for group of villages with direct elections to both bodies.

Zilla Parishad

The Zilla Parishad was to be fully responsible for planning and implementation of all the development programmes in the district. Members of Zilla Parishad were directly elected with 25 per cent of seats for the SCs and STs in proportion to their population (with a minimum of 18 per cent of seats for them). The Adhyaksha and Upadhyaksha were given the status and salary of minister of state and deputy minister of the state government respectively. The official machinery of Zilla Parishad was headed by its chief executive who was called the chief secretary drawn from the Indian Administrative Service. As a deliberate policy, a person senior in service to the deputy commissioner of the district held this post. Besides having an elaborate accounts staff under the chief accounts officer, the Zilla Parishad had a planning unit under the chief planning officer with four or five subject specialists. All the district level officers and the staff of development departments functioned under the Zilla Parishad. There was a segregation of the development and regulatory administration in the district, the deputy commissioner being kept out of the Panchayati Raj setup.

A wide range of functions were entrusted to Zilla Parishad, the general approach being that any activity whose area of benefit did not extend beyond the district should come under it. Besides the overall coordination and integration of development schemes and preparation of the plan for the development of the district, the Zilla Parishads were assigned specific responsibilities in the areas of agriculture, animal husbandry, welfare of SCs and STs and the backward classes, buildings and communication, education, public health, irrigation and ground water resources, horticulture, cooperation, fisheries, rural electrification and distribution of essential commodities. Detailed orders were issued by the state government specifying the schemes, programmes and personnel of each department transferred to the Zilla Parishads. As regards personnel, about 30 per cent of the government employees of whom primary school teachers constituted the largest number, came under the administrative control of Zilla Parishads.

Mandal Panchayat

A mandal panchayat was constituted for a population of eight to twelve thousand (a lower limit of four thousand was imposed for the hilly areas). It consisted of elected members with one member for a population of four hundred, reservation of women, the SCs and STs being provided on the same lines as at the district level. Each mandal panchayat had a whole time secretary appointed and paid for by the Zilla Parishad. Other employees such as sanitation staff, were paid out of its own funds.

Mandal Panchayats were also given considerable powers. Apart from the usual municipal functions and provisions of local amenities they were expected to take interest in agriculture and animal husbandry programmes and in the welfare of the SCs and STs, Mandal Panchayats were also assigned with the implementation of anti-poverty programmes for which they received substantial funds.

Taluk Panchayat Samiti

The Taluk Panchayat Samiti, a coordinating and monitoring body operated at the taluk level. It was headed by a local MLA and had all the mandal pradhans as members. The panchayat samiti had no executive powers except for providing a position for the MLA in the structure. It did not serve any substantive purpose.

Gram Sabha

The gram sabha was given statutory recognition comprising of all the adults of the village. It was expected to meet at least twice a year and at each meeting the mandal panchayat was required to present a report of its activities. Another function was to select beneficiaries under the anti-poverty programmes.

Finances

The zilla parishads did not have any power of taxation while the mandal panchayats had the usual power to levy property tax, tax on vehicles, etc. The state government gave a grant of rupees thirty crore per year to meet the administrative expenses of the parishads and mandals and leave some funds with the latter for local development activity.

Planning at the District Level

The zilla parishads were entrusted with the responsibility of district planning. By the end of July each year the state planning department was required to indicate to the zilla parishads and mandal panchayats the financial ceilings within which their annual plan was to be formulated for the next year. The mandal panchayat convenes a meeting of the gram sabha to know the views of local community and will formulate the plan for ensuring year and forwards it to zilla parishad which in turn will prepare the district plan and forward it to the government. Several meetings are called by the state planning department. District plans are incorporated in the state plan and submitted to National Planning Commission.

The newly elected zilla parishads and mandal panchayats started functioning from 1987. Even though there were signs of improvement in functioning the dominant castes had a huge share of membership and offices. The participation of the weaker sections in decision-making remained very fragile. The zilla parishads had little freedom in determination of priorities. Mandals remained weak and depended on staff of zilla parishad. The gram sabhas did not meet regularly and proved ineffective. The first Finance Commission headed by R.M. Honnavar submitted its report in 1989 with recommendations covering plan and non-plan expenditure and per capita discretionary and incentive grants. But the government did not take any action on the report as interest in panchayati raj had already started falling. Added to this infighting and factional politics within the parent Janata party weakened the panchayati raj institutions. With the return of the Congress party to power in 1990 the zilla parishads ceased to have any role. The share of the district plans in the state plan went down. Finally in 1992 when elections were due, the government superceded the zilla parishads and mandal panchayats and appointed administrators.

The 1993 Act

By the end of 1992 the Congress government which had affirmed its commitment to revive Panchayati Raj institutions took office in Karnataka. This also synchronised with the passing of the Constitution 73rd Amendment Act 1992 by Parliament. The two tier structure in the state had to be replaced by a three-tier structure, the government decided to enact a fresh legislation. Karnataka was the first state to do so after the 73rd amendment. The Karnataka Panchayat Raj Act 1993 came into force on 10th May 1993.

Structure

The Gram Sabha is at the base of the Panchayati Raj structure consisting of all the registered voters in the village. The sabha is expected to meet atleast twice in a year and make recommendations. The annual accounts and administration report of the preceding financial year and current year's proposed development programmes are placed for its consideration. It will also help in mobilising voluntary labour and contributions for community welfare programmes and identification of beneficiaries under developmental schemes pertaining to the village. Every village or group of villages having a population between 5,000 and 7,000 will have a gram panchayat (GP) with one member for every four hundred population. The gram panchayat will have three standing committees which can coopt members of farmers clubs, mahila mandals, yuvak mandals and so on. Every taluk will have a taluk panchayat (TP), one member being elected for a population of ten thousand. Members of the Lok Sabha and the State Legislative Assembly representing the whole or part of the taluk and members of the Rajya Sabha and the State Legislative Council registered as voters in the taluk will be members of the taluk panchayat. One-fifth of the adhyakshas of the gram panchayats in the taluk will also be members by rotation for a period of one year each. At the district level, there will be an elected member of the zilla panchayat (ZP) for a population of 40,000. Members of Parliament and State Legislature and all adhyakshas of the taluk panchayats will be members of ZP by virtue of office. In both TPs and ZPs, the ex-officio members will have the right to vote but not to hold office.

Reservation

Reservations apply to both membership and offices at all three levels. The reservations for SCs and STs will be proportional to their population with a minimum reservation of 15 per cent and 3 per cent respectively. One-third of the total number of seats and offices are reserved for the backward classes. There will be one-third reservation for women under all categories reserved or unreserved.

Functions

The Act spells out in three separate schedules the functions to be performed by panchayats at different levels. These cover all the subjects included in the Eleventh Schedule of the Constitution. Interestingly under the Act, the government may by notification withdraw, amend or add any activity covered by the entries in the schedules.

Taxation and Finance

Gram Panchayats can levy taxes on property, entertainment, vehicles and charge fees on markets and the like. Neither ZPs and TPs have any taxation powers, but they can raise loans with the permission of the government. The government may levy cess on land revenue and additional stamp duty, the proceeds of which will be handed over to GPs and TPs respectively. The Act provides for an annual grant of one lakh rupees to each gram panchayat to meet electricity charges, maintenance of water supply schemes, sanitation and other welfare activities. This will be supplemented by programme related grants. The ZPs and TPs will depend almost entirely on resource transfers by the state government for both maintenance and development activities. Every panchayat will prepare its annual budget. The GP budget can be modified by the TP if it has not been framed in accordance with the Act and the rules. The ZP and the government exercise similar powers in respect of TPs and ZPs. Audit of accounts of ZPs and TPs will be carried out by the Controller and Auditor General and that of Gram Panchayat by the Controller of State Accounts.

Personnel

Every GP will have a secretary paid for by the ZP and other employees paid out of its own resources. An officer of the rank of assistant commissioner will be the executive officer of the TP and he will be supported by officials of different departments. The ZP will have a chief executive officer of the rank of deputy commissioner who will be assisted by the chief accounts officer and deputy secretaries. Officers and staff of development departments at the district level and below specified by government will function under the administrative control of the ZP.

Inspection and Control

The adhyaksha and upadhyaksha of a GP who is persistently remiss in discharge of his duties could be removed from office and even membership, by the divisional commissioner. The secretary of the Rural Development Department and the divisional commissioner could inspect the offices of the ZPs. Similarly, the CEO of the ZP and the executive officer of the TP may inspect the offices of the TPs and GPs respectively. The instructions issued after such inspection must be complied with by the body concerned. There is also provision for technical supervision and inspection by state and divisional level officers. The state government may at any time for reasons to be recorded, institute an enquiry by any of its officers on matters concerning any panchayat. A resolution considered to be unjust or unlawful may be suspended by designated officials in the case of GP and TP and by the government in the case of ZP. If there is abuse of power or persistent default in the performance of duties, the divisional commissioner may dissolve a GP, the state government has similar powers in the case of ZPs and TPs.

Other Provisions

The Act provides for the establishment of the State Election Commission and State Finance Commission as required under the 73rd amendment. It also provides for the Constitution of a District Planning Committee as mandated by the 74th Amendment, the Chairman of the committee being chosen in the manner to be prescribed by the government.

Criticism of the Act

The Karnataka Panchayati Raj Act of 1993 was the first enactment under the 73rd amendment in the country. Yet it has been the most brazen attempt to depart from the spirit of the 73rd amendment. It fights shy even to use the phrase "Self Government" in its preamble. The 1993 Act provides for a Grama Sabha at the base and a three tier structure of Village, Taluk and Zilla Panchayats. It uprooted the earlier Mandal Panchayats and Zilla Parishads. It doubled the number of village panchayats from 2600 to 5641 by reducing their size in terms of population covered from eight to twelve thousand per panchayat to five to seven thousand. This means an increase in establishment expenditure and reduction in their resources to a less viable level. Though the 73rd Amendment intended (section 44) to promote direct election of village panchayat Chairpersons, the 1993 Act strikes to indirect election as earlier. Reservation of seats under it for Panchayats have become highly controversial and litigious. The 73rd Amendment intended reservation for SCs and STs according to their population (Art. 243D), the 1993 Act provides for a mandatory reservation of 18 per cent irrespective of their population (Sections 5, 123 and A62). Also reservations for SCs of 18 per cent, STs three per cent, women one-third of the panchayat size and BCs 30 per cent exceeded the 50 per cent limit for reservations laid down by the Supreme Court. These reservations coupled with the most undesirable portion of the Act and the 73rd Amendment as well i.e. "the reservation of Chairpersonship" created unmanageable and inefficient political and administrative situations, leaders and institutions in rural areas. These made the Act and the 73rd Amendment highly litigation bound with many cases filed in courts.

The 1983 Act's emphasis was on Zilla Parishad and Mandal Panchayat. The 1993 Act laid emphasis on middle tier Taluk Panchayat. Yet the Taluk Panchayat along with Zilla Panchayat was denied powers to mobilise its own resources. At the district level the 1993 Act undoes the powerful Zilla Parishad created by the 1983 Act. Indian Administration at the district level has been the preserve of bureaucracy for too long. The 1983 Act was a bold attempt to undo it and democratise it by giving the elected President and Secretaries of Zilla Parishad higher status and powers. The 1993 Act rebureaucratises the Zilla Development Administration in essence.

So far as functions and powers of Panchayati Raj Institutions the 1993 Act provided three lists of functions which overlap. Resource-wise it displaced the more flexible per capita grant by a lump sum grant of rupees one lakh per Panchayat. The Taluk and Zilla Panchayats without their own independent resources were made to be dependent on government schemes and doles. The 1993 Act provided more "recentralisation" of development administration than the "decentralisation" that existed under the 1983 Act. Control-wise, the spirit of the Panchayati Raj Movement and the 73rd Amendment was to democratise it. The 1993 Act brazenly bureaucratises it. Particularly under sections 193(3), 70(3), 232 to 238 of the 1993 Act, the officials from Village Panchayat Secretary to the Chief Executive Officer of the Zilla Panchayat, the Revenue Assistant Commissioners, the technical Heads of Departments and State Government were given the powers of either inspection, inquiry, supervision, withholding of resolutions passed or actions taken by Panchayati Raj Institutions or of directing of certain actions or ultimately of dissolution of these bodies. The most undesirable Democle's Sword on decentralisation scheme in the 1993 Act is Section 312 under which the State Government i.e. the Executive wing can "omit, amend or add activities and schemes" listed in the three schedules of functions assigned to Panchayati Raj Institutions.

Amendments to the 1993 Act

In the general elections to the State Legislative Assembly towards the end of 1994, the Janata Dal party was swept to power and the new government announced its intention to revamp the Act of 1993 to restore autonomy that existed under 1983 Act. An expert committee (the Nayak Committee) was constituted in February 1995 which submitted its report in March 1996 recommending wide ranging changes in the Act of 1993.

In the light of the recommendations of the Nayak Committee, changes were effected in 1997. Important among them included the following:

- The objective of enabling panchayats to function as units of local self government was made explicit in the preamble.
- A variety of functions relating to the electoral process such as delimitation of constituencies, determination of the number of elected members, reservation of seats for different categories, disqualification of members and publication of the names of elected members were entrusted to the State Election Commission. Earlier these were with the government or designated officials.
- The powers which had been entrusted to the divisional commissioner, deputy commissioner and assistant commissioner (hearing appeals, acceptance of resignation, removal of office bearers of GPs, dissolution of GPs, suspension of resolutions and so on) were withdrawn and they ceased to have any role in Panchayati Raj. While some routine functions were transferred to the executive officer of the TP and chief executive officer of the ZP, the more important powers were vested in the ZPs (in respect of GPs) and the government (in case of ZPs and TPs).
- From the supervisory angle, a hierarchical relationship was established between the three-tiers. The ZP has been given the power to enquire into complaints of non-performance of duty by the TP and give directions for due performance. The TP has a similar role vis-à-vis the GPs.
- Obligatory functions were prescribed for the first time. GPs are mandated to provide sanitary facilities to households, maintain water supply works, achieve universal enrolment in primary schools and universal immunisation among others. The TPs are obliged to improve water supply and to get half-yearly reports on the functioning of GPs. Establishment of health centres, social forestry and prevention of drilling of irrigation wells in the vicinity of drinking water wells are the obligatory functions of ZPs. These functions are complimentary to those listed in the schedules to the Act. But the obligation is subject to the availability of funds.
- Restrictions have been placed on the frequency of no confidence motions against the Adhyaksha and Upadhyaksha (one year in GPs and six months in ZPs and TPs).
- The adhyaksha of the ZP was made the chairman of the District Planning Committee.
- Provision was made for establishing the State Panchayat Council under the Chairpersonship of the Chief Minister with a few ministers and all the ZP adhyakshas as members to act as a forum to discuss matters relating to the functioning of Panchayats in the state.

These amendments have gone a long way in restoring the true spirit of Panchayat Raj in the State though it is still short of what was attempted under the 1983 Act. A feature which stands out by its absence is that there is no provision for establishing own cadres of personnel in Panchayats.

Sum Up

The Panchayati Raj system in Karnataka did not spring out of a vacuum. It is the result of a number of developments which have unfolded over decades. It is a product of evolutionary process. While number of forces have contributed towards creating a climate conducive for devolution there is continuing presence of some problems within the devolutionary system.

The 73rd amendment undoubtedly marks a significant advance but its limitations are also visible. The state law under which the Panchayati Raj bodies are constituted should be so designed as to make participatory local governance possible. But though the law can ensure the form of local government, it cannot guarantee its content. It is the commitment of political parties, the elected representatives and leadership at the national and state levels to devolution of political and administrative power which will determine the character of these institutions. Karnataka has moved steadily towards ensuring greater autonomy for Panchayati Raj Institutions. Hopefully this will promote more participatory governance in future.

Sources

Reports

1. Integration and Coordination Committee for Local Bodies (V. Venkatappa Committee), 1950.
2. Local Boards Enquiry Committee (D.H. Chandrashekaraiya Committee), 1954.
3. Mysore Village Panchayats and Local Boards Act,1959.
4. Committee on Panchayati Raj (Kondajji Basappa Committee), 1963.
5. Report of the Joint Select Committee on the Mysore Panchayat Raj Bill, 1964.
6. Report of the Joint Select Committee on the Karnataka Zilla Parishad, Taluk Panchayat Samitis and Nyaya Panchayats Act, 1983.
7. Report of the Zilla Parishad and Mandal Panchayat Committee (K.S. Krishnaswamy Committee), 1989.
8. Karnataka Panchayat Raj Act, 1993.
9. Report of the Expert Committee on Karnataka Panchayat Raj Act 1993 (March 1996).
10. Report of the Working Group on Decentralisation (Government of Karnataka, 2002).

Secondary

1. Abdul Aziz, (1994): *Decentralised Planning: The Karnataka Experience*, New Delhi, Sage Publication.

2. Abdul Aziz, N. Devendra Babu, Madhushree Sekher and C. Charles Nelson (1998): *Decentralised Governance and Planning: A Comparative Study in Three South Indian States* (Ford Foundation Project Report) (Mimeo), Bangalore, Institute for Social and Economic Change.
3. Abdul Aziz (1998): *"Process of Decentralised Governance and Planning"*, Prashasniko, 25(2), 113-119.
4. Abdul Aziz (1994): *Decentralisation: Mandal Panchayat System in Karnataka*, National Institute of Rural Development, Hyderabad.
5. Arun Ghosh, "The Panchayati Raj Bill", *Economic and Political Weekly*, Vol. XXIV, No. 26, 1 July 1989.
6. Amitava Mukherjee (1994): *Decentralisation: Panchayats in the Nineties*, New Delhi, Vikas Publications.
7. Anand Inbanathan (1994): "Karnataka Panchayats Under Administrators", 1994, *Occasional Paper Series No. 14*, New Delhi, Institute of Social Sciences.
8. M. Babu Devandran (1997): "Decentralised Planning in Karnataka", *The Asian Economic Review*, Vol. 39, No. 2.
9. K.S. Bhat (1977): *A Study of Rural Local Government in Mysore State*, Bombay, University of Bombay Press.
10. B.K. Chandrashekar, "Panchayati Raj Bill: The Real Flaw", *Economic and Political Weekly*, Vol. XXIV, No. 26, 1 July 1989.
11. George Mathew (1986), *Panchayati Raj in Karnataka Today: Its National Dimension*, New Delhi, Concept Publishing Company.
12. George Mathew (1995): *From Movement to Legislation*, New Delhi, Concept Publishing Company.
13. Midatala Rani, "Panchayat Raj System in Karnataka", *Social Science in Perspective*, Vol. 2, Nos. 3 and 4, July-September and October-December 2010, 407-431.
14. Richard Slater and John Watson, 1989, "Democratic Decentralisation or Political Consolidation: The Case of Local Government Reform in Karnataka", *Public Administration and Development*, 9(1), 147-157.
15. M. Umapathy (1998): *Rural Self Governance in Karnataka*, Mysore, Mysore University.

12

New Panchayati Raj System in Tamil Nadu

— *G. Palanithurai*

Introduction

Tamil Nadu had an experience of a century in local governance in the pre-independence period which, in fact, forms the basis of the new local governance in the post-independence era. Though it was intended to create Panchayats as institutions of self-governance, in practice, they were made institutions to implement the schemes and programmes of the centre and state governments. Till the enactment of the 73rd Amendment, the structure of the Panchayat system in Tamil Nadu was of three-tiers and two-tiers in two different periods. In the three-tier Panchayat system, District Boards, Taluk Boards and Village Panchayats constituted the structural arrangement in the pre-independence period. Even after the enactment of the 73rd Amendment to the Constitution of India, discussion was about the two-tier system. But in conformity with 73rd Amendment in 1994, the Tamil Nadu government enacted a conformity legislation in which the three-tier Panchayat system was created. Originally, in the pre-independence period, from 1884 to 1934, it was a three tier structure and, when the Taluk Boards were abolished by the government, the two-tier system came into vogue. In post-independence India, as per the 1950 decision, there were two-tiers, namely District Board and Village Panchayat, through two different Acts. With regard to powers, service functions were entrusted to local bodies during the pre-independence period and development functions were entrusted to local bodies along with service functions in the post-independence period.

It is an irony that at present the two ethnic political parties in Tamil Nadu, namely, the Dravida Munnetra Kazhagam (DMK) and the All India Anna

Dravida Munnetra Kazhagam (AIADMK), never concurred on any issue but both agreed on one issue, namely, opposing the three-tier Panchayat structure at the grassroots for governance. The two political parties are ardent advocates of devolution of powers from the Centre to the State and they call it as 'state autonomy'. Now they do not talk about state autonomy as they are partners in the coalition government at the Centre. But they are the ardent opponents of creating a vibrant three-tier democratic governance structure at the district level and hence they opposed the 64th Amendment Bill and the 72nd Amendment Bill to the Constitution of India. It is only during the DMK and the AIADMK periods that the powers of the Panchayats were eroded. Panchayats came to a stand still only during the 1980s. It is only during the regimes of these parties that the bureaucratic raj was well established under the tight control of the District Collector. A well built bureaucratic culture has been growing in the past three decades.

The bureaucracy has been empowered only during this era. When the Congress Party was in power, if the State Government arranged a meeting and ministers participated, it happened under the Chairmanship of the MLA of the constituency. It has been changed and the District Collector has been made to preside over the meetings during the era of the Dravidian parties. Officials have been empowered in an unfathomable measure. Their opposition to District Panchayats and District Planning Committee is obvious as they don't want to see any parallel power at the district level equal to MLAs, and MLAs are made subservient to the District Collector. The State Government can do and undo things with the help of the District Collector. But when Panchayats are in position at the district level it will be a hindrance to the power of the State Government. This has been the considered opinion of the two Dravidian political parties in Tamil Nadu. This was the belief of the State Congress Party also when it abolished the District Boards. It considered the District Board a threat to State Government. The ethnic political parties (both the DMK and the AIADMK) have looked at the decentralisation process from the ideological perspective. It is to be noted here that powers of states are slowly being eroded and centralised through various means and strategies adopted by the central government. At this juncture, they do not want to strengthen the Panchayati Raj System as a whole. By strengthening Panchayati Raj, they feel that they are weakening the state government. The two political parties could have raised their voice against centralisation. But they are not doing so because of the political compulsions. Instead of strengthening the entire Panchayati Raj System, they strengthen the Gram Panchayat with a view to deliver the services effectively and carry out the programmes of the centre and state governments more effectively. It is the considered opinion of the two political parties that the Panchayati Raj System is only the implementing agency rather than a unit of self-governance.

Whether they accept or reject, the new system of governance at the grassroots ideologically they have to comply with the mandate of the Constitutional requirement and hence the State Government enacted a conformity legislation in the year 1994 after sleeping over the mandate for one year. A historic legislation was passed in the Tamil Nadu Legislative Assembly without any discussion and thereby one can easily judge to what extent the state government attached importance to the new Panchayati Raj System. After enacting the legislation, the government was again looking for reasons to delay the conduct of election. Tamil Nadu is known for giving reasons for postponing the Panchayat elections. After passing the legislation there was no public pressure or political pressure on the State Government to conduct the elections. There were only a few civil society organisations which took the initiative to create awareness among the public about the new dispensation. When the political climate prepared for general elections in 1996, Panchayati Raj drew the attention of the political parties and it was incorporated in the manifesto of the political parties of which the Dravida Munnetra Kazhagam (DMK) gave prominence to the conduct of Panchayati Raj elections in its manifesto. The DMK gave promises during the elections that the DMK would conduct the elections to Panchayats and accused the AIADMK of not conducting the Panchayat elections. Thus, it was the expectation at every level that 1996 would be a turning point for the Panchayats. In the general elections the AIADMK was defeated and the DMK won the election and to fulfill the poll promise it conducted the Panchayat elections at one stroke. The DMK gave life to the Panchayat in Tamil Nadu.

Even before the conduct of the Panchayat elections, the Government of Tamil Nadu constituted the First State Finance Commission. After the elections a high level committee was constituted to devolve powers to three-tier Panchayati Raj System in Tamil Nadu in the year 1996 in the State Planning Commission under the leadership of L.C. Jain. Since elections were conducted for Panchayati Raj System, activities and responsibilities have to be given to them. In the meanwhile steps were taken to give assignments to all the three-tiers of the new Panchayati Raj System. As a result the rural development schemes were distributed among the three-tiers. In the meanwhile, the First State Finance Commission submitted its report. Before finalising the decision on functions and responsibilities among the three-tiers, the State Finance Commission had made recommendations. Subsequently L.C. Jain submitted his Committee's report to the state government in the year 1997. The government did not accept the report fully. But based on the recommendations, some orders were issued with regard to entrustment of responsibilities to the three-tier Panchayats. Arguments and criticism were levelled against the government for poor devolution of powers. As a result, under the Chairmanship of the then Local Administration Minister Ko.Si.Mani, a high power committee was constituted with representatives of the political parties in the year 1997. The above committee also submitted its report. Following the submission, executive orders were issued. Even then criticisms were levelled against the state government for poor devolution of powers, functionaries and finance to panchayats. As a result, yet another high level committee was constituted in the year 2007 under the chairmanship of the Minister for Local Bodies M.K. Stalin to devolve further powers. The above committee has submitted its report in the same year. It is to be noted here that the Government of Tamil Nadu expressed its position on the 73rd Amendment on the Constitution of India. In this regard it passed a resolution in 2006 in Tamil Nadu Legislative Assembly that the Tamil Nadu would press for the amendment of the Constitution seeking a two-tier system of panchayats and the abolition of District panchayats. Further it stressed that the Government of Tamil Nadu believes in direct election. In the same way the Government of Tamil Nadu expressed its views on the status of District Rural Development Agency (DRDA). It strongly argues that DRDA is an instrument delivering development programmes and services very effectively and hence it need not be merged with District Panchayat as District Panchayat is a political institution. This was the policy position of the Government of Tamil Nadu.

Some Vital Statistics on Panchayats in Tamil Nadu

Table 1: Details of Seats and Offices in Panchayati Raj System in Tamil Nadu

1.	Village Panchayat Wards	40,879
2.	Village Panchayat Ward Members	97,458
3.	Panchayat Union Wards	6,570
4.	District Panchayat Presidents	656
5.	Village Panchayat Presidents	12,618
6.	Panchayat Union Chairpersons	385
7.	District Panchayat Chairpersons	29

Source: Rural Development and Panchayati Raj Development. Policy Note 2010 - 2011.

The position regarding reservations in Tamil Nadu as per the provisions in the Tamil Nadu Panchayats Act 1994 and the Tamil Nadu Panchayats (Reservation of seats and Rotation of Reserved seats) Rules 1995 is given below:

Table 2: Reservation of Seats in Panchayats

Category	*Unit of Population used for determining the proportion of seats to be reserved*	*Authority Competent to notify the reservations*
Village Panchayats Ward Member	Village Panchayat Population	Inspector of Panchayats (Collector)
Village Panchayat President	Panchayat Union Population	Government
Village Panchayat President	Panchayat Union Population	Government
Village Panchayat President	Panchayat Union Population	Government
Panchayat Union Ward Member	Panchayat Union Population	Government
Panchayat Union Chairperson	District Rural Population	Government
District Panchayat Ward Member	District Rural Population	Government
District Chairperson	State Rural Population	Government

Source: Rural Development and Panchayati Raj Development. Policy Note 2010 - 2011.

Table 3: Reservation of Offices and Seats for Women, SCs and STs

Sl. No.	*Category of Reservation*	*Total no. of offices/seats*	*Reserved for Women*		*Reserved for SCs*		*Reserved for STs*	
			No.	*per cent*	*No.*	*per cent*	*No.*	*per cent*
1.	District Panchayat Chairpersons	29	10	34	7	24	0	0
2.	Panchayat Union Council Chairpersons	385	140	36	87	23	4	1
3.	Village Panchayat Presidents	12,618	4,275	34	3,143	25	156	1
4.	District Panchayat Ward Members	656	226	34	154	23	8	1

(Contd...)

5.	Panchayat Union Ward Members	6,570	2,302	35	1,534	23	64	1
6.	Village Panchayat Ward Members	97,458	32,638	33	24,630	25	983	1

Source: Rural Development and Panchayati Raj Development. Policy Note 2010 - 2011.

Village Panchayat

There are 12,618 Village Panchayats in the State spread across the 29 Districts and the 385 Blocks. The average number of Village Panchayats per district is 435 and per Block is 32. The Nilgris District (35), Kanniyakumari (99), Theni (130) and Karur (158) are some of the districts with fewer Village Panchayats while Villupuram (1104), Tiruvannamalai (860), Vellore (753), Cuddalore (681) and Kancheepuram (648) are some of the districts with a large number of Village Panchayats. As can be seen from Table below, the populations fall below 500 in some while in others it exceeds 25,000.

Table 4: Classification of Village Panchayats on the basis of Population (2001 census)

Sl. No.	*Population*	*Number of Village Panchayats*
1.	Below 500	66
2.	501 - 3,000	8,418
3.	3,001 - 10,000	3,948
4.	10,001 - 25,000	174
5.	Above 25,000	12
	Total	**12,618**

Source: Rural Development and Panchayati Raj Development. Policy Note 2010 - 2011.

Similarly, wide variations are also noticed in the income levels of the various Village Panchayats as can be seen from Table given below.

Table 5: Income-wise Classification of Village Panchayats

Sl. No.	*Income Range*	*Number of Village Panchayats during 2005 - 2006*	*No. of Villages Panchayats 2009 - 2010*
1.	Upto Rs 50,000	16	0
2.	Rs 50,000 to Rs 1 lakh	142	0

(Contd...)

3.	Rs 1 lakh to Rs 5 lakhs	7,028	1021
4.	Rs 5 lakhs to Rs 10 lakhs	3,718	7146
5.	Rs 10 lakhs to Rs 25 lakhs	1,444	3902
6.	Rs 25 lakhs to Rs 50 lakhs	195	393
7.	Rs 50 lakhs to Rs 1 crore	45	121
8.	Rs 1 crore to Rs 3 crores	29	32
9.	Above Rs 3 crore	1	3
	Total	**12,618**	**12618**

Source: Rural Development and Panchayati Raj Development. Policy Note 2010 - 2011.

Gram Sabha

The Gram Sabha is the nucleus of the New Panchayati Raj System. All the registered voters are members of the Gram Sabha of that Village Panchayat. As per the Act it has to meet thrice a year and at least once in six months. The President of the Gram Panchayat is the presiding officer at the meetings of the Gram Sabha. The Gram Sabha has to give approval to the budget proposal and annual plan of the Village Panchayat. Further it has to give approval to the annual audited statement of the expenditure of the Village Panchayat. One third is the quorum required to transact the business of the Gram Sabha as per the Act. In Tamil Nadu the Gram Sabha is a neglected subject and unit in the local body arrangement as both elected leaders and officials have not shown any interest in it due to many reasons. As per the government orders, even beneficiaries for many government schemes are to be selected only in the Gram Sabha. But in reality it does not happen. Beneficiaries are selected not in the Gram Sabha but in the Panchayat Council, which is violative of the provisions of the Local Body Act of Tamil Nadu. It is a government approved unconstitutional activity. The Government of Tamil Nadu emphasises transparent activities in all government programmes and schemes but there is no way to execute it as the Gram Sabha is made defunct. It is a nightmare to many who have been enjoying power and resources all along. In order to strengthen the Gram Sabha, recently, the government passed an order that all Gram Panchayats have to convene the Gram Sabha meeting four times in a year on 15th August, 2nd October, 26th January and 1st May and transact the activities as per the provisions available in the Act. Further the quorum for the Gram Sabha has been reduced from one-third to one-tenth, as shown in the table given below:

Table 6: Revised Quorum for Gram Sabha

Sl. No.	*Population of a village panchayat*	*Quarum for the Meeting*
1.	Upto Rs 500	50
2.	501 - 3000	100
3.	3001 - 10,000	200
4.	Above 10,000	300

Source: Rural Development and Panchayati Raj Development. Policy Note 2010 - 2011.

Officials from all the government offices related to development will also participate in the Gram Sabha meeting as observers of the meeting and will report the proceedings of the Gram Sabha to the Inspector of Panchayats. The responsibility of the observer is to provide the details of the government schemes and programmes to the people in the Gram Sabha. Recently in the State Legislative Assembly a policy note was placed and the same was approved and in the policy note it is mentioned that participation of women and Dalit Gram Sabha members is a must and for which a quorum has to be fixed. It is to be noted here that with the quorum specified one-third shall be women and the number of SC/ST participants shall bear the same proportion to the quorum as the population of SC/STs bears to the total population of the village panchayats. Recording of Gram Sabha attendance and proceedings through proper registers and keeping photographic record have been made mandatory for the conduct of Gram Sabha. For conducting Gram Sabha expenditure limit has been increased from Rs 500 to Rs 1000.

Village Panchayat

A Village Panchayat or Gram Panchayat is constituted for a minimum of five hundred population. But there 60 panchayats do not have even 500 population. In the Village Panchayat, the Ward Members and the President, are to be elected directly by the voters. The Vice-President of the Village Panchayat is elected indirectly from among the elected Ward Members of the Village Panchayat. The Village Panchayat has to look after subjects like Construction, repair and maintenance of village Panchayat roads, Lighting of public roads and public places, Providing drainage facilities, Extension of village sites and the regulation of buildings, Sinking and repairing of wells, the excavation repair and maintenance of ponds or tanks and the construction and maintenance of water works for the supply of water, Maintenance of parks and reading rooms, Implementation of schemes such as Indira Awaas Yojna (IAY) and National Rural Employment Guarantee Scheme (NREGS), Cleaning of streets, Providing public latrines, Providing burial and burning grounds,

Providing water for washing and bathing purposes and, such other duties notified by the government then and there.

Administrative Powers

Gram Panchayat have been empowered to give administrative sanction and execute individual works upto Rs 2 lakh from their general funds. It has been given powers to execute urgent works upto Rs 2000 at a time and upto Rs 5000 for a year without sanction. The President can draw self cheque upto Rs 500 to meet contingent expenditure. It can attend to repairs and maintenance of hand pumps, power pumps and Rs 7500 per power pump per year without reference to engineer for preparation of estimates or passing of bills. In order to encourage the village panchayats to carry out innovative works in the villages Uthamar Gandhi village panchayat awards are being given to the best adjudged panchayats based on their performance. A citation with Rs 5 lakh cash award is being given to each of the Gram Panchayats.

Panchayati Union

For each development block a Panchayat Union is formed. Each Panchayati Union has a Chairperson and a Vice-Chairperson elected indirectly by the members of the Panchayat Council. Union Council Members are elected directly by the people. For every 5,000 population, one Union Council Member will be elected by the people. Members of Parliament and Legislative Assembly elected from that area are ex-officio members of the Panchayat Union Council.

The duties and responsibilities of the Panchayati Union includes Construction, repair and maintenance of Public roads, Construction of water works for the supply of water for drinking washing and bathing purposes, Establishment and maintenance of dispensaries, Construction and maintenance of elementary schools, Preventive and remedial measures connected with any epidemic, Conduct of fairs and festivals, Veternary relief, Opening and maintenance of Panchayat Union markets, Extension of village sites and regulation of buildings, Maintenance of statistics related to births and deaths, Improvement of agriculture and agriculture stock; Implementing various centrally sponsored and state schemes, Promotion and encouragement of cottage industries, Preventive and remedial measures connected with any epidemic or with malaria and other duties and responsibilities entrusted to Panchayati Union by the government through government notification.

To enable the Panchayat Union to perform its duties the Government of Tamil Nadu has issued a notification to take up the following activities:

(a) Construction and maintaining Panchayat Union roads, irrigation tanks, and lakes, initiating family welfare activities, executing noon meal schemes and implementing schemes for Adi Dravidas;

(b) Works have to be identified from Employment Assurance schemes and they are to be executed;

(c) Draught relief works have to be identified and executed;

(d) M.P. and M.L.A. area development schemes akin to union have to be executed;

(e) Panchayat Union buildings have to be maintained by the union itself;

(f) Panchayat Union can supervise the activities in the domain of public health, primary education, drinking water supply, roads, small culverts, khadi and village industries works, technical training education, libraries, rural electricity and non-conventional energy.

The Panchayat Union administrative arrangement has been modified by which works have been classified into two divisions and entrusted to Block Development Officer and Assistant Block Development Officer. The two sections work independently with their supporting staff. Infrastructural facilities have also been divided and attached to the two divisions.

Panchayat unions cannot levy any tax. The revenue of a panchayat union consist non-tax revenue, assigned and shared revenues and grants.

District Panchayat

The District Panchayat is constituted with directly elected members for every 50,000 population and indirectly elected Chairperson and Vice-Chairperson from among the Council Members. The District Panchayat perform functions like preparation of development plan for the district, Compilation of administrative reports of village panchayats and panchayat union councils of the district and preparation of Annual Report for the District, Planning and review of Agriculture, Land Development, Animal Husbandry, Dairy, Poultry, Fisheries and Rural Industries, Planning and review of Rural Housing Programmes particularly housing for SC/STs and Identification of major water supply schemes.

To enable the District Panchayat to perform the earmarked functions, an administrative change has been effected by which the Divisional Development Office which is nearer to the district headquarters will supervise the District Panchayat activities. Yet another office which is away from the headquarters will look after auditing of the District Panchayat activities and the third one will be attached to the District Panchayat.

The District Panchayat has no taxation powers. Its only source of revenue is from statutory grants like State Finance Commission Grants and development grants under Centrally sponsored schemes.

District Panchayats can sanction and execute works up to Rs 20 lakhs from their general funds without any external approvals. However, in the case of centrally sponsored schemes, prior administrative sanction of the District Collector is necessary.

State Finance Commission Grant

To augment the resources of the local bodies, financial devolution to the local bodies is made on the basis of recommendations of the State Finance Commission (SFC). In the beginning eight per cent of the State's total own net tax revenues (other than entertainment tax) was devolved to the rural and urban local bodies in the ratio of 58.42 respectively. 87 per cent of the allocation for rural local bodies is being shared among the three-tiers in the ratio of 47:45:8 among Village Panchayats, Panchayat Union Councils and District Panchayats respectively. This grant was being released every month to the local bodies. The balance 13 per cent consists of Equalisation Fund (six per cent), Incentive Fund (five per cent), and Reserve Fund (two per cent).

The SFC grant is generally utilised for the following purposes:

(a) Salaries, pensions, office maintenance, etc.; (b) Maintenance of drinking water facilities; (c) Maintenance of street lights; payment of electricity charges; (d) Maintenance of Village Panchayat and Panchayat Union roads; (e) Maintenance of minor irrigation tanks; and (f) Public health, sanitation, etc.

The first Finance Commission recommended devolution of state owned tax resources from eight per cent to twelve per cent by increasing one per cent annually from 1996 - 1997. But the state government decided to freeze it at eight per cent of its resources for the first five years. The second Finance Commission recommended devolution of eight per cent from state owned tax resources for the first two years and nine per cent for the next two years and ten per cent for last one year. But the government issued orders freezing the devolution of funds to eight per cent for each year. The third State Finance Commission recommended financial devolution of ten per cent to the local bodies for the entire award period. But the government ordered devolution of funds from nine per cent to ten per cent from 2007-08 to 2011-2012 in the following order: nine per cent, nine per cent, 9.5 per cent, ten per cent, ten per cent. The State Government consistently violated and contradicted with the recommendations of all three State Finance Commissions in terms of devolution of financial resources due to panchayats. Further panchayats are facing more and more pressure and burden to meet the basic requirements of the people. This has continuously weakened the financial position of the Panchayati Raj. Further, they are made as subservient to the State Government.

District Planning Committee

The Government of Tamil Nadu shall constitute in every district a District Planning Committee to consolidate the plans prepared by the District

Panchayat, Panchayat Union Councils, Village Panchayats, Municipal Councils, and Municipal Corporations in the district and to prepare a draft development plan for the district as a whole. The Committee shall consist of the Collector of the district, members of the House of People who represent whole or part of the district, members of the Council of States, Members of Legislative Assembly whose constituencies lie within the district, the Mayor of the City Municipal Corporation and all Chairpersons of the Municipalities of the district, Chairpersons of the District Panchayats, one-fifth of the total number of chairpersons of the Town Panchayats and Panchayat Union notified by the government every year by rotation, and such number of persons not less than four-fifth of the total number of the committee as specified by the government elected from among the members of the District Panchayat, Town Panchayats, Municipal Councils and Corporations in the district in proportion to the ratio between the population of the rural areas and the urban areas. The Committee shall allocate funds to various schemes in the Panchayats and Panchayat Unions and shall monitor the implementation of the schemes. Now the Government has changed the chairmanship of the District Planning Committee from the Collector to the President of the District Panchayat. It is an irony that the District Planning Committees of the districts have convened their meetings and reviewed the activities of the sectoral departments but never took any step to prepare the District Plan. Further it is to be noted that even in the review meeting, district level officials do not participate. They send their officials to these meetings. It is a routine meeting without much importance.

Reservation

One-third of positions at all levels of the bodies are reserved for women. SC and ST get reservation of positions at all levels of the bodies in proportion to their population. In Tamil Nadu the rotation of positions, especially for women and Dalits, is for once in ten years. It is unique in the whole of the country. This change was due to the pressure given by the women Panchayat leaders through their federation.

Election and Finance Commissions

An Election Commission headed by the State Election Commissioner appointed by the Governor to conduct the local body elections is mandatory. The Election Commissioner enjoys the powers and privileges and status of a judge of the High Court. The tenure of office of the Election Commissioner is two years. However, the Commissioner can be given extension for four more years. In Tamil Nadu elections are conducted on party lines for District Panchayats and Panchayat Unions. Elections to Village Panchayats are not on party lines. In Tamil Nadu elections to Local Bodies, both urban and rural, will be conducted at one stroke. When the election was conducted in few places auctions were conducted, bidding was made, nominations were made by the traditional Panchayat leaders for Gram Panchayat Presidents' posts. After the enactment of the 73rd Amendment, elections were conducted periodically without any lapse or gap. Elections were conducted at one stroke for rural and urban local bodies.

There will be a Finance Commission constituted every five years to review the financial position of the Panchayats and to make recommendations to the Governor to fix the principles to govern the distribution between the state and Panchayats of the net proceeds of the taxes, duties, tolls and fees leviable by the Government and to identify the logistics for making grants-in-aid to the Panchayats from the consolidated fund of the state and the measures needed to improve the financial position of the Panchayats. The Finance Commission shall consist of a chairman and four other members. In Tamil Nadu the Finance Commission was constituted periodically within the stipulated time and so far three State Finance Commissions were constituted. They made recommendations and some of the recommendations were also implemented. Despite all the efforts, panchayats are not strengthened. Panchayats in Tamil Nadu are in form not in spirit.

Critical Evaluation of Decentralisation

The present Tamil Nadu Panchayat Act does not provide much scope for giving life to the spirit of the 73rd Constitutional Amendment Act in Tamil Nadu. Subjects in the 11th Schedule do not find a place in the body of the Act, especially in the chapter on "Functions of Panchayat Bodies." Development officials who work in the Panchayat bodies are declared government officials and they do not come under the perview of local bodies. As a result, the local bodies can not supervise the activities of the officials of local bodies. While comparing the old Act of Panchayati Raj of 1958 with the new one, one finds adequate powers to local bodies in the old act to supervise, regulate and control the officials working in the local bodies. In the new Act the District Collector is vested with the power of controlling the functioning of Village Panchayats. The District Collector's power to suspend and dissolve the Gram Panchayats is against the spirit of decentralisation of powers. The DRDA (District Rural Development Agency) is a registered society, which is under the control of the Project Officer and the District Collector.

The Gram Sabha has not been activated to develop democratic culture in decision-making, to bring about transparency in the activities of the government and to involve the people in the development process of the community. Enactment of legislation and conduct of elections alone will not bring about any change in the functioning of the local bodies. Proper enhancement of the capacity of the leaders, enabling suitable government orders and provision of adequate resources can alone bring about needed change in the functioning of the local bodies.

Steps have been taken to train the Panchayat leaders for which training modules have been prepared. In the meanwhile, training programmes have been conducted by a few institutions. Panchayat leaders have formed their associations to exert pressure on the government for more devolution of powers. Gram Panchayat Presidents have formed an association. Likewise, the elected women representatives of Gram Panchayats have formed their own association. Dalit men and women elected to Gram Panchayats have formed their association. District Panchayat Presidents have formed their forum. Likewise, the Block Panchayat Presidents have formed their association. Even among the Block Panchayat Presidents Dalit Women Presidents have formed their association. All these associations have prepared a charter of demands and sent it to the government periodically. Of the associations, the Gram Panchayat Women Presidents Association is vibrant and active. It is always visible and highly articulate. As a result of the elected women representatives' continuous demand, the Government of Tamil Nadu has made an amendment in the existing arrangements for reservation in Tamil Nadu to reserve the constituencies in all the three-tiers for two continuous terms to the women and Dalits by which whether it be a Ward of the Gram Panchayat or Gram Panchayat or a Ward of the Block Panchayat or Ward of the District Panchayat once reserved for women and Dalits will be reserved for two terms. The concept of rotation of reservation of position in Tamil Nadu is for ten years not for every five years term. The Government issued a directive to all the District Collectors that whenever the elected women representatives organisation demanded a meeting with officials to sort out their problems, the District Collector has to organise such interface and sort out the problems faced by the women leaders. It is exclusively for women leaders.

In terms of resources, the Panchayats have to face a financial crisis due to the changes made in the formula for matching grant. Further diversion of funds, and not facilitating panchayats to get their dues from assigned revenue have weakened the panchayat institutions and evolved their autonomy. Sizeable reduction of resources from the State Government has reduced the activities of the Panchayats. Further revenue from minor minerals and sand quarrying from the Panchayat area has been totally stopped as the activity of sand quarrying has been taken over by the State Government. Dues from Social Forestry is not being given to Panchayat as the money has not been released from the Social Forestry Department.

The next important issue is that of the tariff of the Electricity Board for the electricity consumption of Panchayats. Panchayats have to pay commercial rates for the consumption of electricity. It has been raised from Rs 1.20 to Rs 3.40 per unit for public consumption by the Panchayats. This has increased the expenditure of the Panchayats. The entire electricity charge has been excluded from the State Finance Commission grant which is due to the

Panchayats. The Block Panchayat Councillor is operating schemes which are meant for the village independently without consulting the Gram Panchayats. District Panchayat Councillors are also operating their schemes without consulting the Gram Panchayats. MLAs are operating their constituency development fund without consulting the Gram Panchayats. In the same way MPs are also spending their money without consulting the Gram Panchayats. Apart from the above the sectoral departments have their own funds. They carry out their activities without consulting the Gram Panchayats. Money is being spent in a huge quantities but not on the demands of the people. They spend the money as they prioritize the works. In all the four Gram Sabha meetings people project their felt needs but to meet the felt needs of the people there is no untied fund available at the disposal of the Gram Panchayat. Even the small quantum they get from the State Finance Commission is to be spent for electricity charge remittance. Virtually funds are operated by different agencies on their own priorities and not on the priorities of the people finalised in the Gram Sabha. As a result, the Gram Sabha has been weakened. It is being made a ritual. The District Planning Committee has been constituted and they meet periodically and review the works of the departments. There is no concerted effort on the part of the District Planning Committee to prepare a plan. Neither the District Planning Committee nor the officials show any interest in planning exercise at the grassroots level. The State Planning Commission has developed a module for training in multi-level planning and conducted a training programme also. They have prepared guidelines for the preparation of perspective development plan for the whole of a district. Nothing moves in the absence of political will. Finally the State Planning Commission has given instructions to all District Planning Cells to prepare Village Development Reports (VDR) in select Panchayats. It is a mere compilation of data. In select districts, the Village Development Plan was prepared in select Panchayats with the assistance of the development organisations for which the respective Collectors helped and in turn the District Collectors passed orders to all the sectoral departments to work on the prioritised activities of the plan prepared by the people.

In the context of the non-functioning of the District Planning Committee, the recent notification of the Government Order, G.O.(Ms.) No.140 dated 10.09.2004, is a path breaking event as it envisages a holistic development plan for each and every Gram Panchayat with the participation of the people. The new proposal envisions the participation of the people in the sustainable development of villages and the improvement of the quality of life through good governance and convergence of schemes and programmes. It focuses on resource mapping and community mobilisation for village development, micro planning and prioritisation of needs among village communities, convergence of funds and functionaries of all schemes at the village level, and community led improvement in the overall quality of life.

It is a path breaking exercise in decentralised governance in Tamil Nadu, which is known for its centralised culture in carrying out development activities. It is a demand driven exercise and not a supply driven one. It envisages the participation of the people. It aims at improvement of the quality of life. It strengthens the physical resources for the improvement of the quality of life. It works for the convergence of the schemes and programmes of the government towards the needs of the community as identified by the people. It ensures the participation of sectoral departments in the implementation of the plan prepared by the Gram Panchayats with the participation of the people. It creates a synergy between the schemes and programmes of the governments (both the Centre and the State) and the needs prioritised by the people. It specifically focuses on such sectors as water, sanitation, environment, ecology, education, health, social security and on social issues (elimination of sex selective abortions, prevention of child abuse, age at marriage of women to be not less than 21, prevention of crimes against woman and immoral trafficking, prevention of untouchability and promotion of communal harmony).

The whole exercise is expected to be in a movement mode by carrying out specific campaigns by involving all the stakeholders in the field of rural development. Awareness creation, building and enhancing the skills and capacity of all stakeholders are continuous activities. Each and every Gram Panchayat will have a legal plan document ready for implementation.

Conclusion

It is true that there are many weaknesses in the Tamil Nadu Panchayat Act itself and a variety of existing Acts of different departments do not permit the state to devolve powers. The capacity of the leaders is not so high as to handle all the subjects earmarked for Panchayati Raj and yet leaders are alert and optimistic at present that the Panchayat Raj System is the only solution to solve most of the problems in the rural areas. Steps are on to rectify the defects. Local body leaders are putting out a one point demand to the state government to devolve adequate powers and resources to the local bodies. Expected pressure has come from the people for devolution of powers and the leaders of local bodies have come to a stage to take powers from the state government on their own in the event of denial of powers to the local bodies.

Thus, the Panchayat Raj System in Tamil Nadu is being kept in operation not because of the devolved powers and resources but because of the leadership at the Village Panchayat level. No doubt Panchayats are fulfilling the obligatory functions. A lot of innovations have happened in Panchayats due to the exceptional leadership qualities of the Panchayat leaders. Wherever Panchayat leaders are strong, vibrant, capacitated, and committed they perform very well. Whenever the District Collector and Project Officer, DRDA, is pro-Panchayat, the Panchayats perform very well despite several problems and constraints. District Collectors and Project Officers see this dispensation as very positive as they can achieve the targets in carrying out rural development schemes through the Panchayats. Thus, it becomes a partnership between the district administration and the Panchayats. In Tamil Nadu Panchayats are evolving on their own. Devolution becomes evolution in Tamil Nadu.

Panchayats are instruments of the people created for governance with the participation of the people to achieve development. Though Panchayat leaders are drawn from the place wherefrom MLAs and MPs are drawn they cannot adopt the attitude and behaviour of the MPs and MLAs as they have to work with the community closely. By increasing their capacity and sensitising them on developmental issues, Panchayats can be prepared to achieve development and social justice. Capacity building, continuous support extended by the support structure, forming network with the media and NGOs and providing needed information could make them achievers and path finders. If state governments really want to achieve social development, it can be achieved through the Panchayats. People should be mobilised to participate in the development process. In the long run people will assert and claim their rights and entitlements through the Panchayats.

References

1. Athreya V.B. and Rajeswari K.S. (1999): *Women's Participation in Panchayati Raj: A Case Study from Tamil Nadu,* M.S. Swaminathan Research Foundation, Chennai.
2. Dharampal, (1972): *The Madras Panchayat System Vol-II A General Assessment,* Impex India, New Delhi.
3. Government of India, (1994): *Powers and Functions of Panchayati Raj Institutions: A Framework,* Ministry of Rural Development, New Delhi.
4. Government of India, (1994): *Renewing Local Self Government in Rural India,* Ministry of Rural Development, New Delhi.
5. Government of Tamil Nadu, (1999): *Democratic Decentralisation: Powers Entrusted to Panchayati Raj Institutions,* Rural Development Department, Chennai.
6. Government of Tamil Nadu, (1998): *High Power Committee Report on Entrustment of Powers to Three Tier Local Bodies in Tamil Nadu,* State Planning Commission, Chennai.
7. Jennie Litvack, Junaid Ahmed, (1998): *Rethinking Decentralisation in Developing Countries,* The World Bank, Washington D.C.
8. Palanithurai G., "Building Alliances and Capabilities Among the Elected Women Representatives of Grassroots Institutions", *Womens Link,* Vol.10, No.1 (Jan-Mar 2004) pp.18-25.
9. Palanithurai G., "Towards Participatory Governance at Grassroots: Synergisation of Rural Communities and Institutions", *South Asian Journal of Socio Political Studies,* Vol. 4, No.1 (Dec, 2003).

10. Palanithurai G., (2001): *Capacity Building for Local Body Leaders,* Concept Publishing Company, New Delhi.
11. Palanithurai G., (2003): *Development Role Reversed: From Government to People,* Gandhigram: Rajiv Gandhi Chair for Panchayati Raj Studies.
12. Palanithurai G., Dwaraki B.R. and Narayanasamy S., (Eds), (1997): *Major Issues in New Panchayati Raj System,* Kanishka Publications, New Delhi.
13. Palanithurai G., (1994): *Empowering People for prosperity: A Study in New Panchayati Raj System,* Kanishka Publications, New Delhi.
14. Palanithurai G., *Evaluation of Process and Performance of Gram Panchayat Women and Dalit Presidents in Tamil Nadu,* Gandhigram: Rajiv Gandhi Chair, 2003.
15. Palanithurai G., (1997) : *Grassroots Democracy in Indian Society,* Concept Publications, New Delhi.
16. Palanithurai G., (2000) : *New Panchayati Raj System at Work: An Evaluation,* Concept Publishing Company, New Delhi.
17. Palanithurai G., (1999) : *New Panchayati Raj System at Work: An Evaluation,* Concept Publications, New Delhi.
18. Palanithurai G., (1996) : *New Panchayati Raj System: Status and Prospects,* Kaniska Publications, New Delhi.
19. Palanithurai G., *Panchayats, Communities and Social Development,* Gandhigram: Rajiv Gandhi Chair for Panchayati Raj Studies, 2003.
20. Palanithurai G.,(Ed), (1996) : *Empowering People: Issues and Solutions,* Kanishka Publications, New Delhi.
21. Population Foundation of India, (2001) : *Empowerment of Panchayati Raj Institutions on Issues Related to Population, Health and Social Development, A Final Report,* New Delhi.
22. Rajiv Gandhi Chair, *Functional Efficiency of Gram Sabha: A Report Submitted to II State Finance Commission,* Gandhigram: Rajiv Gandhi Chair for Panchayati Raj Studies, 2000.
23. Rajiv Gandhi Chair, *Problems faced by the Gram Panchayati Leaders,* Gandhigram: Rajiv Gandhi Chair for Panchayati Raj Studies, 2000.
24. Rajiv Gandhi Foundation, *Dialogue on Panchayat: Summary Proceedings of Four Regional Tripartile Interface Interactive Workshops,* New Delhi: Rajiv Gandhi Foundation, 1999.
25. Rajiv Gandhi Foundation, *Panchayati Raj in India: Status Report,* New Delhi: Rajiv Gandhi Foundation, 2000.
26. Rajiv Gandhi Foundation, *Proceedings of the National Seminar on Panchayats,* New Delhi: Rajiv Gandhi Foundation, 1997.
27. Rajiv Gandhi Foundation, *Proceedings of the National Seminar on Panchayats,* New Delhi: Rajiv Gandhi Foundation, 1993.
28. Rajiv Gandhi Foundation, *Revitalisation of Panchayati Raj in India,* New Delhi: Rajiv Gandhi Foundation, 1999.
29. Rajiv Gandhi Foundation, *Voices from Below: Summary Proceedings of Sub-Regional Workshops on Panchayats: Issues and Recommendations,* New Delhi: Rajiv Gandhi Foundation, 2001.

30. Rukmani R., (1996) : *Panchayati Raj Institutions in Tamil Nadu: A Historical Review,* Madras Institute of Development Studies, Chennai.
31. Rural Development Department, (1999) : *Democratic Decentralisation: Panchayati Raj System in Tamil Nadu,* Chennai.
32. Sarasvathi, (1973) : *The Madras Panchayat System Vol. I A Historical Survey,* Impex India, Delhi.
33. Siddartha, Sivaramakrishnan, (1999) : *Panchayati Raj Institutions in India - A Society Study for the World Bank,* World Bank, Washington DC.
34. Siddartha, Sivaramakrishnan, (1999) : *Discussion: Challenges and Opportunities for Panchayati Raj,* World Bank, New Delhi.
35. State Finance Commission, (1966) : *Summary of Recommendations of the State Finance Commission for Local Bodies,* Chennai.
36. State Planning Commission, (1997) : *Report of the Working Group on Decentralised Planning and Panchayati Raj,* Chennai.
37. State Planning Commission, (1997) : *Report on the Entrustment of Powers to Panchayats,* Chennai.
38. The Hunger Project, *Report on the Workshop on Panchayati Raj: Trials and Triumphs, Gandhigram:* Rajiv Gandhi Chair for Panchayati Raj Studies, 2003.
39. The Hunger Project, *Women and Panchayati Raj: The Pathway to Social Transformation and a New Future for India,* Bombay: The Hunger Project, 1999.

13

Continuity and Change in Panchayati Raj Institutions in Andhra Pradesh : An Appraisal

—*M.A. Hussain and A.R. Reddy*

Andhra Pradesh ranks as the fifth largest state in India in terms of territory and population. It is the first linguistic state in the Indian Republic which came into existence on November 1st, 1956 by merging the nine Telugu speaking districts of the old Hyderabad state with the eleven districts of the Andhra State which was separated from the composite State of Madras in 1953. Nearly three-fourth of its population dwells in villages. It abounds in a variety of natural resources, having agriculture as the primary source of employment and income.

Backdrop

Local self-government in Andhra Pradesh flourished right from the days of Satavahana rulers to the days of Vijayanagara Empire. After Independence, Andhra Pradesh, next to Rajasthan, was the pioneering state in implementing three-tier Panchayati Raj system, as a sequel to the community development programme. The Panchayat Raj system came into being in 1959 on the basis of recommendations of the Balvant Rai Mehta Committee as it felt that "rural development and rural welfare are possible only with local initiative and local discretion." Before the introduction of Panchayati Raj system, several concrete developments took place. Of these, the most noteworthy are the Firka Development scheme, the village Panchayat Act, 1950 and the community development and NES Blocks.

The village Panchayat Act, 1950 was passed and the panchayats acquired a more democratic character under it. Even after the State of Andhra Pradesh was formed, the Panchayats in Andhra Area continued to function under the Act of 1950 while those in Telangana area functioned in accordance with the Act of 1956. However, in 1964, all the Panchayats were brought under an integrated Andhra Pradesh Gram Panchayats Act.

A.P. Panchayat Samithis and Zilla Parishads Act of 1959

It was an important landmark in the evolution of Panchayati Raj in Andhra Pradesh. Many of the recommendations of the Balwant Rai Mehta Committee were incorporated in the Act. Accordingly, 235 Panchayati Samities and 20 Zilla Parishads were established. During the tenure of Neelam Sanjiva Reddy elections were held for the first time in 1959. The basic structure of Panchayati Raj remained the same till the mandal system was introduced despite minor alterations made from time to time.

Andhra Pradesh Panchayati Raj Act of 1986

Though generally described as mandal system, based on the recommendations of the Asoka Mehta Committee, the model of Panchyati Raj introduced in 1986 by N.T. Rama Rao in Andhra Pradesh was substantially different from the Ashok Mehta model. The Act of 1986 provided for a three-tier structure with the Gram Panchayats at the base and the Zilla Praja Parishads at the apex. In between the two, there was a Mandal Praja Parishad for each revenue mandal whose population ranged from 35,000 to 55,000. The most radical departure from tradition was the provision for the direct election of the Chairman of the Zilla Praja Parishads and Mandal Praja Parishads by all the voters of their respective areas.

The Andhra pattern of Panchayati Raj was somewhat disappointing when compared to its counterpart in Karnataka. To begin with there was nothing new about the composition of the Zilla Praja Parishads compared to the former Zilla Parishads except that its Chairman was directly elected by the residents of the district numbering about 20 lakhs. Such a popular leader was provided with the status of a Minister of state without executive powers at all. The presence of the Zilla Sameeksha Mandali with Cabinet Minister as Chairman has considerably reduced the importance of the Parishad. The Collector continued to occupy a very pivotal position in the district as the Vice-Chairman of the Standing Committees of the Parishad and as the member secretary of the Sameeksha Mandali. His traditional powers relating to regulatory administration continued to be with him. He also continued to be the rallying point for securing not only coordination between the development officers of the district intense but also between them and Panchayati Raj. The formation of Karshaka Parishads as parallel bodies had given a death blow to Panchayati Raj.

Andhra Pradesh Panchayati Raj Act of 1994

The Congress Party which came to power in 1989 had tried to change the Panchayati Raj system, particularly mandal set-up. It attempted to either abolish or reduce the strength of existing Mandal Praja Parishads. But there was widespread resistance both from the legislators and the rural masses. Therefore, the State Government felt it worthwhile to continue the system with minor changes such as removing the word "Praja" from Zilla Praja Parishads and Mandal Praja Parishads. Meanwhile the 73rd Constitution Amendment Act was passed. Accordingly, in conformity with the Central Act, Andhra Pradesh Panchayai Raj Act (Act No.13 of 1994) was enacted.

Important Provisions of the Act are as follows:

(i) The new Act is a simple comprehensive Act covering all the three-tiers of Panchayati Raj.

(ii) The new Act dispensed with the Zilla Abhivrudhi Sameeksha Mandals which were created at the districts level under the previous Act and planning functions are transferred to the Zilla Parishad to be exercised by it through its standing committees. However, District Development Review Committees (DDRCs) have been set-up under the Chairmanship of a Cabinet Minister nominated by the Chief Minister from outside the district.

(iii) The reservation of seats as well as positions in all the three-tiers are provided to SCs (18 per cent), STs (8 per cent), BCs (34 per cent) and women (33 per cent).

(iv) Sarpanch of a Gram Panchayat is to be elected directly by the people, while the President of Mandal Parishad and Chairman of Zilla Parishad are to be elected indirectly by Mandal Parishad Territorial Constituency (MPTC) members and Zilla Parishad Territorial Constituency (ZPTC) members. Elections to the Mandal Parishad and Zilla Parishad are party-based while those to Gram Panchayats are non-party-based.

(v) Persons with more than two children after one year from the date of commencement of the Act are disqualified from contesting the election to the PRIs.

(vi) Political chiefs of lower tier are made permanent invitees in the next higher tier without the right to vote.

(vii) All the three-tiers are expected to perform such functions and exercise such powers as may be entrusted to them in respect of the 29 items specified in the Eleventh Schedule of the Indian Constitution.

(viii) All the requirements of the 73rd Constitution Amendment Act pertaining to elections, reservations, finances, etc...are duly incorporated in the new Act.

Accordingly, a State Election Commission and a State Finance Commission have been constituted. There are 22 Zilla Parishads, 1092 Mandal Parishads and 20,560 Gram Panchayats in the state.

Some Reflections

A study of Panchayati Raj in Andhra Pradesh indicates that the pendulum has been swinging between a case for greater decentralisation and that of limited decentralisation. The existing structure of Panchayati Raj in the State seems to be weak on the areas which are as follows.

Functions

The precise functions and powers of the PRIs in relation to 29 items included in the Eleventh Schedule of the Indian Constitution have not yet been identified and transferred to them. Moreover the PRIs have lost control over even on the conventional items such as rural roads, rural sanitation, rural drinking water, primary and secondary education, which were hitherto under the control of ZPs before the enactment of Act of 1994. The funds for rural roads emanate from World Bank, NABARD, Special Rural Road Maintenance, RRM and MNP. The proposals for these funds (except RRM and MNP) are directly sent from the Panchayati Raj Engineering Department to the State Government even without the knowledge of the Chairman or Chief Executive Officer of the Zilla Parishad. Even the RRM was about to be diverted to the Janmabhoomi Programme under G.O. 125. However, the G.O. was withdrawn when Cuddapah Zilla Parishad Chairman threatened to resign. In respect of Rural Drinking Water 75 per cent of the work is being done directly by the State Government. Rural sanitation is transferred to the Janmabhoomi Programme. Under primary and secondary education, local bodies have no say on construction of classrooms. They have the power of transferring the teachers only. In this respect too, the State government intervenes by imposing ban on transfers now and then. This kind of transferring local Government functions to the State Government goes against the true principle of democratic decentralisation.

Most of the Rural Development Programmes are kept under control of DRDA, the Chairman of which is the District Collector. Eighty five per cent of plan grants for rural development are channelled through the agency.

Hence, the functions and powers of the three-tiers of Panchayati Raj should be identified and transferred to them. All rural development programmes should be brought within the ambit of the PRIs. As in the case of West Bengal, the DRDA should be made an administrative arm to implement development functions of the Zilla Parishad.

Finances

The finances of PRIs consist of own resources (tax and non-tax revenue), assigned resources (those levied and collected by the State Government and given to the PRIs) and grants-in-aid. The powers of taxation are exclusively given to the Gram Panchayats whereas the middle and top tiers have not been vested with such powers. There is a poor drive on the part of the Gram Panchayats to effectively mobilise these resources. The income from assigned resources is meager. So the PRIs generally look for grants from the State Government. The grants are in the form of per capita population grants @ Rs 2 to the ZP, Rs 5 to the MP and Re 1 to the GP. These grants are utilised to purchase stationary, to pay electricity bills etc. The per capita grant, fixed in 1987, is too low keeping in view of cost escalations. Thus, the position of finances of PRIs has been far from satisfactory.

The State Finance Commission has already submitted its report but it is yet to be accepted and implemented by the State Government.

So the State Government should take appropriate steps to enable PRIs to tap resources as recommended by the Ashok Mehta Committee, the Narasimham Committee and the recent State Panchayati Raj Finance Commission Report. The per capita population grant should be enhanced.

Functioning

- The creation of DRDCs "to review developmental works within the district' is not necessary as the ZPs themselves review the functioning. The DRDCs are not functioning regularly and effectively. Even when they are held, they became battle grounds for rival political parties. Hence, they may be abolished and District Planning Committees may be constituted as envisaged in the Constitution Amendment Act.
- It is indicated that the Mandal Parishad which is the middle tier of Panchayati Raj has become a very weak unit, despite arguments put forth in its favour. In addition to the paucity of staff and finances, more than 50 per cent of the Mandal Parishads do not have regular Mandal Parishad Development Officers. So, depending upon the workload of various Mandal Parishads, the State Government should appoint or recruit the necessary staff without which the Mandal Parishads cannot achieve desired results. As preferred by the Ashok Mehta Committee, the President of Mandal Parishad should be directly elected to avoid horse-trading, to ensure stability and to enhance the political importance.
- The meetings of gram sabhas have not been held regularly. They meet only on paper. Since the objective of Panchayati Raj is to establish participatory democracy, strengthening of the gram sabhas is sine-qua-non.
- Powers and functions of MPTC and ZPTC members are not yet specified. Many incidents were reported where they boycotted their

respective meetings over this issue. Hence, there is a dire need to define their powers.

- The Sarpanch is not a member of Mandal Parishad and the Mandal President is not a member of the ZP. Hence, the Sarpanch and the Mandal President should be made the full-fledged members of MP and ZP respectively to bridge the linkages.
- The staffing pattern of PRIs suffers from certain deficiencies, like deputationist attitude, strong departmental loyalties, lack of commitment to Panchayati Raj, problems of inter-personal co-ordination and official and non-official tensions for some of the serious and continuing problems of the Panchayati Raj personnel. Unless efforts are made to strengthen the personnel working in PRIs, their low morale will continue to affect the developmental efforts at the local level.
- The A.P. Panchayati Raj Act leaves many things to the discretion of State Government. It is feared that such discretion may be misused for partisan political advantage.

The Act ensures full freedom to plan according to the local needs but this not merely requires delegation of powers and resources but also peoples participation.

It has been more than a decade and half since the 73rd Constitutional Amendment Act has come into force in 1994 in Andhra Pradesh and it is necessary to make an assessment on how far the process of democratic decentralisation of governance has progressed in Andhra Pradesh. The National Commission to Review the Working of the Indian Constitution has commented[1] in the following words:

"In Andhra Pradesh, the Gram Panchayat and Mandal Parishads are not required to plan for economic development and social justice. All tiers of Panchayats have been assigned with large number of functions. But, none of them has financial or administrative resources under their control to execute them. The Mandal Parishad has no control over the staff of development blocks, and the Zilla Parishad has no control over the District Rural Development Agency, which controls huge funds over various poverty alleviation programmes."

It is not correct to say that a large number of functions have been given to the Panchayati Raj Institutions in Andhra Pradesh. As per the 11th Schedule, 29 Subjects can be devolved to the local governments, but the Government of Andhra Pradesh has devolved only 17 subjects and that too without transferring either the funds or functionaries along with the functions.

District Planning Committees have not been constituted inspite of a clear constitutional mandate to do so. The District Planning Committee should prepare a district level development plan and forward it to the State Government. In A.P. a district level institution called District Development review Committee has been constituted to review the development activity in the district. The District Development Review Committee does not have any functional linkages with the local governments. It is the MLA and MP, who have a strong say in the functioning of District Development Review Committee. The absence of District Planning Committee and the functioning of District development review Committee in Andhra Pradesh goes against the spirit of the 73rd and 74th Constitutional Amendment Acts.[2]

Till recently, the District Rural Development Agency has also not been integrated with the rural local government. However, after the implementation of the 73rd Constitutional Amendment Act, the functioning of District Rural Development Agencies in Andhra Pradesh, independent of rural local government is contrary to the spirit of the Indian constitution.

The fiscal devolution to local governments has also been minimal in A.P. while Gram Panchayat has taxation powers, Mandal Parishad and ZPs tend to depend on the transfers and grants from the Andhra Pradesh Government.[3] The Government of A.P. claims that almost 10.5 per cent of its rural expenditure has been spent by local government. However, a closer examination of facts reveals that a mere 5.3 per cent of its financial resources have been spent through local governments and the remaining 4.7 per cent was from its own financial resources of local government.[4] There is also absence of accurate fiscal data on the financial devolution of local governments as the World Bank observed in its report.

Government of Andhra Pradesh's figures on the amount transferred to the local government as "planned" are misleading as Janmabhoomi amount is shown as released to the local governments, in reality, it is released directly to the District Collector, who then releases the amount to the Nodal Officers.[5] It is estimated that almost 80 per cent of the financial resources of the local governments goes towards meeting the wage bills. So the Andhra Pradesh Government has been complaining that they may be true of the governments' own current expenditure. However, in their case, the privilege of employment and powers of supervision and control go with the bill. In the case of local government only the bill bears their name while the powers remain with the State Government. However, since these are now shown as local government activities, the onus of non-performance falls on them. In the absence of clear functional devolution and control over functionaries and lack of access to resources, the local governments are unable to function in any meaningful manner.

Janmabhoomi Programme

This is a people-centred development process to revive and reinforce the values of hard work, perseverance, integrity, team spirit and community participation. This programme was introduced by Nara Chandra Babu Naidu, former Chief Minister in Andhra Pradesh during 1997. This programme has three components (1) Prajala vaddaku Palana (Take Administration to the doorsteps of the common man), (2) Shramadhanam and (3) Micro-Planning. Naidu believed that the joint efforts of the people and the government would certainly lead to an over all development of Andhra Pradesh. Each round of Janmabhoomi had a specific theme decided by the State Government. Funds for departmental programmes were channelled through line department. In the implementation procedure, the role of local governments was minimal.[6] The Congress Government led by late Y.S. Rajasekhara Reddy abolished the Janmabhoomi programme in 2005 due to corruption and excessive governmentalisation of the programme with the panchayats being made peripheral bodies. The Janmabhoomi programme was replaced with Rajiv Palle Bata and Rajiv Nagara Bata programmes by the Congress Government under the leadership of late Y.S. Rajasekhara Reddy.

Village Secretariat in Andhra Pradesh

In an attempt to provide various services under one roof in rural areas the Government of Andhra Pradesh led by N.Chandra Babu Naidu in 2002 launched Grama Sachivalayam (Village Secretariat) System. In this system, the Village Secretary is the key person performing as many as 60 functions of various departments such as police, revenue, panchayati raj, health and agriculture. The emergence of an administratively powerful Village Secretary is being seen as an attempt to weaken the local governments[7] in Andhra Pradesh.

E-Panchayats in Andhra Pradesh

The Andhra Pradesh Government under the leadership of Y.S. Rajasekhara Reddy introduced E-Panchayats scheme to provide the better civic amenities to the rural citizens through the electronic governance. Under this scheme, the State Government wanted to extend the E-Sevas to the rural people who are living in 475 Gram Panchayats and an amount of Rs 332 crores was earmarked in the first phase. Through this scheme the State Government wanted to computerize the land records, birth and death certificate particulars and other vital information pertaining to the Gram Panchayats in Andhra Pradesh.[8] The State Government earmarked the amount for the above mentioned scheme and for each Gram Panchayat Rs 70,000, Rs 50,000 for the purchase of computer and Rs 20,000 for computerisation of data. This scheme was implemented in A.P. since November 2005. The E-Panchayats will function under the Chairmanship of the District Collector, Zilla Parishad Secretary and other officials of the Panchayati Raj bodies besides the Village Secretary.[9]

Conclusion

The rural local government institutions were handicapped by paucity of funds, lack of administrative control and confusion regarding the devolution of functions. The emergence of new bureaucratic institutions such as Nodal Officers further weakened the functioning of rural local government institutions and eroded their powers considerably.

The focus on the rural electorate compels the leaders to engage in meaningful implementation of the rural agenda set forth by the 73rd Constitutional Amendment Act. When we take pride in calling our democracy the largest, the reference point is invariably the Central or State Governments, the local government is completely ignored. The time has come now to make this most important fundamental unit of local democratic governance vibrant, efficient and meaningful.

Thus, the Panchayati Raj Institutions in Andhra Pradesh are in a pathetic situation and these rural institutions are starved of powers, finances and staff. In the absence of concerted effort to provide these bodies with appropriate powers and functions backed by necessary financial resources and staff support, they can hardly be re-activated and rejuvenated. For this, a strong and determined political will is required.

References

1. National Commission to Review the working of the Constitution. Institute of Social Sciences, New Delhi, 2001.
2. Dr Jaya Prakash Narayan, Empowerment of Local Governments: *A Lok Satta Report*, Hyderabad, 2004, p. 22.
3. *Ibid.*, p. 23.
4. *Ibid.*, p. 24.
5. World Bank Report 2000, "Overview of Rural Decentralisation in India", Vol.II.
6. M.Ubaidulla and M.A. Hussain, "People's participation in Panchayati Raj: Perspectives on Janmabhoomi Programme in Andhra Pradesh", in Ramesh, K. Arora (ed.) (2001) : *People Centred Governance,* Aalekh Publishers, Jaipur, p. 225.
7. James Manor: "Democratic decentralisation in two Indian States : Past and Present", *The Indian Journal of Political Science*, March, Vol. 63, No.1, 2002, p. 60
8. 'Empowerment of Local Governments', *A Lok Satta Report*, Hyderabad, 2004, p. 27.
9. *Indian Express*, Hyderabad, September 21, 2005.

14

Decentralisation in West Bengal

—*P. Krishnakumar*

Gandhiji defined his vision of Village Panchayat as follows, "My idea of village swaraj is that, it is a complete republic independent of its neighbours for its vital wants and yet interdependent for many others in which dependence is a necessity. The government of the village will be conducted by the Panchayat of five persons annually elected by the adult villagers, males and females, possessing minimum qualifications." Local governance calls for an increased participation of civil society in public activities. It is felt that it will enhance the efficiency of public services and make local government more accountable and transparent. It deepens democracy by complementing representative forums with participatory forums.

West Bengal covers about three per cent of the geographical area of India and supports more than six per cent of the Indian population. It is the only state which has suffered due to the partition of the country at the time of independence. Then it faced the burden of refugees and lost a sizeable portion of its grain producing zones. The state is surrounded by the poor states such as Bihar and Odisha where feudalism still prevails. Poor people from these states come to the capital of West Bengal – Kolkota in search of jobs. This state has a long political tradition. West Bengal is famous for the mobilisation of the rural poor. The Tebhara movement of 1940's and 1950's, the food movement of 1950's and 1960's are some among them.

The Left Front fought elections under the banner of United Socialist Organisation in1952 and in the name of United Front in 1957. West Bengal is the only state in India in which a single political party has been in power in the state for more than three decades without any interruption. The idea of 'political Panchayat' is in tune with the leftist approach to Panchayats. The Left Front government has transferred all developmental activities in the rural areas in the State to Panchayats. Development policy which emphasis redistribution before growth followed by the government in West Bengal helped them to ensure growth with social justice.

Decentralisation During British Period

It is widely believed that modern Panchayat Raj System had its roots in the ancient Indian Social practices. But its origin and early nature is still unknown. During the vedic period village was the basic unit of administration. Thus, the village administration was under the supervision and direct control of the village 'head man' who was called Gramani. He was assisted by an informal council of village elders. In Mauryan period also village was the basic unit of administration. During the Gupta period village councils were made regular bodies in several parts of India. The settlement of village disputes was the major function of these village councils. During the Chola period there existed a well organised village Panchayat system which can be compared with the modern Panchayat system. Village councils were formed by elected representatives and the village administration was done by the council. During the Sultanate period also there was Panchayat system at the village level. Panchayats acted as judicial bodies and they looked after education, health and sanitation of the villagers.

While examining the Panchayat systems in India during the colonial era, Huge Tinker has observed that the Panchayats of the past were rarely representative in character and they were dominated by the superior castes or the ruling family. Besides this, Panchayats has practically nothing to do with civic or developmental functions. They were primarily concerned with the maintenance of order in the village communities.

During the British Colonial Period steps were taken in Bengal to introduce modern local self-governments. The Bengal Village Chowkidari Act was passed in 1870 and statutorily constituted Panchayats were established. The Chowkidari Act had limited scope. The Panchayats were appointed by the District Magistrates. Panchayats functioned as an agency for the assessment and collection of local tax which was used for meeting the expenses of the village police. The Panchayat committees were mostly composed of officials nominated by the District Magistrate. The non-official members had no administrative powers. Several taxes were imposed on rural people and there was great dissatisfaction among people. A glaring example of this discontent was the reaction against the Road Cess Act of 1871.

The most important milestone in the development of local self-government in rural areas is associated with the administration of Lord Ripon. In 1882, Rippon Resolution put forward new-reforms aiming at increasing the non-official representation in local bodies. The resolution recommended in making a non-official member the Chairman of local bodies and giving more financial powers to the local bodies. So Rippon Resolution is sometimes termed as the 'Magna Carta' of Local Self Governments in India.

The Bengal Local Self Government Act 1885 is the outcome of the increased urge for local governments from the people. The Act Set up three tiers of Local authorities – the Local Board, the Union Committee and the District Board. Administrative functions to be performed by each tier were specified. The District Board has jurisdiction over a whole district. The Local Board was meant for each sub-division. The Bengal Administration Report 1891-1892 showed that the elected members were in minority in all the tiers. Those who were elected are Zamindars, legal pracitioners and government servants. Poor people were left unrepresented. It is also observed that the Chowkidari Panchayat and the Union Committee co-existed for a long time in Bengal.

The District Administrative Committee appointed by Government of Bengal in 1914 recommended for reorganisation of village self-government. On the basis of the recommendations of the Committee, the Bengal Village Self-government Act 1919 was enacted. The Act combined the functions of Chowkidari Panchayats with those of Union committees by creating Union Boards. The Act was extended to all the districts. The Boards were empowered to perform several functions related to primary education, health, sanitation, water supply, maintenance of roads and bridges etc. The term of office for the Union Board was fixed as four years. But due to several reasons like inadequacy of funds, irregular functioning, bad accounting systems etc. the Boards failed in due course of time.

In 1935, the Bengal Village Self-Government Act1919 was amended and made much more comprehensive. But the progress of local self-governments since 1938 in Bengal suffered seriously due to the reasons such as the communal policies followed by successive Muslim ministers in the Province, impact of the second world war and partition of Bengal in 1947. As regards the functioning of local self-governments during the colonial period Pranab Bardan and Dilip Mookherjee observed that, "the Union Boards brought village administration into the formal administrative and revenue structure of the colonial state. These Boards made no effort to encourage popular participation of local residents. Their main purpose was to co-opt local elites into the power structure of the colonial state, partly in response to the threat of rising nationalism among the elites." Even though there existed limited scope for the common man to participate in local administration during the colonial period; the efforts discussed above can be considered as the forerunners for the establishment of democratic set up and the present form of local self-government in West Bengal.

Decentralisation in Post-British Period

West Bengal Panchayat Act 1951 has considered Gram Sabha as a direct participatory forum for the people. As per the structural arrangements of the Act, Gram Sabha was at the lowest level and each Gram Sabha covers on an average 800 to 1200 population. It was expected to meet twice in an year to consider the working of the Grama Panchayat and direct it for future activities. Gram Sabha has no power in preparing or publishing its voter list. The voter list of the West Bengal State assembly election is used to identify the voters of the Gram Sabha. Grama Sabha has no executive powers. It was only a deliberative and recommendatory body. Presence of atleast one-tenth of the total number of members of the Gram Sabha is the required quorum of its meetings. Apart from the statutory meetings, extra-ordinary meetings can also be convened. The members of the Gram Sabha elect the members of Grama Panchayat.

Grama Panchayat is the lowest tier in the Panchayat Raj System. Its strength varies between 9 to 15 members. The Act provided provisions for nominating members to Grama Panchayat. The members of the Panchayat in its first meeting elect the Adhyaksha and Upadyaksha among themselves. The term of office of the members and Adyaksha as well as Upadyaksha was fixed as four years. Eventhough the functions of the Adyaksha and Upadhyaksha was not clearly specified in the Act, they performed both statutory and delegated functions. But the non-mentioning of the function of these two persons in the Act has created confusion on the role and performance of them. Due to the non-mentioning of the functions they were unable to take independent decisions in the important village matters.

Above Grama Panchayat, the second executive tier in West Bengal Panchayat systems suggested in the Act of 1957 was Anchal Panchayat. It covers eight to ten Grama Panchyats having 8000 to 10000 populations within it. It was an additional tier in between village and block. The members of Anchal Panchayat were indirectly elected. The Adhyaksha of Grama Panchayats is ex-officio members. The views of the Grama Panchayats were reflected in Anchal Panchayat through the Adhyaksha of Grama Panchayats. The head of the Anchal Panchayat, the Pradhan and the Upapradhan were elected by the members. Anchal Panchayat had to perform statutory and delegated functions. It was responsible for law and order, justice and imposition of some taxes. It has given the power to approve the budget also. The creation of this additional tier in between village and block was questioned by many scholars. The provisions for indirect election to this important body were also questioned. It is argued that this tier has reduced the power and importance of Grama Panchayats.

Anchalik Parishad was the third executive tier of the West Bengal Panchayat system (at the block level). It consisted of five categories of members such as ex-officio, elected, appointed, co-opted and associate. Anchalik Parishad was responsible for the development of agriculture, animal husbandry, cottage industries and construction and maintenance of rural roads. Eventhough the Anchalik Parishad was established, the community Development Organisation (CDO) at the block level was not merged with it.

So a diarchy had been created at the block level and the relationship between the Block Development Officer and the elected members in several blocks was not cordial. Above these three tiers, at the district level, there was a Zilla Parishad. The West Bengal Zilla Parishad Act was passed in 1963. Zilla Parishad was expected to co-ordinate the development works within the district and monitor the functioning of the lower tiers. It is important to note that eventhough Grama Panchayat has been established in West Bengal in 1958-1959, the full-fledged four-tier structure of the Panchayat Raj Institutions was inaugurated only on 2nd October 1964. The entire State except some tea estates of Darjeeling and other districts was covered by PRIs.

Studies conducted by different scholars on the West Bengal Panchayat Raj system after the 1957 and 1963 act revealed that eventhough the Zamindari system was formally abolished under the 1953 Act, the Zamindari system continued to dominate with all its manifestations. It was also noticed that the representation and response of womenfolk in the Panchayat institutions was very poor. Ratheendranath Chatterjee has opinioned that there was no collective will in the villages. Caste and class differences were so pronounced in the village life. During this partyless Panchayat era the effective functioning of the Panchayats were almost absent. Functioning of the Panchayats were badly affected by the lack of political support, inadequate statutes and laws in making the Panchayat representative bodies, lack of delegation of powers, bureaucratic neglect and defective structural arrangements. The failure of this first generation panchyats in West Bengal was also due to the inadequate representation or even the exclusion of backward classes particularly scheduled castes, scheduled tribes and women.

In 1967, the Congress was defeated in the West Bengal Assembly election and the United Front Government was formed. This new government proposed a completely new scheme for Panchayat system. But the government was dismissed and the state was brought under President's rule in 1968. In the next general election United Front was voted to power and they have introduced drastic changes in the existing Panchayat system. They proposed a three-tier structure of PRIs. Their bill was not enacted till the government fell in 1970. Again the state was put under President's rule. In 1972, Congress came to power and they have introduced the West Bengal Panchayat Act 1973. This act replaced the earlier acts of 1957 and 1963. The Act provided for three-tier Panchayat system – Grama Panchayat at the village level, for a group of villages – Panchayat samity; at the Block level and Zilla Parishad at the district level. But unfortunately the legislation was not implemented during the Congress regime. The national political scenario was not conducive to the implementation of the Act. So in West Bengal the Panchayat system was in a moribund state until 1977.

Decentralisation During the Left Front Rule

In June 1977 the Left front led by the Communist Party of India (Marxist) was voted to power. The elections to the Panchayat were held in 1978. Panchayat elections in West Bengal since 1978 have been conducted along party lines and the recommendations of the Ashok Metha Committee report were followed in this regard. Left Front considered Panchayats as a centre to fight against vested interests and to implement development activities. During 1970's Left Front had little influence in the rural areas of West Bengal. They have used the 1978 Panchayat elections to establish their political base in the rural areas of West Bengal. Instead of attempting for a rapid expansion of the party, they have followed the strategy of controlling the Panchayats through Communist Party of India (Marxist). The party leaders played a crucial supervisory role over the local government institutions. The restructuring of the Panchayat system has given the Left Front chances to reduce excessive dependence on the bureaucracy. By handing over the power and responsibility to the Panchayats, to distribute funds of poverty alleviation and other such welfare programme CPI (M) gradually established its political supremacy in the rural areas. The research findings of scholars like Bandyopadhyaya (1999) and Webster (1996) has pointed out that the operation of the panchayat system in West Bengal during Left Front rule has been determined by the political strategy of CPI (M).

Factors that helped the Left to win the elections and establish political and administrative supremacy in the state are the distributional changes made in the state in favour of the poor and marginalised sections of the population. Land reforms implemented in 1980's are also important in this regard. The grassroot level democracy introduced in West Bengal by the Left regime replaced the hierarchical power structure. The poor people were given an opportunity to play a crucial role in the decision-making process at the village level.

Another argument for the Left supremacy in West Bengal is related to the economic crisis faced by the state. Abhirup Sankar has argued that the economic stagnation in the state has helped the ruling Left Front to continue in power. Economic stagnation had reduced the economic opportunities open to the citizens particularly the poor. This situation forced them to be dependent of the ruling party for small favours and survival.

An in-depth analysis of the benefits distributed by the Left Front through panchayats show that the same are usually distributed through panchayats in other states also. But in West Bengal, apart from winning political support and vote, the left front was able to create a situation of political loyalty-cum-clientelism. The clientelist relationship between the Left in power and the electrorate has been created through the benefit distributed by the rulers and received by the voters. Political loyalty towards the Left was more pronounced among the poor, the landless, uneducated, unemployed and socially backward people.

In several studies it has been stressed that the panchayats worked fairly well to uphold the interests of the poor people. Pranab Bardan has pointed out that political awareness and participation is high in West Bengal. These were somewhat higher among the educated and affluent people. The attendance in Grama Sabha show that the poor and Scheduled Caste/Tribe people actively participate in it. Benefits are distributed in favour of these sections of the community. But their involvement in political activities is limited. Negative correlations exist in between the households involved in political campaign and benefits received. The study reported that benefits are distributed in favour of the panchayats where the Left Front is in power. But intra-panchayat level distributive inequalities are not glairing.

In a study conducted by Pranab Bardhan and Dilip Moorkherjee they have observed that inter-village allocation of resources was subject to high level of discretion reflecting both political priorities of upper level governments and the bargaining strength of local governments and local citizens. Villages with more landless people and low caste status and greater land inequality received substantially fewer resources than the others. Allocation of resources and benefits follow political party lines. It was also observed that the extent of autonomy of the panchayats is limited in comparison with the local governments of many countries. The own source revenue of the panchayats are negligible. Panchayats have no elastic revenue base. Activities of the panchayats depend upon the grants from the state and central governments. No conscious effort is made so far to empower the panchayats in raising revenue locally. So the ability of the panchayats to fight against poverty is quite limited.

A study made by four scholars, Pranab Bardhan, Dilip Mookherjee, Abhrup Sankar and Sandip Mitra have tried to examine the nature of inter-village distribution of benefits in West Bengal. They have carried out their investigation in three stages: - 1. Examined the proportions of benefits of different categories (such as housing, drinking water, ration cards etc) going to the poor and socially underprivileged classes. 2. The effect of different variables (like landholding caste, education, political participation) on the distribution of benefits within a village. 3. Distribution of benefits across villages to understand how village characteristics like the proportion of landless and backward classes residing in the villages influence the distribution of benefit.

They have observed that: - (1) Largest benefits were reported for roads (32 per cent) and water (23 per cent) which are non-excludable public goods (2) Among the non-excludable personal benefits beneficiaries from ration cards (12 per cent) and relief of various kinds (12 per cent) topped the list. (3) Fair portion of the benefits went to landless and to SC/ST households.

This study has examined the prevailing clientelist and gratitudal relationships. To look into such relationships the benefits received by the people were further divided into two categories such as one time benefit and recurring benefit. Clientelist relationship between the party and the voter would involve distribution of recurring benefits. If votes are obtained due to gratitude factor both kinds of benefits would be important. The study shows that ST people received more one time benefits than recurring. But for SC population just the opposite happens. So ST votes are based more on gratitude factor where as SC votes are mainly rooted in a clientelist relationship between the party and the voter.

A significant 'U' shaped relationship between left majority in panchayats and per household benefits are seen in the state. The 'U' shaped relationship implies that more resources are allocated to villages were seat allocation were extreme, i.e. either the proportion of Left seats are high or very low. In the panchayats whether it is ruled by the Left or the non-Left, if they have a big majority, they could bring more resources from higher levels of governments. Unfortunately, more evenly contested panchayats could bring fewer benefits per households.

Eventhough several paradoxes can be seen in the decentralised governance in West Bengal, compared to several other states in India it stands at a high pedestal. Single party rule for more than three decades is one reason for it. The recent changes in the political scenario pose new challenges to the decentralisation in West Bengal.

Conclusion

The long lasting political supremacy of the Left in West Bengal received a jolt in the Panchayat elections of 2008 and later in the Assembly elections in 2011 they lost power in the state. The long era of political stability was shaken by various events in the state. Acquisition of agricultural land for industry and the prolonged protest of the poor and the violence that erupted in 2007; the consequent political developments, the withdrawal of Tata motors from Singur and the adivasi agitation in Midnapur were some among them. In 2003 elections to local bodies 71 per cent of the Grama Panchayats, 86 per cent of Samitis and 88 per cent of Zilla Parishads were controlled by the Left. In 2008, these proportions were reduced to 49 per cent, 69 per cent and 76 per cent respectively. It is interesting to note that there has been no indication of this decline, in other words the Left decline in West Bengal was not gradual. The future of decentralised governance in West Bengal depends on the attitude towards it by the new government.

References

1. Ratna Ghosh and Alok Kumar Pramanik (ed), (2007) : *Panchayat system in India – Historical, constitutional and financial Analysis*, Kanishka Publishers, New Delhi.
2. Huge Tinker, (1967) : *The Foundatinas of Local Self-Government in India*, Pakistan and Burma, Lalvani Publications, Bombay.
3. Pranab Bhardhan and Dilip Mookherjee (ed), (2007) : *Decentralisation and Local governance in Developing Countries,* Oxford University Press, New Delhi.
4. Ranjit Chauduri, 'Panchayats and interest Groups: Study of a Bengal village', *Economic and Political Weekly*, Vol. XVI, No. 38, September 19, 1967.
5. S.K. Bhanja and S.K. Dutta, 'Panchayat Raj Institutions in West Bengal', From the Book, *Panchayat Raj Institutions in India: An Appraisal,* NIRD, Hyderabad.
6. Prabhat Dutta, (1998) : *Major Issues in the Development Debate: Lessons in Empowerment from India*, Kanishka Publishers, New Delhi.
7. Pranab Bardhan, Sandip Mitra, Dilip Mookherjee and Abhrup Sankar, 'Local Democracy and Clientelism', Implications for Political Stability in Rural West Bengal', *Economic and Political Weekly*, Vol. XLIV, No. 9, February 28, 2009.
8. Rajarshi Dasgupta, 'The CPI (M) 'Machinery' in West Bengal: Two village Narratives from Kochbehar and Malda, *Economic and Political Weekly,* Vol. XLIV, No. 9, February 28, 2009.
9. Partha Chatterjee, 'The Coming Crisis in West Bengal', *Economic and Political Weekly*, Vol. XLIV, No. 9, February 28, 2009.

15

Democratic Decentralisation in Bihar: A Historical Perspective

—*Manjula Bharathi*

Introduction

The 73rd Constitutional Amendment Act, 1992 conferred constitutional status on the Panchayati Raj Institutions (PRIs) and is a landmark in the history of decentralised governance in the country. The Act provided for devolution of powers and responsibilities upon appropriate levels of the panchayat structure, and envisaged people's participation in planning and implementation with respect to local governance. It necessitated the central and state government ministries and departments to confer the necessary administrative powers to PRI representatives and functionaries to enable them to effectively discharge their new responsibilities.

Bihar has a strong history of local governance. From ancient times, concepts like *sakya gantantra* existed in the state. Before independence, parts of the state were brought within the purview of the Bengal Local Self-Government Act. Afterwards, the Bihar and Orissa Village Administration Act, 1922 enabled the creation of elected union boards and also some elected panchayats. The government in autonomous provinces in 1935 was pro-people and worked towards strengthening the village administration.

Post-independence, through the Bihar Local Self-Government Act, provision was made to make the district board areas smaller than the revenue boards. An amendment in 1950 made provision for elected representatives in local boards. The launching of community development programme in 1952 accelerated the constitution of panchayats in the state. Starting with 25 panchayats per sub-division in 1952, there were 6474 notified panchayats and 2970 unofficial units by 1955. In the same year government decided to introduce two panchayat halka systems, by which a karmachari for revenue collection and a development worker were provided to them. In 1961, the Bihar Panchayat Samiti and Zilla Parishad Act was enacted to create block and district level panchayats. This Act was amended in 1964 so as to shift the focus from village to block and district level units. By 1970, three-tier structures were in place all over the state. In pursuance of the 73rd Amendment of the Constitution of India, the Bihar Panchayati Raj Act was passed in 1993. Panchayat elections were held in 2001 and then in 2006. (State of Panchayats, Bihar, MoPR, 2008).

Panchayati Raj in Bihar is governed by the Bihar Panchayat Raj Act, 2006 as amended from time to time, and as per rules made there under. The three-tier panchayat Institutions in Bihar consist of gram panchayats (8,463 GPs) at the lowest level, panchayat samitis (531 PSs) at the block level and zilla parishads (38 ZPs) at the district level. Elections to PRIs were held, after more than two decades, in 2001. After the 2006 PRI elections, the state has more than 260,000 elected representatives in these PRIs comprising mukhiyas (chairpersons of GPs), ward members, sarpanchs (elected heads of Gram Katchahries at GPs), panchs, pramukhs (chairpersons of PSs), PS members, adhyakhas (chairpersons of ZPs) and ZP members. Through the Amendment of the Bihar Panchayat Act, elaborate provision of reservation, based on caste and gender, has been institutionalised at the PRIs. The reservation policy of the state prescribes fifty per cent seats at every level, including single posts like mukhiyas, and heads of panchyat samitis and zilla parishads, to be reserved for women. Caste-based reservation has also been expanded to provide reservation for extreme backward castes along with Scheduled Castes (SCs) and Scheduled Tribes (STs).

Local Self Governance in the Ancient Period

Bihar's ancient history of local governance is highly intertwined with the Vedic and mythological period. The influence of governance arrangements that prevailed during the Ramayan period is still evident in the culture of Bihar. The Ramayan period had a model of de-centralised administrative structure, which was expected to deal with social and economic issues. The lowest layer of administrative units was the Dashadhipati in charge of ten villages, followed by the Satadhipati in charge of 100 villages and Sahashradhipati in charge of thousand villages. The reporting channel of social issues as well as the revenue issues used to be initiating from the Dasadhipati, and moving through Sahadhipati and Sahardhti before reaching the king.

Ramayan period also shows the illustration for the mukhiya system. The village head or gramadhipati is mentioned as the gramani who is equivalent to the present mukhiya in the panchayati raj system. The post of gramani was considered to be a very prestigious post and as a result there was huge inter dynamics for reaching the post. The king used to act through the gramani in dealing with the matters concerning the villages.

The Maurya period was also a period of systematic local governance. The local self-governance was practiced for the first time during the Maurya period. Kautilya in his Arthshastra assigned the responsibilities of revenue collection to the samaharta who is equivalent to the revenue officer of the modern period. There was also provision of making a union of different villages under the administration of a post created namely, Gope.

The Maurya period also had practice of gram sabhas. The gram sabhas were authorised bodies to prepare and administer legislation necessary for social life in the villages. Agriculture was the source of main livelihood in the villages and the system was self-sufficient. The Maurya period also ensured certain levels of self-governance to these villages. The same situation as well as system of local administration continued during the Gupta dynasty also. The gram sabhas were regular and they had day to day interference in the problems faced by the village people.

Local Self Governance During the Mediaeval Period

The main feature of the mediaeval period with respect to local self-governance is the parallel existence of centralised administrative system as well as the local decentralised self-governance systems. The Muslim emperors did not give much importance to the development of local self-governance system or even improving the existing local governance. A highly centralised imperialistic administrative system was believed to be effective in controlling such a large empire from Delhi. Unlike the British colonial period, the Muslim rulers did not destroy the then existed local governance system in the area. They rather considered the existence of such a system as helpful in administering their empire.

The medieval system of local governance suffered from limitations curtailing the space, economic power and political independence that used to be enjoyed by the local governance units in the ancient period. Still the gram sabhas continued uninterrupted, the mukhiyas continued to be social leaders, and panchayat continued to be smallest unit of administration. There was also a clerical staff to help the mukhiya with the revenue matters and a chowkidar who acted as the village policeman.

Local Self Governance During the British Colonial Period

With respect to the status of local self-governance institutions, the British colonial period could be divided into two distinct periods. In the initial period of British rule, the British colonialists wanted to establish a strong revenue system, which would make tax collection easier for maintaining centralised system of administration. For these reasons, the British preferred a system completely based on officers. Centralised bureaucratic system was encouraged and in this process all the local self-governance and institutions got demolished. This also had its impact on weakening the self-sustainability and self-rule of the villages. Villages started to be dependent upon unsustainable economies. Gram panchayats lost its esteem as social and political unit, thereby making the concept of social self-rule redundant and irrelevant.

It was at the time of widespread rebellion against the British rule all over India that the British acted upon the local self-governance system. The design was not the same as the ancient panchayat system of India but as administrative units, which could become the representative of British empire in the villages. With this view, Lord Rippon advocated for establishment of village panchayats all over India. Later, Sahi Decentralisation Commission in 1907 and Government of India Act 1919 made efforts to rejuvenate the local self-governance system in India but no remarkable progress was made. The apparatus of decentralised governance and ideology of centralised governance hardly were in match with each other, thus curtailing the possibility of an effective decentralised system. It was later in the post-independence period that some progress was made in strengthening the panchayat raj system.

Local Self Governance During the Post-Independence Period

The vision of independent India also shared the vision of people oriented empowerment by strengthening panchayat raj system in the villages of India. With this vision, the first Panchayat Raj Act of Bihar was brought in 1947. As part of the five-year plans, Government of India had designed many village development programmes like Community Development Programme of 1952. Bihar also adopted all these centrally enacted programmes. The rural development programmes expected a high level of co-operation in the rural community, which was vital for reaching the objectives envisaged in these programmes. In 1955, the report of the Central Evaluation Committee revealed that these objectives were hardly met. But the report also indicated that the physical achievement of these community development programmes have been satisfactory, while the expected objective of the construction of an organic village community as a well knit socio-cultural interrelated space was hardly met. This implies that these programmes remained a government programme with only limited participation of people in the process.

In 1957, the Balwant Rai Mehta Committee, which looked into the reasons of this failure, stressed the importance of decentralisation and devolution of power for establishment of real democracy at the village. The commission also highlighted the need of ensuring people's participation while conceptualising, planning and implementing development programmes. For democratic decentralisation, the commission suggested three-tier panchayati raj systems with the gram panchayat at the village level, panchayat samiti at the block level and zilla parishad at the district level. The committee also stressed the importance of providing sufficient resources of the panchayat and intensive training to the panchayat representatives and functionaries. The recommendation of Balwant Rai Mehta Committee was accepted by the National Development Council in January 1958. It appealed to the state governments to establish the panchayati raj system, which would fit into the existing situations in the states. As per this, Bihar came under the purview of panchayati raj scheme in 1959. Under this democratic decentralisation programme, local elected representatives were given the power to prepare plans as well as to participate in the implementation of the same. Under the panchayat raj scheme, gram panchayats were established all over the state. Incorporating the recommendations of the Balwant Rai Mehta Committee, the Bihar Panchayat Raj Act was amended. Bihar Panchayat Samiti and Zilla Parishad Act was passed in 1961. This Act was operationalised in 1963, and Bihar had panchayat raj election in 1963 as well as in 1972.

The Janta Party government appointed Ashok Mehta Committee in 1977 for rejuvenating the panchayat raj institutions. The committee submitted its report in 1978. The committee recommended panchayat election on the basis of political parties. The recommendation was rejected and Bihar had next panchayat election in 1978. Subsequent to this, vested political and bureaucratic interests blocked panchayat elections in Bihar for next two decades.

The Congress government in the centre appointed G.V.K. Rao Committee in 1985 and L.M. Singhvi Committee in 1986. The Singhvi Committee recommended for legalised panchayats and to establish village courts. About the participation of political parties, the commission left it to the consensus of all political parties. The Rajiv Gandhi government reasoned that there was high prevalence of deep-rooted corruption, in the absence of institutions of democratic decentralisation. Sensing the need for decentralisation of power at the panchayat level, the 73rd Constitutional Amendment was made.

Bihar Panchayati Raj after 73rd Amendment

After the 73rd Amendment of the Constitution, Bihar Panchayati Raj system incorporated the constitutional provisions and the Bihar Panchayati Raj Act, 1993 was enacted. The first elections to the gram panchayats, panchayat samiti and the zilla parishads, as per this Act, took place in April 2001. Elections were held for 8471 gram panchayts, 532 panchayat samitis and 37 zilla parishads in the state. Though the Panchayati Raj Act was amended in 1993, the first elections could take place only after eight years, in 2001, because the proposition for reservation of single post like the mukhiya, pramukh and adhyaksh were challenged in Patna High Court and later in the Supreme Court.

Reservations for SCs and STs and women in the Bihar Panchayat Act, 1993 were challenged in the Patna High Court through a writ petition (CW

GC- 3351 /1994 Krishnan Kumar Misra and others).The court, through its verdict in 1996, allowed reservation for SC, ST and women, while ordered that the list of the Backward Class citizens be revised and that reservation for them to be stalled till the new list was re-submitted. The state moved a Special Leave Petition before the Supreme Court and chose not hold elections to the PRI, wrongly interpreting the decision of the High Court as stay on the elections. In the meantime, the Patna High Court, delivering its judgement in a PIL ((Nanth Kishore Singh Vs. the Union of India) asked the state government to hold the elections without further delay. The order was upheld by the Supreme Court, following which elections to the PRIs in Bihar were held in April 2001.This resulted, for the first time in the history of Bihar, an induction of 44,815 EWRs at the PRIs, among who 29,962 belonged to the SC community.

Subsequently, the Panchayat Raj Act, 1993 of Bihar was repealed and was replaced by the Bihar Panchayat Raj Ordinance of 2006, which mandated 50 per cent reservation to women at all levels of the PRIs, and 50 per cent reservation for women in the seats reserved for SC and ST. The same provisions were made in the case of mukhya of gram panchayat, pradhan of panchayat samiti, adhyaksh of zilla panchayat and sarpanch of gram kachahry. The elections in 2006 were held accordingly.

The second elections after the 73rd amendment took place in 2006 whereby 1162 zilla parishad members, 11,566 panchayat samiti members, 11,5479 gram panchayat members, 8463 mukhiya, 8463 sarpanch and 11,5479 panchs were elected. The total number of panchayat representatives in Bihar was 26,0612.

Two important aspects of the Bihar Panchayati Raj System, which has become a model in the entire nation, are the 50 per cent reservation for women and the reservation ensured to the most backward communities. People's participation is the key to the success to the local governance; it increases transparency and reduces corruption. The Parliament and Assembly election has spread democracy but have not ensured the participation of the deprived sections of the society. The Bihar government, by providing reservation to the most backward communities in 2006 elections, widened the spheres of participation. The reservation has ensured the participation of the most backward communities who form 20 per cent to the total population of the state. In the particular situation of Bihar where the upper caste communities and the backward communities are organised in the political process, and the SCs and STs have reservation in the political process, it is the women and the most backward community that are unorganised politically and, consequently, deprived of political participation. The reservation policy in the Bihar Panchayati Raj system has ensured participation of both these sections of the society.

PRIs and Constraints

Bihar Panchayati Raj system suffered from serious political power dynamics in the post-independence period. As a result, the panchayat elections in Bihar have been delayed for a long time. There was a long gap in conducting panchayat elections after the 1978 panchayat elections. Though the 73rd amendment came into operation in 1993, the panchayats in Bihar had to wait for another eight years for the panchayat elections to take place. The debates around reservations for women and the backward castes, the debate around reservations in single posts and the debate on the role of political parties in panchayats etc. had been controversial issues in the political parlour of Bihar. The society of Bihar being divided into two strong groups of forwards and backwards, the political consciousness is high among the people and every discussion in relation to power structure invokes high interest across the state. The historicity of traditionally self sufficient village panchayat system in Bihar made the society to understand and experience deep rooted power relations at the panchayat level. Besides, the people of Bihar went through severe struggles during the pre-independence period for sustaining their traditional panchayat system against the imposed administrative systems of the colonial rule.

The entire history of panchayat raj in Bihar is a male dominated one. Though panchayats were traditionally empowered to deal with social, cultural and economic problems of the village, there is hardly any example of women's issues been discussed or resolved through the panchayat. No woman panchayat head could ever be possible in the highly patriarchal system. Thus, the discussion on the reservation for women in panchayats evoked large scale ripples of political and cultural nature.

The deep-rooted caste-based hierarchy in Bihar society always exercised caste dominance through the panchayats. Traditionally, the panchayat in a particular village used to be completely dominated by the upper caste groups residing in that village. There was hardly any say for the lower caste members in the panchayats. In most of the situations, the panchayat decisions were given in favour of the dominant caste groups. Discussion on caste and gender based reservations indicated a threat to the age old dominance and accepted power structures.

Once the 73rd amendment was through and panchayat elections were held in 2001, all these political, cultural and social differences posed constraints in the way of the panchayat raj institutions. There was widespread tension, conflict and ambiguity in almost all the panchayats during 2001 elections. This kind of tensions was reduced in 2006 elections as the society had made attempt to adjust to the changed power relations in the villages. However, sporadic incidences of violence against women representatives and lower caste representatives continue to occur.

Traditionally, the panchayats had very little people's participation. Though legally established panchayats have completely replaced the traditional panchayats, the culture of imposing decisions prevailed in some parts of rural Bihar. Despite the fact that success of democratic decentralisation rests on the active and dynamic gram sabhas, there is hardly any gram sabha in real sense of the term, thus hindering the process of decision-making, planning and successful implementation by the panchayats.

As per the Bihar Panchayati Raj Act 2006, 29 subjects specified in 73rd amendment of the Constitution of India had to be devolved to the panchayats. Even after devolution of powers to the panchayats, in line with the Act, the PRI elected members find themselves marginally involved in the governance and programme implementation processes. There are also problems related to unclear definitions of jurisdictions of different layers of the panchayat. There are many conflicts existing to be solved between gram panchayats and panchayats samitis as well as between panchayat samitis and zilla parishads on the issue of trespassing into the jurisdiction by the respective institutions.

Though devolution of the power is claimed to have been completed by the government, it is an open fact that devolution of fund and functionary to the panchayats are far from satisfactory. Thus, the panchayats in Bihar are power abodes without proper infrastructure, adequate functionaries or enough funds. Added to this is the inexperience of the elected panchayat representatives on panchayat processes. Corruption at the panchayat level increases under such circumstances and contributes to the failure of PRIs.

The most dissatisfied units of panchayat elected representatives are the ward members, panchs, and sarpanchs. In the mukhiya centric panchayat system, the ward members of gram panchayat have practically no role to play other than holding technically constitutional posts. They feel unrecognised and powerless as they are not able to exercise any control over the mukhiya or have their opinion accepted without the favour of the mukhiya. The gram kachahari is defunct in all the panchayats though the sarpanchs and panchs do exist. This legal authority of the villages has never being used or capacitated to use its powers. The active members in the panchayat are just the mukhiyas; the panchayat samitti members and the zilla parishad members form only less than 10 per cent of the total elected panchayati raj members in Bihar.

16

Panchayati Raj System in Madhya Pradesh: Dynamics and Divergencies

—R. Sreekantan Nair and Ashitha

Introduction

The initiative and political will for the 73rd constitutional amendment was historic and revolutionary in character. The move has brought drastic changes in the political landscape of the nation in a bigger and deeper way. As such the nation has been subject to various types of political and social changes unprecedented to the history of the country. As a result of the move women got a rare opportunity to take part in the decision-making process of the country. The common man became the dispenser of his own social and political destiny. However, the process of decentralisation and participatory governance took various forms and shapes in the process of its application, which was subject to local realities and power relations. For studying the dynamics of local governance in Madhya Pradesh, the article deals with the question of 73rd amendment and its major political implications, the impact of this move on the local governance of Madhya Pradesh and the contradictions in the local governance of the state.

The Concept of Participatory Governance

The concept of participatory governance is very old. Often it is associated with the concept of the **panchayati raj.** As such it was the oldest system of local government in the Indian subcontinent. Modern Indian government has decentralised several administrative functions to the local level, empowering elected gram panchayats. The term "Panchayati Raj" is relatively new, having originated during the British administration. Raj literally means "governance or government." Mahatma Gandhi advocated Panchayati Raj, a decentralised form of Government where each village is responsible for its own affairs, as the foundation of India's political system. Gandhiji's views found articulation in Article 40 of the Constitution. It enjoins that 'the States shall take steps to organise village panchayats with such powers and authority as may be necessary to enable them to function as units of self government'. During the last fifty years, several attempts have been made to bring about effective decentralisation, both political and economic, with limited success. However, the year 1992 marks a new era in the federal democratic set up of the country. The 73rd Constitutional Amendment Act, 1992 conferred Constitutional status on the Panchayathi Raj Institutions (PRIs). It envisages the establishment of a democratic decentralised development process through people's participation in decision-making, implementation and delivery. In order to achieve this objective, the Constitution provides for devolution of powers and responsibilities upon panchayaths at appropriate levels. Twenty nine Subjects listed in the Eleventh Schedule of the Constitution have been identified for devolution to the PRIs. The 73rd Constitutional Amendment Act has created three-tier PRIs in the rural areas with allocation of specific subjects to them. In pursuance of this, States have initiated action to devolve administrative and financial powers and resources to PRIs to enable them to discharge their Constitutional role. It is expected that once the process of devolution is effectively operationalised, resources from the Central and State Governments meant for programmes falling within the jurisdiction of the PRIs would directly get allocated to them.

The Amendment Act of 1992 contains provision for devolution of powers and responsibilities to the panchayaths both for the preparation of economic development plans and social justice, as well as for implementation in relation to 29 subjects listed in the eleventh schedule of the constitution. In the history of Panchayati Raj in India, on 24 April 1993, the Constitutional (73rd Amendment) Act 1992 came into force to provide constitutional status to the Panchayathi Raj institutions. This act was extended to Panchayaths in the tribal areas of eight states, namely Andhra Pradesh, Gujarat, Himachal Pradesh, Maharashtra, Madhya Pradesh, Odisha and Rajasthan starting 24 December 1996. Currently, the Panchayathi Raj system exists in all the states except Nagaland, Meghalaya and Mizoram, and in all Union Territories except Delhi.

Madhya Pradesh is one of the better-governed States in India. In this context, where many experts are comparing Madhya Pradesh initiatives with the successes of two divergent models of governance in Kerala and Andhra Pradesh, it becomes imperative to go beyond the government's stated objectives, rules and regulations, Acts and claims of effective functioning of Panchayaths, and take an earnest look at the ground reality. It also becomes imperative to understand and analyse the socio-economic and political implications and accompanying processes unleashed by the Panchayathi Raj initiatives of the Madhya Pradesh government. Madhya Pradesh pioneered the implementation of the 73rd Amendment by, for instance, conducting

Panchayath elections in 1994. The Panchayath system in Madhya Pradesh has been dynamic and constantly responding to the needs emerging from the field. Through Panchayathi Raj, an attempt is being made to initiate a new era of people's empowerment. An Amendment of the Panchayath Act to introduce the Gram Swaraj system clearly demonstrates this flexibility and commitment. Importantly, the Madhya Pradesh government perceives decentralisation and people's participation as central to its governance agenda, of which the Panchayathi raj system is the most critical building block.

Panchayati Raj System in Madhya Pradesh

In Madhya Pradesh, the second largest Indian state in size with an area of 308,144 square kilometers, there are 50 districts, which are divided into nine revenue divisions for administrative purpose. The strong rural base is reflected in the large number of villages 55,393 that are covered by about 23, 040 Gram Panchayats and 313 Community Development Blocks. A system of village level governance, Gram Swaraj, has been put in place since 26 January 2001, under which Gram Sabha's have been bestowed with considerable powers for development of villages and welfare activities.

In the post-73rd Amendment phase different States have responded with varying degrees of enthusiasm. Madhya Pradesh has responded with innovativeness and remarkable commitment to making the system sustainable and successful. The State's effort to institutionalise the system is evident in the number of amendments that have been made to the State Panchayat Act as a dynamic response to the problems at the ground level.The process of implementation of the Panchayati Raj Institutions (PRIs) has raised several vital questions linked to the institutional and structural mechanism of governance; it also raises fundamental questions regarding the nature of the Indian state. The PRIs also have far reaching implications for the political and social processes. Through a study on the status of Panchayats in Madhya Pradesh an attempt can be made to comprehend and analyse these implications and processes. Madhya Pradesh is a good case study also because of its diversity and plurality, and its wide geographical and cultural base. Significantly, it has a substantial tribal population with their own traditional governance systems and cultural uniqueness leading to interesting interaction with the PRIs. Further, the State's underdeveloped status can provide interesting insights to the development perspectives and paradigms.

Madhya Pradesh was the first State to organise elections to the Panchayats after the Constitutional Amendment and constitute these as institutions of local self-governance. The Madhya Pradesh Panchayath Act aims at making significant changes by introducing the system of Gram Swaraj.The Madhya Pradesh Panchayathi Raj Act drastically altered the existing governance system and constitutionalised grassroots democracy. Panchayati Raj institutions, working as agents of change, are altering rural society. Madhya Pradesh, a pioneer in the implementation of the Panchayati Raj Act, presents a good case study on the basis of which larger trends and implications for decentralised rural self-governance can be identified.

The traditional Panchayaths – the caste and village Panchayaths – were vibrant in Madhya Pradesh. With modernisation and functioning of modern maximalist state, the strength of the traditional Panchayats has slowly diminished, though to a lesser extent in the tribal areas of the State. Efforts have been made by enacting laws that further the cause of decentralised governance. The Madhya Pradesh Panchayath Act, 1962, was one such effort based on the recommendations of the Balwant Rai Mehta Committee. In 1978, this Act was amended to reduce the age of voters from 21 to18 years of age to allow more citizens to exercise their franchise during Panchayath elections. A new Panchayathi Raj Act was enacted in 1981, which was later amended in 1988 to provide reservations of seats for SCs, STs and women in Panchayaths. These institutions were given extremely restricted local-maintenance functions and had no developmental responsibilities, which made them largely ineffective. Elections to these bodies were not held regularly, and the bodies remained under the control of government-appointed administrators.

The Madhya Pradesh Panchayathi Raj Act, 1990, attempted to revitalise the Panchayathi Raj institutions and transfer power to the people to ensure their effective participation. The key features of this Act were direct elections to these bodies, involvement of political parties, and the transfer of resources and developmental machinery to the Panchayaths.The Madhya Pradesh Panchayathi Raj Act, 1993, was enacted to cover lacunae in the existing laws for the establishment of Panchayath institutions. This Act was drafted in conformity with the objectives, substance and directives of the 73rd Constitutional Amendment. The Act provides for a separate and independent audit organisation (under the control of the State government) to monitor the audit of Panchayat accounts; a State Election Commission to supervise, direct and control the preparation of electoral rolls and to conduct elections to the Panchayaths; and a State Finance Commission (SFC) to recommend to the State government any grant-in-aid as may be needed by the Panchayaths. The Act was given the Governor's assent on January 24th, 1994.

The primary objective of the Act is to strengthen and empower the Panchayath institutions and to ensure effective involvement of these institutions in local administration and development activities. The idea is to make Panchayath institutions more democratic through people's greater participation, democratic decentralisation and effective local self-governance, and agents of economic and social justice. This Act provides the backbone for all changes and development in the sphere of Panchayaths in Madhya Pradesh.

Structure of the Gram Panchayat

Each village or cluster of villages is required to have a Gram Panchayat (23,012 Grama Panchayats) with tenure of five years. The Gram Panchayats are divided into a minimum of 10 wards, and if the population of the village is more than 1,000, the number of wards can be more than 10 but should not exceed 20. Every Gram Panchayat consists of elected Panches from the wards, an elected Sarpanch and Upsarpanch. The seats to be filled by direct election in every Gram Panchayat are reserved for SCs and STs in proportion to their population in the Gram Panchayat, on a rotational basis. A Gram Panchayat with 50 per cent or less of seats reserved for both SCs and STs has 25 per cent seats reserved for the Other Backward Castes (OBCs) on a rotational basis. The Sarpanch is directly elected and is the key functionary of the system. The seats of Sarpanch are reserved for SCs and STs in proportion to their population in the block. If the total population of SCs and STs in the block is less than 50 per cent, then 25 per cent of the Sarpanch seats are reserved for OBCs. Significantly, the Act reserves one-third of the total number of seats of Sarpanches within a block for women. This reservation for women is a reservation within a reservation for SC, ST and OBC seats, implying that one-third of the reserved seats will be reserved for women of these categories. The Upsarpanch is elected from the elected Panches, and if the Sarpanch is not a SC or a ST, then the Upsarpanch is elected from this category. A no-confidence motion against the Sarpanch and Upsarpanch can be passed by a resolution with a majority of not less than three-quarters of Panches present and voting, and if such a majority is more than two-thirds of the total number of Panches constituting the Gram Panchayath. A meeting of Gram Panchayath discussing a no-confidence motion is presided over by an officer of the government. Each Gram Panchayat is required to have standing committees not exceeding three, and these committees exercise powers as assigned by the Gram Panchayat. A Gram Panchayat creates a Gram Panchayat fund, and all sums received by the Panchayat are part of this fund. The fund is utilised for developmental activities of the Panchayath, or for other expenses approved by the government. The State government appoints a Secretary to a Gram Panchayat for keeping and maintaining records of the Gram Panchayat.

Structure of the Gram Sabha

The Gram Sabha consists of all people in the voter list of every village or village cluster. A Gram Sabha should meet at least four times in a year; an extraordinary meeting can be called if required by the Janpad or Zilla Panchayat Collector, or if one-third of the total members of the Gram Sabha request it in writing. The required quorum is one-tenth of the total members of the Gram Sabha. The Sarpanch or Upsarpanch presides over the meeting, and the Secretary of the Gram Panchayat convenes the meeting. Under the Gram Swaraj Act 2001, Gram Sabhas were also empowered to constitute up to five Standing Committees. However, this has now been restricted to two committees—the Development Committee (Gram Vikas Samiti) which looks after the overall development of the Panchayat, and the Construction Committee (Gram Nirman Samiti) which takes care of all the construction activities in the Panchayat. The Sarpanch chairs both the committees.

Structure of the Janpad Panchayat

The Janpad Panchayat, (313 Janpad Panchayat) the second tier of the Panchayath Raj system, is constituted at the block level, and consists of members elected from the constituencies; members co-opted from the marketing societies or cooperatives, and all members of the State Legislative Assembly representing constituencies of the block. The government divides the constituencies for the Janpad Panchayat, and each constituency has a population of not more than 5,000. The total number of constituencies should not exceed 25, and these are single-member constituencies. The reservation of seats for SCs, STs, OBCs and women is in accordance to the principle adopted for Gram Panchayat. Every Janpad Panchayat makes five Standing Committees from its members. These Committees are General Administration Committee, Agriculture Committee, Education Committee, Communication and Works Committee, and the Cooperation and Industries Committee. The Janpad Panchayath establishes a Janpad Panchayath fund similar to the Gram Panchayat fund, and the funds are utilised for developmental activity or other expenses as approved by the government. A Chief Executive Officer (CEO) appointed by the government will be responsible for keeping and maintaining the records of the Janpad Panchayat.

Structure of the Zila Panchayat

Every district has a Zila Panchayath (50 Zila Panchayath) with a term of five years, consisting of members elected from the following constituencies: Chairperson of District Cooperatives and Development Bank; all members of the Lok Sabha representing the district partially or wholly; all members of State Legislative Assembly returned from districts; and members of Rajya Sabha returned from the State whose names appears in the voter list of a Gram Panchayat within the district. The government divides the constituencies; constituency is a single member constituency and has a population of 50,000. The total number of constituencies does not exceed 35. The President and the Vice-President of the Zila Panchayat are elected for five years and the procedure of election is similar to that of the Janpad 14 Panchayat. Reservation of seats of Zila Panchayath and for the office of President and the Vice-President of Zila Panchayat is according to the principle adopted for reservation in Janpad Panchayat. The Zila Panchayat controls and supervises the administration of the District Rural Development Agency (DRDA), and all functions and schemes assigned to DRDA by the State government should be implemented under the supervision of the Zila Panchayaths.

Structure and constitution of panchayath in MP

Level of panchayat	*No. of panchayat*	*Name for Chairpersons / Deputy Chairpersons*
Gram Panchayath	23,012	Sarpanch and Up-Sarpanch
Janpad Panchayat	313	Adhyaksh and Up-adhyaksh
Zila Panchayat	50	Adhyaksh and Up-adhyaksh

Source: Ministery of Panchayathi Raj, Government of India, 2012.

Functions of Panchayat

The meetings of Panchayaths called by the Sarpanch or the President should be held every month, failing which the Secretary or the Chief Executive Officer (CEO) issues notice of the meeting 25 days after the last held Panchayat meeting. The quorum of the Panchayat meeting is half the members constituting the Panchayath. If the quorum is not complete, then the competent authority postpones the meeting, and for such postponed meeting, a quorum is not required but no new subjects can be brought for consideration. A notice of the meeting is pasted at the Panchayat office. The Secretary and the CEOs of the Janpad and Zila Panchayat place a report about the income and expenditure of the Panchayat before the Panchayath respectively.

The Madhya Pradesh Panchayati Raj Act, 1993, provides for a separate and independent audit organisation, i.e. the State Finance Commission, under the control of the State government, to look after the audit of accounts of Panchayats, The State Election Commission supervises, directs and controls the preparations of electoral rolls and conducts all elections to Panchayats.

The State government may vest in the Panchayaths any property vested with the State government. It may assign to a Panchayath such taxes, tolls, fees levied and collected by the State government, and may make grant-in-aid from the consolidated fund of the State for such purposes and subject to such conditions and limits as the State government may deem fit. The State government shall make grant-in-aid to the Panchayats as may be decided on the recommendations of the State Finance Commission. The State government is empowered to make rules to regulate the imposition, assessment, collection and sharing of taxes for Panchayats. It can also dissolve Panchayaths for default or abuse of power. A dissolved Panchayat is to be reconstituted within six months in accordance with the provisions of the Act. The State government also regulates the relations between Panchayaths and other local authorities in matters in which they are jointly interested. The State government makes the rules for implementing various provisions of this Act. It may, from time to time, make model bylaws for the guidance of Panchayats. The Act and the

Panchayath system in Madhya Pradesh have not remained static but evolved in the last five years. A dynamic and adaptive Panchayat system has ensured the success of Panchayati Raj institutions in the State. This adaptiveness is reflected in the various Amendments made to the Panchayati Raj Act, 1993, and the ever-evolving office orders issued to operationalise and institutionalise the Panchayath system. For a comprehensive status report of the Panchayat system in Madhya Pradesh, it is essential to understand the operational status of the Panchayat institutions and the evolutionary processes and measures undertaken in the Panchayat arena. It is also imperative to understand the environmental factors, their implications and contribution to the success of Panchayati Raj in Madhya Pradesh.

Amendments to the Madhya Pradesh Panchayati Raj Act, 1993

The Amendments have given much-needed elasticity to the system and have contributed to the success of the Panchayati Raj system in Madhya Pradesh as institutions of grassroots democracy. A dynamic system where information flows upward from the bottom, and a system that responds and adjusts to these stimuli, is a truly democratic and representative system. This Amendment clearly reflects the government's desire to institutionalise and empower the system. The Amendments deal with teething problems of the system via the Amendments, the State government has tried to overcome limitations that had cropped up during implementation of the Act. In accordance with the provisions of the Constitutional Amendment Act, 1992, the Madhya Pradesh Government was the first in the country which enacted the Madhya Pradesh Panchayat Raj Adhiniyam in 1993, "with the objective of consolidating and amending the law relating to the establishment of panchayaths for ensuring effective involvement of panchayaths in local administration and developmental activities." The Act has been amended several times to overcome difficulties faced in its implementation and also for making improvements in the light of experience gained.

For example, it was realised that women did not attend the Gram Sabha despite it being a crucial forum for public debate and decision-making on village and Panchayat isues. The lack of women's participation in Gram Sabha despite reservation for women in elected positions of Panchayats was viewed detrimental to the objectives of Panchayati Raj. Madhya Pradesh government amended Article 6 of the State Panchayat Act to make it mandatory to have one-third of the quorum as women members. Another interesting example is the Amendment of the Act, which barred any Member of Parliament (MP) or Member of the Legislative Assembly (MLA) who represents a completely urban constituency from being a member of the District or Block Panchayat. This was clearly done to protect the interests of rural areas in relation to urban areas. The aim, in addition to strengthening the Panchayath is also to articulate and define the functional space of these institutions. A constant endeavour is to define the function of these institutions and devolve more administrative and financial powers to the Panchayaths simultaneously; the Amendments try to guarantee socio-economic change in favour of the marginalised, as envisaged in the 73rd Constitutional Amendment. The State government, through the Amendments, has tried to operationalise the Panchayats consistent with an ideology of 'power to people' and democratic decentralisation.

Gram Swaraj: New System and its Implications

The State government continuously devolved powers and authority to the Panchayati raj institutions and initiated innovative measures to empower, strengthen and institutionalise the Panchayati Raj institutions. Unfortunately, the distortions of the existing political systems at the State and Union levels were replicated at the Panchayath level and a new class of elite and power centres led by the Sarpanches emerged within the Panchayathi Raj system undermining the spirit of democratic decentralisation. The state government recognised the growing distortions in the Panchayath system and they were reflected in the open criticism of the existing Panchayat system by the former Chief Minister, Digvijay Singh, who once said that 'the Panchayati Raj has degenerated into Sarpanch Raj'. A comprehensive process of evaluation and assessment was initiated by the state government to address the deformity in the Panchayat system and to look for possible solutions. The new system of Gram Swaraj is a result of this process.

On 21st January 2001, Madhya Pradesh government amended the Madhya Pradesh Panchayath Raj Adhiniyam (Act), 1993, to rename it as the Madhya Pradesh Panchayat Raj (Sanshodhan). The addition of words 'Gram Swaraj' in the citation of the amended Act notifies a significant paradigmatic shift in the fundamental principles of governance in Madhya Pradesh. In fact, the new system of governance Gram Swaraj, enacted by the Madhya Pradesh Panchayath Raj (Sanshodhan) Adhiniyam 2001 and operationalised from 26th January 2001, is the most significant change and experiment in the system of governance since the adoption of representative parliamentary democracy in India. The operationalisation of Gram Swaraj in Madhya Pradesh will herald the beginning of a new system of governance based on 'direct democracy' instead of indirect representative parliamentary democracy. The experience and operationalisation of Gram Swaraj will also have serious implications for discourses on governance, democracy and modernity. Gram Swaraj is a new system of local self-governance at the village level, which moves from indirect to direct democracy. It is based on the premise that in a village people can assemble and sit collectively. Therefore, representatives to represent the views, aspirations, needs and interests of the people are not required. The new system intends to give power to the people and not to their representatives. To operationalise this system in the field, it has been decided that Gram Sabhas shall be strengthened, which under the new structure will exercise all the powers of Gram Panchayats and many more powers will also be devolved to Gram Sabhas.

Panchayat Raj Avam Gram Swaraj Act clearly states that "the powers, functions and duties of the committee shall be such as may be entrusted to it by the Gram Sabha from time to time. Every committee shall be responsible and accountable to the Gram Sabha and shall work under its control and supervision." The framers of Gram Swaraj are completely aware and conscious of the hierarchical social order and inequitable power relations in the village; therefore to protect Gram Swaraj from becoming a fiefdom of the privileged few, certain provisions have been inserted as safeguards to protect the interests of the larger community in general and deprived categories in particular. Firstly, the quorum of a Gram Sabha should not be less than one-fifth of the total number of members of the Gram Sabha. Importantly, of these, not less than one-third should be women, and the SCs and STs shall be represented in proportion to their population in the Gram Sabha.

This clearly indicates that a generic quota for the deprived, which can be short-circuited, has been discarded and a more stringent safeguard to ensure the participation of deprived communities has been built in. Second, according to the new Act, the Gram Sabha is not empowered to take decisions in any circumstance if the meeting lacks quorum. It is essential and obligatory to fulfil the quorum requirement before proceeding with the process of decision-making.Thirdly, it is hoped that Gram Sabha will take most of the decisions unanimously, however in cases of difference of opinion, the matter should be decided only through a secret vote. The operative word in this provision is 'secret' to provide space to the marginalised voice. Fourthly, the representation of women and marginalised communities in the standing and ad-hoc committees is ensured by reserving a minimum number of seats for them in these committees. Finally, considering the oppressive village reality, a provision of appeal to a three-member committee constituting Division Officer, Janpad Panchayat Adhayaksh and a member of Janpad Panchayat of that area against the Gram Sabha decision is also present. This provision was incorporated in the Panchayat Avam Gram Swaraj Act to safeguard the rights and interests of deprived and marginalised groups. Another progressive innovation of the new Gram Swaraj system is to organise separate Gram Sabhas for each village. In Madhya Pradesh, a Gram Panchayat is often constituted of more than one village. To do justice to each village and to make the system of Gram Swaraj effective it was imperative to recognise the Gram Sabha of each village as independent. However, to resolve issues affecting the whole Gram Panchayat a provision of joint Gram Sabha has also been inserted. The Sarpanch of the Gram Panchayat will chair the Gram Sabha meetings and every committee formed by the Gram Sabha (standing and ad-hoc) will have a Gram Panchayat member, although it would be required that the Panch is a stakeholder of the work assigned to the committee. ThePanchayat Secretary will function as Secretary of the Gram Sabha. In the new system the funds will be given to Gram Panchayat and then the funds will automatically flow to Gram Sabhas.

Gram Swaraj has emerged from an extensive process of deliberation, refinement and dialogue. It is also a result of the grassroots experiences of Panchayati Raj functioning coupled with Madhya Pradesh government's stated commitment to democratic decentralisation. The Gandhian ideological framework (although not in its entirety) inspired the basic structure and body of this new system of self-governance.

Challenges of Panchayati Raj System in Madhya Pradesh

The decentralisation of power to the people through the 73rd Amendment created a significant shift within institutions and existing power relationships. The newly elected Panchayat representative's in all three tiers have a mandate to participate in the development process of their constituencies. This has implications for the functioning of development administration, especially for functionaries at the lower level and the established political leadership – representatives from the Parliament and the Assembly – to provide space to Panchayati Raj institutions in earnest spirit. The emergence of Panchayats has also put pressure on voluntary organisations to define a new set of relationships to work with the community, which is truly represented in the Gram Sabha.

Intra-institutional Power Dynamics

In the new Panchayat system, it is interesting to note that the three different tiers have an evolving intra-institutional relationship. These tiers have representatives from different backgrounds with different roles and functions. The Panchayat system does not have a model of functioning; therefore, relationships and functional processes are evolving with experience on a daily basis. Unfortunately, due to a lack of orientation and capacity building, conflict emerges, largely due to structural problems such as concentration of powers in the Sarpanch and lacks of significant powers in the upper two tiers. On the basis of field experience, it emerges that intra-institutional linkages, although well defined, are not being practised at the ground level and need serious attention.

The Community Feedback

With the exception of a few places, the community largely felt discontent about the efficiency and effectiveness of the bureaucracy and the Panchayat Secretary. It felt that the bureaucracy is neither supportive nor sympathetic. Most villagers felt that block level officials visit villages only to organise and conduct Gram Sabhas. The Below Poverty Line (BPL) list is considered bogus by people as they find the actual poor excluded from it. In many places, the community also complained about the Sarpanch and other Panchayat members. According to several villagers, the Sarpanch acts only in the interest of his supporters and not in the interest of the village. Often, there is factionalism in the village and unfortunately the Panchayat Secretary and the bureaucracy support one or the other group, leading to considerable tension and very little development in the village.

Attitudinal problems in the bureaucracy and Panchayat functionaries is one of the root causes of conflicts, especially while preparing the beneficiary list, identifying construction activity or its monitoring and evaluation. The caste and gender of the Sarpanch dictate the willingness of the bureaucracy to interact with him/her. The bureaucracy has used information as a fulcrum for power and shared it very selectively to suit their own purposes. People view bureaucracy as a 'necessary evil'. Moreover, bribery seems to be a universal feature, while corruption in the bureaucracy or among Panchayath members has the potential to de-legitimise the system.

The bureaucracy uses its control over resources as a method of controlling Panchayaths. The capacity of Panchayat functionaries, as well as the bureaucracy, needs to be enhanced to understand the intricacies and technicalities of a local government system. The village representatives are from the grassroots and are unable to understand the legal and administrative processes, especially when it is compounded by bureaucratic apathy. Thus, there is a need to simplify the processes and make decision-making and follow-up less cumbersome. The Panchayath bureaucracy relationship seems to be governed by the need to sanction funds rather than by a desire to strengthen the PRIs. There is confusion at all three tiers regarding intra-institutional dynamics and attempts by the upper two tiers to transgress clearly defined functional boundaries. A system of local self-governance will not be effective if people at the grassroots level feel it is not responsive to local reality. Moreover, excessive dependence on government agenda by Panchayat representatives, rather than developing an agenda based on local needs, will prevent Panchayaths from evolving as autonomous units. Gaps between the actual amounts of resources allotted to Gram Panchayaths and the aspirations of villagers place officials in a difficult position. A widespread feeling of discontent prevails in the community. The community knows that the government is making a sincere effort to activate Panchayaths but it also recognises internal impediments posed by a skeptical bureaucracy. The community has started distinguishing between the will of Government and that of the bureaucracy. This is an unhealthy trend and the bureaucracy should commit itself to implementing the broader agenda of the government. Several problem areas remain, such as corruption, lack of willingness to delegate powers to Panchayats, respect for the authority of Panchayaths etc., and therefore strategic intervention for strengthening and institutionalising the Panchayat system is required.

The 73rd Constitutional Amendment is a landmark since its objective is to empower women by creating space for them (with a 33 per cent reservation of seats). The significance of this can be gauged from the fact that the number of women in politics at the grass root level is now higher than in the past. However, as these Acts operate in a highly complex and entrenched patriarchal/hierarchical socio-economic fabric, women are interwoven in it. This creates, in its wake, contradictory trends and gaps between the potential and actual realisation of women's empowerment. Now 50 per cent seats are reserved for women but women have faced several challenges to perform their functions. The process of socialisation clearly demarcates spaces: private for a female, public for a male. Thus, when women cross over their traditionally assigned private space and take on leadership roles in the public realm, hostile attitudes take various forms. The widespread view in the community was that women are neither capable nor interested in attending Gram Sabha and Panchayath meetings. Moreover, women were portrayed as submissive. They are not meant to be active and outspoken, particularly in the presence of men and elders. Though the Panchayathi Raj institutions are based on democratic values and equality, any attempt by a woman to go against male dominance results in usurping of their power.

Conclusion

Democratic decentralisation is often founded upon the notion that the democratisation and empowerment of local political bodies will create institutions that are more accountable to local citizens and more appropriate to local needs and preferences. The experiences of the Panchayat system across India have been varied, depending on several factors including political will, nature of bureaucracy and prevalent socio-economic conditions in the region. However, one could find divergent peculiarities and indigenous situations in each and every context of the region. The picture is not distinct in the case of Madhya Pradesh.

The strong political will and government support to the Panchayat system can be clearly seen in the framing of progressive Acts, and continuous delegation and devolution of powers, authority and roles to Panchayat institutions. Despite these efforts and initiatives in Madhya Pradesh, the Panchayat system continues to be plagued by immense difficulties and faces stiff resistance from several quarters.

On the one hand, there is very progressive legislation, policies and guidelines for the Panchayats backed by strong political will. On the other hand the ground reality clearly indicates weak and ineffective implementation of the Panchayat system, leading to little progress. First is resistance and non-cooperation from the bureaucracy and the existing institutions of governance, evident inadequate financial devolution, the framing of rules contradicting the spirit of Panchayats, and red tapism and corruption. In effect it indicates that the state and the ruling classes are still not ready to devolve powers and authority to another level of governance due to diverse vested interests developed over time and therefore they use multiple strategies and mechanisms to stall the process of democratic decentralisation. The second set of factors are resistance from the political class, and the socio-economic and political élites of rural Madhya Pradesh, which view Panchayats as a serious threat to their interests and hegemony. These classes in alliance with the bureaucracy and the political class are working to make the Panchayat system ineffective. For example, these could be representing the patriarchal forces or the feudal caste forces disturbed by the election of women and dalits to position of dominance. Finally, the third set of factors are lack of capacities at grassroots, lack of information among common people about Panchayati Raj and lack of political education among the ordinary people whose political role is critical for effective Panchayat functioning.

The cases of empowerment of women, dalits, collective community decision-making, altering the development priorities in favour of the people's needs and aspirations are all very significant examples and raise hopes for the Panchayat system, despite its shortcomings. These achievements in the context of a state largely constructed on a colonial model and unequal non-democratic social and political order are extremely significant. As proactive participants in the process of democratic decentralisation it becomes critically important to highlight these successes. In tune with this perspective, a large number of civil society actors have identified the problems and successes of Panchayats and are working to consolidate the gains from the Panchayat system for people-centric development and effective democratic self-governance.

Madhya Pradesh government has been extremely receptive to ground realities about the inadequacies of the Panchayat system and has continuously striven to devise strategies for making Panchayats effective institutions of local self-governance. The establishment of Gram Swaraj is a testimony to this spirit of innovativeness and sincerity to the process of democratic decentralisation. This new system has attempted to address several of the shortcomings of the previous system of local self-governance and has the potential to facilitate the achievement of the primary objectives of economic growth, people-centric development and social justice.The state of Madhya Pradesh is yet to carry forward its strive for achieving a better democratic social order for realising the full potentials of democratic decentralisation and participatory democracy.

Notes and References

Rohit Mullick and Neelam Raj, 9 September 2007, "Panchyath system in to Kangaroo courts": *The Times of India.*

India 2007, p. 696, Publications, Divisions, Ministry of Information and Broadcasting, Government of India.

Panchayath.nic.in

Datta, Prabhat Kumar (1996): 'Rural Development through Panchayats: The West Bengal Experiences', *Kurukshetra*, 44(7): 65, April.

Datta, Prabhat (1995): 'Village self-government in Post-colonial India', *Kurukshetra*, 43(7): 52, April.

Dwivedi, R. S. (2000) : *Madhya Pradesh Panchayat Raj Adhiniyam.* Bhopal: Suvidha Law House.Government of Madhya Pradesh (1996) Gramin Vikas Ka Mahatvapurna Aadeshon Aur Nirideshon.

Ka Samakalan, 1 (1994–1996): Government of Madhya Pradesh Panchayat Avam Gramin Vika Bhopal: Government Press.

Datta, Prabhat (1995): 'Village Self-government in Post-colonial India', *Kurukshetra*, 43(7): 52, April.

Government of Madhya Pradesh (1996): Gramin Vikas Ke Mahatvapurna Aadeshon Aur Nirdeshon.

Capacity Assessment and Capacity Development Strategy Report for Strengthening Panchayathi Raj Institutions in Madhya Pradesh : http//www.pri-resources.in

Institute of Social Studies (1997): ISS Manuscript Report–II, Panchayati Raj Training in MP – An Evaluation. New Delhi: Concept Book Publishers.

Evolution of local self government: http//www.mp.gov.in /finance Institute of Social Studies (1995): *Status of Panchayati Raj in the States of India 1994*. New Delhi:Concept Book Publishers.

Kabeer, N. (1994): *Reversed Realities: Gender Hierarchies in Development Thought*. Verso, London.

Evolution of local self government: http//www.mp.gov.in /finance

Amitabh Behar and Yogesh Kumar: Decentralisation in Madhya Pradesh India from Panchyathi raj to grama swaraj (1995-20001) http/www.odi.org/UK/sites/odi.org.UK/files/odi-asset

Kurian, G. (1998): Empowering Conditions in the Decentralisation Process. Centre for Policy Research and Advocacy, Bhubaneshwar.

Maheshwari, S. R. (1994): *Local Government in India,* Laksmi Narain Agarwal, Agra.

Amitabh Behar andYogesh Kumar, Decentralisation in Madhya Pradesh India from Panchyathi raj to grama swaraj (1995-20001) http/www.odi.org/UK/sites/odi.org.UK/files/odi-asset.

Kaushik, S. (1995): Panchayati Raj in Action: Challenge to Women's Role, Friedrich Ebert Stiftung, New Delhi.

17

Negotiating the Politics of Presence: Gendered Citizenship and Rural Local Governance in Maharashtra

—*Manjula Bharathy*

Decentralised governance has recently been accorded a central place in the discourse on development. Theoretically, the normative appeal of arguments for local democracy has resided in the belief that the quality of political participation and therefore of public life itself will be substantially transformed only when people gather to debate and deliberate on issues of common concern collectively, and are provided with decision-making powers to give effect to their shared concerns (Niraja Jayal, 2006). While discussing on the subject of Local Governance, Mohanty (2007) discusses two divergent perspectives: one sees it as an arena for transforming an unequal local society into a democratic community; while the other treats it as an agency or the channel to implement centrally formulated policies and programmes.

The Panchayati Raj Institutions (PRIs) in India, with 537 district Panchayats, 6097 intermediate Panchayats and 2, 34, 676 village Panchayats form one of the largest constitutionally elected local governance institutions in the world. One of the most vexing contradictions of the Indian scenario of Panchayti Raj Institutions is the continual lip service provided to it right through the colonial rule and then in the five decades following independence as self-reliant republics. The aim for decentralisation in India was the normative-political project of greater inclusion and the representation of historically disadvantaged or marginalised groups. Gopal Guru (2009) argues that 'Dalits in India are exiled citizens,' and the purity-pollution logic has extended into the formal public sphere. Similarly, women, despite their presence and intervention in the public sphere, are confined largely to the private sphere, or at best to its margins.

The privileges of a citizen are restricted to those who are bestowed with the status of being 'full members of community' (Yuval-Davis, 1997). Once we recognise that citizenship is beyond 'given' privileges of equality, (because in fact, communities are not equal), we also need to recognise that there is a dynamic nature in the formation of citizenship. With the evolving notion of community, the individual goes through a process of acquiring citizenship. In reformulating the question of democratic citizenship, it is interesting to look at Murdock's definition of democratic citizenship, in which he defines the 'fundamental prerogative of citizenship as the right to participate fully in social life with dignity and without fear, and to help formulate the forms it might take in the future' (Murdock, 1999). The notion of the 'full participation' is co-terminus with that of 'adequate citizens'.

To use Anupama Roy's (2005) terminology, women have been, both in historical and the present-day contexts, 'inadequate citizens'. It is necessary to emphasise here that one is not bringing in the 'blaming the victim' concept to account for the woman herself as the reason for her inadequacy, and this again does not imply that the onus to come out of this inadequacy needs to be on the woman herself. The inadequacies in the status of a woman's citizenship arise because of the structural aspects of the social relations, she engages in her lifetime as an individual, and over generations within contexts of caste, class, race and nationality.

The questions that we face in the socio-economic context of inequality where we are located are at various levels: Who are the citizens? Who is excluded from being a citizen? What are the various levels or tiers of this exclusion? What sort of process does an individual go through in the course of becoming a citizen? How does the perception of herself change in the course of her becoming a citizen? Is the process of becoming a citizen a democratizing process? This paper tries to understand the idea of gendered citizenship - as how these women travel from being 'inadequate citizens' to (if at all) achievable 'citizens' with the deepening of democracy in the context of rural local governance in Maharashtra. The analysis is based on a research study to understand the process of engendering governance at ten panchayats in Maharashtra covering three geographic zones of the state - Western Mahrashtra, Konkan, Vidarbha, which are obviously diverse in its socio-cultural and political power relations.

Gendered Governance

Five decades of developmental plans, initiatives and programmes had not produced significant impact on the gender empowerment of women in India. Women, who comprise half the population, in general, still remain marginalised and invisible in the socio-political and economic spheres of life. When exclusion takes place on the basis of historically deprived and socially ascribed identities like women, inclusion becomes complex, ambiguous and challenging. In many instances inclusion simply comes to mean seeking legitimacy, both from the state and from society. However, seeking legitimacy is only a preliminary effort to level the playing field for the larger struggle for inclusion. The critical issue is how to compete as equals or to carve out a course of action in a game, which is essentially between the powerful and the powerless, especially in a patriarchal society.

It is in this context that the notion of gendered citizenship acquires importance. Gendered citizenship requires citizenship to be conceptualised by taking into account the experiences of those whose inclusion remains problematic. This is crucial because gendered citizenship is not merely an extended conceptualisation of citizenship; it also strives to turn citizenship into a set of practices. It thus becomes imperative to look at citizenship from the vantage point of marginalised collectives, so that their experiences of exclusion can help guide their action for inclusion. In other words, gendered citizenship comes to privilege citizenship from actors' point of view.

The 73rd amendment brought in women into the 'public' space of local governance in large numbers. The use of quotas and reservations to bring in women in large numbers into the political institutions is based on the understanding that a few women, no matter how strong they might be, cannot engender a system, and that equal or roughly equal participation is needed to ensure that both men's and women's voices are heard. The criterion of numbers has thus been largely met for these institutions. (Sudarshan, 2008). More than fifteen years after this inclusion, a historical and analytical understanding of the gendered governance and its significance in altering the hegemonised gender equations in the socio-cultural and political web of the state becomes relevant. It is against this macro context of complexities prevalent in the gender relations that one needs to understand the engendering process at rural local governance in Maharashtra.

The Social Reform Movement in Maharashtra

In the nineteenth century western education had an impact on the elite of Mumbai and Pune. This gave a great impetus to the social reform movement. Reformists tried to examine their social system and religious beliefs with a critical eye and gave priority to social changes over political freedom. In their reform efforts, they had to contend with stiff opposition from the conservatives.

Foremost among the reformers were Balshastri Jambhekar (1812-1846), who condemned Sati and female infanticide; Gopal Hari Deshmukh (1823-1892) who, through his *Shatpatre* attacked orthodox Brahmins who opposed social and religious reforms; and Jyotirao Govindrao Phule (1827-1890) who revolted against an unjust caste system and upheld the cause of untouchables and that of education for women of lower castes.

Ramakrishna Gopal Bhandarkar (1837-1925) and Justice Ranade (1842-1901) were the pioneers of Prarthana Samaj, an organisation for general, social and religious reform. Gopal Ganesh Agarkar (1856-1895) prioritised social reform, while Dhondo Keshav Karve (1858-1962) devoted his life to the cause of women's education. Behramji Malbari (1853-1912), a Parsi from Bombay, started Seva Sadan for the care of women of all castes.

Vithal Ramaji Shinde (1873-1944) fought for the eradication of untouchability through his Depressed Classes Mission, while Chhatrapati Shahu Maharaj of Kolhapur (1874-1922) defied the caste system, championed the cause of the untouchables and promoted education in his state. Karmaveer Bhaurau Paigonda Patil (1887-1959) was the architect of the Rayat Shikshan Sanstha. Dr Bhimrao Ramji Ambedkar (1891-1956), the chief architect of the Indian Constitution, created social and political awareness among the Scheduled Castes of India.

The social reform measures brought about a renaissance and social-awakening in Maharashtra. Women reformers too emerged in this period - Savitribai Phule (1831-1897), Pandita Ramabai (1858-1922), Kashibai Kanitkar (1861-1948), Ramabai Ranade (1862-1924), Rakhmabai (1864-1955), Dr Anandibai Joshee (1865-1887), Anandibai (Baya) Karve (1866-1950), Yashodabai Joshi (1868-1948), Lakshmibai Tilak (1868-1936), Tarabai Shinde and Parvatibai Athavale (1870-1955) - to mention a few. They shed centuries of traditions and patriarchal hegemony to cross what Meera Kosambi calls 'multiple thresholds' in order to be educated, and later, to work in the public sphere. Writers, a doctor, teachers and reformers - these women covered a wide spectrum of roles with the vocations they chose for themselves. Their entry into the public space and the public gaze broke many social taboos and challenged the patriarchal structure of contemporary upper caste Hindu society. They attracted censure, ridicule, public scorn, and also - as in the case of Savitribai Phule - verbal and physical abuse. The much debated reservation for women at legislative institutions has to be seen from the historicity of these struggles and resistances by both men and women for enhancing the status of women in the society.

Contexualising Engendering Local Governance : Quotas for Women: Arguments For and Against

Women's reservation is an issue that has since the earliest days of its conceptualisation excited deeply divided opinion, as much on grounds of ethics as around form. Therefore, before we venture to explore how our own findings in Maharashtra intervene with these concerns, and what they may have to suggest to gender and governance theory, it would be useful to briefly map out significant themes/ theoretical perspectives that have emerged over the years in the sphere.

As early as 1931, Sarojini Naidu and Muthulakshmi Reddi in a letter to the British prime minister refused 'preferential treatment', stating (in an accompanying declaration), "we look upon nominations, reservation of seats, and the co-option in any sphere of activity as a pernicious and humiliating system which must run counter to any real progress" (cited in Dhanda, 2008). In more recent times, Vina Mazumdar, member secretary of the Committee on the Status of Women in India (CSWI) admitted that as 'daughters of independence' her generation had been skeptical of special representation but gradually 'found our understanding of nation-building changing radically' (Mazumdar, 1997).

But if those such as Mazumdar have come to acknowledge abstract citizenship as cover for privilege, there are feminist stalwarts such as Madhu Kishwar who continue to vigorously oppose quotas for women, as measures that would feed into existing faulty structures of governance instead of reinventing them. Rai (cited in Dhanda, 2008) while sharing Kishwar's skepticism on the use of gender quotas as envisaged in its current form, suggests that the frame of discourse around affirmative action would benefit from a shift from the language of 'power' to that of 'empowerment'. With its emphasis on 'power to' rather than 'power over', empowerment rephrases access to power as enabling, as competence rather than dominance. As it is in its current form however, political representation would be (to quote Fraser) a strategy of recognition rather than redistribution, restricting its transformative potential. The group as basis of representation however is ridden with its own set of questions, by no means amenable to easy resolution. Menon (2000) cautions for instance that if identities emerge in and through political mobilisation, we then need to guard against the possibility that these identities may themselves freeze into new formations of power, blocking the emergence of new identities and new alignments. To quote Habermas - cautioning against the possibility of collective rights 'overtaxing' the theory of rights tailored to individual persons - group rights could represent a kind of preservation of species by administrative means. "To guarantee survival would necessarily rob the members of the very freedom to say yes or no if they are to appropriate and preserve their cultural heritage (Habermas, 1994: 130)."

Any attempt to summarise arguments for and against reservations would be quite incomplete without touching upon the theoretical contribution of Anne Phillips, whose work on the subject has been reflected, debated or contested in almost every paper on the subject subsequently (including most of those quoted here).

Phillips has a fairly straightforward case. There are particular needs, interests, and concerns that arise from women's experience and this will be inadequately addressed in a politics that is dominated by men. While they may find a few powerful allies among the men, they cannot really expect, as she puts it, 'the degree of vigorous advocacy that people bring to their own concerns' (Phillips, 1995). This takes on particular pertinence when a history of political exclusion has made it hard even to articulate group concerns. In such contexts there is little to turn to other than the people who carry the interests, and who does the representation then comes to be of equal significance with what political parties they represent. Phillips terms this a shift from a politics of ideas to a politics of presence. The politics of ideas suggests 'a broadly secular understanding of politics as a matter of judgement and debate, and expects political loyalties to develop around policies rather than people'. A politics of presence on the other hand, privileges the question of 'who' rather than 'what' and demands equal representation of women, ethnic minorities, and other groups that see themselves as excluded (Phillips, 1995).

The politics of presence has found its predictable criticisms. Louise Vincent (2004) for instance paints a cynical picture of the real use of quotas based on the experience of South Africa. The improved presence of women in South Africa's national legislature due to the African National Congress's quota has, she says, done little more than advance the careers of a select group of already well-educated, politically highly well-connected women. In the prevalence of a culture of tight party controls, 'simply having members of marginalised groups present when unjust decisions are taken serves to legitimise these decisions because legitimacy is thought to rest not on what is decided, but on who was present when it was decided' (Vincent, 2004: 84).

Philips acknowledges the possibility of failure to know particular women's interests (perhaps even more likely in India where a single constituency may be sharply divided along caste-class-ethnic lines), as even the as likely (conscious and unconscious) conflict(s) of similar (class, ethnic, linguistic or other) identities between elected women representatives and their (female) electorate. She also acknowledges, if cursorily, the possibility of (all too real, or perhaps more visible in South Asia) issues of failure of accountability as arising out of conscious dereliction of commitment, or corruption. There is indeed some evidence that women, once elected, may in fact be more attuned to the so to say, universal interests of women such as childcare or labour relations (Philips, 1995). Nevertheless in the absence of enough empirical data on what kind of factors actually inspire/ drive women to stand for election to such councils, and once in positions of power what would in fact motivate them to stick it out, even try for subsequent terms in office, would it be anything short of conjecture to surmise women as likely to per se make more ethical or committed legislators?

Phillips answer is a pragmatic yes, but unlikely. The case for gender parity among our political representatives as she sees operates in 'a framework of probabilities rather than certainties... Changing the gender composition of elected assemblies is largely an enabling condition (a crucially important one, considering what is *disabled* at present) but it cannot present itself as a guarantee'. Having asserted the need for representational governance is not enough in itself. One also needs to understand the role of the representative in representing her community. The role of representatives in governance is of great significance because they don't just bring forth issues. More importantly, they engage in the politics around the issues. Representatives are not only expected to articulate issues of local concern, but are part of the formation of a political discourse. Thus, representatives play an important role in determining the very *nature* of governance in a structure. In a governance system that is dominated by upper class and upper caste men, issues of mass concern will be interpreted through a hegemonic lens. The resulting political structure will, accordingly, be highly unequal. It is obvious that the discourse of equality in conditions of inequality only results in deepening inequality. Most of history is a thing of the past invisible to us, as written history is that of the privileged. Reservation is argued for as positive discrimination for historical correctives seeking to subvert regressive structures.

Nevertheless with or without 'guarantee of good intent', as Phillips puts it, discourse on quotas for women at least in India, is no longer really grappling today as much is the question of its desirability. The terrain of debates - both academic and political - is quite clearly now around its possible form and details, and its likely ramifications for women as well as for governance in general. In the post-1990s context, the political and socio-economic scenario of the country has undergone much change, with a transition of the nation-state that was taken for granted in the post-independence era. Lower caste, minority and gender politics have moved substantially from existing patterns with a rise of various contradictions. Feminist voices have emerged, not in academic spaces, but also in the day-to-day lives and politics of citizens. Women's movements have reflected the unfolding nature of the citizenship. The conceptualisation of reservation has emerged now in changing contexts - that of the post-Mandal agitation on reservations for OBCs, emergence of caste parties like the Samajwadi Party (SP) and the Bahujan Samajwadi Party (BSP), widespread emergence of Naxal ideology, the demolition of the Babri Masjid and the communal violence that followed in its wake.

The women's issue had never been exclusive of the concerns of caste and religion, and in this era, the overlaps were even more obvious. Thus, a monolithic understanding of the term *patriarchy* is no longer viable, and the need of the hour is to understand the *diverse* patriarchal forces that come into play in making the representation of women unequal. Mary John asserts the need for 'a complex articulation of *unequal patriarchies*' (Mary E John, in *Dhanda* (ed.), 2008, p. 54, italics original).

The argument against reservation is in that women representatives elected through reservation could end up only as token representatives who are actually represented by their husbands. The question of proxy governance is a serious issue and has also been observed in the course of this study. This has to be seen in the context of the hierarchized division of labour within the family and the lack of women's access to education or control over resources. However, the argument that we want to stress on is that empowerment is not a one-step event. On the contrary, it is a long process, often accompanied by violent backlash. A woman is not singularly 'empowered' when she is elected as a representative. That is just a step in facilitating the further assertion of her agency in a patriarchal system. Reservation can further act as potentially powerful tools of redistribution, not only of economic resources but also of political spaces that have traditionally been dominated by upper class, upper caste men in patriarchal governance systems.

There are certain core themes that emerge recurrently in the otherwise diverse narratives of elected women representatives spoken to in Maharashtra. Predominant among them are those of caste, local administrative corruption, alcoholism/ prohibition, domestic violence/ repression, definition/ reorganisation of 'women's work', school education, availability of and access to water, village infrastructure (toilets, roads etc). Many or in fact most of these are (gendered) concerns they already had with them in prior identities as daughters, wives, mothers, (caste) community members, citizens and so on.

This section seeks to theorise how women's inclusion into the hitherto unavailable domain of 'formal politics' intersects, and often intervenes with their existing alternate identities and concerns. How do these women in new found locations of power in the public sphere negotiate with old power structures of caste, class and gender in their local contexts? How if at all does such affirmative action alter the existing structures of governance? How do women's experiences as elected women representatives relate to existing discourses on gender and governance?

Gender as Counterpublic to Caste

Caste would seem to be a powerful marker of social identity and status in most regions surveyed in Maharashtra, recurring as it is in narratives of individual respondents as well as in focus group discussions. Geeta, an elected representative of a Gram Panchayat who spoke to this study in a focus group discussion for instance recalls how she was asked to keep standing by other members as her husband was a peon in the Panchayat. Another Elected Women Representatives (EWR), Pratibha recounts how when a statue of the Dalit icon Babasaheb Ambedkar was to be erected in the *chowk* opposite her house, the proposal was refuted as people from all (upper) castes would pass by *chowk*. When the statue was being erected, 'others' threatened a repeat of the Khailranji incident. Caste also appears as the predominant concern in narratives of at least four (of a total of nine) EWR's interviewed in Maharashtra. While three of these four women (Ratnamala, Jyoti Meshram, Mayadevi Sorte) are from underprivileged castes (SC), the fourth (Anuya Kulkarni) is interestingly, upper caste. (The narrative of another respondent, Rita Sukhdev (also SC) also dwells on the subject of caste, but more in the retrospective of positive change she has seen over the last two decades.)

The strength of caste structures in these regions is perhaps evinced best from the fact that despite holding elected positions of power in local councils (at the gram panchayat/ higher level), these women were subjugated to open discrimination and humiliation. Mayadevi of Vadval Nagnath village in Latur district (elected member of Grama Panchayat since July 2000) recalls facing years of discrimination as a Dalit social/political worker in the village. For instance when she and her (upper caste) colleagues would go to people's houses to meet women (to organise Self Help Groups or SHG's) her tea cup would always be kept separately.[1]

Jyoti recounts on the other hand how in the very first Gram Panchayat meeting after being elected Sarpanch (the post was reserved for SC women) the upper caste 'opposition' passed a resolution preventing her from carrying out any financial transactions of the Panchayat. She challenged this resolution and sought justice from the Panchayat Samiti district officer and the Commissioner, and after seven months was finally awarded the right to financial transactions.[2] In the very next month after she had procured an order that the resolution was illegal and began to work, a no-trust motion was again proposed against her, accusing her of not taking the Panchayat members into confidence as well as of not undertaking the approved work. Jyoti managed to obtain a stay against it, and six months later a decision in her favour, allowing her to continue in office.

However, the hostility from her upper caste colleagues continued unabated. When seven or eight Sarpanches proposed Jyoti's name for the post of president of a Sarpanch organisation which was being revived in Gadhchiroli, some upper caste Sarpanches objected, and prevented her from becoming the president. Again, traditionally, when the festival of 'bail-pola' (worship of the bull that tills the farm) is celebrated in Kotgal, an *aarti thali* from the Sarpanch's house is brought with great revelry, marking the beginning of the festival. In the five years that Jyoti was Sarpanch, not once was the *thali* brought from her house. She was merely invited as a guest for the function. Worse, on the morning of January 26 - three months after Jyoti took over as Sarpanch and the day when for the first time a Dalit woman was to hoist the flag in the village - her husband was accosted and beaten up at daybreak at the public water pump.

Gender on the other hand shows up as much, if not more visibly in narratives of the EWR's studied as a powerful, and in many ways more insidious structure of oppression that has always divided their worlds into (more than haves and have-nots) into the 'deserving' (of voice, power, resources) and 'undeserving'.[3] Though narratives of *all* respondents of this study across caste-class - ethnic identities portray evidence of such gendered stratification, for our purposes here, let us look more closely specifically into the narratives of caste-oppressed women to understand how access to political power (via assisted entry into Panchayat Raj Institutions in Maharashtra) has played with their gender identities, and interestingly, therefore caste status.

Let's take for instance the case of Ratnamala - a Dalit, and an ordinary woman who when her mother-in-law developed a heart condition, was labelled as 'Pandharyapaychi', literally 'a woman with white feet' or a witch. But thanks to efforts by her husband's uncle (Nasik Raoji Tirpude who had been the Deputy Chief Minister of Maharashtra) Ratna stood for elections and won a (reserved category) seat in the gram panchayat. Her narration of an incident during her tenure as an EWR is significant to understanding exactly how gender when brought into play from a hitherto powerless category to a (newly) *empowered* category is capable of being effectively pitted against another powerful category of social repression such as caste.

Ratnamala recalls that when she was in hospital for some treatment, the sarpanch started repairing a sewer in her ward without the consent and signatures of all the members. This was against the rule and when she heard about it she asked him to show her the signatures and the consent of all the members of the Gram Panchayat. The sarpanch - who was of Teli caste (OBC) - told Ratnamala, 'People from my caste don't even urinate in the mouth of people from your community (SC). How have you gathered the courage to speak to me and look at me in the eye?' Angered, Ratnamala grabbed him by the collar, slapped him and then also went to the police station and filed a complaint against him for abusing her on the basis of her caste. Though the sarpanch also demanded that she be arrested, he was informed that he could be booked under the Prevention of Atrocity Act (a non-bailable offence). Predictably he withdrew his complaint and also requested Ratnamala to withdraw hers, which she did after he had apologised to her.

Let's also revisit the case of Mayadevi, the Dalit EWR who had grappled with poverty, untouchability as well as gender discrimination since her earliest years. Her parents were landless agricultural labourers. When her father married for a second time, Maya and her mother were abandoned. She recalls that she had an upper-caste friend whose house she used to visit and even eat with. Her friend's grandfather loved Maya as his own grandchild, and she was grief-stricken when he died. Yet at his funeral, as she moved ahead to pay her respects, people objected to her presence and refused to let her do so. A confident, extroverted child, she was also married off barely in her early teens early as according to her relatives, she needed to be 'tamed'. (As consequence of the taming, she became a mother when barely a child herself.) Yet today as an elected woman representative of the gram panchayat, she has been able to alter an age old purity-pollution practice in the village. Every year a religious ceremony is performed in the temple of Nagnath and people are fed *prasad*. On this occasion a common dinner is organised for all the villagers with the fund collected from the entire village. However, the Dalit families were served at the end, after everybody else was done. They were served by an upper-caste person but had to bring their own plates and glasses. By the time it was their turn to eat, it would be almost midnight. Maya Tai, who had always hated the discrimination, now (as an EWR) advised the Dalit community to boycott the *prasad* as a symbol of protest. It worked, and today the entire village participates together in all the festivals and rituals.

Finally, let us also look again at Jyoti's narrative. Despite initial resistance she could finally manage to push back opposition and non-cooperation by other (male, upper caste) members of the panchayat. Though with great difficulty (her husband was beaten up), she could also finally reach the Panchayat, and hoist the republic day flag in her village.

All is not perfect for these women, or at least not yet. Ratnamala for instance lost the next round of elections as a day before, the ex-Sarpanch distributed pamphlets that alleged that she was a prostitute and had slept with various men to get developmental work done in the village. Nevertheless her story (that of a Dalit and a woman, who slapped an upper caste man who also happened to be the Sarpanch of the village and still completed her term unharmed) and similar ones of her colleague may have some lessons for transformative possibilities.

They were women, and also Dalit, ostensibly a category of citizens doubly oppressed. Yet as evidently, an '*empowered gender*' identity in fact worked in the case of caste oppressed women as a powerful, strategically useful tool, actually capable of being pitted against (oppressive) caste 'others', and winning.[4] Political empowerment based on gender status in fact worked as quick route to bring women in circumstances as structurally constrained as theirs not just into the restricted domain of state policy and initiative, but actually gave them space and voice to emerge as effective 'subaltern counterpublics' (Fraser, 1990) in the larger public sphere (s). That they are state representatives in current context and time should not matter[5] if we see affirmative action (in this case through forums of the state) as creating (a possible set of – there may be others) core conditions that enable the emergence and development of counterpublics, and therefore discursive contestation for times to come.

Politics of Being

'He is the Subject, he is the Absolute, she is the other' wrote Simone de Beauvoir (1949, xxviii), summing up why the visibility of the self is such an important issue for women. The main thesis of *The Second Sex* revolves around the idea that woman has been held in a relationship of long-standing oppression to man through her relegation to being man's 'Other'. Women are consigned to selflessness - to invisibility, subservient passivity and self-sacrificial altruism (Burman, 1998). Most often this happens in an unconscious way as the hegemony of gender is strongly internalised by women, supporting their current status quo by providing visible roles to men, while women assume invisible roles in all spheres of life. The reservation of women at the PRIs and the politics of reservation assumes interesting dimensions in this inter-sectionality of politics of being, which is embedded in the 'phenomenology of absences' and 'politics of presence', which brings in forth an 'epistemology of presence'.

Intermeshed with the politics of reservation is the politics of identity and the divergent ways in which political agents regard their various, often contending, identities. Social beings are characterised by multiple selves and identities, and by complex relations between their selves and identities. One's self is not a coherent whole, rather it is a multilayered structure of one's own historicity - class, caste, ethnicity and gender. The politics of identity involves the manifestation of the multiple selves, and how individuals shift between selves to express group identities, and particular group identities over others. Our concern here is in understanding the process of political decision-making that women go through, having positioned various vulnerabilities within these multiple selves.

Within the multiple identities of the individual, political expressions involve giving priority to one over another. A woman who is a Dalit, rural, wage worker might have a strategic advantage of asserting one identity, often at the cost of another. Looking at the relationships conversely, within one group (say Dalit) one identity (say male) is dominant over another (namely, the female), and thus within the group identity where both the man and woman both belong, the other identity - that of gender, creates a hierarchy. There are central-peripheral relationships within a vulnerable group, and women emerge in the periphery of the periphery. There are areas where identities are collapsing, and within the converging identities, there are other identities that are diverging. The politics of reservation (on the basis of group identity) is inclusive of this politics of collapse and divergence.

To take an ideological position on the politics of identity one needs to ask the question: from where does an individual get the authenticity and legitimacy to claim/represent a particular identity? Identity politics confines the space of representation of a particular group to individuals with common historicity. What arouses the consciousness of identity in an individual? One aspect of identity is created and enhanced by the ontology of the individual, the consciousness of one's ontology and the perception of threat from other groups. In such cases, group identity becomes more overwhelming than individual identity, and one group identity is given priority over another. Such affiliations however result in violent assertion of group identity, often resulting in aggressive exclusion of others from processes and the complete negation of anyone else entering the group. Does just the ontology of being in a particular group give one the authenticity to represent that group? There is also the need to critically approach this question as we discuss the politics of reservation.

The process of becoming citizens results in many changing and conflicting identities. Each changed identity is a rupture from the existing identity and these ruptures are often very violent indeed. The ruptures in these women's lives in these multiple roles are in contradiction, and the process of various contradictions coming together dialectically brings about continuity in the process of struggle. These struggles are important events in the women's lives and they change the perspective of the women's beings and citizenship. In many cases, the problems within their private lives become the trajectory of their struggle.

The story of Dhakuli Gundu Naik, better known as Dhakuli Maushi, an Adivasi (Naik) woman from Halkarni Village in Kolhapur district elucidates this. The process of politicisation for Dhakuli Maushi happened as a reaction to alcohol abuse within her family. Dhakuli Maushi's struggle began as one against the menace of alcoholism in her village. Her long struggle started off from the personal level and moved on to become a political one. Her struggle was seen as a micro-movement, wherein she mobilised the collective consciousness of women. This demands its merit and significance at the level of the local politics of the village. The caste and gender equations of Dhakuli Maushi's village have changed considerably from the time when she started her struggle. Women's mobility has increased considerably and they are a lot more politically aware and conscious. Now more women participate in the Grama Sabha and other committees.

At this juncture we return to the question of empowerment of women through reservation. One of the enduring contributions of women's activism and feminist theorising is the challenging of the definitive political boundaries between public and private politics. Feminists argued that public political life was built on the absence of women from it, that the exclusion of the private sphere was essential for the primacy of the public. By expanding the definition of politics to encompass both public and private spheres - indeed by asserting that these two are mutually constitutive - feminists have been able to challenge the dominant understanding of the politics itself, and therefore of democratic practices and discourse. This Gramscian ideology, deconstructed the hitherto Marxian notion of public-private divide and it did reformulate the dialectic nature between the public and the private. Dhakuli Maushi herself has never contested the Panchayat election (citing illiteracy as the reason). However, the oral narrative of Dhakuli Maushi positions her as strong actor in the village, bringing in her political subjectivity in her real life world, despite her not being the member of GP. This notion of gendered citizenship is interesting and illuminating as the epistemological discourses are transcended beyond the institutional structures. Similarly, Razia Sultana has ensured that gender dynamics within her highly conservative nuptial family has changed considerably ever since she became politically mobilised. Her relationship with her husband has changed for the better and she proudly announced that the gender based violence and discrimination within her family had stopped, and that respect for women in general had gone up. It is important to note here how the micro politics of oppression within families work to reinforce patriarchal state structures and how women confront these structures. Travails in the women's daily lives act as motivation for change, and their positive role in governance is often seen to have increased their power of negotiation within the microcosm of their family.

This is of course to be noted with a word of caution. Often the patriarchal structures within the family are far too violent for the women to feel empowered with the new role as elected women representatives. Many women feel that this is an additional burden to their already heavy burden of housework.

There is a clear inter-relatedness between the economic and political spheres. There is an assertion of agency through a sense of control of their own access to economic and other resources, which in turn redraws the lines of the political spaces. We in our case studies have witnessed cases where women representatives not only managed to ensure more access to resources within the family, but also engaged other women in the struggle to claim property rights. Anuya Kulkarni from Sherpe Grama Panchayat motivated 22 women from her village to claim joint ownership of their houses with their husbands and made efforts to transfer land in women's names at the Grama Panchayat.

Another area where the woman representative's role is significant is in trying to ensure a higher level of nutrition within the family by pressurizing ration dealers to provide women with their entitlement. Women representatives seem to have a positive influence in countering the feminisation of poverty. Unequal distribution of resources within and outside the family, coupled with patriarchal social norms, results in women and children being the most vulnerable to poverty and malnutrition. Gender division of labour within the household renders ensuring enough food at home the woman's concern, and accordingly, as has been observed in the case of Maharashtra, female representatives concern themselves with ensuring nutrition for household members.

Politics of Recognition

The usual approach to the politics of recognition transposes what Nancy Fraser calls the 'identity model'[6] onto the cultural and political terrain. In this view to belong to a group that is devalued by the dominant culture is to be 'misrecognised', to suffer a distortion in one's relation to one's self. As a result of repeated encounters with the stigmatising gaze of a culturally dominant other, the members of disesteemed groups internalise negative self-images and are prevented from developing a healthy cultural identity of their own. In this perspective, the politics of recognition would aim to repair internal self-dislocation by contesting the dominant culture's demeaning picture of the group, by members of misrecognised groups collectively producing and publicly asserting a self-affirming culture of their own to (re)gain the respect of society at large.

Fraser proposes an alternative approach to address recognition: as a question of social status. From this perspective, what is important is not group-specific identity but the status of individual group members as full partners in social interaction. Misrecognition, accordingly, then does not mean the depreciation and deformation of group identity, but social subordination in the sense of being prevented from participating as a peer in social life. To redress this injustice still requires a politics of recognition, but in Fraser's 'status model' this is no longer reduced to a question of identity, but is a politics aimed at overcoming subordination by establishing the misrecognised party as a full member of society, *capable of participating on a par with the* (*italics mine*). Unlike the identity model, Fraser's status model then understands social justice as encompassing two analytically distinct dimensions: a dimension of recognition, which concerns the effects of institutionalised meanings and norms on the relative standing of social actors; and a dimension of distribution, which involves the allocation of disposable resources to individual social actors.

If we go along with Fraser - and it is difficult not to – it is easy enough to agree that patterns of cultural value while undoubtedly significant have in fact not been the only obstacles to participatory parity for EWR's in Maharashtra. Given the (deeply stratified, rural) social context of the respondents of this study, 'maldistribution' is an old structural reality impeding parity of participation in social life. While 'equal participation' as Fraser sees it is still a distant dream for most respondents, the first few steps to its realisation were taken only when actors were given - in the form of quotas to PRI in this case – necessary local resources to interact with others as peers.

But while Fraser dismisses proponents of the identity model who transpose it to the cultural and political terrain where recognition is a relation *between groups*, and will ostensibly be rectified by undoing the misrecognition of the group (in our case that of gender), her own thesis on 'recognition' too somewhere is incomplete. Can we really theorise recognition without factoring in the matter of what individuals in the 'group' in fact see it as? What if we were to ask for instance, why do women really want parity, or what do they in fact *value* as a result of that parity of participation?

Initially, many EWR's, who were stepping into the public space for the first time, found it difficult to cope. But eventually – as evident from their own narratives again – most of these women not just coped but delivered to the imperatives of their role as political administrators with initiative and vision. Yet much more than the visible, material benefits of a foothold in the local political sphere, narratives of women EWR's throw up a deep sense of personal confidence, satisfaction and *individual fulfillment* that these women developed by factor of their entry into PRI, and thereby into the public domain.

A simple but telling instance, when these newly empowered women, especially those from the oppressed castes speak at functions and programmes in the presence of Taluk officers and village people, it is a matter of great pride and joy to them and their families. Fulma is proud that she could address as many as 250 women (not so different from her) at a 'Melava', telling them about Gram Panchayats and Grama Sabhas, and answering their questions confidently in Hindi. She believes she is good at handling people and is strategic in her dealings with them - that she speaks Hindi well and is aware of urban mores and way of life (having also lived outside the village) add to her strengths as a leader. In her own words, she had the 'spark' even before joining the MRA. For most problems in Jamunnala village, Fulma is the first person people go to, because she is always willing to help out. In fact, Fulma is more active than the Sarpanch and often makes decisions herself. She is now a leading personality in the taluka.

Fulma also later contested elections in the Panchayat Samiti in 2007, though she did not win. When asked about her future plans, she says that she wants to work at the district level in the Zila Panchayat. Several other respondents of this study too aspired for higher 'posts' and larger spheres of influence. Jyoti plans to stand for elections at district level. Rita's wants to now be an MLA (member of legislative assembly). She says she is happy that 'she has gained so much respect' - not from the 'other' but from community, from her peer group.

Do these answers perhaps have more to do with self actualisation than equalisation? Narratives of women EWR's in Maharashtra do seem to indicate that (access to) these multiple public spheres are also important sites for the construction/ reconstruction of *individual* identities of people in oppressed groups, along pathways not always predictable by the imperatives of the group itself.

Gendered Governance: Intersubjectivity to Consensus?

At one level we can see women's inclusion in PRI in the all too real, 'this-worldly' terms of Fraser's multiple publics, contesting against other publics for space and voice, and thereby facilitating enriching democratic discursiveness. At another level however it is as possible - and perhaps more tempting - to view this inclusion as a step that not just aids the creation of conditions for shared understanding, but also perhaps holds the kernels of hope of manufacturing political consensus based on trust and truth, a matter of no small relevance in our contested times.

To understand the domain assumptions of the first project (of shared understanding), perhaps there has been no one better than the Vienna born phenomenologist Alfred Schutz. The core assumption underlying Schutz's work was his thesis of 'intersubjectivity', whereby he delineated how people interacting in small groups develop a certain shared understanding. This interaction is not covered symbolically but one of physical encounter. It is this physical encounter that leads to social meanings.[7]

For Schutz, the knowing subject, and the constitutive, creative nature of the human mind was exceedingly important. Nevertheless for him intersubjectivity did not mean 'subjectivity', but in fact occurs when we are able to transcend our subjectivity and meet each other on a common platform. His intersubjectivity is in other words a shared objectivity.

It does not take much conjecture to see the implications of his theory for women's inclusion into Panchayat Raj Institutions. A quick way to look at it would possibly be that while women already have a certain shared understanding with women of their own (caste/class/ethnic) community in these micro worlds (villages), the entry of women into local councils of governance engenders increasing intersubjectivity with women of other caste-class-ethnic groups, facilitating better governance. This is indeed borne out in narratives of most EWR's this study engaged with in Maharashtra.

Take for instance the case of Anuya Kulkarni, an (upper caste) member of the Sherpe Gram Panchayat and a District Organiser of the MRA, who successfully built a Mahila Mandal of 120 women in Sherpe across all castes.[8] Though many powerful people in the village were against it and tried to pressurize her, she continued working on it for several months, conducting meetings in each and every community. Finally, about ten to fifteen women from each community were ready to join the Mahila Mandal. This was the first attempt at removing caste barriers in the village. Anuya organised the women in four or five neighbouring villages too, and built an organisation called 'Sindhudurg Mahila Vikas Sanghatana'. The Sanghatana eventually succeeded in banning liquor from all those villages. Women from nearby talukas like Devgad also joined the organisation, drawn by the common cause of *darubandi*, or the campaign against alcohol. The Sanghatana's numbers swelled to about 800.

Schutz's theory of intersubjectivity is in fact very instructive to understanding Anuya's attempts to break through caste barriers in her village. Anuya formed SHGs of women *across communities* to help bring them together, so that they could share thoughts and see how similar their situations are. Caste differences are strictly followed in the Konkan, with untouchability still in practice. For instance, separate cups and plates are used for Dalits in upper-caste homes. Therefore, while working here, the MRA has used strategies like get-togethers and luncheons across communities, organising meals in the Gram Panchayat, etc. On Dr Ambedkar's birth anniversary, her organisation, Vikas Prabodhini, puts together lunch and a programme among Dalits and the other village women. Ten women from *different communities* of the village have been trained by Anuya Tai to work in her absence. She has also trained women from nearby villages. Despite threats from people of her own caste, Anuya and other women could take the issue of untouchability forward and managed to remove the practice at least in the public domain.

Or take the case of Dhakuli Gundu Naik, an illiterate social worker known as 'Dhakuli Mavshi' to the people of Halkarni in Kolhapur district.[9] Many people here - some as young as 12 and 14 - are addicted to cashew liquor. Dhakuli was successful in organising not just Adivasi women, but Maratha women as well into a united front. It was again the increasing intersubjectivity between women of different communities in Halkarni that became the driving force behind a successful women's movement that was in turn therefore empowered to resolve a complex local issue like alcoholism in Halkarni.

While deepening woman to woman ties of understanding are borne out amply in our research (and will perhaps have a higher probability of developing in contexts elsewhere as well), our findings with women's (assisted) entry into local councils of governance in Maharashtra are in fact indicative of a promise - even if very nascent - of the possibility of (or at the least better chances of) such 'shared understanding' developing also in the larger public sphere/s (in the small world local context), in other words between men and women as well. Take for example Fulma's example again. Illiterate, tribal, and a woman, she is nevertheless the first person people – men and women - now think of when in trouble in the village. She herself says the *villagers* are now united and cooperate with her. Mayatai Sorte (of Kharola village in Latur district) too says she now has (thanks to small but significant works in the village) the people's support. She has also been able to win the confidence of different pressure groups in the village and encourage them to join hands in developmental activities.

Habermas takes Schutz's case for intersubjectivity to another level of possibilities, with his magnum opus '*The Theory of Communicative Action*' (1981). Habermas was pushed towards a focus on intersubjectivity and mutual understanding by his practical concern with the possibility of rational moral and political discourse in the public sphere of modern societies. His analysis of intersubjective communication was driven by a notion of emancipation as involving the demolition of systematic obstacles to understanding. Habermas then broaden's Chomsky's theory of linguistic competence into a theory of 'communicative competence', a universal pragmatics whose task would be to identify and reconstruct universal conditions of possible understanding. Acts of linguistic communication, for Habermas, presuppose four validity claims: that what we say is comprehensible, that it is true, that it is right (i.e. that there is a normative basis for the utterance), and that it is a sincere expression of the speaker's feelings. The 'background consensus' between speaker and hearer includes the fact that they implicitly make these claims and could if necessary justify them. Finally, Habermas argues that we can only distinguish as a matter of principle, between a genuine and a false consensus if we presuppose the possibility of an unconstrained dialogue to which all speakers have equal access and in which only the 'force of the better argument prevails'. This is what he calls the ideal speech situation.

It is undoubtedly easier to prove the applicability of Schutz's thesis of intersubjectivity in the context of our own findings in the micro world rural context of villages in Maharashtra. Habermas's is a humanistic promise, or rather hope of truth and consensus that is much harder to exemplify in practice. Nevertheless in a politics among whose deepest concerns today are guile, deception and corruption, it is perhaps worthwhile asking whether the entry of women into local governance in Maharashtra has at all any implications for 'ideal speech conditions' as Habermas would have seen it?

Based on the narratives we have with us, perhaps to some extent yes. As Anuya Kulkarni put it (in a somewhat different context), 'If women do not bring about such change, then there will not be any difference between the methods used by men and the methods used by women.' It does look like at the start of the new revolutionary road, women engaged with women/ other publics in the multiple discourses of governance are more likely to seek political discourse with a 'background consensus' of truth. Not because women are more truthful or not because they care more, but because at this moment in time, gender empowered and (as important) *inspired* by political voice – and with very little to lose - makes for a powerful opponent, capable of, and desiring of dismantling not just existing structures of gender oppression, but other parallel structures of oppression as well.

Conclusion

Governance is presumed to be gender neutral. But in fact, the discourses, procedures, structures and functions of governance remain heavily skewed in favour of men in general. This unequal sharing of power leads to an unequal sharing of resources - time, income and property - between men and women. As discussed before, women at the grassroots level politics in Maharashtra did made a dent in the hegemonic power structures of the socially stratified structures of the village, and challenged the invisibility of women in political and public spaces. But the study also argues that Panchayats replicate the rural power structures. The deeply embedded patterns of dominance and the inequalities on women's lives are mediated by their class and caste positions. Interestingly EWRs had bitter experiences of being labelled 'immoral' or 'non-womanly' when they crossed the thresholds designed to curtail them. They were called 'inadequate' when they were well within the boundaries of patriarchal societies.

To quote Archana Jatkar, a Sarpanch: "I wonder why they insisted on humiliating me in spite of the fact that I was a responsible Sarpanch. Was it because I am a woman? Wasn't a woman capable of this kind of work?" This double gaze is problematic when one has to engage with the governance and family structures in both 'public and private' domains in day-to-day engagements. Despite these hurdles, one cannot ignore the positive changes in the socio-political lives of EWRs, where some of them are playing meaningful roles in the current PRIs and their process of self-responsibilisation. Their experiences of leadership and collective action need to be channelised to form a political resistance.

But at the same time, it is equally important to mention that most often the uncritical use of the term 'empowerment' in development discourses disguises a problematic concept. Power relationships reproduce themselves, regardless of how participatory or democratic a setting is, unless a conscious, sustained effort is undertaken to alter them. This becomes more relevant in the case of Elected Women Representatives and their participation in the process of democratic decentralisation. There is an important caveat to be entered between representation and participation, for the former is necessarily the first, but by no means a sufficient guarantee for the latter. Authentic participation of women in the decision-making bodies is a long-term and complex process. The ubiquity of historically entrenched patriarchal practices is the most formidable social constraint on women's participation.

The experiences of the Peoples' Planning Campaign (PPC) in Kerala - the largest of its kind in the local democratic decentralisation process in India - showed that one can in no way argue that the PPC completely changed the internalised structures of patriarchal subjugation and the invisibility of women. Challenges and problems highlighted by various studies (Chatukulam and John, 2000, Vijayan and Sandhya, 2004, Radha and Roy Chowdhary, 2002) need to be read along with the successes scored by at least some EWRs in Maharashtra, both as participants in local governance and as representatives articulating the interests of women. Patriarchy is not overturned or even significantly eroded, overnight. But the entry of women into public spaces via grassroots institutions means that they are leaving behind the private and circumscribed spaces of the home. That they are - to an extent at least - neglecting the question of '...Who will make the chapattis' (Datta, 1998) is an important indicator of change. Many EWRs shared the feeling of an enhanced sense of social and personal status within and outside the family.

While the fact that the EWRs are now invited to weddings in upper caste/class families and that their men were willing to share household responsibilities, might seem trivial at the level of macro analysis, but at the micro level, it becomes a significant gain (B Manjula, 2008).

A dialectic view of truth must include the notion that there are always emerging possibilities that are not yet visible. A new trend of micro politics is emerging as part of this engendering process in rural Maharashtra. This could be the seed of a new democratic formulation.

Notes

1. Maya Devi's village, like most others in the region is clearly divided into Dalit and Patil (upper caste) households with stark differences between the allocation of resources and living standards of both. All essential resources like bore wells, roads and electricity supply were concentrated in the area where the upper castes lived. The Dalit area had neither roads, nor electricity nor water sources. Dalit women had to walk three to four kilometers to fetch a pot of water.
2. The Zila Panchayat looked into her complaint after about two and a half years, and the nine Gram Sabha Panchayat members who had passed the resolution were suspended on grounds of hampering development work. (However, they in turn challenged the suspension and obtained a stay order on it.)
4. Cumulative effect of unmarked identities.
5. For Fraser - as for Habermas - participation in the public sphere was conceptualised as activity outside of the domain of state politics.
6. The identity model of recognition takes off from the Hegelian idea of identity as constructed dialogically through a process of mutual recognition. For Hegel, recognition designates an ideal reciprocal relation between subjects, in which each sees the other both as its equal and also as separate from it. Recognition from others is thus essential to the development of a sense of self, and to be denied recognition or be 'misrecognised' may result in both distortion of one's relation to one's self as well as injury to one's identity.
7. Schutz explains this *vis-a-vis* his theory of 'appresentation': how all physical encounters in micro worlds are immediately transcended by social identification.
8. It probably helped that Anuya's father had been of an activist bent and never believed in inequalities. As a Gramsevak, he too had met with stern disapproval of the other Brahmin families when he shared food with 'lower caste' villagers.
9. Next to the Marathas, the Adivasi Naik comprise a large segment of the population in Halkarni where almost every family has dry irrigated land (about half an acre to one acre) on which they grow rice. The Naiks also work as farm labourers and brew liquor from the abundant cashew in the region.

References

1. Dhanda, M (ed.). (2008): *Reservations for Women,* New Delhi: Women Unlimited.
2. Foucault, M. (1981): *Power/Knowledge. Selected Interviews and Other Writings 1972-1977*. (Ed.) Colin Gordon. New York: Pantheon Books.

3. Foucault, M. (1988): 'The Ethic of Care for the Self as a Practice of Freedom', in J. Bernauer and D. Rasmussen (eds.), *The Final Foucault*, Boston, Mass: MIT Press.
4. Foucault, M. (1991): 'Governmentality' in Graham Burchell, Colin Gordon and Peter Miller (eds.) in *The Foucault Effect: Studies in Governmentality*. Chicago, IL: University of Chicago Press.
5. Foucault, M. (1993): 'About the Beginning of the Hermeneutics of the Self' (transcription of two lectures in Dartmouth on Nov. 17 and 24, 1980), (ed.) Mark Blasius in *Political Theory*. Vol. 21, No. 2. May: pp. 198-227.
6. Fraser, Nancy. (1990): 'Rethinking the Public Sphere: A Contribution to the Critique of Actually Existing Democracy'. *Social Text*. No. 25/26: pp. 56-80.
7. Fraser, Nancy. (1998): 'Social Justice in the Age of Identity Politics: Redistribution, Recognition and Participation'. *The Tanner Lectures on Human Values*. (Ed.) Grethe B. Peterson. Salt Lake City: University of Utah Press.
8. Fraser, Nancy. (2000): 'Rethinking Recognition'. *New Left Review*. May-June.
9. Habermas, Jurgen. (1981): *The Theory of Communicative Action*. Vol.1 and 2, Heinemann, London.
10. Habermas, Jurgen. (1989): *The Structural Transformation of the Public Sphere: An Inquiry into a Category of Bourgeois Society*. Cambridge MA: The M.I.T Press.
11. Habermas, Jurgen. (1994): *'Struggles for Recognition in the Democratic Constitutional State.'*
12. Amy Gutman (ed) : Multiculturalism: Princeton University Press, Princeton.
13. Hindess, Barry. (1996): *Discourses of Power. From Hobbes to Foucault*. Blackwell, Oxford.
14. Kishwar, Madhu. (1996): "Women and Politics: Beyond Quotas', *Economic and Political Weekly*, Vol. 31, No. 43, 26 October.
15. Mazumdar, Vina. (1997): 'Historical Soundings'. *Seminar*. 457.
16. Menon, N. (1997): 'Reservations and Representation', *Seminar*, Special Issue on 'Empowering Women', No. 457 (September): 41. September: 15-16.
17. Menon, N. (2000): 'Elusive 'Woman': Feminism and Women's Reservation Bill'. *Economic and Political Weekly*. WS 35, 28 October: 3835-43.
18. Philips, A. (1995): *The Politics of Presence: The Political Representation of Gender, Ethnicity and Race*. Clarendon Press, Oxford.
19. Schutz, Alfred. (1967): *The Phenomenology of the Social World*. (Trans.) Walsh G. and Lehnert F. Evanston, Northwestern University Press.
20. Schutz, Alfred (with Luckmann T.) (1973): *The Structures of the Life-World*. (Trans.) Zaner R. M. and Engelhardt T. Evanston: Northwestern University Press and London: Heinemann.
21. Vincent, Louise. (2004): 'Quotas: Changing the Way Things Look without Changing the Way Things Are'. *The Journal of Legislative Studies*. Vol. 10. No. 1. Spring: 71-96.

18

Democratic Decentralisation in Rajasthan: A Historical Overview

—*Manjula Bharathi*

A historical overview of democratic decentralisation in Rajasthan reveals that village panchayats were central to the ideological framework of the Indian national movement. Gandhi had called village swaraj a complete republic where village panchayats would be based on perfect democracy and individual freedom (Gandhi, 1942). The emergence of Gandhi at the head of the Indian national movement was, in fact, the unfolding of the subdued expectations of India's village at the conscious level of political processes. His concept of decentralisation was derived from his concern for the village (Pyarelal, 1958). Gandhian concept of *sarvodaya* describes a democratic socialistic pattern of economies and institutions suited to the conditions, realities and needs of the Indian society. He stressed for village reconstruction rather than urban industrialisation. In practice, this was an attempt to produce powerful village communities by initiating participatory development, developing self-reliant village republics in the form of panchayats, enforcing reform of land ownership and encouraging the development of rural industries.

Panchayats, in one form or the other, have been an integral part of rural socio-political life in Rajasthan. Between 1939 and 1948, seven princely states of Rajasthan passed resolutions and accorded statutory recognition to the panchayats. Later, the Rajasthan State Legislative Assembly consolidated the panchayats at the state level and enacted the Rajasthan Panchayat Act, 1953. A tehsil panchayat at the intermediate level and district boards at the district level were constituted through this enactment.

Rajasthan was the first state in India to inaugurate panchayati raj on October 2, 1959, when the then Prime Minister of India Jawaharlal Nehru hailed the system as "the most revolutionary and historic step in the context of new India...democracy at the top would succeed if only it is built from below" (Nehru, 1959). Article 40 of the Directive Principles of the Constitution of India states that the state should take steps to organise village panchayats and endow them with such power and authority as may be necessary to enable them to function as units of self-government (GoI, 1950). This implies grassroots democracy and 'Power to People.'

All theoretical analyses understand the concept of power as located not on the surface of society's structure but as deeply woven into a complex contextual social web. Theorists like Althusser, Gramsci, Foucault, Habermas and Friere analysed the concept of power from socio-cultural, psychological, political and structural perspectives. Power, effected through an unconscious subjection to ideology in an Althusserain framework, power in the Gramscian hegemony, which involves the colonisation of popular consciousness or common sense through the articulation of specific social practices and positions within ideological codes or chains. Foucauldian notion of power as crucial to the construction of reality, language, meanings and rituals of truth, the power resulting from knowledge in an information economy according to Habermas, all analyse the concept of power.

1.4 (a) Pre-73rd Amendment: PRI Scenario in Rajasthan

Panchayati raj functionaries gained importance in rural areas since 1959. Many local development works like drinking water wells, panchayat and school buildings, gram sevak quarters, village roads, culverts and drains were constructed as per local needs and aspirations of the villagers. People's participation was significant with 50 per cent contribution coming from the village community. People offered *Shram Dan* (voluntary labour) in many cases. Extension officers from departments of agriculture, animal husbandry, industries, cooperation, education, social welfare, etc. all were placed at the disposal of panchayat samiti, which was like a mini-government at the block level. There was great enthusiasm and team synergy at the intermediate panchayats. District level officers, including collector, attended monthly meetings of panchayat samiti and quarterly meetings of zilla parishad. The state posted IAS officers as Block Development Officers. Several block chiefs/ *pradhans* rose to become MLAs. *Pradhans* also became Ministers and *pramukh*(s) and Chief Minister. In certain quarters, however, Panchayati Raj Institutions were perceived as a constant threat to political authority of state level leaders, who tried to weaken panchayati raj in the state.

Second generation panchayats led to withdrawal of departmental extension officers from panchayat samitis. Besides, various other developmental agencies like Small Farmer Development Agencies (SFDAs) and District Rural Development Agencies (DRDAs) came into existence for initiating rural development, employment generation and implementation of poverty alleviation programmes. Funds also started flowing directly to such agencies by-passing the panchayati raj. This was a step towards weakening of panchayati raj. Panchayati raj was also weakened by irregular elections of these bodies; elections were not held between 1965 through 1978. This period saw Block Development Officers (BDOs) as administrators in panchayat samitis and collectors as administrators in zilla parishads. In 1978, only Panchayat elections were held. The subsequent elections were held in 1981 and in 1988. In 1991, gram sevaks became administrators in panchayats, BDOs in panchayat samitis and collectors in zilla parishads. These bureaucratic administrators continued till 1993 when constitutional amendment made it compulsory to hold elections every five years through the State Election Commission.

1.4 (b) Institutionalisation of Panchayati Raj

Though panchayati raj was a state subject, the union government took the initiative to make panchayati raj system a part of Indian Constitution by making the 73rd amendment to the Constitution of India. (GoI, 1993). "The amended Constitution requires the states to constitute panchayats as institutions of self-government not only for villages, but also at intermediate and district levels. Consequently, there will henceforth be three strata of government: the union, the states and the panchayats." (Mukarji, 1993)

Rajasthan has shown the pathway for decentralised governance as it enacted the Panchayat Raj Act even before the amendment to the Constitution. The Rajasthan Panchayat Raj Acts of 1953 and 1959 were the initial legislations in this regard.[2] However, the initial enthusiasm of decentralised planning and participation of people were lost due to political and administrative reasons. As noted by Sharma and Anita (2007), the increasing support to the village level leaders was perceived as a threat to political authority of state level leaders who tried to weaken the Panchayat Raj in the state. Before the 73rd amendment, in most parts of the nation, the control of village Panchayats was in the hands of well-off and big landlords. The case of the state of Rajasthan was also not different as panchayats were controlled by the upper castes for long. The marginalised sections of society, like women and Dalits, were excluded by the upper caste male members from the political sphere too. Irregular elections, corruption and bureaucratic administration were the pre-73rd amendment scenario at the local level institutions. Hence, marginalised sections of society such as women and Dalits were 'invisible' in the earlier development process.

It was after the enactment of 73rd and 74th amendments to the Constitution of India that the participation of women and Dalits was appreciated in the country that made one-third reservation for women at all levels of village level institutions, and for Dalits, in proportion to their population, mandatory. Apart from this, participation of marginalised women and Dalits at all levels of planning and decision-making process was also ensured. This provided them an opportunity to raise their issues in public forums, participate in the development process and contest elections at all levels of the Panchayat.

The case of Rajasthan is also peculiar in the articulation of women's and Dalit human rights groups, which have shown a pathway to the Indian democracy in terms of Women's Development Programme (WDP), Right to Information (RTI) Act, Right to Food campaign and NREGA. The women's movement, women and human rights organisations and NGOs have played a crucial role in making decentralised planning transparent and accountable.

1.4 (c) Structure and Functioning of Local Self Government in Rajasthan

In pursuance of the constitutional mandate, Rajasthan Panchayti Raj Act, 1994 was enacted in April 1994 (GoR, 1994). Prior to promulgation of the Constitution (73rd Amendment) Act, Panchayati Raj institutions in Rajasthan were governed by Rajasthan Panchayat Act, 1953, and Rajasthan Panchayat Samiti and Zilla Parishad Act, 1959. Many amendments were necessary in both these Acts in the wake of mandatory constitutional provisions contained in the Constitution (73rd Amendment).

However, enactment of the Act was not seen as an end in itself by the government. Devolution of powers and functions were also considered necessary. As a background to the amendment, a High-powered Committee, headed by Development Commissioner, was set up in August 1993 to suggest powers and functions, along with resources, to be entrusted to PRIs consequent to the 73rd Constitutional amendment. It recommended the merger of panchayati raj and rural development departments. It was also in favour of PRI's administrative control over all the concurrent officers concerned with rural development at district and block levels. It allocated schedule I, schedule II and schedule III for functions to panchayats, Panchayat samitis and zilla parishads, respectively. A subsequent committee headed by the Development Commissioner, in May 1999, recommended transferring of 16 subjects (of the 29-included in XI schedule of the Constitution) to Panchayati Raj Institutions. The state cabinet approved it in January 2000. Thus, an ordinance was issued that devolved some powers on PRIs for the first time. A village monitoring committee, headed by a sarpanch, was formed for recommending disciplinary action and transfer of village level employees on account of absence from duty.[3] A cabinet sub-committee could only review decisions related to transfer carried out at the recommendation of village committee. This has, definitely, increased the power and status of sarpanch among village level officials. Devolution of powers to Panchayat is a continuous process. In this process, the government of Rajasthan has taken several steps, since June 2003.

1.4 (d) Administrative Powers

The Rajasthan Panchayati Raj Act's amendment of January 2000 provides for grama sabha's control over functions and functionaries of various social development institutions. Village level officials are expected to attend gram sabha meetings, get their attendance verified and leave sanctioned by the sarpanch and inform him/her of their tour programmes. These are significant departures from the previous regime. However, the task force in January 2001 found that departments were hardly complying with these directives. Though the officials of revenue, medical and health and women and children departments have been attending gram sabha meetings, they still do not get approval of tour programmes etc. from the sarpanch, as required.

The State Cabinet, on January 2, 2000, placed village extension workers of agriculture, animal husbandry sub-centres with staff, 'D' class staff of fisheries tanks, khadi supervisors of industries department, assistant engineer and junior engineer (PHED) in District Rural Development Agency, chief medical officer, doctor in-charge of primary health centres, sub-centre staff, anganwadi workers and Child Development Project Officers (CDPOs) of Integrated Child Development Services (ICDS) and staff of social welfare hostels under PRIs' control. However, owing to change of political regime and bureaucratic resistance, administrative control of functionaries and finance remained under the control of respective departments. Though fresh orders were issued in June 2003 for transfer of funds and functionaries, the BDO and the Chief Executive Officer (CEO) still have to countersign the salary bills. The budget control continues to vest in respective departments. On the matter of penalising the transferred staff for minor offences, PRIs have been devolved some powers without amending the relevant rules. Government has stayed the transfer of staff of Public Health Engineering Department (PHED), Food and Civil Supplies, Public Works Department (PWD). This testifies to the half-baked overtures to empower the PRIs in Rajasthan.

Patwari has been made the main assistant in proceedings of Finance and Taxation Standing Committee of gram panchayat, since June 2003, and has been attending panchayat meetings and getting mutation attested by panchayat. But his administrative control and resultant loyalty continues to rest with revenue department rather than to the PRIs.

Gram panchayats are expected to supervise working of fair price shops. Sarpanch has the authority to check distribution of articles and verification of the registers. The licence dealer has to submit the account of receipt/ distribution, etc. of materials to gram panchayat and send monthly information directly to the panchayat samiti which, in turn, sends them to the District Supply Officer (DSO). The BDO sends monthly-consolidated report to the DSO.

Block Education Officers and District Education Officers have been placed under the control of panchayat samiti and zilla parishad, respectively. Director, Elementary Education, deals through zilla parishads rather than departmental officers. Powers of transfer and Rajasthan Civil Service Rule 17 CCA (Classification, Control and Appeals Rules) regarding transfer of teachers is vested with Administration and Establishment Standing Committees of panchayat samiti and zilla parishad. Recruitment of teachers also has to be done through standing committee of zilla parishad, since June 2003. Thus, PRIs have been delegated with complete administrative control over elementary education, though periodic technical directions have to be followed by them regarding syllabus, examinations, holidays, etc., as issued by the administrative department. But the real situation is totally at variance from what the issued orders entail. Education department has usurped all the powers in violation of the orders.

All the activities of agriculture/agriculture extension, hitherto performed by agriculture supervisor, have now been transferred to panchayat samitis along with agriculture supervisors and assistant agriculture officers. All the activities of soil conservation and watershed also stand transferred to zilla parishads.

All the activities executed by District Social Welfare Officers at the district level have been transferred to zilla parishads. District Level Probation Officers/ Social Welfare Officers, Assistant Directors/Deputy Directors will work under zilla parishad. Gram sabha selects eligible beneficiaries for old age, widow or handicapped category pensions, and BDO sanctions them. Zilla parishad is now expected to approve the list of all the applicants desiring benefits under Prime Minister's Rozgar Yojana (PMRY). Besides, proposals for small industries will now be placed before concerned standing committee of the panchayat samiti. It is expected that the draft list of potential industries prepared, annually, by Industries Department should be discussed in the standing committee meeting and all suggestions are to be incorporated.

Zilla parishad now has the jurisdiction of decision of villages in respective districts for consideration of Renewable Energy Development Authority (REDA) for supply of non-conventional energy-based electrification. Concerned zilla parishads will select villages in respective districts for electrification and forward the list to Electricity Corporation for action.

Since August 2003, DRDA has been renamed as Rural Development Cell of zilla parishad, and the sixth standing committee has been constituted as Rural Development Committee of zilla parishad through a Government Order. However, the rules have not been amended. District Women Development Authority (DWDA) and Small Farmer Development Agency (SFDA) have also been merged with zilla parishad. Zilla pramukh is chairperson of all the bodies.

1.4 (e) Financial Powers

It is heartening that three types of financial powers have been devolved to the PRIs, besides the above mentioned administrative powers. A gram panchayat has power to issue administrative and financial sanction upto Rs 2 lakh under Rule 176(1) and 214(1) of Rajasthan Panchayati Raj Rules, 1996 (GoR, 1996). Finance and Taxation Standing Committee, constituted under Section 56 of the panchayat samiti, has the right to sanction Rs 2 to 4 lakh from the own income of a gram panchayat. The power to sanction Rs 4 lakh and above rests with the zilla parishad or Finance and Taxation Standing Committee, constituted under section 57. This is subject to resolution of gram sabha and technical sanction as per Directory for Rural Works, 2002, effective since June 2003. The above delegation of financial powers for use of own resources is practicable only in case of PRIs having own income from farms, shops, banks or other natural resources. It is an affirmative step towards self-governance of PRIs.

Rights of recovery of irrigation tax and its use also now rest with PRIs. Since June 2003, it is maintained that gram panchayat /panchayat samiti will undertake maintenance /repair works on priority basis out of funds received under Sampoorna Grameen Rozgar Yojna.

Besides, the control of 'D', 'C' and 'B' class fishery tanks have been transferred to gram panchayats, panchayat samiti and zilla parishad, respectively. Concerned PRI can auction, and can use the auction income. However, PRIs have to maintain these tanks with the income thus generated. Auction notices are being issued by respective PRIs. Panchayat Samiti has control over installation and repair and maintenance of hand pumps, tanks and piped-water supply schemes. Budget to this effect would be transferred to them. Besides, the sarpanch will now verify the salary of the hand pump mechanic. PRI can now organise agricultural fairs, but the financial compliance still has not been implemented.

Under the new dispensation, BDI/CEO countersigns salary bills of the agriculture officers. Firewood, fodder and minor forest produce related income to forest and non-forest areas are now PRIs' income, but it will have to ensure compliance of concerned forest acts and rules and departmental circulars. In case of tendu patta, the income net of administrative expenses stands transferred to PRIs.

Thus, as per the spirit of 73rd amendment, functions, functionaries and funds have begun to be transferred to PRIs. In reality, however, the progress is very slow in many instances to render these institutions of self-governance effective. Transfers, attendance, sanction of leave and tour approval powers rest with the PRIs. Disciplinary action power, regarding minor penalty, up to stoppage of two grade increments, has also been vested with PRIs. However, status quo is maintained with regard to budget drawing and disbursing salary to officers. State government will allot budget to departments. But as per activities transferred, budget for the same has to be transferred to the concerned PRI. The concerned zilla parishad/panchayat samiti has the administrative and financial sanctioning authority now. But this budget transfer clause is yet to be implemented.

The state of Rajasthan has slowly begun to empower PRIs by devolving the functions, functionaries and funds in small measure after a lapse of 10 years. PRIs do have the potential to become institutions of self-governance — provided intensive and sustained training of elected representatives and transferred officials are ensured along with devolution of the four Fs, i.e., functions to be transferred with functionaries, funds and the freedom to function.— to inculcate a positive, proactive and responsive attitude,

1.5. Civil Society and PRI Empowerment

Civil society, which has emerged as an inseparable partner of the development, also plays a decisive and crucial role in articulating these spaces of power. Though there were initiatives by different scholars to position civil society as a third sphere, the viability and feasibility of the civil society to intervene and engage with the state and the people need to be consciously understood, especially in the context of the forces of globalisation. The much claimed autonomous status of the civil society needs a critical analysis, especially in lieu of its diverse and debatable character.

In India, post-independence decentralisation and devolution had given a centric position in development approach. The proliferations of grassroot organisations, community-based organisations and self-help groups have to be viewed against this development context of the state. PRIs can be viewed as a link between the formal public spaces and the informal private spaces at the local level where we could see a synergy between the state apparatus and voluntary organisations working along with each other, that way hitherto considered as state domains. One has to agree that in the contemporary context of market dominance and state minimalism, the civil society has taken a facilitative role to achieve the beneficiary functions along with the state and the market.

Right to information is an issue which has gained considerable importance in recent years. People are increasingly beginning to feel the need for greater access to information, which had been in the exclusive domain of the government, even though it relates to the well being of the individuals or the public at large. Growth of democratic values has led to the feeling that the government must be made accountable in order to make democracy meaningful. The right to information is also being viewed as a possible potent instrument for minimising corruption, transparency and inefficiency within government. Civil society in Rajastan with NGOs like MKSS has really initiated a new dialogue in the democratic discourses with events like Janvani, which brings clientilism and corruption as open topics for debate in the public sphere.

1.6. Gender and Development

In the development trajectory of India, goal with stability in the 60s was changed to growth with social justice, thereby showing concern and caring towards the marginalised. Women, in general, despite half the population, are considered marginalised in the society irrespective of their class, caste, gender or race. Their social position is asymmetric and the scenario is much worse in the case of rural women. Even though India's perspective on gender development has been articulated clearly in the Constitution and the relevant strategies were envisioned, there exist a definite gap between ideas and practice if one follows the postulates of Amartya Sen (2000). This gap between an idea (participated democracy) and its institution envisaged for PRIs and the manifested practices in these local governing institutions indeed shows a gap. It is very difficult to estimate using conventional indicators the gap difference as it tend to expand and collapse at various context based on the lens with which you are looking at the gap.

While, national policies and plans have reflected a vision of progress and there has been an increase in the spaces available for women in India, there exists a paradox: on the one hand there are significant gains, on the other, gender-based inequalities prevail in almost all spheres and across different states. Translating the goals of gender equality into reality continues to be a challenge.

In the 1970s the main focus was on understanding issues related to women/ girls within the Women Integrated Development (WID) framework. One can also see that the practice of WID is also characterised by a discursive professionalisation, bureaucratisation and institutionalisation. It also produces instrument effects that affect women's life – the women who are the objects of interventions are much the women planners designing the programme. The body of knowledge thus formulated constructs a stereotypical version of the women, especially the women of the third world rural areas. This in a way re-casted the colonial gaze back to the rural women identifying their issues and prescribing their solutions.

The situation of women as producers in their own right, and not merely in their role as child bearers, present or potential, was not recognised. Gradually, issues related to women's work and employment, women's role and social change, education of women and children, health of women and children and violence against women gained increasing centrality.

Beginning with the launch of the Women's Development Programme of the Government of Rajasthan in 1984, a shift in attention from 'delivery mechanisms'—that so far had looked at women as objects of compassion and welfare— to that of subjects in the development process was made. A State Policy for Women was introduced in March 2000. A State Policy for children was also drafted in 2003. The panchayat legislation enacted in the wake of the 73rd amendment facilitated a new presence of rural women in the institutions of local governance, and has been heralded as a silent revolution. While there is evidence of new energies, women's role in the panchayat continues to be fiercely debated. The increasing number of women in public spheres has demonstrated that reservation challenges the societal image of women's roles. It has also given recognition to the need to increase women's spaces and for support structures to enable their effective political participation. The importance of women's political participation is, therefore, to be understood in the context of their socio-cultural subordination. It can, however, be argued that while it is true that traditional social and political structures continue to subordinate women even after they are elected to the positions, the opportunity to participate in the public arenas is itself a great leap forward for women in Rajasthan. The increase in reserved seats for women to 50 per cent in 2010 has once again given rise to mixed reactions.

19

Decentralised Local Governance : The Case of Andaman and Nicobar Islands

—*S.S. Sreekumar*

The post-Second World War era witnessed the adoption of growth centred model for development by the newly independent states. In this model the state assured the moral and political responsibilities for the development of society. The growth centred model mainly aimed at economic growth and increased Gross Domestic Product (GDP) of the country. However, some nations could achieve these goals at great social and environmental costs. But experience in various nations reveal that this model had bypassed large sections of the society, leading to a greater disparity, further marginalising the deprived sections. The special programmes initiated for the weaker and vulnerable sections failed to make an impact since people were treated as mere beneficiaries and objects of development. A crucial debate has been relevant in developing nations regarding the degree of control that central governments should exercise over development planning and administration. The past experiences of planned development among developing nations including India reveals that it has raised doubts regarding achievement of welfare objectives, removal of poverty and social inequalities, economic growth and social justice. The disillusionment prevailing in highly centralised planning resulted in economic inequalities, regional disparities and increased poverty. Hence, the basic premises of development theory come into question during 1970s.

A growing realisation among policy analysts that as government activities expanded, it became difficult to plan and administer development activities effectively from the centre. In this context, local autonomy in making decision of primary concerns to the locality and greater responsibility for designing and implementing development programmes became a necessity. This revived interest in the notion of decentralisation. Decentralisation has to be viewed as a theory of development which requires variety of institutions for empowering and uplifting the marginalised and the poor. It is expected to work for building up of an administrative space at the cutting edge level where the felt needs of the poor could be ventilated. Decentralisation is a prime mechanism through which democracy becomes truly representative and responsive.

Decentralisation leads to the empowerment of the local people through devolution. Decentralised governance seeks to tap local in initiatives and practices by involving grassroots organisations. Representative and participatory democracy become possible through decentralised governance. Another important feature of decentralised governance is *interactive policy making* which leads to decentralised decision-making. Inter-active policy is a process where government and non-governmental sectors such as private sector, non-governmental organisations communities, grassroots organisations, pressure groups all participate in decision-making. Hence, decentralised governance is an alternative strategy for development. A primary objective of decentralisation is to maintain *political stability* in the face of pressure of localisation. When a country finds itself deeply divided, especially along geographic or ethnic lines decentralisation provides an institutional mechanism for bringing opposition groups into a formal, rule-bound bargaining process. In South Africa and Uganda decentralisation has served as a path to national unity. In Sri Lanka it offers a potential political solution to the Civil War. It is an instrument for deflating secessionist tendencies in Ethiopia, Bosnia and Herzegovina. In Columbia, centralised party elites relied on decentralisation to gain grassroots support particularly in area of under rebel control.[1]

One argument in favour of decentralisation is that it *increases the efficiency* and *responsiveness* of government. Locally elected leaders know their constituents better than authorities at the national level and so should be well positioned to provide public services as per the requirements of local residents. Moreover, physical proximity makes it easer for citizens to hold local officials accountable for their performance. The extent to which decentralisation *exacerbates 'income differences'* among regions or becomes a positive force in efforts to alleviate poverty depends on two factors. The first is horizontal equity or the extent to which the sub-national governments have the fiscal capacity to deliver equivalent level of service to their population. The second can be described as within state equity. This relates to the ability or willingness of sub national governments to improve income distribution within their borders.[2]

Decentralisation if handled poorly can *threaten macroeconomic stability.* Fiscal decentralisation reduces the central government's control over public resources. Deficit spending by local governments can also thwart central government efforts to cool the economy by restraining public expenditure. The threat of macro economic in stability is a serious issue only in countries where, sub-national governments control substantial resources, i.e, usually large federations or highly decentralised wealthy countries. Several studies suggest that decentralisation has not undermined stability in the U.S. or in Western European countries. In Latin America sub-national governments' contributions to the national deficit was negligible in most countries, except in federal ones.[3]

Another argument raised by Gerry Stocker is that a decentralised government has the capacity to *win public loyalty*. It can better meet local needs and win support for public services, because it allow 'choice'. It facilitates a matching of local resources and local needs. By making the governments less remote and more manageable makes it more comprehensive, enabling a clear and balanced choice to be made over the extent to which people wish to promote community values.[4] Decentralisation encourages greater political participation and increased responsiveness among government institutions and in the path of development. Decentralised governance as a mechanism ensures people's participation in planning and implementation and therefore state becomes more participatory, accountable, effective and efficient.[5] G. Shabbir Cheema and Dennis A. Rondinelli in their pioneering work enumerated the following advantages of decentralisation:

(a) tailor-made plans as per the needs of heterogeneous regions and groups are possible;

(b) it can cut red-tape;

(c) closer contact between government officials and local population is possible;

(d) it can allow better penetration of national policies to areas remote from the national capital;

(e) it will ensure greater representation of political, religious, ethnic and tribal groups in development decision-making that could lead to grater equity in allocation of resources;

(f) capacity of local institutions and their managerial and technical skills will develop;

(g) top management would be relieved for routine jobs and devote time to more important jobs;

(h) it will ensure better coordination;

(i) it will institutionalise the participation of the citizens and exchange of information;

(j) it will offset the influence of the elite people;

(k) it will lead to a more flexible, innovative creative administration;

(l) local people can execute, monitor and evaluate better than the central agencies;

(m) increased political stability will be ensured by increasing the participation of the local people in decision-making; and
(n) it will also reduce the cost of planning and increase the number of public goods.[6]

A new framework of decentralised governance for the society can be laid down by taking the following measures:

(i) Providing people the opportunities and the forums to articulate their views and perceptions;
(ii) taking the points of service delivery closer to the peoples; and
(iii) strengthening the local bodies as self-government institutions.

In the context of the third world, decentralised governance has crucial significance, because the target group of development in these nations is the poor people. The World Bank Reports indicate that all about 12 of the 75 developing countries with more than five million inhabitants have implemented some form of decentralisation, with varying degrees of financial and political power. Parallel to these developments establishing legal frameworks and institutional mechanisms for people's participation at the local levels have been developed in countries like Philippines, India, Honduras, Bolivia, Namibia, Uganda, Tanzania, Brazil and Nigeria.

Decentralisation is especially important in developing countries where rapid expansion of public services greatly increases the number of government transactions and consequently the hindrances and wasted efforts resulting from centralisation of controls. During the 1970s and 1980s many of the new nations faced serious economic and political crises. It was justified that decentralisation is a way of managing natural, economic and political developments more effectively. Decentralisation can provide better service to local preferences, strengthening local accountability and supporting local economic development.[7]

Post independent India adopted a democratic system of governance. The provisions of democracy found their place in the Govt. of India Act 1909, 1919 and 1935. Mahatma Gandhi, Jawaharlal Nehru and Jai Prakash Narayan described democracy as government that gives power to the people. Regarding decentralisation there are broadly three views. The Balwant Rai Mehta Report favoured the Block as being nearest to the people (1957). The Sukhamoy Chakravarty (Economy Advisory Council, 1984) Report on decentralisation of planning considered even the district to be too small for proper area planning. The Ashok Mehta Report (1978) on the Panchayati Raj, however, categorically favoured the district because historically it had been the pivot of local administration for centuries and also because the requisite expertise for planning and related purposes could be mustered at this level and not lowers. The Dantwala Report (1978) on block level planning and the

Hanumantha Rao Report (1984) on district planning endorsed this view in essence. In political parties too thinking has crystallised on the district as the most appropriate level for first-stage decentralisation from the state level. The principal thrust of Balwant Rai Mehta Committee Report was towards decentralisation on democratic institutions in an effort to shift decision centres close to the people to enable their active and continuous participation under local popular control. The Ashok Mehta Committee's principal thesis was the functional necessity for decentralisation of administration level closer to the people. Both Balwant Rai Mehta Committee and Ashok Mehta Committee reports can be considered as landmarks in the history of democratic decentralisation in India. With the introduction of the 73rd and the 74th Constitutional Amendments, the decentralisation has been democratised and the scope of democracy has expanded to include women, Other Backward Communities (OBC) and Dalits at the grassroot level. Prior to this, the dominant social groups exclusively dominated the institutions of the local self-governance. This defeated the very purpose of democracy. Democracy can be termed as the substantive democracy. In the past two decades, in India substantive democracy has found a significant place in the discourse on democracy.

Andaman and Nicobar Scenario

The Union Territory of Andaman and Nicobar Islands comprises more than 306 named and unnamed islands and over 260 named and unnamed rocks. However, only 36 islands are inhabited. Of these, 24 are located in erstwhile Andaman District and 12 in Nicobar District. At present there are three revenue districts in the island territory-i.e. South Andaman District, North and Middle Andaman District and the Nicobar District. Nicobar District is mostly inhabited by tribes and is declared as tribal area. There are seven tehsils and 547 revenue villages.[8]

The population of these islands can be classified into two categories – the aborigines and immigrants. As per 2011 census, the total population of islands comes to 379944 of which 202330 are males and 177614 are females. The literacy rate of the island territory is 86.27 per cent and the sex ratio 878.[9] Bulk of the population of the islands are non-aborigines which are categorised into three streams. First category includes the descendants of convicts from India and Myanmar who immigrated to the islands before 1942 and popularly known as *locals.* Second category includes the refugees and repatriates resettled and rehabilitated in various islands and generally called as *settlers.* The third group is the voluntary migrant population from mainland India who came here seeking employment in government service, merchants and their employees from mainland and labourers. People of this category are known *as mainlanders.*

Five linguistic groups constitute majority of this non-aboriginal population of the islands. Bengali-speaking people form the largest group, followed by Tamils, Hindustanis, Telugus and Malayalees. These five groups constitute 80.78 per cent of the non-aboriginal population. Besides these five major linguistic groups, there are persons speaking Punjabi, Urdu, Marathi, Oriya, Kannada, Nepali and other languages. They constitute 9.87 per cent of the total population. The Nicobari language spoken by the Nicobarese, the largest tribal community in the Islands constitute 9.34 per cent of the population.

Among the total population, 67.37 per cent are living in rural area and the remaining 32.63 per cent in urban area. Religion-wise classification of the population of the islands reveals that Hindus constitute 69.24 per cent, Christians 21.67 per cent and Muslims 8.22 per cent and other religious communities 0.769 per cent[10].

The Union Territory has no legislature. Till 1967, the Member of Parliament representing this Island was nominated by the President. A Pradesh Council was existing in the islands from July 1979 to 1994. The Pradesh Council was composed of 29 members out of which 24 were elected. There was also provision for representation of women, if no women were elected to the council. The term of the Pradesh Council, when dissolved, was four years.

Local self-governing institutions began in the islands in 1957 with promulgation of Andaman and Nicobar Islands (Municipal Boards) Regulations, by the President of India. Under the Regulation, a Municipal Board at Port Blair, the loan urban area, was established. This body started functioning in 1958. Majority of its numbers were elected. To cater to the civic needs of rural area, the Andaman and Nicobar (Gram Panchayats) Regulation,1961 came into existence. The Regulation provided for establishment of Gram Panchayats and Nyaya Panchayats in these islands. Since the population of Nicobar Group of Islands is predominantly tribal, they have their traditional Panchayats and village Captain who are able to settle local matters and problems amicably.

With the passing of the 73rd and 74th constitutional amendment, further decentralisation was introduced in the islands in the 1990s. In 1994, the Municipal Regulations of 1957 and the Panchayat Regulation of 1961 were repealed by the Andaman and Nicobar (Municipal) Regulation, 1994 and the Andaman and Nicobar (Panchayat) Act, 1994 respectively. The Port Blair Municipal Council consists of 18 wards. As per 73rd Amendment of the Constitution of India, the new Panchayati Raj Institutions (PRIs) began to function with a three-tier system. Accordingly, at present there are 69 Gram Panchayats at village level, seven Panchayat Samities at Block level and two Zilla Parishads at district level. Provision for reservation for women has also been effected as provided in the constitutional amendment.

The following table shows the position of Panchayati Raj Institutions in the Islands:

Table 1: Position of Panchayati Raj in the Islands

Tehsil /Panchayat Samitis		*Gram Panchayat*		*Panchayat Samiti Members*	*Zilla Parishad Members*
Diglpur	North &	15	132	15	06
Mayabunder	Middle	08	81	08	03
Rangat	Andaman	14	141	14	07
Ferrargunj	South	15	163	15	06
Prothrapur	Andaman	10	113	10	05
Little Andaman		04	46	04	02
Campbell Bay		03	31	03	02
Total		**69**	**707**	**69**	**31**

Source: Andaman and Nicobar Gazette Extraordinary, 24th September 2010.

Under the new Andaman and Nicobar Islands (Panchayats) Regulation, 1994, the three-tier panchayati raj system was constituted. The three tiers are Gram Panchayat, Panchayat Smithi and Zilla Parishad. Seats are reserved for Scheduled Tribes and Women according to the Regulation. Elections to the officers of Gram Panchayats are also to be held directly. The Pramukh and Up-pramukhs of Panchayat Samithies are to be elected from amongst the elected members of Panchayati Samithi. The tenure of Panchayats and of Gram Pradhans, Pramukhs and Uppramukhs is five years. The Adhyaksha and Upadhyaksha are to be elected from amongst elected members. Reservation in the offices of the Pradhan of Gram Panchayats as also in the offices of Pramukhs of Panchayat Samithies for the Scheduled Tribes and Women have been provided according to the constitutional provisions. The office of the Adhyaksha for the first and third year of the Zilla Parishad is to be reserved for Women.

The first election to the newly constituted Panchayati Raj Institutions (PRIs) of these islands was conducted in September 1995. Second time elections were held in September 2000 and the third in September 2010. A brief review of the functioning of the PRIs reveals the following scenario.

Along with other State and Union Territories this Island Territory also implemented the three-tier panchayati raj system from 1995 onwards and the seeds of democratic decentralisation have been drilled. The Andaman and Nicobar Administration had already taken all administrative measures to transfer functions as per the 73rd and 74th amendment to enable the PRIs and lone urban area i.e. Port Blair Municipality to function as institutions local self-government. The concerned Departments of the Administration have been given direction to issue orders to transfer the functionaries and assets to the respective PRIs. The present position of the functioning of the PRIs is as follows:-

1. Funds have been already devolved to the local bodies.
2. Regarding functions, some activities in the sectors such as agriculture, veterinary, fisheries, public works (civil), pre-primary education have been already devolved and come within the purview of local bodies.
3. Functionaries also have been transferred to the PRIs at three levels.
4. Capacity building measures have been already initiated by the local administration with the cooperation of National Institute of Rural Development, Hyderabad. Majority of the functionaries and PRI members were imparted training regarding the functions of the local bodies. Non Governmental Organisations (NGO) are involved in the training programmes. Organisations such as Yuvasakthi, ACANI, and the Nehru Yuvak Kendra are among those which are active in the field.
5. Committees have been formed in all PRIs for the functioning of the devolved activities.
6. Steps have been taken from the part of local administration to have proper coordination and liaison with the concerned Departments wherever necessary.

Inspite of the measures undertaken by the local administration, the following ***problems exists in the field of decentralised local governance*** in the Island territory:

(1) Some functions as per the amendment are yet to be devolved. In this category includes the sectors of education and health. Full devolution of activities in the sectors have not been done.

(2) Many elected members of the PRIs lack perception regarding the notion of decentralisation. They lack knowledge to tackle the problems of people in some sectors.

(3) Though literacy rate is high in the Island territory, the general public lack correct perception regarding the working of the PRIs. They *lack a participatory approach.* This is one of the reasons for the lack of active civil society organisations in the islands.

(4) As mentioned above, some Non Governmental Organisations are working actively in the field of rural development. They carry out works relating to formation of Self Help Groups, training for youth development and other functions concerned with local governance. However, their work is not spread over the Islands and not includes

all sectors of development (i.e. not covering the whole geographical area and major socio-economic sectors).

(5) Field observations reveal that due to lack of clear perception and maturity among the elected members of the Panchayat Raj Institutions regarding the notion of decentralised governance, some of them unnecessarily interfere in the working of government institutions. This is especially observed in the fields of education and health.

Suggestions

(1) It can be revealed that ***political parties*** are not active. They have to educate the public so as to inculcate democratic values. This will help the rural mass to participate in Gram Sabha meetings and to get involved in socio-political activities. The political parties have to take steps to ***aggregate the interests*** of the people.

(2) Field experience of the researcher reveals that ***capacity building measures*** undertaken by local administration has not attained the desired results. It has been observed that even after '*formal*' devolution of functions, the public has to depend upon concerned Departments for benefits of the implementation of welfare schemes.

(3) The Department of Local Self Government has to take steps to study the ***problems*** faced by some Panchayats in the sectors of ***education and health***. These two being relevant social sectors, problems in these sectors may have crucial impact on social life of rural mass.

(4) The local administration has to ***conduct studies*** regarding the extent to which results of the welfare programmes are reaching the beneficiaries. These studies can be conducted in collaboration with NGOs and National Institutes like NIRD. The studies in this context are to be conducted from a geographical perspective to observe disparity in socio-economic development.

Concluding Observations

Decentralised governance is the only way to empower people at grassroots level. In developing societies like India, women constitute nearly half of the population. Several research studies reveal that with the implementation of 73rd and 74th amendment, women's participation indicates a positive increase. This can be considered as a positive indicator for formation of social capital.

Gram Sabha has to be regarded as a forum for discussion and deliberation of the issues of the rural people. There is an impression among the people that Gram Sabha is a forum for poor people to get distributed the schemes. It has been observed that the educated middle class refrain from attending the meetings. This has to change. The relevance and need to participate in

Gram Sabha meetings have to be inculcated among the people especially the middle class who have to act as agents of socio-economic change.

A truly decentralised governance can open avenues for full democratic expansion and political reform. However, there is an urgent need to inculcate especially among the womenfolk the advantages of decentralised governance and get them politically socialised.

References

1. World Bank, (2000): *World Development Report,1999 -2000,* Oxford University Press, New York, p.108.
2. *Ibid.*
3. *Ibid.*
4. Gerry Stoker, (1988): The Politics of Local Government, Macmillan, London.
5. (a) Conyers, Conyers, " Decentralisation: The Latest Fashion in Development Administration", *Public Administration and Development,* 3(1), pp.97-109.
   (b) Friedman, H, "Decentralised Governance in Asia: Local Political Alternatives for Decentralised Development", in G.S. Cheema and D. Rondinelli (eds), *Development*, Sage, Beverly Hill.
   (c) Manor, J, "Democratic Decentralisation in Africa and Asia", *IDS Bullett in,* 26(2), pp. 1-2.
6. Rondinelli, D and G.S. Cheema, (1984): *Decentralisation in Developing Countries: A Review of Recent Experience,* World Bank, Washington, D.C.
7. Baker, J.L, (1997): *Poverty Reduction and Human Development in Caribbean : A Cross Country Study*, World Bank, Washington D.C.
8. Andaman and Nicobar Administration, *Basic Statistics, 2007-2008,* Directorate of Economics and Statistics, Andaman and Nicobar Administration, Port Blair, 2009.
9. Andaman and Nicobar Administration, Basic Statistics, of 2011, Directorate of Economics and Statistics, Andaman and Nicobar Administration, Port Blair.
10. Andaman and Nicobar Administration, *Andaman and Nicobar Islands at a Glance 2007*, Directorate of Economics and Statistics, Andaman and Nicobar Administration, Port Blair, 2007, p.13.

20

Democracy, Decentralisation and Development : A Retrospect on the Performance of Panchayati Raj Institutions in India

—*T. Rajan*

Of all the innovative forms of government, democracy is the most appreciable one. The Greeks, who were endowed with a sharp intellect and a philosophical quest, in their pursuit of perfection in terms of virtues, gave birth to a new form of government called *democracy*. But, whether it was their concern for the best system of governance or a crave for virtue, to treat all as equals, to make the system reasonably and logically operational, that compelled them to arrive at the destination of democracy is not clear. However, there is consensus as to the existence of the virtue of equality or at least a presumption as to its existence in a democracy even at present and that emphasises its inevitability for the survival of democracy. Thus, there is *the virtue* at its base and but for the same democracy would be a farce. This is an accepted fact both in theory and practice. The Constructivist Vision at the root of the Doctrine of Human Rights fully endorses this when it postulates: "Traditional societies have two ways of safeguarding their norms- by punishing offenders or by promoting certain virtues in society" (Nalini Rajan, 2002:24-25). But, the Greeks could cast this new adventure in perfect governance only against the background of smaller territorial units called *city states*. Later, the growth of civilisation and unavoidable circumstances of human life compelled the modern generation to recast the same structural device of governance against the larger environment of nation state system. Despite the difference in the background against which this structural device of perfect governance is cast, fundamentally the system presupposes equal participation of people in the policy-making process and a control over its implementation. It is this rationale of democracy that prompted Cleon, the

Athenian Politician, to define democracy as "that shall be democratic which shall be of the people, by the people, for the people." (Hoyeda Abbas, Ranjay Kumar, 2012:394). Close to his heels, in the modern period, Abraham Lincoln defined democracy as government of the people, by the people, for the people in his famous Gettysburg speech on November 17, 1863.

When democracy thus made a shift from its classical attire to modern suit, people became sufficiently large and governmental machinery absolutely complex. Direct participation by the people was found impractical and the inability on the part of the layman to imbibe the spirit of the complexities of modern government made him to embrace representative government. Meanwhile, the Seventeenth Century Europe saw the decay and death of many absolutist monarchies and the rise of popular Governments. The close of Eighteenth Century heralded three major revolutions: the English (1688), the American (1776) and the French (1789). In the intellectual sphere, the political ideas of John Locke and Jean Jacques Rousseau also gave a philosophically democratic base to these popular movements. However, the craze for equality was maintained all throughout.

Representative democracy with its thrust on equality was thus born and still reigns the world. 'The inevitable death of communism', as the triumphalist would speak of it, in the 1990's once again definitely proved democracy's superiority and its success over communism. This triumphalist version clothed in a pseudo philosophical perception finds its expression in the historic statements of Francis Fukuyama. In his article, 'The End of History', he suggested that "capitalist democracy represents the final and highest stage of the development of human political and economic institutions. Capitalist democracy has not yet been realised on a global scale, and perhaps may never be; but never the less that is the goal to which all developing and modernising societies tend and aspire, however fiercely the tendency may be resisted by reactionaries on the one hand, and socialists and communists on the other (Anthony Arblaster, 1994:1). To the western world democracy is their brain child. But, even the communists and the fascists speak about their own style of democracy. Cleaved between these two extremes, one finds it difficult to understand democracy. Whatever mockery the communists made of democracy, there were traces of democracy in their theory and practice too. Their version often offered an alternative conception of what democracy would mean which did offer some kind of challenge to the western world.

However, it is vibrant and current despite the oppositions and challenges. Its currency itself is its importance. But, its systemic comprehensiveness alludes to it's difficulty in understanding. It is a concept because it is a fact. As a fact it has transcended the boundaries of time and space and also varies from situation to situation. Thus, it is susceptible to many definitions. Fundamentally, democracy is identified with popular sovereignty or majority rule: a system of governance in which the people choose their leaders through the process of election. Also known as electoral democracy, this definition describes the process by which a government derives its authority or mandate. In other words, it simply means 'how' a government is formed. This is only one side of the picture. What the government does with the mandate and how it rules are also needed to be analysed. Thus, democracy brings within its wings governance by rule of law, protection of human rights of the people or what it does to promote the wellbeing of the people. Therefore, the practical version of the ideal of democracy combines both the 'How' and 'What' of government. How the two components are to be compromised? Arguments may differ and the stature of democracy may vary. However, it is widely accepted that a true democratic system must compromise both. The extent to which it does so will determine its quality and appreciability and acceptance and durability. On this score Dorothy Pickles visualises a democracy as meaningful which "...must first be able to elicit as accurately as possible the opinions of as many people as possible of who should be their representatives" (Dorothy Pickles,1970:13).

Regarding the first part of the meaning it should be stated that a democracy presupposes election at its base as a process for constituting a government. But, elections as such cannot be considered as the sine qua non of democracy. Elections were there in the erstwhile state of Soviet Russia, El Salvador or the Philippines under President Marcos. Such elections were not free since the people didn't have a choice open to them. The 1984 Nicaraguan regime under Sandinista though claimed popularly elected was not acceptable to the Western bloc and the United States as popular regimes. Therefore, for all practical purposes elections should be free and fair. It should be free from all the vices such as corruption, communalism, sectarianism, muscle power, money and mafia intervention, either direct or indirect. Again, in contemporary democracies, it is generally accepted rightly or wrongly that a government means government by the people or at least by the people's elected representatives. But, on account of the increasing apathy on the part of the people and the possible divisions among the people, the government is likely to be representative, but not of all people and in some cases of the minority as clothed in a coalition for the sake of power grabbing. "Even in national political systems today the rate of non-participation is often high"[1] (Robert A. Dahl, Bruce Stinebrickner, 2003:104). Therefore, preponderance of opinion always favours a representative government with a sound majority base constituted on the basis of free and fair elections. This sound majority base should be built from the bottom level in order to make democracy lively in terms of participation.

Initial thinking on the part of the modern generation during the course of development of democracy always favoured centralisation of powers for security, stability, efficiency and cost effectiveness. But, centralisation despite precautions, always tends to promote arbitrariness and authoritarianism. Moreover, centralisation brings in lack of accommodation, of accommodating the multifarious local interests which characterise the people, and retarded development at an equitable pace among the various localities or regions and even among divergent segments in the society. Its ramifications are unthinkable in a plural and diverse society like India. Thus, democracy to be development-oriented should be decentralised. Only such a decentralised democracy can set the goals of development in the larger context of the nation states. Gandhi showed an uneasy attitude towards democracy when he said: "It was abstracted from society, centralised, bureaucratic, obsessed with homogeneity, and suffused with the spirit of violence" (Vaishali Jain, 2009:31). From a Gandhian perspective centralisation is not only synonymous with violence but also hinders development. It also nullifies equality. True democracy, to him meant, a *shasanmuktha* state, a state free from domination and coercion: a state that is institutionalised and nurtured on *lokshakti* or people's power. Thus, the Gandhian thesis upholds the natural truth that centralisation is opposed to true democracy. That is why all democratic orders the world over preferred to have decentralisation within their democratic frame.

Administration is said to be decentralised when "the lower levels are allowed the discretion to decide most of the matters which come up, reserving comparatively a few bigger and more important problems only for those up" (M.P. Sharma, 1975;121-122). Decentralised administration is known for the active participation of the people and avoidance of delays and jurisdictional disputes because co-ordination is done at the field itself. "Decentralisation is the transfer of planning, decision-making or administrative authority from the central government to its field organisations, local administrative units, and semi-autonomous para statal organisations" (G.S. Cheema, D.A. Rondinelli [ed] 1983;18). It should not be delegation of administrative functions with financial powers to implement the policies that the central authorities cannot undertake or authorises to do. What makes it meaningful is the authority to take decisions themselves and to raise funds themselves. Thus, democratic decentralisation combines administrative decentralisation, political decentralisation and fiscal decentralisation (Meera Chandhoke, Praveen Priyadarsini [ed]: 2009; 247). Moreover, the spirit of democracy alludes to democratic decentralisation a human right perspective. Once power tends to be concentrated, it comes to be corrupted. This may assume multiple dimensions ranging from arbitrary exercise of power by the state to absolute denial of rights to the people at large. In any sense, it undermines the popular base of democracy. Technically speaking, centralisation takes its practical shape from the top to bottom. Therefore, the chance is always in favour of limiting the scope of equality at the top sphere only. Further, this process of confining equality augments severity especially when the vast majority are illiterate and uneducated.

The philosophy that lies behind democratic decentralisation is the age old doctrine of popular sovereignty. People are the sovereigns: they are the ends and means of administration. Therefore, the administration should be responsive, responsible and accountable to the people. To make it conform to the above standards, people should involve themselves in the administration: they should have a role in taking decisions which bind them. Moreover, the source of finances for the government is the tax paid by the people. Hence, people should have the legitimate right to expend the money for their own benefits, in their best interests. They are the judges of what is the best for them. Mahatma Gandhi, the exemplary champion of decentralisation, understood this even before the inauguration of Indian Republic itself. Hence, he stood adamant on its inclusion in the Constitution. Democracy should comply with the needs and aspirations of the people. Generally, it does so. But more important is the question: Does democracy help the people to reap its fruits? Proper service delivery, qualitative improvement in tribal administration, women empowerment gender justice etc could be achieved properly only in a decentralised democratic set up. Further, to set development at an equitable pace among the various sections of the people as well as various regions, decentralisation is necessary. "The huge untapped potential of local initiative needs to be unlocked in every district, block and village, for speedy and context relevant socio-economic development" (V.N. Alok, 2011-12: Forward). Therefore, decentralisation is suggestible as an anti-coagulant in democracy. It is an antidote to bureaucratic authoritarianism.

The very purpose of placing 'the virtue' at the centre of democracy is (i) to effect an equitable distribution of the productive forces in the society and (ii) to achieve and maintain the wellbeing of the people. Together they form the primary step to development. Therefore, 'development' becomes all the more significant. A democratic regime should always aim at and focus on the development of the people. The liberal philosophy finds the inevitability of the state in the rationale of the wellbeing of the people. There should be enough room for the moral and material growth of the *masters*. Therefore, the inevitable outcome is a sound philosophy of 'development' which should be people oriented or pro-people. Invariably, development involves two aspects: It should take care of the present needs of the people as well as their future needs. Moreover, the fruits of development need to be distributed equitably not only among the people in general but also in relation to the needy depending upon the degree of their requirements so as to bring them at par with the general societal standards. Automatically, this entails a process of development through decentralisation. Only this makes administration to "maintaining coordination and communication between the people and the administration" (P.S.N. Sinha (ed), 1991:5). In short, development should aim at decentralised good governance. Former Prime Minister, Manmohan Singh in an address said: "We perhaps need to architect a uniform vision for rural development that can respond differentially and purposefully to development situations in different States and different regions...Many development challenges are [therefore] not uniform national problems any more, but problems of selected States (Prime Minister Manmohan Singh's Speech at the Conference of Chief Ministers, 2004). 'Development' when brought in compatible with decentralisation becomes decentralised development. It was Rajiv Gandhi's realisation, of course absent on the part of the leaders till his date, that impacted upon "to create an environment in which local people participated in development activities," through Panchayati Raj Institutions (PRIs) (Morley Mohan Lal, 1994:3). Since the time of Hellenic civilisation till date the power behind democracy happened to be equality which analytically perceived hints at three implications: (i) equal participation; (ii) equal access to reap the fruits of administration and (iii) equitable pace in development. Only a proper amalgamation of these trio could turn democracy positively. The process of amalgamation should start from the bottom level itself if democracy is to be meaningful.

The PRIs: A Historical Vision

Only democratic decentralisation and decentralised development provide an opportunity to resolve the problems inherent in the working of our system. It is with much credit that our history unravels the merits of democratic decentralisation in ancient India.. "The village organisation in ancient times functioned as a centre of community life independent of the state, which followed a policy of non-interference as long as it received its share of land revenue, its main source of income" (Morley Mohan Lal, 1994:4). In Modern India, it all started with the Bengal Chowkidiri Act 1870 introduced in the erstwhile Bengal presidency.[2] However, its sound foundation was built up on a resolution on local governments adopted by Lord Rippon in 1882.[3] Since then local self-government system took its slow pace in India. But, restricted suffrage based on property and status not only vitiated but also kept it away from its ultimate object. However, it was most unfortunate for post-independent India to witness a heated discussion and sharply divided opinions in the constituent assembly itself over its omission in the new constitution, followed by Gandhi-Ambedkar controversey. Gandhi rightly claimed that the soul of India lives in villages and believed that sovereignty resides at the grassroot level.[4] Anyway at the instance of the majority, Dr Ambedkar finally gave way for Santhanam's proposal. Thus, the present constitution included a provision on organisation of village panchayats as a directive (The Constitution of India, Article:40). Finally, though the Constitution came in to force in1950, for a decade the directive as incorporated in Article 40 practically remained unattended.[5] Experience with the past, however, prompted the authorities to constitute a committee to streamline the activities in this direction. Thus, a committee headed by Balwant Rai Mehta was appointed by the Central

Government to suggest measures for strengthening panchayat system to make them operationally at par with the need of the hour.

The Balwant Rai Committee submitted its report in 1957 and recommended for a three-tier system of local governance from the village to the district level; adequate devolution of power and responsibility to them and transfer of adequate resources. Further, the Committee stressed that all development plans and programmes at these levels should be implemented through them. Indirect election from the grassroot level was advised for the constitution of the block level samiti. The Zilla Parishad should be constituted with members from the lower tier with the District Collector as chairman. The system visualised by this Committee was accepted by the Central Government and endorsed by the National Development Council on January 12, 1959.[6]

The period from 1959-1964 witnessed the ascendancy of PRIs. During this period 90 per cent of rural population were brought under its periphery: about 2.25 lakh panchayats were set up, covering a population of 44 crores. Of the 4,974 blocks, 4,033 had panchayat samitis and 266 out of the 399 districts had Zilla parishads. The extent and form of democratic decentralisation, however, varied from state to state (Morley Mohan Lal,1994:8). However, the period from 1965-1969 saw a period of stagnation. The next eight years witnessed a steady decline in the status and functions of the PRIs. The year 1977 heralded a new era in the political history of India. One party dominance was overthrown: the Congress was routed from power and the Janata Party acceded to power with a thunderous majority at the centre. The new government appointed a Committee under the chairmanship of Ashok Mehta to review the working of panchayathi raj and suggest measures for qualitatively improving the system both infrastructurally and functionally. The Committee submitted its report in 1978 and the Chief Ministers conference (1979) convened at Delhi endorsed it with certain reservations. The major suggestion advanced by the Committee was the replacement of the three with a two-tier. Its recommendations were so crucial for the future development of India that the panchayathi raj should be viewed as a 'government' in its own right at the grassroot level (Amreshwar Avasthi, Anand Prakash Avasthi, 2002:564). A bill was also drafted for the purpose of imparting unity for the system throughout the country. But, due to the collapse of the Janata Government, it was shelved. Out of the factions and feuds of the Janata camp, Indira Gandhi came back to power in 1980. To attract the people especially from the bottom level and to strengthen vote banks, she introduced certain programmes.[7] When Rajiv Gandhi came to power, he added a new dimension to this programme in 1986 by including the preservation and protection of environment.

Suggestions as to removal of the intermediary block level bodies and direct party based election to the PRIs as recommended by the Ashok Mehta

Committee were not liked by a good number of states. Subsequently three more committees were set up—G.V.K. Rao Committee (1985), L.M. Singhvi Committee (1987) and the Thungon Committee (1988). The Thungon Committee for the first time recommended constitutional status for the PRIs. Accordingly the 64th Constitutional Amendment Bill was placed before the Parliament in 1989 under the aegis of Rajiv Gandhi. The Bill was passed in the Lok Sabha but could not be passed in the Rajya Sabha. It opened countrywide deliberations and discussions. On the basis of the overall consensus, the Constitution (Seventy Third Amendment) Act,1992 was passed which constitutionalised the PRIs. Thus, democracy, decentralisation and development are corollaries and contributories: their culmination could be seen only in the PRIs. PRIs, therefore, stand out as exemplary and unparalleled institutions of Indian democracy.

The Constitution (Seventy Third) Amendment Act, 1992

Warranted by the best genius of time and situation, this Amendment heralded a new era in the history of India by providing constitutional status for PRIs in India. The amendment was not a response to pressure from grassroots, but the result of an increasing recognition that the institutional initiatives so far designed and implemented in the preceeding decades had not delivered; that the extent of rural poverty was still too large and thus the existing structure of government needed to be reformed.

The amendment which came in to force in April 1993 introduced Part IX (Articles 243-243 O) and Eleventh Schedule covering 29 subjects over which the PRIs can legislate. It was binding for all states to pass Conformity Acts within one year of the commencement of the said amendment. The Constitution of India, Article 243(d)) defines Panchayat: "Panchayat' means an institution (by whatever name called) of self government constituted under Article 243-B, for rural areas." Art 243 B specifies that "There shall be constituted in every state, panchayats at the village, intermediate and district levels in accordance with the provisions of this part." Thus, the Act provided for a three-tier system throughout India.

The Act in Operation

The concept of democratic decentralisation has dominated the dynamics of development discourses and a matter of serious concern in independent India over the last half a century. It became a policy of concern, discussion and deliberation in many Asian, African and Latin American countries since 1960s. Democratic decentralisation, as already stated, presupposes decentralisation at three spheres: Political, administrative and financial. Ever since the adoption of the Constitution (Seventy Third Amendment) Act,1992, political decentralisation had been sought to be installed at the Indian democratic framework. At the infrastructural level, the Act provided for a three-tier system of PRIs. The following Table illustrates the infrastructural pattern of political decentralisation at the all-India level.

Since 1993 PRIs at the district level, intermediate level and the village level have come to stay in India. The lowest unit in almost all states is called the Grama Panchayat. The name of the intermediate rung differs from state to state.[8] The PRIs at the district level is called the District Panchayat or Zilla Parishad (ZP)/ Parishad in many states.

Table I: Table showing the number of Elected Panchayat Institutions in India by States/Union Territories as on March, 2012

Sl.No.	*State*	*Village*	*Intermediate*	*District*
1.	Andhra Pradesh	21807	1097	22
2.	Arunachal Pradesh	1779	161	16
3.	Assam	2202	185	24
4.	Bihar	8442	531	38
5.	Chhattisgarh	9734	146	18
6.	Goa	189	0	2
7.	Gujarat	13945	223	26
8.	Haryana	6083	119	21
9.	Himachal Pradesh	3243	77	12
10.	Jammu & Kashmir	4139	212	24
11.	Jharkhand	4423	259	24
12.	Karnataka	5627	176	30
13.	Kerala	978	152	14
14.	Madhya Pradesh	23012	313	50
15.	Maharashtra	27937	351	33
16.	Manipur	165	4	6
17.	Meghalaya(a)	0	0	3
18.	Mizoram(a)	707	0	0
19.	Nagaland(a)	1110	0	0
20.	Odisha	6236	314	30
21.	Punjab	12775	143	20
22.	Rajasthan	9177	248	33
23.	Sikkim	165	0	4
24.	Tamil Nadu	12524	385	31
25.	Tripura	511	23	4
26.	Uttar Pradesh	51914	821	72
27.	Uttrakhand	7555	95	13
28.	West Bengal	3351	333	18

(Contd...)

29.	Andaman & Nicobar Island	69	7	2
30.	Chandigarh	12	1	1
31.	Dadar & Nagar Haveli	11	0	1
32.	Daman & Diu	14	0	1
33.	NCT of Delhi (b)	0	0	0
34.	Lakshadeep	10	0	1
35.	Puducherry	98	10	0

Source: MoPR, Govt. of India.

(a) For traditional village and autonomous district councils exist in these states

(b) Panchayat has yet to be revived

Altogether, there are 2,39,946 Grama Panchayats, 6174 Intermediate Panchayats and 570 District Panchayats in India as on March, 2012. Among the Indian States, Uttar Pradesh with 51,914 Grama Panchayats stands at the top, followed by Maharashtra having 27,937. At the lowest rung of the ladder stand both Manipur and Sikkim with 165 Grama Panchayats. Coming to Union Territories (UTs), Puducherry bags the first place with 98 followed by Andaman and Nicobar Island with 69 Grama Panchayats. Lakshadeep having 10 Grama Panchayats stand at the bottom level. While Uttar Pradesh has 2,988 population per village, Maharashtra got a population of 2,203 per village. In respect of the total number of village panchayats, there is a wide discrepancy between the two states, the difference being 23,977.

Political Decentralisation

Political decentralisation is the innate trait of democracy. But, when the original Hellenistic notion of democracy was rescheduled in the wider context of the nation state system, it became representative by losing its popular basis at the functional level.[9] Consequently, political decentralisation has come to be confined to universal adult franchise which though builds up a society of politically equals, ignores the ubiquitous participation of the people. It is to rectify this defect that the idea of political decentralisation has been rejuvenated to mean letting the masses directly to involve themselves in both policy formulation and implementation. People are the best judges of their likes and dislikes: they are the masters of their own environment. Therefore, they should have a say, not that much alone, actual control over policy and administration.

The question that arises at this point of time is the effectiveness of these Grama Panchayats in terms of political decentralisation. How effective and efficient are the Grama panchayats in effectuating the will of the people at the grass root level? Such an analysis should be made at two levels- infrastructural and operational or functional. In the infrastructural side, everything is okay as shown in the Table. At par with the requirements of the Act and at the behest of the Central Government almost all the States have put in to effect the mandatory requirement of establishing Gram Sabhas in the manner provided in the Constitution. The second question need be answered in the wider context of the process of implementation itself. Therefore, it should start with the factors influencing the election process itself. Periodic elections at an interval of every five years is postulated by law itself. But, there were instances of elections being postponed by the state government itself on very many occasions in different states. Assam, one of the pioneer states that introduced PRIs way back in 1948[10] itself happened to experience such a situation. The tenure of the PRIs expired in 1997. Instead of holding elections at the earliest, it was put off on ground of budget session in 1997, monsoon in 1998, law and order situation, and census operation in subsequent years and thus kept delayed till 2002. Similarly, in Bihar despite the adoption of the Bihar Panchayat Raj Act,1993 subsequent to the Constitution (Seventy Third Amendment) Act,1992, elections were held only in 2001. Similarly, elections were held in Jharkhand and Jammu and Kashmir after decades (Report of the Task Force, 2011:4). Delay in holding elections remains a regular feature of the PRIs in almost all states in India, the only variation being in the span of time among the states in respect of delay.

Close to the heels of delayed elections comes the question of free and fair elections. Are the PRI elections free and fair? As per Articles 243K (The Constitution of India, Article 243K), the superintendence, direction, control and conduct of elections to the Panchayat shall be vested in a State Election Commission (SEC) consisting of a State Election Commissioner. The SECs are to function independently of the state government concerned. The SEC cannot be removed from office except in like manner and on like grounds as a judge of a High Court. The Governor is mandated by the Constitution to make available to the Commission such staff as may be necessary for the discharge of his duties. Subject to these provisions, the Constitution empowers the State legislature to make laws regarding elections to Panchayats. The powers, and responsibilities vested on the SEC are identical with that of the Election Commission of India in regard to elections to Parliament and State Legislatures. Here, the intention of the Constitution is clear. The Constitution expects that the SEC should be an independent body.

But, the approach of the various states towards the SEC is different. In the Constitutional framework, laws regarding Panchayat elections are framed by States, and therefore, there is a great deal of variation across States. Several SECs face constraints in conducting free and fair elections.[11] "Even though the third tier of government has a constitutional status now, all State Governments are not able to give State Election Commissions the priority they need and deserve for ensuring a fair and equitable operation of democracy" (Report of the Task Force, 2011:3-4). Inadequate legal, administrative and financial powers account for this state of affairs. Election Jurisprudence has evolved well in India over the years in relation to Parliament and State Legislatures. Legally and constitutionally the same is applicable to PRIs also. But, for want of in-house legal personnel, law officers and libraries, the SECs are practically incapable to assert their stand in courts. Application of benefits and fruits of information technology (IT) which facilitates speedier and effective governance in all walks of governmental business are not being used by the SECs for want of ample IT personnel, knowhow in hardware and software.

Despite the Amendment and subsequent laws made, the SECs do not enjoy a uniform status throughout India. The status accorded by the states to their respective Commissions determine their potency. In fourteen of the Indian states, the SECs are given a status of the High Court Judge. The State of Maharashtra had conferred upon the SEC a status equivalant to that of a High Court Judge. The following Table provides an overview of this.

Table II: Table showing the status, tenure and age limit in respect of SECs in the States and Union Territories

Sl.No.	*Name of state/UT*	*Status*	*Tenure*	*Age limit*
1.	Andhra Pradesh	HC Judge	5	65
2.	Arunachal Pradesh	,,	,,	,,
3.	Assam	,,	4	62
4.	Bihar	Chief Secretary	5	65
5.	Chhattisgarh	HC Judge	5	,,
6.	Chandigarh	Not defined	3	,,
7.	Delhi	,,	,,	,,
8.	Gujarat	Addl. Chief Secretary	5	Not Fixed
9.	Goa	HC Judge	,,	65
10.	Haryana	,,	,,	,,
11.	Himachal Pradesh	Not defined	,,	Not fixed
12.	Jammu & Kashmir	A senior officer holding addl.charge of Secretary	Not defined	Not fixed
13.	Jharkhand	HC Judge	3	64
14.	Kerala	Chief Secretary	5	65
15.	Karnataka	HCJudge	,,	Not fixed
16.	Maharashtra	Equivalent to HC Judge	,,	,,
17.	Madhya Pradesh	,,	6	66
18.	Manipur	Law Secretary holding addl. Charge	3	62
19.	Mizoram	Chief Secretary	,,	Not fixed
20.	Nagaland	,,	,,	,,
21.	Odisha	HC Judge	5	65

(Contd...)

22.	Punjab	HC Judge	5,	65
23.	Puducherry	Secretary to Govt.	3	,,
24.	Rajasthan	Chief Secretary	5	,,
25.	Sikkim	HC Judge	,,	67
26.	Tamil Nadu	,,	2	No limit
27.	Tripura	Equivalent to Prl. Secretary, Govt.of Tripura/Addl.Secretary	5	62
28.	Uttar Pradesh	HC Judge	,,	65
29.	Uttrakhand	,,	,,	,,
30.	West Bengal	,,	,,	66
31.	Andaman & Nicobar islands,Lakshadweep, Dadra & Nagar Havali, Daman & Diu	Secretary to Govt.of India/ Chief Secretary	,,	65

Source: MoPR, Govt. of India

In Bihar, Kerala, Mizoram, Nagaland and Rajasthan, the SECs enjoy a status of the Chief Secretary. The status of the SEC in Gujarat is that of an Additional Chief Secretary. In Tripura, it is equivalent to Principal Secretary, Government of Tripura/Additional Chief Secretary. Both in Jammu and Kashmir, a senior officer of the government holds additional charge of the SEC. The most unfortunate thing is that even in Delhi it is not defined till date. In Union Territories, the respective SECs are given the status of Secretary to Government of India/Additional Chief Secretary

Similarly, there is no upper age limit for holding the post of SEC in Tamil Nadu. In states like Gujarat, Himachal Pradesh, Karnataka, Maharashtra, Mizoram and Nagaland their upper age is not limited.

Absence of infrastructural facilities also bars the SECs in certain states from enjoying an autonomous status. "In some states, the State Election Commissions are housed in State Government Secretariats creating the impression as if they are part of the state government or one of its departments" (Report of the Task Force, 2011:5). Situations like these do not conform to the independence and impartiality the ESCs. "Apart from many other things, the involvement of parties makes the entire election process far more complex, given the fact that State Election Commissions are not that powerful and effective as the Election Commission of India (The Hindu, October 1, 2013).

Party-based election, though recommended by the Ashok Mehta Committee, was not accepted by the best brains for the Indian PRI frame-work initially. Experiences over the years, however, show that in all the states in India PRI elections are being fought on party lines. This party based elections disunite the people at the grassroot level on ideological basis and on other common party lines. Often, it takes the form of state patronage when the same party happens to rule the state as well as the PRIs. The worst impact of this patronage is the exclusion of a large chunk of local people from participating in the activities at the local level. Moreover, it also tends to exclude the people from equitably sharing the benefits of administration. In short, party based democracy prevents en masse participation, a vital ingredient of grassroot democracy.The recent statement made by Master, Lakha Singh, the State Office Secretary of the International Democratic Party on the eve of PRI elections in Punjab in May, 2013 sounds seriously in this context. The State Officer said: "the move will decrease the functionalism at village levels, the pillars of democracy…if the elections are contested without going under the banner of political parties, the elected representatives could be free to think for the development of village level institutions than going in for factionalism" (The Times of India, April, 21, 2013). It is on this score that T. Ramakrishnan, a veteran Media person said: "One aspect that ought to have been included in any debate on local governments is the desirability of continuing with the existing system of direct participation of political parties" (The Hindu, October 1, 2013). Despite the higher literacy rate and other development indices, even the State of Kerala cannot keep itself fully aloof from this situation.

Attempts at attributing potentiality to the principle of political decentralisation started with the Guwahati Round Table (November, 2004). It made several recommendations on Panchayat Elections. At the outset itself it was suggested that since the Indian voter is one and indivisible, there must be parity in the electoral process between Parliamentary, Assembly and Panchayat elections. Therefore, the MoPR recommended frequent and intermittent consultations between the Chief Election Commissioner and the State Election Commissioners and also favoured evolving a common electoral roll for elections at all the three levels (A Mid-Term Review and Appraisal, 2006:41).

At the functional side, as with other elections at the national or state level, it has come to be observed that "…with increased devolution of funds and functions, the use of money power in elections to LSG has increased." (Report of the Task Force, MoPR; 2011,17). It is ironical to see that in the midst of India's unchallengable status as the largest democracy in the world, her politics has come to be throttled by money power. Money makes its way in to politics when the voter turnout is comparatively low. The impact of money power is likely to be less if polling is higher. However, the middle class is comparatively free from the impact of money. But, at the grassroot level votes are actually bought by political parties (Ashat Kandelwal, 2013:14).

The election procedure at the PRIs' level is also not free from peculiar power relationships that exist in India. "The developments of the twentieth century have forced intellectuals in India to look beyond the institutionalised structures of power" (Mahendra Prasad Singh, Subhendu Ranjan Raj[ed], 2012:49). At the societal level power is distributed among social relationships in the form of caste, class and gender. These are status groups. Their speciality is that they tend to bind the people of the same status in to specific groups negating political affiliations and ideological commitments. Despite our status as the largest democracy, caste still continues to evade through in these groups. The recent brutal attack on dalits by caste Hindus in Bihar, that too, on the independence day exemplifies the all pervasive nature of caste perversion (The Hindu, August, 21, 2013)." In the 1950s and 1960s, caste had been a silent factor in Indian power politics. Now, with the rise in backward-caste movement and dalit movement, the entire discourse on power has changed. They are considered as vote banks..." (Mahendra Prasad Singh, Subhendu Ranjan Raj [ed], 2012: 49). This is the result of a social upsurge which India experienced in the 1980s and 1990s: the dalits, adivasis, women and peasants emerged as new potential centres. The finest example is the State of Madhya Pradesh (MP). From the place of a social group caste has permeated the very vitals of MP politics. It is not politics that is caste ridden, it is caste that gets politicised in MP (Deol, J.S,1978:161). To repeat the lines of Rao, caste plays a twin role in MP-in rural areas it acts as political groups and in urban areas as social groups (Lekshman Rao,1979:8).Therefore, members of the dominant castes get a better chance of securing seats from the national parties than members of the non-dominant castes. Often party tickets are distributed on the basis of caste. There, members of the forward castes get a better chance of securing party tickets. Again, within the party itself caste plays a vital role sometimes bringing it to the brim of collapse as in 1980.[12] This is not an isolated instance in MP alone. Generally speaking, even the most advanced states in India like Kerala is also not free from this vicious circle. Even at the grassroot level elections caste plays a vital role. The very emergence of the Dalit Human Rights Movement (DHRM) in Kerala reminds us of a burning issue in caste polarisation in Kerala Politics.

Again, Mafias, in their search for resources, are tightening their grip over villages. Land mafias, sand mafias and criminal gangs are conducting themselves in such a manner as to have a hand on the grassroot administration. On the otherside, the innate inclination for money among the ruling structures also brings them closer to these mafias. Thus, as an extension of the general scenario, in villages too "ruling structures are coming under the influence of strong-armed mafia and lumpen elements, accompanied by the rise of money power and growing criminalisation and corruption..." (Rajni Kothari, 2005:3). Again, it is not too remote to forget about the allegation raised by Aiyar, the Union Minister in-charge of Panchayat Raj from 2004-2009 that all levels of panchayats across the country are involved in corruption. All these tend to deactivate the spirit and purpose of political decentralisation at the PRI level in India. Moreover, the traditional landscape of Indian federalism also poses a danger to the serenity of political decentralisation. The upper echelons of elected representatives often have a feeling of superiority and they consider the PRIs, at least in rare instances, as a challenge to their authority. The after effects of globalisation have reduced these elites and bureaucrats in to the status of mere tools to woo the common man at the bottom level. The mining magnate, Bharat Aluminium Company Ltd (Balco) decided to have 50 acres of forest land in Taraimarh village in Chhattisgarh. It is also in the process of acquiring 1,070 hectares of land granted as part of a mining lease in Dharmajaigarh block for its intended power plant at Korba in the same state.This will cause to disappear three villages.They tried to intrude in to the villages through the Tehsildar with the connivance of certain MLAs and MPs. However, the serious Gram Sabhas resisted their design (The Hindu, September 30, 2013). There are certain likely situated instances, though stray in sequence, in which Gram Sabhas effectuated themselves. An exemplary situation recently emerged from Kerala shows how potential the Gram Sabha is in view of its broad based participatory character. When there was a move to resume functioning of a granite quarry in Pathanamthitta under police protection at the instance of the district collector disregarding the refusal of licence by the grama panchayat, people en masse revolted against it, finally forcing the withdrawal of the permission granted by the district collector (The Hindu, October, 5, 2013). However, on the whole, a sound judgement on a reasonable perception compels one to say that political decentralisation has not attained maturity at the PRIs level in India. Delay, that too unnecessary and unwarranted, in the conduct of elections, elections conducted remaining far from being free and fair, escalating role of caste politics, intrusion of money and muscle power and allied and emerging perverse forms of politicisation together with infrastructural flaws especially the one in respect of the status of the SECs are evidentially pointing at the insignificant impact of political decentralisation. Whatever the Gram Sabhas have achieved over the years are definitely far less than their shortcomings.

Administrative Decentralisation

Administrative decentralisation that comes next to political decentralisation stands for devolution of administrative responsibilities from top to bottom. It indicates a genuine transfer of power and responsibility to these institutions of local government with adequate resources. Democracy can become truly participatory only if administration is decentralised. It helps to create a sense of nearness between the people and the seat of authority leading to their involvement in all walks of administration. Moreover, sharing benefits of administration by the people is also made more fruitful by administrative decentralisation. Decentralisation, being the antithesis of concentration, helps the people, to a certain extent, to be free from governmental arbitrariness. Moreover, decentralisation enables the people to enjoy human rights in an unhindered manner. In fact, political decentralisation and administrative decentralisation are two sides of the same coin. Democracy could achieve meaning and relevance only if there is convergence between the two.

Only administrative decentralisation takes development to the grassroot level. The philosophy that suggests a common remedy to the many ills of India advances the doctrine that development should begin from the bottom level. Accelerated development can be provided only if governmental efforts are adequately supplemented by direct and indirect involvement of the people at the grassroot level.

Article 243G (The Constitution of India, Article:243G) mandates the States to endow the Panchayats with such powers and authority as may be necessary to enable them to function as institutions of self-government and to effect devolution of powers accordingly on the items specified in the Elevanth Schedule. The aim of this devolution should be (a) the preparation of plans for economic development and social justice in the context of the Panchayat and (b) the implementation of schemes for economic development and social justice as may be entrusted to them including those mentioned in the Eleventh Schedule. The inferences that follows from any reasonable interpretation of this Article are: (i) devolution of powers and functions are the responsibility of the State and (ii) the Panchayat can undertake to implement such schemes including those in the Eleventh Schedule only if it is entrusted to the Panchayats. Clearly, the State Government has an upper hand in the matter of devolution of powers and responsibilities. When this pucca fact is corroborated with the absence of a clear cut division of powers between the States and Panchayats as in the case of the Union and States, the problem assumes a larger dimension. Moreover, the Eleventh Schedule also brings in complexities in the wake of duplication and overlapping between the State List and Concurrent Subjects. This had forced the Central Government to step in to expedite the process of devolution.

Administrative decentralisation got momentum at an augmented pace with the establishment of the Ministry of Panchayati Raj (MoPR) in 2004 which evolved a series of clear and dedicated action plans.[13] In the First Round Table held at Kolkata in July, 2004, the delegates concentrated on how to strengthen Gram Sabhas. It was resolved that States would work towards devolving powers and responsibilities in relation to all matters listed in the Eleventh Schedule. It was also decided that devolution should be based on mapping of activities at the three levels in order to bring clarity in tasks and responsibilities at each level. The key outcome of the Round Table was the resolve on the part of the delegates to complete activity mapping in all states by April, 2005. The Second Round Table held in Mysore (August, 2004), decided to speed up the process of activity mapping and evolve steps to save the PRIs from being bypassed. Parallel structures at state and district levels for the implementation of centrally and state sponsored schemes and registered societies are found to bypass the PRIs.[14] But, the focus was to constitute District Planning Committees (DPCs) in all districts where these had not so far been constituted by April, 2005.

A long eight years have elapsed since the Round Table Conferences. Still the governments at the upper two levels, especially the Central Government, have not been able to achieve as much as they visualised. Devolution, activity mapping, Planning Commissions at the district level etc were constituted. The Task Force constituted in the Fifth Round Table at Srinagar (October, 2004), recommended that " All parallel bodies created by or through scheme conditionalities of Centrally Sponsored Schemes (CSSs) should be wound up or merged with Standing Committees of the PRIs" (Mid-Term Review and Appraisal, 2006:46). This was initiated to avoid any instance of bypassing the PRIs by the scheme functionaries. But, till date that was not effectuated in the manner as thought for.

An attempt at 'rationalising policy in respect of Centrally Sponsored Schemes 'as included the Eleventh Schedule' of the Constitution' was undertaken by a Group of Ministers (GoM) with the Union Minister for Human Resource Development (HRD) in chair. The GoM stipulated that two mapping exercises by the Central Ministries and the States, respectively, should be carried out in co-ordination with each other (Mid-Term Review and Appraisal, 2006:46). Similarly, the Chandigarh Round Table (October, 2004) resolved that in terms of Article 243N of the Constitution, State legislations must incorporate a Memorandum of Local Government to every new law so as to harmonise and reconcile legislation relating to the Panchayats with other legislation impinging on the same issues (Mid-Term Review and Appraisal, 2006:40). Consequent up on the stern will of the Central Government, new avenues for strengthening decentralisation were carved out in various fields in the administrative sector. In the field of education, the role of the Panchayats in the planning and monitoring of Sarva Shiksha Abhiyan (SSA) has been formalised. Mid Day Meal (MDM) Scheme was cast in such a way as to provide for the centrality of the PRIs (Mid-Term Review and Appraisal, 2006:47). The PRIs are also assigned a positive role in the implementation of the National Rural Health Mission (NHRM).[15] In rural infrastructure building also the PRIs are given a sure hand. Popularly known as Bharat Nirman, the programme concentrates on developing rural infrastructure in six areas.[16] Again, PRIs were directly involved in public distribution system to the extent it supervises the fair price shops. The guidelines for village Grain Bank Scheme have been revised giving centrality to panchayats.

Thus, when perceived from a straight away plane, it can be said that we have achieved administrative decentralisation. But the innermost of the story reverberates with certain hard realities, all of which tell about the sad demise of the spirit of this administrative decentralisation. Though the propensity of state domination in the matter of devolution has been buttressed by central initiatives, absence of any clear cut division of powers between the states and panchayats, the complexities posed by the XI schedule in the form of duplication and overlapping and the presence of parallel bodies altogether cause to nullify its spirit and soul. Moreover, the ghost of the traditional bureaucratic mind still pervades through the landscape of administrative decentralisation. They are not in a mood to accept the significance of or the spirit inherent in the PRIs. Not only that many of the projects designed for the people are found to be practically of little help to the people. Even at present, the sponsored schemes, both central and state, tend to bypass the PRIs by virtue of the over enthusiasm or callousness of the bureaucrats. In the much accomplished State of Kerala itself the situation is grim. Recently, the Kerala Government has started a Grow Bag Scheme for attaining reliance in vegetable production. The scheme was essentially planned and implemented by the state to the exclusion of the PRIs except in the field of advice to cultivators. The Attappady Irrigation Plan in Kerala started in 1980 for Rs 400 crores with the object of irrigating the hills, supply drinking water to the tribal hamlets and generate power, though dormant over a period of more than 30 years, was finally rejuvenated in the 2012-13 budget but only to abandon it (Hindu, October 21, 2013). Had it been conceived on par with entry 3 of the XI schedule, it should have been done by the Panchayat itself and the Panchayat would have done it and benefitted by it. This is an instance of the State overstepping Panchayats in the matter of development, thus eroding the very spirit and purpose of administrative decentralisation. Again, many a children had lost their lives in Attappady in a series of instances of death mainly due to malnutrition and spread of epidemics. Of late, it has been reported in the media that 59 children have lost their lives within 16 months in Attappady (Deshabhimani, November 3, 2013). This should be weighed against the background of assigned duties of the panchayats in the health sphere. This is another instance of failure of administrative decentralisation.

A recent study conducted by the Rajiv Gandhi Institute of Development Studies in Neyyar (Kerala State) concluded that Panchayats are not able to cater to the needs of the people because of the additionally imposed duty of welfare pension distribution. Of these, the most important schemes that disturb the normal work of the Panchayats are the distribution of benefits in lieu of Unemployment Scheme and Karshaka Thozhilali scheme (Farmers' Welfare Scheme). The survey assessed the total number of loss of panchayat working days in this regard as 18 and 8 respectively. Other findings of the study relate to the failure of panchayats in protecting water sources and waste processing (Malayala Manorama, October 8, 2013). The total work paralysis caused by pension distribution is due to the lack of staff. This tendency of imposing additional work load without providing adequate staff definitely affect the capability of panchayats for which none other than the State Government is to be blamed. Needless to speak about the failure of the local bodies in preserving water resources and waste management. Water resources are exhausted or polluted in Kerala and elsewhere in India. Keralites would not have forgotten the Plachimada Issue in which the panchayat itself played from behind. No concerted and effective effort has been taken so far even by a single panchayat in the whole of India in the matter of tackling pollution of water resources. Similarly, waste management, the gravest concern of the present day still remains to be unsolved and unresolved at the hands of the panchayats. In the northern states, caste atrocities and economic disparities are on the rampage in villages. All these glaring instances tend to question the very viability of administrative decentralisation as an effective tool of participatory democracy in India.

Financial Decentralisation

It is an accepted principle of administration that there should be a match between functions and finances. Only the balance between the two will help any organisation to realise its goals or objectives. The translation of policies in to functions itself is an exercise in expenditure which, in turn, mandates an assignment in revenue. Thus, comes the preponderant role of finance and the need for independence in the realm of finance. The demand for financial autonomy for local government is a subject of debate and discussion in various countries of the world. Recently, it has become contentious in both Malasia and Nigeria. In India too, the foremost among the multiple causes that lay embedded in the PRIs framework is the question of financial autonomy itself.

A fair degree of financial autonomy is the sine qua non for the PRIs to function effectively as self-governing institutions. What has been couched as financial autonomy is simply the right for local governments to have direct access to funds. Such funds can be raised by way of taxation, through borrowing powers, sharing taxes and duties and receiving grants-in-aid. In the context of the PRIs in India, financial autonomy means that the units at the bottom level should have their own taxation, borrowing powers and a share in state's taxes and duties and grants-in-aid from higher levels. It speaks of an independent status in the matter of raising, borrowing and spending of money.

As per Article 243-H of the Indian Constitution, the legislature of a state may (a) authorise a Panchayat to levy, collect and appropriate taxes, duties, tolls and fees; (b) assign to a Panchayat such taxes, duties, tolls and fees levied and collected by the state government; (c) provide for grants-in-aid to the Panchayat from the Consolidated Fund of India and (d) provide for the constitution of Funds for crediting all such moneys received.

Moreover, Article 243-I provides for the constitution of a Finance Commission at the state level to review the financial position of the Panchayat within one year from the commencement of the Constitution (Seventy Third Amendment) Act,1992, and thereafter at the expiry of every fifth year. The Commission can make recommendations as to the principles which should govern (a) the distribution between the State and Panchayats of the net proceeds of the taxes, duties, tolls and fees leviable by the State and the allocation of their respective shares between Panchayats at all levels; (b) the determination of the taxes, duties, tolls and fees assigned to or appropriated by the Panchayats; (c) the grants-in-aid to the Panchayats from the Consolidated Fund of India. It can also recommend (i) on the measures to improve the financial position of the Panchayats and (ii) any other matter referred to this Commission by the Governor in the interests of sound finance of the Panchayats. Provision for proper accounting, maintenance of accounts and auditing of accounts shall be made by the Legislature vide Article 243-J of the Constitution.

The chief sources of revenue of PRIs constitute (i) tax revenue; (ii) non tax revenue; (iii) shared tax revenue and (iv) plan assistance to local governments. In the category of tax revenue comes property tax, profession tax, entertainment tax, advertisement tax, service tax and show tax. Non-tax revenue includes license fee, gate fee, income from property in the form of rent, income from property other than rent, permit fees, registration fees, service user charges, income from ferries and fines and penalties. Shared tax comprises maintenance grant and general purpose fund. Lastly, comes plan assistance to local governments for both centrally sponsored and state sponsored schemes. Despite the multiple sources and care taken by the Central Government, the fact remains that no state could acquire financial stability viable enough to achieve financial independence. Moreover, misappropriation, misuse, political patronage and corruption among the bureaucracy tend to create situations hampering the very financial independence of the PRIs.

Eversince the introduction of the Ministry of Panchayat Raj in 2004, the Ministry has been urging all State Governments to quickly follow up Activity Maps with fiscal devolution patterned on the model of Kerala and Karnataka[17] by the end of 2007-08 fiscal year. The Ministry also advised already advanced states in fiscal devolution to undertake reviews to further improve their pattern and content of devolution. Imbibing the spirit of past experience the Ministry stood in favour of a "Bing Bang Approach", that is to say, the governments at the Central and State levels should place confidence on substantial devolution rather than moving incrementally towards devolution.

Efficient use of finances requires a well built planning process at the grassroot level. "Thus, district planning, as envisaged in the Constitution, is not a romantic notion but a practical, feasible and desirable process of participative, democratic, grassroots governance through which, as stipulated in Article 243G, Panchayat Raj institutions come in to their own as institutions of self government" (A Mid-Term Review and Appraisal, 2006:8). At par with the spirit of grassroot planning, Article 243ZD provides for the constitution in every state at the district level a District Planning Committee to consolidate the plans prepared by the Panchayats and the municipalities in the district and to prepare a draft development plan for the district as a whole. The Constitution provides for an elected District Planning Committee (DPC) at each district to the extent of 80 per cent (Four-fifths) membership, by and from and among the elected members of the district level panchayat and municipalities within the district. The rest 20 per cent is caused to be nominated by the legislature to assist the DPC in the technical and administrative complexities of planning. The process of planning itself is designed in such a fashion as to confer up on the bottom units wider discretion. These units are to undertake planning based up on their local needs and environment. It is stated that DPCs are required to "consolidate" and not prepare the draft district plan. Invariably, this proposition carries three necessary implications: (a) Plans must emerge from the bottom level; (b) Plans, thus, emerging from the grassroot level, when they reach the DPCs, are to be consolidated and put in to a draft. Here, Article 243ZD imposes on the DPCs a duty to prepare the draft and not the final plan and instructs them to forward these drafts to state governments for finalisation and (c) At the consolidation level, for clarifications and avoiding conflicts DPCs should be backed by the district level bureaucracy, a team of dedicated technical experts and civil society activists. Thus,funds and the way in which they are put to use are more or less in conformity with the spirit of the PRIs. But, due to constraints of practical realities we couldn't achieve financial independence.

In the collection of tax revenues the PRIs couldn't make any headaway. On perusal with computational data from various studies, it could be discerned that even Property tax, a major source of revenue for the PRIs was neither scientifically assessed nor periodically collected. Both political and bureaucratic patronage extended to the defaulters together with lack of infrastructure in the form of staff constitute the major cause for failure of timely collection. A scientific assessment of the said tax remains long due in the vast majority of states including Kerala. More or less similar is the situation in respect of all taxes in this category except profession tax. In the non-tax revenue category, the PRIs often fail to elicit compliance from the commuters. Even when there is compliance, there is a stinch of falsification of data, making the PRIs the losers. This compels the PRIs to look to the upper stairs for finance, solely putting them in a state of dependence. Failure to have adequate infrastructure and lack of expertise in planning and preparation of plans also hamper the financial stability of the grassroot level. The delay in preparing the Detailed Project Report (DPR) for securing funds under the Jawaharlal Nehru National Urban Renewal Mission (JNNURM) and consequent expected failure to obtain funds to the tune of Rs 15,000 crore to the State of Kerala is material in this context (The Hindu, November 3, 2013). The reason for this is stated to be the incompetency of many local bodies to prepare DPR in time coupled with the inefficiency or callousness of the state government. Again, the fate of the Attappady Valley Irrigation Project (AVIP) in Kerala visualised in 1980 and its non materialisation even at present despite an allocation of Rs 400 crore in the budget of 2012-13, shows the disinterested state approach towards the PRIs in providing finances.

Globalisation and the forces that it left had played havoc with the finances of the national states. Multinationals and corporates have found their way in to India. This had badly affected the status of national governments. The very same forces have put institutions at the grassroot level under constraints, the major constraint being the lack of funds itself. As usual misappropriation and misuse of funds, political patronage and corruption among politicians and bureaucrats also tended to negate financial autonomy of the PRIs.

Taking Cognisance

Our system is a highly centralised one. Perhaps more centralised than Communist China itself. Amidst ideological and administrative centralisation, China happens to have the fortune of augmenting rapid economic progress by enlisting the support and active participation of local governments. Employment and exports in China are powered by the millions of Town and Village Enterprises (TVEs) with the help and support of local governments. Geographic compulsions, historical facts, British legacy and the diversity of India in its multiple walks of life contributed extensively for a higher degree of centralisation so as to keep her intact. The innate dangers involved in such an unparalleled and unethical centralisation often made the rare and few geniuses in India to bargain for decentralisation. That is the reason why the floor of the Constituent Assembly itself witnessed conflicting opinions on the inclusion of Panchayat System in the Constitution. From the date of commencement of the Constitution on 26th January 1950 to the adoption of the Constitution (Seventy Third Amendment) Act, that provision in Part IV remained rather dormant at the operational level and an amendment itself became necessary to enforce it.

At present decentralisation at its best is achieved in India at the theoretical plane with the grassroot level emerging as a power symbol. Grama Sabhas at the bottom most level are capable of according not only representation but also ensures participation to the people. Perusing the infrastructural standards as somewhat okay does not mean to accept the disabilities and limitations at the functional side. Flaws within the electoral system, role of money power and mafia influence, increasing considerations of class and caste and the like have arrested the Gram Sabhas' potential growth. Party-based democracy, which is mainly representative only, limits the scope of those bodies to participation to segments and not the whole population. Involvement of political parties at the bottom most level tends to promote political sectarianism which hampers the very spirit of Grama Sabhas. Instead of bringing the people together, they tend to disunite the people. Again, to boost their morale at the time of elections and to strengthen their vote banks, political parties unscrupulously bring in class and caste considerations. Delay and postponement of elections on flimsy grounds also pose a major threat to grassroot democracy.

Once elections are conducted, schedule of meetings are not strictly adhered to in many instances. Aggravated form is the fabrication of evidences to show the conduct of such meetings on time. Despite these negative trends, on the whole Grama Sabhas went a long way in augmenting unity to the people of a village. There are instances of the Vllage en masse supporting or opposing a particular move which they do not like or dislike. Thus, the inference that can be drawn is that political decentralisation has not attained a state of maturity as is expected of it.

On the question of administrative decentralisation, almost all states have devolved down powers to the local units. To make the devolution perfect, states have resorted to Activity Mapping at the instance and initiative of the Central government. DPCs have been constituted to make administrative decentralisation more effective. Bypassing of PRIs in the context of central schemes, though decided to be done away with, still pervades the scenario. In the process of effecting devolution, many bureaucrats have found a shift in their office from the higher to the lower levels and remote areas, quite contrary to their will. Though they joined the grassroot administrative cadres, still they are neither prepared to accept the reality nor are they ready to forgo the age old bureaucratic culture. This to a large extent dilutes the very spirit and purpose of the PRIs. Again, though the states were eager to effect devolution at the instance of the centre, in many cases there is the dearth of employees. Moreover, absence of clear division of powers between the state and the PRIs and complexities caused by duplication and overlapping in respect of the XI schedule, and the over burdening of responsibilities imposed upon them at the instance of the state – all tend to minimise the potentialities of administrative decentralisation.

Coming to funds and finances, the worst problem is the inability of the PRIs to collect own resources at the appropriate time itself. The only tax that is collected properly is the profession tax. Even in this field evasions are not seriously addressed. Tax on property, a major source, is not updated properly at par with time or steps have been evolved to collect it in a befitting manner. Always looking upwards for funds is not positive. Political considerations often intrude in to the realm of usage of funds. Moreover, misuse and misappropriation of funds also pose a serious handicap. Examination of many instances show that despite the introduction of decentralised planning, local potentialities are neither scientifically studied nor investigated on a large scale.

As reported by the MoPR in a study where DPCs are properly constituted, they are not operational: in other states district planning is operational but DPCs are not constituted and in some other states a parallel process of planning prevails. Under the People's Planning, the State of Kerala achieved something commendable. But, the general performance at the national level is not credible.

Globalisation and its aftermath have generated a cluster of forces antagonistic to the survival of PRIs. National Governments have suffered a lot in their domain of sovereignty: corporate and multinationals have crept in and trade barriers vanished. At the instance of the National Government itself many corporates have come to India with large industrial designs, many of which negated and nullified the very spirit of decentralised planning. In certain cases, there were intrusions from the Corporates itself to dupe the PRIs to their advantage as done by Balco. On the whole, the PRIs in India have succeeded but, they couldn't achieve as much as expected or couldn't achieve as hoped and worked for.

Notes

1. A team of Political Scientists conducted a comprehensive study among Americans which revealed a substantial degree of variation across acts of political participation. A similar comparative study among States of the world like United States, UK, West Germany, Netherlands and Austria also advanced the same proposition. For details, see Robert A. Dahl and Bruce Stinebrickner (2010): *Modern Political Analysis,* PHI, New Delhi, pp. 111-112.
2. This Act introduced a system of village policing in the erstwhile state of Bengal, the cost of which was met from the funds raised by the panchayats. A whole body of nominated members constituted the panchayats.
3. Lord Rippon introduced Local Boards consisting mainly of elected members.
4. Gandhian thesis always upheld the independence and integrity of the villages. To him growth in industry means decay of villages and increase in towns means degeneration of villages.
5. However, there were certain attempts at improving the life of the rural people: the Community Development Programme,1952 and the attempts at establishing a just and integrated social structure in rural areas under the Second FiveYear Plan are certain examples.
6. The Report of the Committee heralded a new era with discussions and deliberations for strengthening the PRIs. In order to meet the financial burden associated with its implementation the Central Government appointed a Study Team on Panchayati Raj Finance in July 1962 with Santhanam as its chairman.The government also appointed a Study Group on Budgeting and Accounting Procedure of Panchayati Raj Institutions with M. Ramakrishnayya as chairman. The report of this Committee was significant for it suggested ways and means for systematising and rationalising the budgeting procedure of PRIs in India. Their reports submitted to the Central Government in 1963 were not only accepted by the Central Government but also sent to the states with direction to implement them as far as possible.

7. The Twenty Point Programme was launched by the Central Government to raise the economic condition of the common man, particularly the depressed and backward classes.
8. It is known as Mandal Parishad in Andhra Pradesh, Anchal samithi in Arunachal Pradesh, Anchalik Panchayat in Assam, Janapad Panchayat in Chhattisgarh and Madhya Pradesh, Taluka Panchayat in Gujarat and Karnataka, Panchayat union in Tamil Nadu, Block Panchayat in Uttar Pradesh, Uttarakhand and Kerala, Panchayat Samitis in other states including Bihar, Haryana, Himachal Pradesh, Jharkhand, Maharashtra, Odisha, Punjab and Rajasthan.
9. Here, the emphasis is on the distinction between theory and practice in democracy. Democracy theoretically presumes that the people are the sovereigns. In practice, it is their representatives who are assembled in the legislature who wield and exercise this sovereignty. This negates the very purpose and spirit of democracy, throwing the people at a far away distance from policy-making, implementation and even from reaping the benefits due to the people.
10. In the State of Assam, Panchayat system was introduced way back in 1948 itself by the enactment called The Assam Rural Panchayat Act,1948.
11. In the 2008 PRI election in the Makokchung Town Council in Nagaland, there was an instance of a group of males surrounding the office of the Returning Officer to block the entry of women for filing nomination. Even in 2011, there was a similar show of strength in Puducherry. Instances of violence were there in UP, Jharkhand and Jammu and Kashmir on many times on the eve of PRI elections. See the *Report of the Task Force*, 2011, p. 4.
12. In 1980, in the State of Madhya Pradesh the Congress (I) witnessed an intra-party contest between two of its senior candidates-Mr.Solanki, an adivasi and Mr Arjun Singh, an upper caste.
13. The MoPR swung in to action barely after one month of its constitution in 2004. The Ministry in conjunction with the union Ministry of Rural Development organised a Conference of Chief Ministers on Poverty Alleviation and Rural Prosperity through PRIs at New Delhi on 29-30th June, 2004. In the inaugural session itself, the Prime Minister highlighted the exemplary role of the PRIs in poverty alleviation.To speed up the process and chalk out details, seven Round Tables were convened.
14. Central Ministries and state departments concerned with various rural development schemes and programmes such as agriculture, health, education and so on are setting up parallel structures. The line ministries at both levels also undertake schemes. These schemes have staffs of the state's line departments going right down from block to village level, often bypassing the PRIs.
15. In the sphere of National Health Rural Mission the PRIs were assigned certain specific responsibilities- the selection and mentoring of Asha workers, planning and implementation of the scheme through the Village Health and Sanitation Committee and provision for a revolving fund are some of the highlights.
16. The areas were irrigation, rural roads, drinking water supply, rural housing, rural electrification and telephone connectivity. In each sphere, a special programme was initiated.
17. The State of Kerala had set a mark of its own by devolving 40 per cent of its plan outlay to the panchayats during the period just prior to the period under review by the MoP in 2006.

References

1. Nalini Rajan,(2002): *Democracy and the Limits of Minority Rights,* Sage, New Delhi.
2. Hoveyda Abbas, Ranjay Kumar (2012): *Political Theory*, Pearson, Delhi.
3. Anthony Arblaster (1994): *Democracy*, World View, Delhi.
4. Dorothy Pickles (1970): *Democracy*, Basic Books, New York.
5. Robert A. Dahl and Bruce Steinebricker (2010): *Modern Political Analysis*, PHI, New Delhi.
6. Vaishali Jain (2009): *Crisis in Indian Democracy and Gandhian Alternatives*, Regal Publications, New Delhi.
7. Sharma M.P (1975): *Public Administration in Theory and Practice*, Kitab Mahal, Allahabad.
8. G.S. Cheema, D.A. Rondinelli [ed](1983): *Decentralisation and Development: Policy Implementation in Developing Countries,* Sage, New Delhi.
9. Meera Chandhoke, Praveen Priyadarsini [ed] (2009): *Contemporary India-Economy, Society, Politics,* Pearson, Delhi.
10. V.N Alok (2012): *Devolution to Panchayats in India: Ranking Functional Environment at Sub-National Level-Empirical assessment, 2011-12*, IIPA, New Delhi.
11. P.S.N. Sinha [ed] (1991): *Studies in Development Administration*, Vol 5, Commonwealth Publications, New Delhi.
12. G. Morley Mohan Lal (1990): *Rajiv Gandhi and Panchayati Raj Democracy and Development at the Grassroots*, Konark, Delhi.
13. *The Constitution of India* [Bare Act].
14. Amreshwar Avasthi, Anand Prakash Avasthi (2002): *Public Administration in India*, Lakshmi Narayan Agarwal, Agra.
15. *Report of the Task Force*, (2011) MoPR, Government of India.
16. *A Mid-Term Review and Appraisal* (2006): MoPR, Government of India.
17. Mahendra Prasad Singh, Subhendra Ranjan Raj [ed](2012): *The Indian Political System*, Pearson, Delhi.
18. J.S Deol,(1978): *State Politics in India*, New Academic Publishing Company, Jullundhar.
19. Lakshman Rao, (1979): *Internal Migration and Political Change in India*, National Publishing House, New Delhi.
20. Rajni Kothari, (2005): *Rethinking democracy*, Orient Longman, New Delhi.
21. Akshat Khandelwal (2013): *Baiting the Ballot*, The Caravan, Vol.5, Issue 10, p. 14.
22. News papers

    The Times of India.

    The Hindu

    Malayala Manorama (Mal)

    Deshabhimani (Mal)
23. http://www.augusto.com

Appendix

Local Governance: An Inspiring Journey into the Future

(Extract from the report of Second Administrative Reforms Commission (ARC) GOI, 2009)

The Core Principles

While the State Government continues to have an important and significant role, appropriate to that level, the Commission considers the core principles in the reforms of local governance to be: application of the principle of subsidiarity; clear delineation of functions of local governments vis-a-vis State Governments and among different tiers of local governments; effective devolution of these functions and resources accompanied by capacity-building and accountability; and the rural-urban dichotomy and integrated view of local services and development through convergence of programmes and agencies and above all, 'citizen-centricity'.

Common Issues

The principles governing democratic decentralisation are the same for both rural and urban areas.

The Constitutional Scheme

The issue of whether a firm constitutional directive compelling State Legislatures to empower local governments effectively is desirable has been a matter of much public debate over the last decade. Clearly, there is need to empower local governments. Happily, an impressive political consensus on this issue among political parties across the spectrum exists. However, when it comes to action, many States seem to feel that the balance of convenience lies in favour of minimum local empowerment. Given this backdrop a strong constitutional provision mandating effective empowerment of local governments seems both desirable and necessary. However, there are difficulties in such an approach. First, the autonomy of States must be respected in bringing about major constitutional amendments. Second, the situation varies from State to State and the uniform approach could be detrimental to the objective of local government. Third, the matters listed in the Eleventh and Twelfth Schedules could not be fully handled by the local governments even in the best of circumstances.

The Commission examined the desirability of reviewing the two Schedules. However, these lists are merely illustrative and in any case, there is need for further functional delineation between the State Government and local government in respect of most of these matters. Therefore, the Commission is of the considered view that the two Schedules need not be revised, but that the fact that they are not exhaustive and are only illustrative should be recognised.

The Commission is of the considered view that while Article 243G and 243W need to be strengthened, it is desirable to lay down general principles of empowerment without unduly restricting the States' freedom of action. In particular, two principles need to be stated in the Constitution so that the State Legislature can make laws based on these governing principles. First, devolution should be based on the broad principle of subsidiarity, and local governments at the appropriate level should be vested with adequate powers and authority to enable them to function as institutions of self-government in respect of functions that can be performed by the local level. Second, as matters listed in Eleventh Schedule are not intended to be wholly transferred to local governments, the empowerment of local governments should be for functions, which can be performed at the local level.

Presently, most of the States do not have Legislative Councils. After the enactment of the 73rd and 74th Constitutional Amendments, a third tier of Government has been created in the form of the local bodies. The Commission feels that this third tier of Government should also have a stake in making laws in the State Legislatures. Apart from constituting Legislative Councils (where they do not exist), the existing Legislative Councils may be recast as a council for local governments.

Imposing the presence of Members of Parliament and the State Legislature in the Panchayats would dampen the emergence of local leadership which is a sine qua non for development of vibrant local governments. Therefore, the Commission is of the view that Members of Parliament and State Legislatures should not become members of local bodies. This would endow the local bodies with decision-making capabilities.

The Commission feels that States should be free to decide the composition of Panchayats and the manner of election to suit their local conditions best.

However, the Commission is of the view that in the States which opt for indirect membership of Intermediate Panchayat and District Panchayat, whereby the Chairpersons of the lower tiers became members of higher tiers, and there are no directly elected members, it is desirable to have the Chairperson directly elected. In other words, in each tier, either the members or the Chairperson should be directly elected so that the people will get proper representation at different levels.

One important feature of the constitutional scheme of local government is the empowerment of the SC, ST, women and where the States choose so, OBCs through a system of reservations. Already evidence shows that women and weaker sections elected to Panchayats and Municipalities have performed very creditably. The resultant empowerment of these sections has been one of the most noteworthy features of local government.

Elections

The Electoral Process

In many States, the powers of delimitation of local government constituencies have been retained by the Governments. As a result, in many cases, particularly in urban areas, the SECs have to wait until a delimitation exercise is completed by the State Governments. The Commission is of the view that a separate Delimitation Commission for local governments is unnecessary. Independent SECs, especially when appointed as Constitutional authorities, can easily undertake this exercise and the government can provide the broad guidelines for delimitation either by law or by Rules.

The Commission is of the view that reservation of constituencies should also be entrusted to SECs. In respect of the Lok Sabha and the Legislative Assemblies, both delimitation and reservations are decided simultaneously by the Election Commission. It would be better if the rolls for the Legislative Assembly are used as the basis for local bodies elections also. It however needs to be emphasised that the electoral rolls for the Legislative Assembly cannot be used straightaway for local bodies elections because of two reasons: (i) a local body area may not be exactly the same as the area covered by the electoral roll of a Legislative Assembly; (ii) the voters' list in case of local bodies elections have to be prepared ward-wise whereas the voters' list of the Legislative Assembly is a part-wise and as a unit a 'ward' is completely different from a 'Part'.

It has been experiensed that 'Parts' are not always compact geographical units because of which it becomes difficult to use them as the basic unit for the purposes of delimitation of municipal and village wards (constituencies). The Commission is, therefore, of the view that a 'Part' should be defined to be a compact geographical unit. Then a "Building Blocks" approach can be used so that a ward comprises one or more integral parts.

The Commission is of the view that local government laws in all States should provide for adoption of the Assembly electoral rolls for local governments without any revision of names by SECs. For such a process to be effective, it is also necessary to ensure that the voter registration and preparation of electoral rolls by the Election Commission of India is based on geographic contiguity. Similarly, the electoral divisions for elections to local bodies should the Building Blocks approach.

Rotation of reservations becomes necessary given the complexity and high percentage of reservation of seats. However, frequent rotation denies to the elected representatives, an opportunity to gain experience and grow in stature. Considering these facts, the Commission is of the view that reservation of seats should be in a manner that leads to effective empowerment and not numerical and notional representation. This can be accomplished through the following three broad approaches:

First, the rotation can be after at least two terms of five years so that there is possibility of longevity of leadership and nurturing of constituencies. In Tamil Nadu, this approach has been adopted. However, with multiple reservations this may lead to large sections being denied the opportunity of reservation for a generation or more.

Second, instead of single-member constituencies, elections can be held to multi-member constituencies. Several seats can be combined in a territorial constituency in a manner that the number of seats allocation for each disadvantaged section remains the same in each election in that constituency. Elections can then be held by the List System so that parties get representation in proportion to votes obtained. Alternatively, members may be elected on the basis of votes obtained individually. In either case, the law should clearly specify the required number of members to be elected from each reserved category. The 1952-57 Lok Sabha/State Assembly elections were conducted in two or three member constituencies. Maharashtra has adopted multi-member constituencies for elections in Panchayats.

Third, if the office of the Chairperson/Chief Executive is elected directly by popular vote there is greater pool of talent available from the disadvantaged sections and leadership can be nurtured and developed. The Commission's recommendations to give the States the flexibility in the composition of Panchayats and the manner of elections would address this problem.

In most States, DPCs/MPCs have not been constituted. As per Article 243 ZD, at least 80 per cent of members of DPC shall be elected by and from amongst the elected members of the Panchayat at the district level and of the Municipalities in the district in proportion to the ratio between the population of the rural areas and of the urban areas in the district. In case of MPCs, at least two-third of the members shall be elected by and from amongst the elected members of the Municipalities and Chairpersons of Panchayats in the

Metropolitan area in proportion to the ratio between the population of the municipalities and of the Panchayats in that area (Article 243ZE). This process involves giving weightage to the votes proportional to the population and timely conduct of elections. The Commission, therefore, feels that the conduct of elections for the elected members of these bodies should also be entrusted to the SECs.

Constitution of the State Election Commission

There is no doubt that State Election Commissions must discharge their functions in a totally 'neutral' manner. Moreover, the Commissioner should be a person with impeccable credentials. The Election Commission should have enough autonomy and powers to resist all extraneous 'pressures'. The Commission is of the view that the SEC should also be appointed on the recommendations of a collegium comprising the Chief Minister, the Speaker and the Leader of Opposition in the Legislative Assembly.

The Commission strongly believes that an effective institutional mechanism should be evolved and strengthened to bring the Election Commission of India and the SECs on one platform. This will facilitate regular interaction, logistical coordination, infrastructure sharing and technical support to the SECs. It will also help SECs draw upon the institutional strength and credibility the Election Commission of India has established over the decades.

The Constitution had laid down provisions for delimitation of constituencies after every census so that the population-seat ratio is maintained. The increase in population has not been uniform throughout the country. Moreover, the high rate of rural to urban migration has increased the population of urban constituencies much faster than their rural counterparts. As a result, on an average the number of electorates in an urban constituency is much higher than in rural constituencies. The freeze imposed by the Forty-second Amendment and further extended by the Eighty-fourth Amendment, on the total number of seats in the House of the People and the Legislative Assemblies is quite understandable, as it seeks to help the objectives of family planning. But within the number of seats allotted to a State, it would be desirable to carry out the adjustment of such seats.

Such an exercise would set right the imbalance between the urban and rural electorate and would help in getting the focus of legislators on urban issues along with the rural issues.

Functions of Local Governments

Devolution of Powers and Responsibilities

The overriding intention of Articles 243G and 243W is that powers and authority may be so devolved as to enable Panchayats and Municipalities to function as institutions of self-government. For this, they may also be empowered to prepare local plans for economic development and social justice and to implement schemes/perform functions including those listed in the relevant Schedules.

In this respect, there is need to identify practical steps for effective empowerment of local governments, in addition to strengthening the constitutional provisions of Article 243. There are two areas which need special attention. First, Article 243N and 243 Z F mandate that all laws which are "inconsistent" with the provisions of Parts IX and X of the Constitution shall continue to be in force until such laws are suitably amended to bring them in conformity with the Constitutions or repealed, or until the expiration of one year from the dates of the 73rd and 74th Constitutional Amendments coming into effect. Most States have not even identified all the statues which are inconsistent with Parts IX and X of the Constitution. Clearly, when the architecture of governance is fundamentally altered, several existing laws need to be suitably amended and alternative statutory arrangements made.

The Commission is of the view that a fresh, more comprehensive, set of functions should be laid down for urban bodies, to include all the activities that need to be performed at the local level. In addition to the functions already listed in the Twelfth Schedule, functions like school education; public health including community health centres/Area hospitals; traffic management and civic policing activities; land management, including registration etc. may also be included.

Framework Law for Local Bodies

In spite of the Constitutional provisions, and observations made by several expert groups and even by Parliamentary Committees, empowerment of local governments in the real sense has not taken place. Under such circumstances, it becomes the responsibility of the Union to ensure that the 73rd and the 74th Constitutional Amendments are implemented both in letter and spirit. This becomes all the more necessary as major development schemes, funded largely by the Union Government, are being implemented by the local governments.

Local governments fall under the rightful domain in the States. It would not be desirable to bring this subject in the Concurrent List in order to empower the Union to enact a 'framework law' for the local governments. The Commission is, therefore, of the view that a 'Framework Law' may be passed by Parliament under Article 252 (power of Parliament to legislate for two or more States by consent and adoption of such legislation by other States). The remaining States may then be persuaded to adopt this law. This law should spell out the rights and duties of the citizen in relation to the local authority and also those of the local body *vis-a-vis* the citizen. It would also provide broad principles for detailing of activities at the third tier. Equally importantly, the model law must lay down guidelines for devolution of responsibilities, powers and functions, by the States.

Devolution of Funds

Finances of Local Governments

The local bodies are heavily dependant on State Governments for financial inflows, because the proceeds of various buoyant taxes like State Excise, VAT and Motion Vehicles Tax form part of the Consolidated Fund of the State. The major sources of income for local governments like property tax etc. are woefully inadequate to meet their obligations both due to their inherent nature and inefficiency in collecting them. This asymmetry between the taxation power and the responsibility to provide civic amenities necessitates transfer of funds from the State to the local governments either through untied grants or through a share in other State Taxes or as part of various development schemes.

The State Finance Commission (SFC)

The Twelfth Finance Commission examined the functioning of the State Finance Commissions in great detail and made some very important recommendations. One of the important recommendations of the Twelfth Finance Commission (TFC) pertains to the time span for setting up of the SFCs, the time allowed for submission of its report, time limits for action taken report and synchronisation of its award period with that of the Central Finance Commission.

The recommendations of the Central Finance Commissions are not mandatory but from the beginning, successive Union Governments have established a healthy tradition of accepting the devolution package suggested by the Finance Commission. In effect, therefore, these recommendations have become mandatory. However, this tradition has not been established in the States. The healthy precedent established by the Union Government in generally accepting the devolution proposals made by the Union Finance Commission should also be followed by the State Governments with regard to the recommendations of the State Finance Commissions.

With the Thirteenth Finance Commission likely be constituted in 2007/2008, it would be appropriate to advise that all States appoint their State Finance Commissions in advance so that the reports of the State Finance Commissions are available for the consideration of the Central Finance Commission. This Commission, therefore, feels that State Finance Commissions should be set up with the periodicity of five years as required by the Constitution, but equally importantly, that they should be set up in time across the country, so that, as recommended by the Twelfth Finance Commission, their recommendations can be taken into consideration by the Central Finance Commission. The Commission also agrees with the recommendations of the Twelfth Finance Commission that each State should prescribe through an Act the qualifications of persons eligible to be appointed as Member of the State Finance Commission, on the lines of the Central Act. The proposed "framework law" may cover this aspect also.

The task of the State Finance Commissions is undoubtedly complex. The Commission is of the view that the State Finance Commissions should link the devolution of funds to the level/quality of civic amenities that the citizens could expect. This approach would also help to bring about some uniformity in the quality of services provided by different local bodies.

Although SFCs, while making their recommendations about devolution of funds also give their recommendations on other matters affecting the resources of the local bodies, there has not been adequate emphasis on the outcomes of such devolutions. Local bodies focus their attention on getting the maximum possible funds from the State, and in the process, other recommendations which seek to enhance the resources of the local bodies such as improvement in their own tax base, higher efficiency in tax collection, economy in expenditures, reduction of surplus staff etc do not get due attention. As a result, the recommendations of the SFCs do not get implemented in totality and the outcomes are therefore sub-optimal. The Commission is of the view that the SFCs do not get implemented in totality and the outcomes are therefore sub-optimal. The Commission is of the view that the SFCs should carry out a more thorough analysis of the finances of local bodies and make concrete recommendations for improvements in their working. In case of smaller local bodies, such recommendations could be broad based, but in case of larger local governments such recommendations would need to be more specific.

A substantial portion of the revenues of the local bodies goes towards meeting the establishment expenditure. The SFCs should evolve norms for expenditure on establishment for different local bodies.

Monitoring the implementation of the recommendations of the SFC has generally been weak. It is necessary that a mechanism is put in place which reviews the implementation of all the recommendations of the SFCs. An Action Taken Report must be tabled in the State Legislature within six months, and this should be followed up with an annual statement on the devolution made and grants given to individual urban bodies, through an appendix to the State budget documents. If considered necessary, the devolution of funds could be made conditional to local bodies agreeing to implement the recommendations of the SFCs.

Capacity Building for Self Governor

It is clear that sustained, well planned 'enabling exercises' need to be undertaken to ensure that the implementing agencies have the capacity and the capability to deal with the challenges in undertaking and implementing these major national programmes apart from being able to fulfil their statutory functions.

Organisational capacity building would include designing appropriate structure within the organisation, re-engineering internal process, delegation of authority and responsibility, creation of an enabling legal framework, developing management information systems, institutionalising reward and punishment systems and adopting sound human resource management practices.

Organisational capacity building should not be taken to mean that the organisation acquires all the skills and knowledge required to perform its tasks. Prudence demands that any organisation should have the capability of tapping such skills rather than spending a large amount of resources in acquiring such skills themselves. Evolving partnerships, developing networks and outsourcing functions are all methods of enhancing the capability of an organisation.

The Commission also believes that adequate staffing of local bodies is a matter that requires considerable attention of the State Finance Commissions.

The State Finance Commissions, therefore, need to be vested with the responsibility of suggesting 'staffing norms' for various levels and categories of local bodies to determine the optimum or desirable degree of outsourcing of functions. Failure to take a holistic view of this approach is often responsible for outsourced functions (particularly in the sphere of public health and sanitation) becoming a source of public dissatisfaction.

While State Institutes of Rural Development and other institutions involved in training Panchayat functionaries have been imparting training to the 'target beneficiaries', these are generally limited to areas like Panchayat and Municipal laws, rudiments of book keeping, account codes and office procedures. Clearly, much more is required for capacity building and skills-inculcation beyond such routine measures.

The 73rd Constitutional Amendment provides for minimum of 33 per cent reservation of women in elective posts, thus putting over one million women in positions of leadership. However, because of entrenched gender bias, there are still many instances of women Panchayat members encountering obstruction and exclusion and lacking self-confidence as also adequate knowledge of their duties and responsibilities. There is still need to give special attention to capacity building of women panchayat leaders and members so that they are truly equipped to carry out their envisaged role in the third tier of government.

There is a clear need to bring about a 'networking' of the existing training institutions in various subjects like financial management, rural development, disaster management and general management to formulate compendia of training methodology and training modules to build institutional and individual capacities. There is a strong case for the Union Ministers of Panchayati Raj and Urban Development to initiate funding of specific 'key' training programmes. It is equally important that training should be mainstreamed in the activity mapping of organisation so as to be a continuing activity.

Activities like applied and action research, case studies, documentation of major initiatives and evaluation of important interventions need special focus. Further, some of the larger, better endowed local bodies may be in a position to commission and finance academic initiatives and they should be encouraged to take action in this field. The primary responsibility in this behalf must rest with the State and Union Governments through funding under suitable state/national schemes. The research and higher education funding establishment must also play a role to provide encouragement to 'purely academic' research on topics with implications for the functions performed by local bodies.

As a result of decentralisation, local bodies have become responsible for a number of services. One of the difficulties they face is the lack of specialised and technical skills required for these services pertaining to engineering design, project management, maintenance of high-tech equipment, accounting etc. It would, therefore, be appropriate if a common pool of such expertise is maintained either by a federation of local bodies or by professional agencies which can be accessed by local bodies on demand and payment.

Planning at the District Level

There is also considerable confusion about the district plans. One type of confusion relates to its nature: is it a collection of the Panchayat and Municipal plans? What are the things that cannot be addressed at the micro-levels of Gram Panchayats, Intermediate Panchayats and the Municipalities, but require a macro-view for proper appreciation of the problems and issues? Settled answers to these questions are not yet available. The other type of confusion relates to the domain of planning. Will the district plans consists of only those functions which have been devolved to the local bodies? Should such plans also accommodate the activities of the State Government that are not devolved to the local bodies, because they may have an impact on the economy, society or the physical environment of the district? In other words, is there a need for congruence between the perception of the higher level government and that of the local governments in preparing a development plan for a district? In case of conflict, how should this be resolved? For districts with substantial urban areas, where Development Authorities now carry out town planning functions by stature, the issue of parallel planning bodies working in isolation also arises. In this context, it is necessary to introduce more clarity in the concept of the district plan. The real essence of the district plan has to be in ensuring integrated planning for the rural and urban areas in the district and not to view it as a collection of urban and panchayat plans.

In a regime of multi-level planning, providing knowledge and skills to different levels is a problem that needs to be addressed. The idea of establishing a dedicated centre in each district for providing such inputs to the local bodies may be considered. Closely associated to this, is the need to ensure a two-way process of flow of information from the higher levels of governments to the local governments and vice versa. In an era of advanced information technology, this should not be difficult.

The National Planning Commission has recently issued guidelines to ensure that the concept of planning from below, as envisaged in the Constitution, is realised in practice. The guidelines envisage preparation of a vision document for the district by the District Planning Committee in consultation with the local government institutions. Among other things, this document will analyse the progress of the district in different sectors, identify the reasons for backwardness and indicate interventions for addressing the problems. The document will thus provide a framework for preparation of plans by the local government institutions.

Decentralised planning should involve a process of decentralised consultations and stock taking exercise followed by a planning exercise at each local body level and then the consolidation and integration exercise. The vision should be articulated at every level of local governance. The Expert Group on Planning at Grassroots level headed by Shri V. Ramachandran has gone into great detail regarding the planning process at all levels viz. Gram Panchayat level, Intermediate level and the District level. Their recommendations have been accepted by the Ministry of Panchayati Raj and the Ministry is strictly monitoring its implementations. Specifically, with regard to the measures needed to strengthen the capacity of the DPCs, the Expert Group has made detailed recommendations.

Rural-Urban Divide and Long-Term Role of DPC vis-a-vis District Council

The Commission is of the view that of all the institutions created by the 73rd/74th Constitutional Amendments, the District Planning Committee (DPC) is one, which in most States, has so far failed to emerge as an effective institution. Some States have not formed the DPC. Besides, there are some inherent problems with this institution. In a developmental State, planning is an essential function of government at any level. Creating a separate authority independent of the structures of governance for undertaking the exercise of development planning has no logic. The DPC is the only body in the decentralisation scheme of the Constitution where up to one-fifth of the total members can be nominated. A nominated member can also be the Chairperson of the DPC. Nomination could be used as a convenient tool available to the ruling party of a State to induct members on narrow political considerations. Some state have the system of nominating a minister as head of the Committee, thus converting the DPC into a power centre that is stronger than the elected local bodies. Also, the DPC is a stand-alone committee within the Panchayat-Municipal system and there is no organic linkage between the two. Being constituted partly through indirect election and partly by nomination, it is neither accountable to the people directly, nor to the PRI-Municipal system. With all these weaknesses, the DPC in its present form is hardly able to make any contribution on the process of democratic decentralisation. The situation is compounded by the fact that separate 'district plans' are required to be prepared for each of the major Centrally Sponsored Schemes.

District Council – Relevance vis-a-vis DPCs

It is urged in some quarters that in the strict sense of the term, only the Gram Panchayat and the Municipality qualify for being regarded as local governments. It is also significant that powers of taxation, which is an indicator of governmental authority, is enjoyed by these two bodies among all the local bodies. On the other hand, traditionally, the district has been an indispensable unit of our country's administration. Hence, if democratisation of local administration is the goal, then there has to be a representative body at the district level. Therein lies the justification for having a District Panchayat or Zila Parishad, as it is called in most States.

The urban areas on the other hand have a separate local government system in the form of municipalities or corporations. There are institutional linkages between different tiers of Panchayats, the chairpersons of the lower tiers being members of the higher tiers. Urban local bodies, on the other hand, function independently and remain detached not only from each other but also from the Panchayat system.

The institutional arrangement under which Panchayat cater to the rural areas and the Municipalities to the urban areas only, may work at the micro-level of villages and towns. When it comes to the level of the district, the distinction disappears. A development plan for the whole district, for example, has to take into consideration both rural and urban areas. A district plan is something more than the two sets of separate plans – one consisting of micro-plans for rural areas and the other comprising plans for individual towns. As one moves from the micro-levels to the meso-and macro-levels, perspectives and priorities of plans change. The Constitution recognises this and accordingly prescribes that the district plan, as distinguished from the individual Panchayat and Municipal plans, should have regard to 'matters of common interest between the Panchayats and the Municipalities'. This, in other words, means that the development needs of the rural and urban areas should be dealt with in an integrated manner and, therefore, the district plan, which is a plan for a larger area consisting of villages and towns, should take into account such factors as 'spatial planning', sharing of 'physical and natural resources', integrated development of infrastructure' and 'environmental conservation' [Article 243ZD(3)]. All these are important, because the relationship between villages and towns is complementary. One needs the other. Many functions that the towns perform as seats of industry, trade and business and as providers of various services, including higher education, specialised healthcare services, communications etc have an impact on the development and welfare of rural people. Similarly, the orderly growth of the urban centre is dependent on the kind of organic linkage it establishes with its rural hinterland.

In the decentralised regime, there is thus need for a body which can coordinate between the individual rural and urban local bodies and at the same time take the responsibility of such tasks of local administration as cannot be discharged by the individual local bodies. The DPC is an inappropriate institution for this. In this context, the concept of district government becomes relevant. It is felt that the District Panchayat or Zila Parishad can be perfectly fitted into the role of district government by expanding its jurisdiction to the whole district. Its members may be elected by the people of both rural and urban areas. Under such a scheme, the rural-urban distinction among local government institutions will remain for individual municipalities and the Panchayats up to the intermediate level. At the district level, the distinction will disappear and the local government institution at that level will represent rural as well as the urban people. The present office of the District Collector may be converted into the Chief Officer of such a District Government fully accountable to the elected District Government in all local matters.

A committee dedicated to the task of planning will, however, be necessary for coordination of the planning exercises of various local bodies, providing technical guidelines to them, examining the local plans for ensuring technical and financial viability and for preventing overlapping and duplication of schemes and for preparation of the district plan. Such a committee may function under the district council.

For the metropolitan areas, which often encompass more than one district, an alternative institutional structure in the form of a Metropolitan Planning Committee has been mandated by the Constitution and its planning functions will have to be harmoniously dovetailed with the DPC/District council framework.

Planning for Urban Areas

Multiplicity of Planning Authorities

At present, we are in a transitional phase where urban spatial planning in most cities involves a multiplicity of agencies whereas the constitutional provisions appear to broadly envisage local level planning by local bodies and regional planning by the DPCs and MPCs. Government of India's conditionalities under the JNNURM scheme are, however, helping States to accelerate the transition to a regime where ULBs gain full jurisdiction over town planning functions.

For the metropolitan areas in particular, there is an additional issue of how the two committees i.e., the District Planning Committee and the Metropolitan Planning Committee (DPC and MPC) would interface with each other in different scenarios. Urbanisable area for particular metropolitan cities could extend to more than one district and the setting up of DPCs and MPCs without delineating their jurisdictions, may only lead to confusion. The difficulty with MPCs is also that they have a peripheral outreach that extends into rural areas. There are also issues of externalities. Some of the urban facilities have a larger clientele outside its area or a source which is outside its jurisdiction. It would be useful to dovetail the views and interests of the rural district, which is its immediate hinterland, into the Metropolitan Planning Committee. Another aspects is the future relationship between the two, and the "ownership" in Government of these two institutions. In the Government of India, for example, the Ministry of Urban Development is responsible for MPCs while 'district planning' is with the Ministry of Panchayati Raj. In most States, there is a similar problem of coordination. Clearly this would be even more acutely a difficulty in the field. Presently, a Zila Parishad has jurisdiction in certain matters that extend into the cities. Should there be a difference of opinion between an MPC and a neighbouring DPC, who would be the decision-maker?

One possible option would be for the State Government to notify the jurisdiction of the MPCs in such a manner that all districts falling within its fully urbanising (peri-urban) boundaries would come under one MPC and no DPC for such districts/portions of districts need be constituted. This would ensure that there will be a single planning authority for the entire metropolitan area to be duly notified by the State Government, with no competing DPC. And to further ensure integration of the planning function, the planning resources in terms of technical and human resources of the existing Development Authorities for these metropolitan areas may be integrated with the secretariats of the concerned DPC/MPC. Taking into consideration the need for coordination, it may also be necessary to have Chairpersons of Panchayats and of the local bodies in the MPCs. For this purpose, the Presidents of the neighbouring Zila Panchayats concerned and the Chairmen of the adjacent District Planning Committees (or District Councils) should be ex-officio members of the Metropolitan Planning Committee. This principle, of a single planning authority, will apply even if the DPC is conceived not as an independent planning body, as is currently laid down in the Constitution; but as an adjunct planning office reporting to a representative District government (whether such district government is called the District Council or District

Panchayat or Zila Parishad). In that scenario also, for the Metropolitan areas whose urban footprint encompasses several districts, an MPC alone may be constituted with representation from the District Councils/Zila Parishads/ District Panchayats that fall within its urban-peri-urban boundaries. In any case, there would be no need for a DPC for these areas.

Accountability and Transparency

Need for Effective Accountability

Since power is prone to corruption and abuse, there is need for effective instrument of accountability to be able to check abuse of power and give citizens a voice in improving the quality of services.

Institutional Mechanisms to Ensure Propriety

The first requirement of ensuring accountability in local bodies is to provide for robust institutional mechanisms. Such mechanisms would basically relate to audit, State Government control and an independent grievance redressal body.

It may, therefore, be desirable to consider introducing some of the best practices of good governance prescribed for the corporate sector into the public sector. One such practice is the appointment of an audit committee by the State Government with independent members of proven integrity and professional competence and with appropriate oversight powers.

The Commission is of the view that the audit committee must have independence, access to all information, ability to communicate with technical experts and accountability to the public. Once the District Councils are formed, a special committee of the District Council may examine the audit reports and other financial statements of the local bodies within the district. This committee may also be authorised to fix responsibility for financial lapses. In respect of the audit reports of the District Council itself, a special committee of the Legislative Council may discharge a similar function. The audit committee should report to the respective local body.

Legislative Oversight: Howsoever independent the third tier of governance may become, it should still be responsible to the State Legislature. The Commission is of the considered view that legislative supervision can be ensured by institutionalising a separate Committee on Local Bodies in the State Legislative. This Committee may also function in the manner of the Parliamentary Public Accounts Committee as recommended in this Report while dealing with 'Accounts and Audit'.

Independent Grievance Redressal Mechanism (Local Body Ombudsman)

Apart from the above, there is need for institutionalising a grievance redressal mechanism which would address complaints regarding elected functionaries and official of the local bodies. This would provide a platform to the citizens for voicing their complaints and also bring out the deficiencies in the system for suitable remedial action. The Commission in its Fourth Report on "Ethics in Governance" was of the view that a local body Ombudsman should be constituted for a group of districts to look into complaints of corruption and maladministration against functionaries of local bodies, both elected members and officials. The Ombudsman should have the authority to investigate cases and submit report to competent authorities for taking action. Such competent authorities should normally take action as recommended. In case of disagreement, reasons must be recorded in writing and be placed in the public domain. These would require amendments in the respective State Panchayat Acts and the Urban Local Bodies Acts to include provisions pertaining to the local body Ombudsman.

The Commission further feels that the local body Ombudsman should be a single-member body. The Ombudsman may be appointed by a Committee consisting of the Chief Minister of the State, the Speaker of the State Legislative Assembly and the Leader of the Opposition in the Legislative Assembly. The Ombudsman should be selected from a panel of eminent persons of impeccable integrity who should not be serving government officials. The Commission is also of the view that in case a group of districts has a metropolitan city in its fold, then a separate Ombudsman may be constituted for the metropolitan local body, that is, in addition to the Ombudsman for that group of districts.

In case of complaints and grievances against a local body in general or its elected members with regard to corruption and maladministration, the local body Ombudsman should have powers to investigate into the matter and forward its report to the Lokayukta who shall further recommend it to the Governor of the State. In case of non-acceptance of the recommendations made by the Ombudsman, the reasons for doing so should be placed in the public domain by the State Government. Time limits may be described for the Ombudsman to complete its investigations into complaints.

As far as complaints related to infringements of law governing elections to these local bodies are concerned, the State Election Commissioner (SEC) would be the appropriate authority to investigate in the matter. The SEC should submit its report on such matters to the Governor of the State who shall act on his/her advice.

Measures to Improve Responsiveness of the Local Bodies to the People

Delegation of Functions: To make the lowest functionary accountable and to inculcate responsibility at the cutting edge level, there has to be delegation of functions to the lowest possible functionary in the local bodies. This would make the local bodies responsive in their interface with the common man.

In-house Mechanism for Redressal of Grievances: While audit and governmental control are necessary for making the local bodies accountable and an independent grievance redressal body would provide the citizens with the much needed instrument for enforcing accountability, the local bodies themselves should be in a position to learn from mistakes and mould themselves according to the needs of the people. This would require a robust in-house mechanism for redressal of grievances.

Social Audit

Institutionalising a system of social audit is essential for improving local service delivery and for ensuring compliance with laws and regulations. An effective system of social audit will have to be based on two precepts; first, that service standards are made public through citizens' charters and second, that periodic suo motu disclosure is made on attainment of service delivery standards by the local bodies. The suggestions of the Expert Group on 'Planning at Grass Roots level' in this regard are endorsed by the Commission.

Transparency

Suo motu disclosure of information, especially with regard to duties, functions, financial transactions and resolutions should become the norm for all the local bodies as provided under the RTI Act, 2005. Several local bodies have developed there own transparency mechanisms (see Box 3.7). Such practices may also be adopted by other local bodies.

Evaluation of Performance of Local Bodies

Evaluation of the performance of local bodies may also be attempted from the viewpoint of the citizens. This essentially brings the concept of 'feedback mechanism' to the fore. The feedback could consist of indicating a satisfaction score on the categories mentioned above. The collation of these feedbacks would provide a 'Citizens' Report Card' on the performance of the local bodies. The Commission feels that such methods of a participatory nature which are now recognised the world over as a means of improving governance, service delivery and empowerment should be increasingly adopted as accountability tools.

Accounting and Audit

The Ministry of Urban Development, Government of India in association with the Office of the Comptroller and Auditor General of India, has have brought out a National Municipal Accounts Manual (NMAM) for the ULBs. The accounts of the ULBs are now to be prepared on accrual basis as prescribed under NMAM. The Ministry of Urban Development has prescribed the procedure for formalising these standards. The Commission is of the view that this Manual should be adopted by the State Governments for use by the urban local bodies.

In order to ensure transparency, professional competence and accountability in the process of certification of accounts, the Commission is of the view that the C&AG should prescribe guidelines for empanelment of Chartered Accountants like, qualification of members, length of existence and experience of firms, number of partners, etc. Further, it is also felt that for the proper conduct of audit, detailed guidelines would also be required to be prescribed by the C&AG as is the practice in the case of the Companies Act. It needs to be kept in mind that the audit to be done by the Local Fund Audit or the C&AG in discharge of their responsibilities would be different and in addition to this audit.

As of 31st March, 2007, out of 24 States where the 73rd and 74th Constitutional Amendments are applicable, full entrustment of the role of providing 'Technical Guidance and Supervision' (TGS) over audit and accounts of PRIs and ULBs to C&AG has been made by 19 States. Given the enormity of the task of maintenance of accounts and audit of all the PRIs and ULBs in the States and the concomitant technical requirements, the Commission is of the considered view that the entrustment of technical supervision over the maintenance of accounts and audit of PRIs and ULBs should be institutionalised through a provision in the respective laws governing the local bodies and the accounting formats and standards may be provided by way of Rules. Similarly, the accounts and budget formats of PRIs prescribed by C&AG have been accepted and formal orders issued by 11 States, though 22 States have positively responded. The format developed for PRIs is basically a simple receipt and payment account on cash basis accompanied by key statements that take care of the items of accrued income and expenditure. The format ensures that all the functions which have been devolved or are likely to be devolved by the States to the Panchayats are properly classified. It is also in synchronisation with the classification codes at the State and National level. The Commission would like to emphasise upon what has already been recommended in the Sixth Round Table of the Ministers in-charge of Panchayati Raj held in November 2004 at Guwahati – the formats for the Panchayats should be simple and comprehensible to the elected representatives.

The Commission is of the view that the role of the C&AG should be limited to technical guidance and supervision and not extend to details. In fact, there is a case for institutionalising the independence of the Director of Local Fund Audit (DLFA) so that it could function as a specialised body devoted to the audit of the accounts of the local bodies. This would enhance the stature of the DLFAs with a positive impact on the quality of audit and on accountability. The Commission feels that to achieve this, the head of the body responsible for Local Fund Audit should be appointed by the State Government after selection from a panel vetted by the C&AG. Further, to strengthen the arrangements for providing technical guidance and supervision by the C&AG, release of Finance Commission Grants to local bodies be made conditional on the acceptance by the States of such arrangements.

Apart from the statutory audit performed by the DLFA or such other designated authority of the State Government, audit of certain local bodies in a State would come under the purview of Section 14 of the C&AG's (Duties, Powers and Conditions of Service) Act, 1971. In terms of this Section where anybody or authority is substantially financed by grants or loans from the Consolidated Fund of India or of any State or of any Union Territory having a Legislative Assembly, the C&AG shall audit all receipts and expenditure of that body or authority. For the purposes of this Section, if the grant or loan is not less than rupees twenty five lakhs and is not less than 75 per cent of the total expenditure of such body or authority, it would be deemed to be substantially financed. In case of bodies receiving grants or loans not less than Rupees one crore in a financial year, the Section provides that the C&AG may, with the previous approval of the President or the Governor of a State or the Administrator of a Union Territory having a Legislative Assembly, audit all receipts and expenditure. The Commission is of the view that the final decision on the matter should be left to the States.

Accountability requires that corrective action is taken promptly on audit reports so as to increase the effectiveness of the local government. The audit reports on local bodies should be placed before the State Legislature and these should be considered by a separate Committee of the State Legislature constituted on the lines of the Public Accounts Committee. The access to relevant information/records to DLFA/designated authority for conducting audit or the C&AG should also be ensured by incorporating suitable provisions in the State Laws governing local bodies.

In order to match the above standards with regard to accounts and audit, local bodies particularly the PRIs will need to be suitably strengthened by making skilled professionals available to them. The States should take up appropriate capacity building measures so that the PRIs and ULBs are able to cope with the audit of these institutions.

With the progressive increase in capacity of the local bodies and reliability of the audit mechanism, a system of performance audit should also be gradually introduced. For this purpose, suitable parameters should be developed. This would strengthen the functioning of the local bodies and bring in elements of much desired accountability.

Technology and Local Governance

Information and Communication Technology

Information and Communication Technology provides tools which could be utilised by the local governments for simplifying cumbersome process, reducing contact between the cutting edge functionaries and the citizens, enhancing accountability and transparency and providing single window service delivery for a variety of services.

The Commission is of the view that the local governments should also utilise the facilities provided by space technology to prepare an information base and for delivery of services through resource centres.

Rural Governance

Institutional Reforms

There is need for States to re-examine Gram Panchayat delimitation so as to aim for greater efficiency of scale in delivery of services. Many of the Gram Panchayats are too small to function as autonomous institutions of local government. In order to be an economically viable administrative unit, capable of discharging multiple responsibilities, a Gram Panchayat needs to have a minimum population size. Since there is no data on this issue, it is difficult to give a definite recommendation as to what should be the optimum size of a Gram Panchayat. But it can be emphasised that a tiny Gram Panchayat will not be able to discharge the role envisaged for it under the present decentralisation plan. The factors that would have to be taken into consideration for determining the minimum size of a Gram Panchayat are : (a) potentiality for resource generation, (b) sustainability of the staff structure, (c) suitability as a unit of planning for core functions, (d) geographical cohesiveness, (e) terrain conditions and (f) communication facility within the Panchayat area.

It is imperative that States with small-sized Gram Panchayats undertake a detailed exercise to reconstitute them after considering the factors mentioned above.

Ward Sabha – Its Necessity

The Commission is of the view that in order to have effective popular participation at the micro level, the large Gram Panchayats should be split into a number of wards / areas. Representing a unit of smaller habitation or cluster, the Ward Sabha will provide a platform where people can directly discuss their needs and prepare an area specific local plan. The Ward Sabha can exercise certain powers and functions of the Gram Sabha and also some powers and functions of the Gram Panchayats may be entrusted to them. If possible, the territorial division of a Gram Panchayat Member may be made coterminous with jurisdiction of the Ward Sabha. A simple amendment in the respective State Panchayat Act can introduce this provision.

Panchayats as the government at the local level, should have their own staff. They should have full powers with regard to recruitment and service conditions of their employees within a broad framework of State laws and certain standards.

Purely as a transitional measure, till the personnel structure of PRIs takes a definite shape, the employees of the State Government may be taken on deputation, but such deputation should be made after the consent of the borrowing Panchayat.

In all the States a detailed review of the staffing pattern on a zero based approach should be undertaken within the next one year. The Zila Parishads, particularly, should be associated with this exercise. The 'ownership' of those working for local bodies must lie with these bodies.

PRIs and the State Government

The power of the State Government to suspend or remove elected Panchayat representatives needs closer scrutiny. There have been many instances of arbitrary use of this power. In some States the higher tier of Panchayat is either consulted or given the authority to exercise this power in respect of office bearers or members of the lower tier. The Commission is of the view that this provision is inappropriate because all the tiers of Panchayats are institutions of self government and, as such, there cannot be any hierarchic relationship between them.

Deviant behaviour, maladministration, violation of fiscal responsibility norms, irregular/illegal transfer of Panchayat property, abuse/misuse of authority, corruption and nepotism are some of the situations which may warrant action against the PRIs or their elected representatives. It is also the responsibility of the State Government to ensure that the Panchayats carry out their activities in accordance with law within their autonomous domain. But it is also necessary to ensure that this 'responsibility' does not translate into administrative supervision or control over the functioning of the Panchayats. As far as election related issue are concerned, the Constitution itself provides for creation of a 'State Election Commission' in each State. For any grievance or complaint relating to election law infringements, this institution should be the authority to take a final decision and send it to the Governor. Further, the Commission has recommended establishment of an independent grievance redressal mechanism in form of 'local Ombudsman' for a group of neighbouring districts. Whenever a complaint is made against a Panchayat or any of its members to the local Ombudsman, he will examine the matter and will send his report through Lokayukta to Governor of the State.

There can also be a situation where there is an absolute breakdown of administrative and legal machinery at the level of a Panchayat and the elected body concerned needs to be immediately suspended or dissolved. Even in such cases, the State Government would need to place the records before the local Ombudsman for investigation and appropriate action as detailed above. In all cases of disagreement with the recommendations made by the local

Ombudsman/Lokayukta, the reasons will need to be placed in the public domain.

Position of Parastatals

Parastatals are institutions/organisations which are wholly or partially owned and managed by government (either autonomous or quasi-governmental). They may be formed either under specific State enactments or under the Societies Registration Act. Since activities of many of these organisations are in the matters in the Eleventh Schedule of the Constitution, their separate existence with considerable fund and staff at their disposal, is an impediment to effective functioning and empowerment of local government institutions.

Some of the important parastatals are District Rural Development Agency (DRDA), District Health Society (DHS), District Water and Sanitation Committee (DWSC) and the Fish Farmers Development Agency (FFDA). At the higher levels, some of the parastatals are the State Water and Sewerage Board, the State Electricity Board, Khadi and Village Industries Commission (KVIC) and the State Primary Education Board. Their functions impinge directly on the local institutions.

The most important parastatal at the district level is the DRDA. The Commission is of the view that since the process of democratic decentralisation is now firmly established in the districts and Panchayats with elected representatives being in place at all the three levels, there is no justification for having a separate agency as the DRDA in the district.

Similar is the case with the District Water and Sanitation Committee (DWSC) which deals with the rural water supply and sanitation schemes. The Commission is of the view that since as democratically elected institutions, Panchayats are responsible for these functions to the citizens in the rural areas, DWSC should be a committee of the District Panchayat. A committee at the block level may also be needed to monitor this programme. If so, this committee should be a body of the Intermediate Panchayat. Besides, many of the States have also created a high level organisation called State Water and Sewerage Board to look after both urban as well as rural drinking water supply schemes. Barring a few large investment schemes which need high grade technical and professional support, the rural water supply system can be very conveniently handled by the Panchayats. Hence, the presence of the State Water and Sewerage Board in the rural areas needs to be substantially pruned.

Currently, a district also has a District Health Society (DHS) to look after the programmes of the National Rural Health Mission (NRHM). A major part of its functions concerns the rural sector (e.g. running hospitals, primary health centres and dispensaries). These functions are listed in the Eleventh Schedule and hence this Society has to be responsible to the PRIs for these activities. Similarly the Fish Farmers Development Agency (FFDA) may have a separate existence, because its activities do not coincide totally with the activities of the PRIs. However, keeping in view the potentiality of fish farming as a livelihood programme in the rural areas, this body also needs to work in close collaboration with different tiers of Panchayats especially the Gram Panchayat.

The parastatals should not be allowed to undermine the functions and authority of the PRIs. Some of the existing committee may need to be subsumed in the Panchayats and some of them may be restructured to have an organic relationship with them (Panchayats). The Union and the State Governments should not normally set up special committees outside the PRIs. However, if such specialised committees are required to be set-up because of professional or technical requirements, and if their activities coincide with those listed and devolved, they should function under the overall supervision and guidance of the Panchayats. Similarly, Community level bodies should not be created by decisions taken at higher levels. If considered necessary the initiative for their creation should come from below and they should be accountable to PRIs.

Functional Devolution

The Union Government has significant influence on the devolution of functions and funds upon Panchayats, because of the large fiscal transfers it undertakes to States in the functional domain of the Panchayats, mainly through Centrally Sponsored Schemes and Additional Central Assistance (ACAs). The Ministry of Panchayati Raj has been examining guidelines of old and new Centrally Sponsored Schemes and suggesting changes to make them compatible with the functional assignment to Panchayats. However, at the conceptual stage itself, Ministries will need to undertake Activity Mapping delineating what is to be done at the Union, State and Panchayat levels.

Activity Mapping can become a trigger for ensuring that Panchayats are on a sound footing. When Panchayats are assigned clear tasks, devolved funds and made accountable for their performance of these newly assigned responsibilities, they have a big incentive to demand the capacity required for effective performance. Thus, role clarity catalyses capacity building from being supply driven to demand driven, which is a huge benefit. Empowered Panchayats with clear roles assigned through activity mapping would begin to also demand the staff required for effective performance. Therefore, activity mapping can spur appropriate placement of functionaries for better service delivery.

In order to ensure smooth completion of activity mapping at both State and Union levels, there is a need to avoid misunderstanding and misinterpretation of the exercise. Care must be taken to avoid activity mapping to be (a) either construed as a 'sharing of the spoils' exercise, or (b) an exercise 'disempowering' line departments. The following approaches may dispel any misgivings in this regard:

(i) Undertaking extensive participatory exercise to bring Panchayats and Line departments together to arrive at a consensus as to what activities should be devolved to Panchayats,

(ii) Ensuring transparency in the process and developing trusts among different stakeholders,

(iii) Considering the capacities of Panchayats, prioritising different subjects for step-wise activity mapping,

(iv) Strict adherence to the objective principles described in this report, while approaching the matter of activity mapping,

(v) Simultaneously linking activity mapping with (a) mapping of capacity building, (b) financial requirements and (c) administrative requirements, so that there is a smooth transition and activity mapping can be immediately operationalised,

(vi) Encouraging for reasons of stability, legislative sanction for activity mapping, by eventually including it as part of the law.

The Commission is of the view that every State should take up comprehensive activity mapping with regard to the matters mentioned in the Eleventh Schedule of the Constitution. While doing so the principles discussed in the preceding paragraphs should be kept in mind. The progress made so far in this area is far from satisfactory and therefore, it is desirable that each State should constitute a special task force to complete this work in a time bound manner. Similarly, the Union Ministries will also need to intensively carry out activity mapping for all the Centrally Sponsored Schemes with priority on flagship programmes.

Devolving Regulatory Functions to the Panchayats

Since Panchayats are an integral part of the government at the local level, their activities cannot be confined solely to development programmes. To begin with task like issuing birth, death, caste and residence certificates, enforcing building byelaws, issuing of voter identity cards, enforcing regulations pertaining to weights and measures would be better performed by local governments. The Gram Panchayats can play an effective role in community policing because of their close proximity with the people. Regulatory functions which can be devolved to the Panchayats should be identified and devolved on a continuous basis.

Panchayat Finance

Fiscal Decentralisation

For fiscal decentralisation to be effective, finances should match expenditure assignments related to the transferred activities. This calls for a two-fold approach – first demarcation of a fiscal domain for PRIs to tap resources directly both tax and non-tax and second devolution of funds from the Union and State Governments.

In the Indian context, the concept and practice of local government taxation have not progressed much since the early days of the British rule. Most of the revenue accrual comes from taxation of property and profession with minor supplement coming from non-tax receipts like rent from property and fees for services. The Commission is of the view that a comprehensive exercise needs to be taken up in this sector on a priority basis. The exercise will have to simultaneously look into four major aspects of resource mobilisation viz. (i) potential for taxation (ii) fixation of realistic tax rates (iii) widening of tax base and (iv) improved collection. This could be one of the terms of reference for the Thirteenth Finance Commission.

Exploring Additional Sources of Revenue

Most of the State Acts vest Panchayats with public properties such as irrigation sources, ferry ghats, waste land, community lands, orchards and fairs. Vehicle stand charge and market/shop/cart fees are some of the other sectors which need to be tapped effectively by the PRIs. Thus, all common property resources vested in the Village Panchayats should be identified and made productive for revenue generation.

Apart from exploring new areas for taxation/levies and productive use of common properties, gradually the Panchayats could be encouraged to manage some important utilities. This would be particularly relevant for the higher tiers of Panchayats. They will need to collect realistic user charges for all such services.

The royalty and other income from minerals such as dead rent, fees, cess and surcharge is a major source of revenue for the State Government. Conceptually royalty is charges for letting the lessee consume the wealth belonging to the lessor where the wealth gets depleted over time. Therefore, the local community represented by the local Panchayat should have prime right over the income from royalty accrued to the State Government for mining in that area. State Finance Commissions should bear this in mind while finalising devolution of grants to the rural local bodies.

Apart from allocating substantial share of royalty to the local bodies, the State Government may also consider empowering them to levy local cess on the royalty so accrued to the State Government.

Incentivising Better Performance

One of the effective and fair tools to improve revenue collection of the local bodies is to incentivise their efforts. Panchayats which have shown positive results must be suitably rewarded. This can be done by linking the

Union Finance Commission and State Finance Commission grants to their own revenue generation efforts. States may also promote Panchayats to collect revenue by providing bonus payments at specified pre-announced rates to Panchayats which have demonstrated exemplary collection performance.

The Commission is of the opinion that Village Panchayats must have primary authority over taxation within the tax domain assigned to PRIs. However, where a unit of assessment for imposition of taxes is larger or such taxation has inter-Panchayat ramifications, the higher formations – Intermediate Panchayat and Zila Parishad should be given concurrent powers subject to a prescribed ceiling. Running of small power projects, large scale mining activities, ferry services on a large river, are some of the areas which could be subjected to taxation by higher tiers. However, whenever a tax/fee is imposed either the Zila Parishad or Intermediate Panchayat, such tax or fee should be collected by the concerned Village Panchayats as if it were a tax or fee imposed by them.

Transparency / Transfer / Allocation of Funds

With regard to devolution of funds to the local bodies from higher tiers of government, the Commission holds the view that such transfers need to be unconditional so that the PRIs are able to take care of the local priorities. The approximate quantum of funds to be transferred for a block of five years should be indicated to the local bodies in advance so that the Panchayats can set minimum standards for delivery of services and for attainment of certain minimum levels in poverty reduction, education, healthcare etc. for the period of the allocation.

The Commission is of the view that except major Centrally Sponsored Schemes of the Union Government or special purpose programmes of the States, allocations to PRIs should be in the form of untied funds so that the PRIs can have some degree of flexibility in expenditure. The allocation order should contain only a brief description of objectives and expected outcomes. Also while releasing funds, the States should not impose conditions of utilisation, except those prescribed by the Finance Commission.

Budget Procedure and Transfer of Funds

The Commission is of the view that the budget indexing and accounting procedure for allocation of funds by the State Government to PRIs needs to be simplified and made user and audit-friendly. The Panchayats also need to maintain their accounts with transparency at a low cost. Therefore, there should be a separate Panchayat sector line in the state budget.

The State budget under each head should be divided into State-wise allocation and District-wise allocation. The allocation for each district should be shown separately in the district-wise allocation. District allocations under various heads should be brought together which will evolve into a district budget.

In 2005, the Ministry of Panchayati Raj set up a committee to examine the feasibility of electronic fund transfer to Panchayats. The committee recommended that it was indeed feasible to transfer funds rapidly to approximately 2.4 lakhs Panchayats across the country through banks. The Ministry of Panchayati Raj has developed a software on this process. State Governments should be encouraged to adopt it and speed up their fund transfer procedure.

The State Government should take steps to release grants to the PRIs according to a prefixed time-table so that it becomes possible to utilise the funds during the currency of the year. The fund release could be in the form of equitably spaced instalments. The release could be made in two instalments; one at the beginning of the financial year and the other by the end of September of that year.

PRIs and Access to Credit

Over the years, the demands of the rural sector have shifted from the basics to potable water, power for irrigation, education, improved healthcare services, physical infrastructure and agricultural inputs and services. Apart from making efforts to increase revenue realisation (both tax and non-tax), Panchayats may also need to borrow from banks/financial institutions. The State Government should encourage such initiatives. The role of the State Government should remain confined to fixing the limits of borrowing as per the guidelines of the State Finance Commission.

Local Area Development Schemes

In addition to the regular State Government departments and the three levels of Panchayats, the rural areas of many districts are also being serviced by Area Development Authorities/Rural Development Boards. These organisations receive sizeable grants from both the Union and the State Governments. This arrangement is anomalous. With popularly elected grass roots institutions, Panchayats, in place to take care of the local development needs, there can be very little justification for existence of separate Development Authorities and Boards.

The system of MP and MLA Local Area Development Funds is unethical. The fund gives the sitting MP or the MLA an added advantage over his rival candidates in brightening his electoral prospects and denies the opposition candidates a level playing field. Accordingly, the Commission recommended that schemes such as MPLADS and MLALADS should be abolished.

In view of the above, the flow of funds to public bodies for development of rural areas should be exclusively through the Local Government Institutions.

Rural Development

Centrality of PRIs in the Centrally Sponsored Schemes

Most of the Centrally Sponsored Scheme deal with matters earmarked for Panchayats under Article 243 G and the Eleventh Schedule of the Constitution. Some examples are the National Rural Employment Guarantee Scheme, Sampoorna Gramin Rojgar Yojana, Sarva Siksha Abhiyan, National Rural Health Mission, Integrated Child Development Services, Mid-Day Meal Programme, Drinking Water Mission, Total Sanitation Campaign, Indira Awas Yojana, Swarna Jayanti Gram Swarojgar Yojana, Pradhanmantri Gram Sadak Yojana, Rajiv Gandhi Grameen Vidyutikaran Yojana, Adult Literacy and the Remote Village Electrification Programme. Out of this long menu, nine major programmes take up nearly Rs 65,875 crores during the year 2007-08. Since a large quantum of resources flows through these schemes to the States, efficient implementation of these programmes is critical for the States' economic development. In the long run, the schemes taken up under such programmes also need to find place in the overall development plan of the Panchayat body. It is, accordingly, essential that the centrality of Panchayats is recognised in fulfilling the objectives of these programmes. While some of the schemes do give a crucial role to the PRIs in their implementation, some bypass them and create separate structures. Even the schemes which allow the participation of Panchayats, often do not give them enough flexibility in decision-making. Such flexibility is essential to take care of the local specificities, which strait-jacketed schemes designed from above cannot accommodate.

The Commission is of the view that in due course the present system of release of funds to the CSSs should be substituted with a system where majority of the allocation is in the form of untied grants. The State and local governments should have flexibility in designing project components and implementation mechanism to achieve the overall objectives of a sectoral programme.

Analysis of some major Centrally Sponsored Schemes (CSSs)

Monitoring and review of Community and Primary Health Centres (CHC, PHC) and Sub-centres need to be a routine work of the Panchayats/ and Standing Committees. Such monitoring and review should cover all parameters enunciated in the vision, goal and strategy documents of the NRHM. The present practice of installing a centre-wise managing committee may continue but the practice of separate village committees for each of the three major components (Public health, Women's health and Child health) under departmental command needs to be dispensed with. There should be a single village committee constituted by the Gram Sabha to look after all the above three aspects of the rural healthcare system. At the intermediate and district levels too, the Block Committee and Zila Parishad themselves should be the implementing and monitoring agencies. At the district level, there could be an advisory body consisting of sectoral experts to guide the Zila Parishad from time to time.

Integrating SSA with the PRI system is necessary not only for getting better outcomes from the project, but also for sustainability of processes and the institutions introduced by it.

Integrated Child Development Scheme (ICDS)

The Commission is of the view that the ICDS programme has to be looked at as a part of the comprehensive healthcare delivery structure. By skilfully integrating other components of the system, namely immunisation, ante-natal care, family planning and vector control in the mainstream of healthcare, a composite healthcare machinery for children and women could be built up in the rural areas. This can be done by transferring the responsibility of the local level activities of all these components and the management of the local institutions related to such components (for example, health sub-centres, anganwadi centres) to the PRIs.

Mid-day Meal Programme

A national programme of nutritional support to primary education was formally launched in 1995.

Many of the States have not involved the Village Panchayats in managing this programme, even though most of them have devolved primary education to these institutions. Disassociation of the Panchayats from this important programme has caused an institutional vacuum; implementing agencies at the micro levels have been left alone. In the absence of participation of the PRIs, the monitoring of this programme has remained weak. The programme guidelines need to be revised urgently so as to bring it directly under Panchayat monitoring.

The role of the Panchayats vis-a-vis the Centrally Sponsored Schemes is not yet in line with the commitment of the 73rd Amendment. The CSSs have to shed their separate vertical identity and be part of the overall development plan of the Panchayat Raj system.The Commission feels that there has to be territorial/jurisdictional/functional convergence in their implementation. The centrality of PRIs in these schemes must be ensured if they are to deal with matters listed in the Eleventh Schedule. The Gram and Ward Sabha at the lowest level and the Panchayat Samiti and Zila Parishad at the higher levels have to be the structures looking after all their activities in terms of implementation, monitoring and social audit. In the programmes, where the activities percolate to areas and habitations below a Panchayat/Ward level, a small local centre committee should be formed to support these activities. Such a local committee will only be a deliberative body with responsibility to provide regular feedback to the Gram Sabha / Ward Sabha and be accountable to it. Even while formulating such projects, the Union and State Governments need to include elements of flexibility so that they could be moulded as per local conditions and requirements. The Ministries concerned should only issue guidelines and the implementational flexibility should be left to the local bodies. In order to assess the socio-economic impact of these programmes periodically, a system of outcome monitoring must be put in place. The National Sample Survey Organisation (NSSO) on being suitably strengthened can be given this responsibility.

Information Education and Communication – IEC

The Commission is of the view that different modes of communication like the print media, the visual media, electronic media, folk arts and theatres etc, should be utilised to create awareness among the rural population. As mentioned earlier, it should be ensured that there is a convergence in approach to achieve synergies and maximise reach. District level rural broadcasting should become a full-fledged independent activity of the All India Radio. To achieve this, apart from covering issues related to Panchayati Raj Institutions and peoples' participation in local governance, these broadcasts should also focus on issues related to agriculture and rural development, which concern mainly with the rural areas and combine it with programmes on the citizens' Right to Information. The mechanism for this should be evolved by the Union Ministry of Information and Broadcasting in coordination with the Union Ministries of Panchayati Raj, Rural Development, Agriculture and other related Ministries.

Role of Panchayats in Delivery of Services

The following steps are required to ensure the centrality of PRIs in service delivery programmes:-

- Unbundling the service into activities.
- Assigning clear responsibilities for different aspects of service delivery to agencies including PRIs – the role could range from planning to supervision and feedback.
- Placing the resources required for service delivery, both human and financial, with PRIs.
- Setting standards for services both institutional and otherwise. This has to be modulated according to available facilities and manpower
- Preparing service delivery plans by the PRIs based on these standards in respect of each service, in consultation with the stakeholders and in accordance with the resources and facilities available. Milestones in upgradation of services in terms of quality and quantity. Service Delivery Plans could be prepared by institutional committees consisting of stakeholders, officials, elected representatives and

experts in respect of institutions like hospitals, schools and anganwadis. In respect of other services, the plans could be prepared in consultation with user groups.

- Publishing the elements of Services Delivery Plans in the form of Citizen Charters which would indicate the levels of assured services; measurement and feedback systems and grievance redressal systems.
- Putting in place a community-based monitoring system including user groups, SHG networks and civil society groups to monitor the implementation of Service Delivery Plans and provide inputs for further improvement.

Resource Centre at the Village Level

Resource Centres at the Village Panchayat level should utilise the potential of educated local youths in documenting and mapping local resources; soil types; drainage pattern; cropping and animal husbandry practices; water resources; land and farm holding; susceptibility to natural disasters – documentation of impact, recurrence, rescue, relief and settlement requirement; rural infrastructure etc. This locally generated information base should be corroborated through satellite imagery and other space-enabled services.

Once these Resource Centres become operational, they should also be utilised for documenting in detail, local traditional knowledge, especially about medicine, natural resource management and agricultural practices; local arts and crafts; folk memories – ranging from folk tales and lores to local memories about historical events, movements, people and monuments; community festivals, gatherings, events and folk cultural practices etc. before they vanish into oblivion.

The Commission feels that seting up space technology enabled Resource Centres at the Village and Intermediate Panchayat levels all across the country should be on the priority agenda of the government. This would require substantial capacity building at the local level. This would, in essence, also necessitate a shift from the currently available generalistic education at the post-school level, to a skill and technology-based system which focuses on farm and animal husbandry practices, computer applications, commercial cropping and soil and water management.

Local Government in the Fifth and Sixth Schedule Areas

Local Government in the Fifth Schedule Areas

For decentralisation of governance in these areas, government enacted a special legislation – the Panchayati Raj (Extension to Scheduled Areas) Act in 1996 which extends to all the notified scheduled areas located in nine States of the country.

PESA and the Union / State Laws

Nine States have amended the respective Panchayati Raj Acts to match them with requirements of PESA. However, much remains to be done with regard to subject laws and rules which also need to be modified suitably in accordance with provisions of PESA. Technically under Section 5 of the PESA Act all such laws have automatically become invalid after December 12, 1997. But in practice these laws are being still followed by the State Government machinery. Similarly, there is a large number of Union legislations which need to be hormonised with the provision of PESA.

Since PESA is a Union legislation and a local extension of the Fifth Schedule, a duty is cast upon the Union Government to see that the provisions are strictly implemented. In case of reluctance by any State in implementing the provisions of PESA, specific directions can be issued by the Government of India under Proviso 3 of Part A of the Fifth Schedule of the Constitution.

PESA and Specific Policies of the Government / Centrally Sponsored Schemes

There is a large number of Centrally Schemes which are not compatible with PESA e.g. Policy on wastelands, water resources and extraction of minerals. The policies, as interpreted and implemented, have given rise, on occasions, to confrontations between the tribal people and the administration. Similarly, the National Policy on Resettlement and Rehabilitation of Project Affected Persons, 2003, National Water Policy, 2002, National Minerals Policy 2003, National Forest Policy, 1988, Wildlife Conservation Strategy 2002 and National Draft Environment Policy, 2004 would also require detailed examination from the viewpoint of ensuring compliance to the provisions of PESA.

Effective Implementation of PESA

The PESA has been in existence since last eleven years, but the response of the States towards its implementation has been rather slow.

The Commission is of the view that due importance must be given to regular annual reports from the Governors as stipulated in the Fifth Schedule, Part A(3) of the Constitution.

In tribal areas, though, the society and economy is closely woven around womenfolk, their involvement at the Village Council/Gram Sabha level is minimal. Special efforts need to be taken to raise their status in this respect. There is need to make suitable provisions in the PESA Rules and Guidelines making it mandatory that the quorum of a Gram Sabha meeting would be acceptable only when out of the members present, at least thirty three per cent are women.

For effective compliance to legislation and protection of tribal rights. Special measures have to be taken to strengthen the local administration both in terms of intellectual enhancement and skill upgradation. One such measure could be constituting a group in each State to look into strengthening of the administrative machinery in the Fifth Schedule Areas. This group can consider important administrative issues such as creation of separate cadres of employees for the Fifth Schedule Areas, provision of hardship pay/allowance and other incentives, preferential treatment in accommodation and education etc. and make suitable recommendations to the State Government. Considering the importance of this exercise, the funds required for this purpose should be made available by the Union Government under Article 275 of the Constitution.

Effective Implementation of the Tribal Sub-plan (TSP)

Since last many years, the tribal sub-plan has been a regular feature of the planning exercise in a State, it has been implemented in a ritualistic manner and treated just as an adjunct of the State budget. The performance has not been very encouraging, on account of both poor planning as well as weak implementation. Technically and professionally qualified personnel who are the sheet anchors of the development process, are reluctant to work in such areas. For government employees, a posting in these areas is considered to be a punishment. The situation is further compounded by lack of data; there has been little attempt in the past to have an impact assessment made. Then, finally, one has to contend with the problem of extremism which prevails on a large scale in some of these States. The Commission feels that both the Union as well as State Governments have to take special steps with regard to (i) creation of a special planning unit for scheduled areas in a State; (ii) special financial stipulation for the sub plans; (iii) incentivisation and capacity building of government employees; (iv) impact assessment of the past schemes; and (v) effective monitoring / social audit of the current programmes.

Urban Governance

Urbanisation and Growth

Trends in Urbanisation

Nearly 20 years have passed since the first National Commission on Urbanisation submitted its report. During this period, the importance of the urban sector and its contribution to the national economy and employment has increased manifold while the infrastructural constraints in our cities have become more acute. While the urban growth has been slower than anticipated by the National Commission on Urbanisation, the problems identified still remain valid. Indeed the magnitude and complexities of urban problems have increased and with that the urgency to reform 'urban governance'. The

Commission is of the view that a new National Commission on Urbanisation should be set up to take a holistic and long-term view of the entire range of policy instruments required to deal with the rapid urbanisation, including the large cities and to bring about more balanced and efficient urbanisation in the country.

Structure of Urban Governance

Different Types of Urban Local Governments: The 74th Constitutional Amendment lays down three types of municipal bodies:

1. *Nagar Panchayat (by whatever named called):* This is for a transitional area, which is transforming itself from being a rural area into an urban area;
2. *Municipal Council:* This is for "a smaller urban area"; and
3. *Municipal Corporation:* This is for "a larger urban area."

Implicit in the above classification of urban local governments is the recognition of the need for variation in the functional domain and requirements depending on the size of the population they need to serve.

The Constitution does not lay down the parameters for categorising the urban local bodies into Nagar Panchayat, Municipal Council and Municipal Corporation. This prevents a uniform pattern of categorisation across the States. The Commission recognises the fact that the situation in the States varies and that there is a wide range of structures and systems. The Commission would recommend a common categorisation which might be useful to reduce the lack of clarity help in adoption of a structured and approach leading to a more systematic national planning process and in the devolution of funds through National and State Finance Commissions.

Proposed Basic Structure – Ward Committees and Area Sabhas

Need for Greater Citizen Participation

The Commission has examined the various structures that exist today, in statutes and in practice. The existing system has two important lacunae. First, there is very little role that the average citizen plays in his/her own governance. The second is that the elected representatives as well as the officials are not sufficiently accountable and this often undermines both efficiency and transparency.

The representation ratio between citizens and their elected representatives is almost ten times larger in urban areas. The Gram Sabha gives every rural citizen the opportunity to participate in local issues. In contrast, the Ward (or Wards) Committees, proposed for urban bodies have not yet been constituted in some States. And even where constituted in some States. And even where constituted, they are hampered by the combination of various factors. It is necessary to accept the direction in which demography and habitation trends are moving and push to continue the steps initiated by the 74th Amendment towards citizens' participation in urban affairs. It is towards this end that the following structure is proposed for urban local bodies.

The three tiers of urban local body governance should be as follows:

(a) Municipal Council / Corporation (by whatever name it is called);

(b) Ward Committees; and

(c) Area Committees or Sabhas.

However, in Town Panchayats, there is no need to have three tiers, given the small size and population of these local bodies.

Area Sabha

An Area Sabha would cover the citizens who are voters in one or more polling stations, but preferably not covering more than, say, 2500 voters.

Role of the Area Sabhas: An Area Sabha should be the functional equivalent of the Gram Sabha in villages.

Members of the Area Sabha: Every registered voter of a polling booth would be a member of that Area Sabha. Each Area Sabha would elect, once in five years, a small Committee of Representatives. The Committee of Representatives would elect one person who would chair the meetings of the Area Sabha and would represent the Area Sabha in the relevant Ward Committee. The election of the Committee of Representatives should be held by the State Election Commission along with the election of Councillors and their term should be coterminus with that of the Councillors.

Ward Committees

The present system of having a Ward Committee for more than one ward is not logical and must be given up. There must be a Ward Committee for every ward, each effectively representing one local political boundary. The Chairpersons of the Area Sabha included in the wards would constitute the Ward Committee. The Commission is of the view that in smaller towns also, with population of less than three lakhs, it is necessary to have formal mechanisms for citizen participation and local decision-making through Ward Committees.

The Ward Committee members must have regular meetings with the citizens they represent, through Area Sabhas, to review programmes, their planning and implementation. There must also be regular meeting of the Committee with elected members from Area Sabhas. The Committee must have legitimate functions and appropriate financial devolution. These should cover all the relevant activities that may be delegated by the Legislature or the Municipal Council.

In urban areas, it is not only the individual voter who needs to be involved, but also non-residential stakeholders, such as businesses. These non-residential stakeholders could be given some representation at the Ward Committee level, preferably through their business associations.

Delineation of Functions in the Three Tiers: Just as there is delineation of functions among the different tiers in rural local governance, similar delineation would have to be done in case of urban local bodies also. While doing so, the principle of subsidiarity should be followed. A process of activity mapping similar to the one taken up for PRIs should be carried out for all ULBs.

Zonal System for Large Cities

Within one large city, a number of zonal office should be set up. Such zonal offices do exist in many cities, but, generally do not have adequate delegated powers. The powers of the city government, covering all decision-making for administrative purposes, can be delegated and exercised in the zones. Broadly, one zonal office for every five lakh (or less) population, could be considered. The system could be introduced in all Municipal Corporations within the next three years.

The Office of the Mayor/Chairperson

It is desirable to choose the Mayors/Chairpersons through popular mandate in a direct election. Such a Mayor should have a fixed tenure of five years. The Council should have powers of budget approval, oversight and framing regulations and major policies.

Role of the Mayor/Chairperson

Separation of the functions of Chairperson and Mayor at the city and local level is unnecessary and cumbersome. The Mayor acting as Chairperson will facilitate harmonious functioning between the council and the executive. In a local government, the focus of authority should be unified and clearly defined. The Commission therefore recommends that the elected Mayor should function as both the Chief Executive and the Chairperson of the Council.

The Commission is of the firm view that executive power must be exercised by the elected Mayor/Chairperson because basic democratic legitimacy demands that power is exercised by the elected executive. The Mayor/Chairperson should be the Chief Executive of a city or urban government, and the city government should have the power to appoint all officials including the Commissioner and to hold them to account.

Some form of cabinet system with functionaries appointed by the Mayor exercising authority on his behalf in various department of the executive branch is desirable.

In a city government, the imperatives of separation of powers should be tempered by the need for greater harmony between the elected council and the Mayor. The Commission recommends that a Mayor's 'cabinet', chosen by the elected Mayor from among the councillors, should be constituted in all municipal corporations. The size of this cabinet should not exceed ten per cent of the strength of the council, or fifteen, whichever is higher. Such a cabinet will function directly under the control and supervision of the Mayor.

Management Structure of Urban Local Governments

The Commissioner

The elected Mayor/Chairperson is accountable to the electorate. This accountability should also have commensurate authority over the staff of the local government. The Mayor/Chairperson should, accordingly, have a final say in the matter of appointment of the Commissioner/Chief Officer. However, in order to ensure that the right person is selected, the State must lay down, by law, the procedure and qualifications for selection and appointment to this post.

The responsibility for selection and appointment of the Commissioner may be given to the Metropolitan Corporations and Municipal Corporations within a period of two years. For all other ULGs, this should be possible in three years' time. Selection could be done by the Mayor from a panel of names, which could be prepared by a bipartisan Committee to be set up by the Council/Corporation. Appointment should be for a minimum period to be extended based on performance. During such time as the Commissioners/Chief Officers are deputed by the State Government, selection of the Commissioner should be from a panel of names, from which the Mayor could select an officer.

Staffing of Municipalities

Ultimately all municipal bodies should have the power to appoint their own staff. State Governments may, however, lay down the procedure and the principles of making such appointments. The existing State-wide municipal cadres may continue for the present but no fresh recruitments need be made to such cadres.

Some States also have Directorates of Municipal Administration. The present system of the Directorate of Municipal Administration exercising supervision over the local bodies intrudes into the autonomy of the ULBs. Organisations like Directorates of Municipal Administration come in the way of true decentralisation and should be abolished.

Urban Finances

Property Tax Reforms

The Commission is of the view that the Union Government should pursue the matter with the States to ensure that all States switch over to either the 'unit area' or 'capital value' method in a time bound manner. The categories of properties exempted from property tax need to be revisiting and minimised. In order to ensure that unauthorised constructions do not escape the tax net, State laws should stipulate that levy of tax on any property would not confer any right of ownership in case the property has been constructed in violation of any law. Property tax details for all properties should be placed in the public domain to avoid any type of collusion between the assessing authority and the property owner. State laws should also provide for tax on properties belonging to the municipal authorities, but which are given on lease. Similarly, the law should provide for levy of service charge on properties belonging to the Union and State Governments.

A periodic physical verification of the properties and taxes levied on them should be carried out in each municipal area by a separate wing directly under the control of the Chief Executive. Besides, randomly selected cases of assessment should be audited by the government auditors as is done by C&AG in case of Union and State taxes. As both the 'unit area method' and the 'capital value method' are based on the principles of self-assessment, the law should provide for exemplary penalties in cases of suppression of facts by property owners.

Octroi

In terms of administrative efficiency, Octroi breeds delays in the movement of goods and is neither transparent nor efficient. Octroi should be abolished, but at the same time, States should evolve mechanisms to compensate the local bodies for the loss in revenue as a result of such abolition.

Other Taxes

Professional Tax has the potential of generating significant resources for the local governments. The upper ceiling of Rs 2500, on the tax rate prescribed under the Constitution Article 276(2) limits the potential of this tax. There is need to amend this Article to enhance the upper limit on the professional Tax. The Commission recommends that certain principles should be followed in the administration of taxes. These principles are – (i) The levy of tax should be made totally transparent and objective, (ii) the cost of collection for the local body and the cost of compliance for the tax payers should be reduced to a minimum, (iii) there should be an independent unit under the Chief Executive to monitor the collection of all taxes, and (iv) as far as possible, all levies should be based on self-declaration of the tax prayer but this should be accompanied by stringent penalties in case of fraud or suppression of facts by the tax payer.

Non-Tax Revenues

This Commission is of the view that the levy and collection of appropriate user charges must be encouraged. For this, a significant portion of grants to the municipalities may be linked with their own efforts at resource raising.

The 'User pays' principle is applicable to a large number of services. But there are services where the individual use is not identifiable and the services are of a collective nature. In such cases, recourse should be made to 'Betterment levy'. A good example of a levy on 'Polluter pays' principle would be traffic congestion. It is, therefore, necessary to carry out an impact study for all major developments, and a 'congestion charge' may be levied which could then be used to take steps to ease congestion.

In several types of cases pertaining to the violation of civic laws the power to impose spot fines should be given to the municipal authorities. Another reason for poor compliance of civic laws is the relatively non-deterrent nature of penalties prescribed. Therefore, the punishment prescribed for all civic offences need to be revisited and modified.

Borrowings

The Commission would recommend that municipal bodies should be encouraged to raise their own resources. Any borrowing, be it term loans from financial institutions or market borrowings, could be adopted by the municipal bodies depending upon their capability. Initially, borrowings appeal attractive as they improve the liquidity of these bodies in the short run. But it need to be ensured that the deployment of resources is in economic activities. State support would, however, be required by smaller local bodies. Such bodies would need to be given State guarantee or in the alternative pooled financing mechanisms would have to be put in place.

Leveraging Land as a Resource

Municipal bodies often have a wide range of assets on their balance sheets ranging from infrastructure networks to public buildings, from housing to municipal shopping centers as well as land. In view of the recommendation of this Commission that development authorities should be merged with concerned ULBs and their technical/planning manpower subsumed with the DPCs and MPCs; the substantial land holdings of the development authorities should also eventually come under municipal ownership. With spiralling prices of land in cities, it is extremely necessary that these assets are managed properly.

Sale of public urban land in India is dominated by development authorities and has neither been instrumental in fiscal decentralisation to the local level nor have they contributed significantly to the municipality's capital budget.

In economic terms, municipalities have to not only leverage land as a resource but also avoid the fiscal risk of becoming dependent upon asset sales for covering their recurring costs (and delaying politically difficult decisions on users' charges). They must use the proceeds of land sales mainly to finance investment and capital works.

Most municipal bodies have a large number of properties given on rents or lease. However, the earnings out of these properties are quite low. This is primarily because of litigations by the current occupiers who neither pay the market rent nor vacate the premises. Respective municipal laws should provide that any built up property of municipal bodies shall not be given on rent for more than a period beyond five years and after expiry of the prescribed period the property shall be given on rent only through a competitive process.

A basic necessity for leveraging land for revenue generation is the proper upkeep of land records. The increasing population density and real estate prices in urban areas underlines the importance of proper land management systems in urban areas.

Infrastructure and Service Provision

Types of Services Provided by Urban Local Bodies

Deficiencies in urban infrastructure are a major bottleneck for economic growth. The stress created by inadequate services and facilities compounded by weak governance adversely affects the quality of life of all citizens. Urban services can be broadly classified into three categories:

(a) Regulatory services;

(b) Infrastructural service; and

(c) Social services.

The Commission believes that improvements in the availability and accessibility of these services would result in qualitative improvement in the daily lives of urban citizens.

Regulatory Services

Objectivity: In most of the regulatory functions performed by local governments, it is possible to minimise, if not totally eliminate discretion. Assessment of property tax is one such example. Where it is not possible to eliminate discretion, then the exercise of such discretion should be bound by well-defined guidelines.

Convergence: Different services are provided by different departments of local governments, agencies of State Government and parastatals. This multiplicity of service providers, forces citizens to access each one of these separately. Certain of 'one stop service centers' can address this problem besides expediting processing of requests of citizens.

Speedy Disposal: All applications for regulatory approvals must be disposed off within a specific time frame. A citizen's charter laying down specific deadlines for disposal of different categories of applications should be prescribed. The charter should also specify the relief available to the citizens if the charter is not adhered to.

To avoid delays by the functionaries in processing applications, a system of deemed sanctions after the expiry of self-imposed time limits should be adopted. A system of voluntary compliance backed up with stringent penalties for violations should be put in place. For example, in respect of approval of building permits, a system of self-certification by registered architects (particularly for residential units) followed by approvals over the counter, should be made mandatory.

Infrastructure Services

Creating a Responsive Institutional Framework

Allocation of responsibility and accountability between the urban local bodies and the State Government departments/parastatals has to be clearly demarcated. To an extent, the larger State Government agency may have a final responsibility and ownership, at least of those services and utilities which have a presence beyond the ULB jurisdiction. But wherever, and to the extent it is possible to demarcate the managerial and technical "boundaries" of a civic activity, it should be possible to earmark responsibility to a local body.

In other words, all 'downstream activities' of a particular utility, within the jurisdiction of a ULB should ideally become the activity of the ULB. In a Metropolitan Corporation, for example, the distribution of water should primarily be the responsibility of the local body. This task could be undertaken by the local body itself or through an agency such as the Water Supply Board. In such cases, the head of the Water Supply Board should be responsible to the Mayor for all activities related to distribution of water. In other words, the functionaries of the parastatals have to accountable to the Municipal Council.

Water Supply

Management of water supply should be the primary function of a municipal body. The Commission has recommended that in respect of all downstream activities of a particular utility, as soon as they enter the geographical and administrative boundary of an urban local body, the Government utility / parastatal should become accountable to the ULB. In general, water supply boards are financially more autonomous and have built up higher levels of technical capacities as compared to Municipal Corporations other than the very large corporations such as Mumbai. Therefore, the transfer of these responsibilities from parastatals to the ULBs would have to be appropriately phased in with capacity building of the ULBs. Thus, while the largest Corporation should certainly take charge of the entire gamut of water supply from development to distribution, for most local bodies a phased transfer of responsibilities for management of the distribution networks within their territorial jurisdiction while leaving source development to the parastatal agency would appeal to be the most feasible arrangement.

Tariff: There is understandable reluctance on the part of local governments to pass on the actual costs to consumers. The gap between the revenues and costs of water supply prevents the municipal bodies from making any substantial investments on improving or even maintaining the quality.

The Commission has recommended that the SFCs should carry out a more thorough analysis of the finances of local bodies and make concrete recommendations for improvements in their working. This should necessarily include detailed analysis of water supply systems of the local governments. The SFCs should lay down principles for fixation of water tariffs and its periodic revision. The underlying approach should be the recovery of at least full running costs of these services.

Water supply schemes have to be environmentally sustainable. With a burgeoning urban population, the traditional water sources are inadequate to meet the requirements. As a result, new sources have to be developed, but this raises the cost of water. Local bodies need to prepare infrastructure development plans which should be integrated with the CDPs. In order to reduce the strain on the urban water supply systems, the demand could be tempered by adopting water harvesting measures and recycling of waste water for non-potable purposes. Municipal bye-laws should initially provide incentives for the adoption of such practices and progressively make them compulsory for all buildings.

Sewerage Management

Sewerage systems along with treatment facilities are capital intensive. While granting approvals to new lay-outs, it should be ensured that adequate provisions for internal sewerage systems are made and enforced. Local bodies may even impose a cess on the property tax or development charges in order to raise resources for expansion and capacity enhancement of the existing sewerage systems. In order to motivate the local governments to generate additional resources for sewerage management, matching grants may be provided by the Union and State Governments.

The Commission recommends that a separate user charge be introduced in all municipalities, even as a minimum levy, for sanitation and sewerage, as distinct from water charges. It is necessary to emphasise the need to redeploy these funds into operation and maintenance of the sewerage system.

The Commission notes that the provision of water and sanitation within the slums is skewed very strongly towards notified slums. In the case of latrines,

17 per cent of people in notified slums do not have access to latrines, while the percentage is 51 in the case of non-notified slums. In some States, the situation is abysmal. This is an area of concern, as certain basic steps to prevent human degradation cannot be based on notification of areas.

Several NGOs and civic society groups have set up 'pay and use toilets', especially in slum areas. Co-production of sanitary services has been tried successfully in slum areas. The concept includes setting up of a CBO (Community Based Organisation) at the grassroots, carrying out IEC activities, collecting a significant percentage of the initial capital cost from the beneficiary followed by the construction of a collective toilet block. Such efforts need to be encouraged by municipal governments by providing appropriate incentives. Sewerage facilities have to be provided in slum areas on a priority basis by the municipal bodies.

Solid Waste Management

The management of waste has three basic components: (a) collection (b) segregation for different types of disposal and (c) disposal. The first lends itself to community participation and also privatisation and must be made a part of the activities of Area Sabhas and local NGOs/CBOs who may charge for this. A large number of community-based systems of garbage collection have been tried in different cities. These need to be scaled up. The second component requires segregation into categories for different types of disposal. Unfortunately, our pattern of disposal is mainly one of indiscriminate dumping. It is essential to initiate a civic programme especially in the larger cities to segregate household waste according to its degradability. This would ease the burden on civic authorities. The third component is that of efficient disposal, which can also be carried out either by the local bodies themselves or with private sector participation. The Municipal Solid Wastes (Management and Handling) Rules, 2000 prescribe the manner of disposal of solid wastes. It is important that before any task is outsourced, municipal bodies develop the capacity for managing such contracts.

Scavenging

The Commission is of the firm view that national urban renewal and manual scavenging should not and cannot co-habit the same space. Intensive surveys should be carried out by the State Local Governments to identify manual scavengers and estimate the number of dry latrines in existence within six months. Following this, separately earmarked funds should be allocated to address and remove this abomination within a one year time frame. Central Assistance to States Annual Plan should be tied to this. Funds allocated under the JNNURM should also be linked to it.

Power Utilities and Municipal Bodies

An option could be to hand over distribution of power to the municipal bodies; however, with the existing organisational and technical capabilities of the municipal bodies, this may not be possible. Therefore, as a pre-requisite, the capacity of the municipal bodies needs to be enhanced, and then in a phased manner they could take over the function of power distribution, starting with small manageable areas within their jurisdiction.

Municipal bodies can also play a major role in proper planning of the distribution networks along with other networks like water supply and telecommunication. Common ducts could be planned by the municipal bodies for all these networks and even charges could be levied on the users of these ducts. The local bodies can also help in the power conservation efforts by incorporating power conservation features in the building bye-laws.

Services for Human Development

Education

Irrespective of whether schools for the common people are run by the government or the local bodies, the biggest challenge is to impart quality education. Data indicates that basic facilities such as blackboards, furniture and recreational as also toilet facilities, especially for girls, were inadequate in most schools run by government agencies though interestingly, more of the problem in government schools than in municipal ones. It is necessary that all schools are made functionally self-sufficient, in as much as the basic facilities and classroom requirements are provided in all urban schools within the next two years.

Attempts must be made also to recruit better teachers. Since an appropriate salary is difficult for the ULBs to provide, it should be increasingly necessary for the municipalities, especially the larger ones, to seek the help of NGOs and individual volunteers. Indeed, it would be useful to initiate a voluntary service element to our social sector to improve service delivery.

Crafting a credible service delivery system requires a shift from a system that provides employment guarantees to the service providers to one that provides service guarantees to the citizens. Accountability in such a new system should lie with local governments and local Institutions/Societies/Management committees.

Public Health

Private healthcare plays a critical role in bridging a need gap for the urban population. The trend in urban areas to shift towards private healthcare needs to be seen as an opportunity by the city authorities. It gives them an opportunity to concentrate on public health as distinct from clinical services, and on preventive and not only curative aspects of healthcare.

Public health is dependent on primary healthcare systems, nutrition, safe drinking water, and sanitation and health education. The Commission, therefore, feels that convergence of these services is as important as upgradation of primary healthcare in urban areas. There should be a task force in each local government responsible for all services which impact public health, with members from the State Government and other agencies in the field of public health.

Schools and hospitals require more financial resources to improve performance but they also require institutional autonomy and flexibility to deliver guaranteed service outcomes. The role of the head of the institution has to be strengthened in a framework of decentralisation that allows for accountability to local communities. Flexibility in meeting local needs within a framework that guarantees certain minimum service delivery standards also requires a shift from non-accountable State level recruitment to accountable local government and local institution level recruitment.

For all services provided by the local governments there is need to develop a set of performance indicators. The existing set of performance indicators, wherever they exist, are not sufficient to monitor all important aspects of service delivery. The emphasis in these indicators has to be on quality of service and reliability. A closely linked aspect for improving the quality of services is maintenance of reliable database about all the municipal services at the District, State and National level. This would also help in monitoring of these services as well as taking important policy decisions.

Urban Transport Management

The Commission recommends that, in keeping with the national policy, in each Metropolitan Corporation, a Metropolitan Transportation Authority should be set up with appropriate powers, so as to integrate and coordinate city transport systems. Thus, a single Authority, by whatever name or structure, must become the repository of all responsibility and authority within the municipal limits for all transportation related activities and decision-making. The national policy talks of a United Metropolitan Transport Authority (UMTA) in metropolitan cities for coordinated planning of urban transport. But what is also required is a common ticketing and fare system for different modes of public transport and their integration so that they complement and not compete with one another. To make that happen, UMTAs will need powers to regulate all modes of transport, decide on routes for each operator, fix fares, service standards, etc. In addition, UMTAs will need financial powers and resources to give financial support to operators on unviable routes.

Introduction of mass transit systems has to be carefully conceptualised as the investments required are quite large as is their socio-economic impact. All such systems should be meticulously planned. This requires a high degree of administrative and professional competence amongst officials handling the project. Therefore, capacity building of concerned officials is extremely important. Moreover, mass transit systems should not be planned and implemented in isolation. A holistic approach is necessary. An integrated transport system has various dimensions. In its widest sense it requires:

- Coherence between transport, land use and other social and economic policies.
- Consistent resource allocation criteria between transport modes.
- Consistent budgeting across all modes and services.
- Rational pricing, including externalities.
- A coherent multi-modal system of regulation.
- Design of services and facilities to reflect their individual strengths.
- Facilities for easy interchange between modes and services.
- Common fares and ticketing.
- Co-ordinated timetabling where practicable.
- Multi-modal passenger information.

Public-Private Partnership in Public Transport: Involving the private sector in public transport helps in bringing in capital as well as managerial efficiencies. Various models of public-private partnership are possible. These are 'tendering of routes', wet lease of buses and outsourcing of specific services. Several similar projects have been funded under JNNURM. The pre-requisites for a successful public-private partnership are a meticulously structured agreement between the two parties and complete transparency and objectivity in the selection of the private partner and enforcement of the agreement.

JNNURM – A Reform Process

The implementation of JNNURM is just picking up; however, certain aspects of the programme and consideration. The first aspect, indeed, is the requirement of funds and the funding pattern.

According to the CDPs prepared by 43 cities, that is just two-thirds of the project cities, the cost of projects would be of the order of Rs 211,348 crores. On the same per capita basis, the total investment needs projected for all 63 cities and towns in Rs 3,39,902 crores.

The per capita project costs vary drastically across the States, both in total terms and under different infrastructure segments.

It can be a matter of debate as to why one State should get more than twice the amount per capita than another State. But that may happen if, say, the cost of supplying safe water per person is higher in one State than in another. But the need to balance the distribution of scarce funds remains an imperative. And the first, essential priority must be certification by the States that drinking water and sanitation needs, on the lines of the millennium development goals, have been met.

While the demand driven approach that underpins JNNURM has much to commend itself, it is imperative that its limitations too are taken note of. A study reveals that the predominant share in projects under the Scheme belong to the urban transport sector. This has worrying implications for other equally important sectors like sanitation. Further, the stipulation of the urban local body raising the prescribed share of investment cost, irrespective of the sector has similar implications. The Commission therefore feels that for sectors like sanitations, that have broader social and environmental benefits, there need to be earmarked outlays with lower requirement of share of the ULBs.

Capacity building within the ULBs is critical for successful implementation of the scheme. Even ULBs not yet included in the Scheme must benefit from capacity building initiatives as this has marginal additional costs with benefits of a very significant order.

A Critical and Urgent Area of Reform – Regulating the Real Estate Sector

There is one critical and urgent area of reform without attention to which all others will not achieve the objectives. This relates to the regulation of real estate sector by an independent regulatory authority. Existing laws on land registry, transfer of property, contracts and related matters are themselves inadequate, are implemented by different authorities and they cast no responsibility (or liability) on the builder / developer for observing certain core norms in the contracts with home-buyers. Builders/Developers investing above a certain sum in real estate, in notified urban and urbanising areas, should be required to register and bind themselves to specified core norms of contract and for compliance with all relevant laws and regulations applicable to land and construction in such areas. There should be civil and criminal liability for breach and the regulatory body should also have power to impose fines, deregister and/or black list offenders and publish the names.

Mega Cities – Metropolitan Corporations

Re-Forming Mega Cities

For India, it would be useful to define all cities with a recognised metropolitan area and a population of five million as a megacity and plan for its future with a long-term perspective of at least 30 years.

Redevelopment of the Existing Cities: For land developers, the cost of redeveloping inner city properties – brownfield redevelopment – is much higher than green field developments. At the same time, for the city, 'brownfields redevelopment' is a fiscally-sound way to bring investment back to neglected neighbourhoods, cleanup the environment, reuse existing infrastructure that is already paid for, utilise existing markets and labour pools, and relieve development pressure on our urban fringes and farmlands. Consequently, there must be incentives to encourage better development in the cities, rather than in the distant suburbs.

Developing 25-30 World Class Mega Cities in India

India has to focus on developing at least 25-30 world class mega cities across the country in the next decade in order to give a boost to planned urbanisation in the country. The Jawaharlal Nehru National Urban Renewal Mission (JNNURM) has in a sense, made a beginning in this direction by taking up urban renewal projects in mission mode in 63 selected cities.

However, any such programme also has to be backed by a zero-tolerance regulatory regime, one that enforces all civic laws, major and minor, in an impartial and unforgiving manner so that the present climate of impunity that prevails in our big cities can be brought to an end.

A zero-tolerance strategy towards violations of civic laws will help to forestall the kind of widespread and blatant violations of building bye-laws and landuse norms that led to the Delhi demolitions. For this to happen, in addition to the decentralisation oriented reforms that form the conditionalities for fund flows under the JNNURM, there is need to focus on encouraging and inducing cities to mount a massive crackdown on civic violations of all kinds so that infrastructure development under schemes such as the JNNURM is combined with genuine civic regeneration in our mega cities.

Authorities for Metropolitan Corporation

All cities with population above one million should have Metropolitan Police Authorities. This Authority should have powers to plan and oversee community policing, improving police-citizen interface, suggesting ways to improve quality of policing, approve annual police plans and review the working of such plans.

Metropolitan Transportation Authority: Unified Metropolitan Transport Authorities must be set up in the six largest cities within the next year on priority.

Metropolitan Planning Commerce: The Commission is of the view that for the megacities, it would be useful to have the Chief Minister as the Chairperson of the MPC. This would give the requisite impetus and priority to the process of formulating and implementing the city development plans and will also obviate the need for the CDP/Master Plans to be submitted to the State Government for approval.

Metropolitan Environmental Authority: An environment authority may be set up in each city with a population above five million in the first instance, for urban environment management, with powers as appropriate to be delegated by the State Government. Certain activities can be delegated over time to smaller bodies also. Basically, while the laying down of the regulations and the overall inspection powers would remain with the Pollution Control Board or any other appropriate body, the actual effort on the ground must, as far as is feasible, be undertaken by the Municipality/Corporation itself.

Urban Poverty

Beneficiary Identification

The 'Report of the Eleventh Five Year Plan (2007-12) Working Group on Urban Housing with Focus on Slums' (Union Ministry of Housing and Urban Poverty Alleviation) lays stress on the need for an exhaustive survey to identify the poor. It has been pointed out that such a survey should be city specific correlating with the specific conditions of the urban poor in that area and the parameters should be such that are easily comprehensible to the general public and should be made public before conducting the survey. This Report also suggests that after identification, the beneficiaries may be issued multi-utility cards. The Commission feels that the parameters for identifying the beneficiaries should be such which could be ascertained in an objective and simple manner during a survey without any discretionary element. The basic parameters should be spelt out at the national level. The identification should be based on a door-to-door survey and the survey teams should include at least one person from the concerned Area Sabha.

Measures for Poverty Alleviation

Once the poor have been identified, the issue of urban poverty alleviation would have to be addressed in a systematic and time-bound manner by adopting the mission mode approach. The main thrust area should be on providing skill upgradation and training to the poor. The urban local bodies should also have their own poverty alleviation schemes with adequate backward and forward linkages and convergence. The schemes should have adequate flexibility with regard to type of projects and amount of finance keeping in mind the forces of demand and supply. For training the urban poor, self-employment training institutes on the lines of RUDSETI's may be replicated in urban areas.

Providing education in poor urban areas cannot be viewed in isolation and there has to be convergence between socio-economic development and education. This convergence can be brought by the local bodies. The municipal bodies should ensure that the basic amenities are provided to such areas immediately and also ensure that the basic amenities are provided to such areas immediately and also ensure that adequate space is provided for setting up of schools. The education plan should form an integral part of the development plan for the city.

Health and Nutrition

For improving the lot of the urban poor, urban local bodies should adopt the concept of providing Primary Health Care Centres as is being done in the rural areas. These should preferably cater to slum areas where the urban poor are concentrated and should include community based auxiliary health staff to focus on reduction of IMR and MMR.

Slums in Urban Areas

The total allocation for housing for the urban poor has been grossly insufficient and must be increased substantially. It would be essential to improve the entire area covered by a slum rather than spend on individual hutments. If it is accepted that there is no ownership of property individually in a slum, then it gives scope for the authorities to easily prepare an integrated, socially inclusive colony covering the entire area.

The Commission has given due consideration to this complex issue and recommends that the following suggestions could be kept in view while preparing slum development policies or specific schemes:

(a) All projects for slum redevelopment must be finalised only after sufficient disclosure and discussion with the slum dwellers and their representatives. The felt needs of the beneficiaries must be noted and no top down enforcement approach should be adopted.

(b) The maximum possible floor area may be provided to the beneficiaries. The present limit of four floors on slum/poor housing reconstruction also needs to be reviewed.

(c) Only a small percentage of the land may be offered for profit-based development and all needs of public spaces must be built into the scheme. The facilities to be provided should include total sanitation, adequate water supply, and depending on factors such as space, location, population and proximity to existing facilities; schools, crèches, libraries, dispensaries, cultural activities centres, transport shelters and relevant civic offices.

(d) A small percentage of the cost of the dwelling unit can be met by the beneficiary.

Land Use Reservation for the Urban Poor

It has to be expected that further migration and population increase could create more slums. To avoid this, and to improve the housing stock for the poor, it is necessary to earmark and reserve a certain percentage of land in each town and city for the urban poor. This must be a part of the spatial planning process and must apply to all private developers as well. If a particular construction cannot allocate housing for the poor, the developer must, at his own cost, provide suitable housing in any other appropriate place acceptable to the authorities.

Shelter for Pavement Dwellers: Parallel to housing for slum dwellers, a part of all programmes must include housing for pavement dwellers. An immediate requirement would be construction of night shelters, which could be built by the State Governments and the civic bodies, and handed over to NGOs to run. A detailed programme needs to be drawn up in all cities, beginning with large cities having Metropolitan and Municipal Corporations for implementation.

Urban Planning

The Town and Country Planning Act (s)

It needs to be emphasised that urban planning can be conceptualised at three levels, at the level of a broad perspective plan for a large urban or urbanising area (usually called the master plan), at the level of zonal plans within that area (where the actual detailing of land use patterns is done) and the layout level (where the focus is on neighbourhoods and the linkages with infrastructure service networks become explicit). In the context of the 74th Amendment, the inference thus is that the DPCs and the MPCs have to do the function of preparing plans for the regional levels (master plan and zonal plans) while the layout plans have to be prepared by the local bodies (Panchayat and Municipalities / Corporations). The Commission has already made it clear that DPCs and MPCs should be the sole planning authorities for urban areas (and for bridging the rural-urban divide) in the country.

The Commission wishes to reiterate the imperative need to mainstream disaster specific concerns in the process of urban planning. Special attention is invited to the recommendation about making the National Building Code (NBC) available free of cost and to prepare pamphlets and handbooks on local building bye-laws etc. Making municipal building bye-laws, NBC complaint is an urgent need.

Mere drawing up of good spatial plans is not sufficient. Violations of the zoning regulations are common in our cities. The Commission is of the view that once the City Development Plan (CDP) is finalised, no authority should have any discretion to grant any exemption or waiver. The CDP should have a thirty-year perspective to be revised after every ten years through a participative and transparent process.

With land prices in cities soaring the tendency to encroach on public lands is very common. Such lands include water bodies, natural drains etc. Such encroachments also threaten the ecology of the region and aggravate the problems during any crisis or disasters. The municipal authorities should undertake a special drive to clear such encroachments. Responsibility should be fixed on officials in whose jurisdiction such encroachments take place.

Peri-urban Areas

Wherever townships including satellite towns have been set up by the development authorities, a clear cut time table for transfer of jurisdiction of these planned colonies from the development authorities to the concerned municipal bodies has to be ensured.

Private Townships

The new private housing colonies are not really in the direction of "private cities." They are much smaller and are only private or gated colonies. Apart from bulk receipt of services and utilities, they have no other contact with the local civic authorities. All internal maintenance is done by the developer. It is necessary that the establishment of these colonies must be allowed only within the broad parameters of the large regional urban planning process where the development plans must clearly indicate spaces for private expansion and integrated into the availability of water, sewerage etc. A part of the land must be earmarked for housing the poor who, in any case, would provide various services to the "township." With underground water becoming a fast depleting public resource, such townships which cater to the urban rich, need to be allowed with caution. Most importantly, the gated townships must be placed squarely under the jurisdiction of the concerned local body and be subordinate to their rules and laws.

Special Economic Zones (SEZs)

Local bodies should have full jurisdiction with regards to enforcement of local civic laws in the SEZs. A degree of autonomy for the SEZs to enable them to provide infrastructure and civic services in their areas would be desirable. Taxes raised by the local bodies from the SEZ area can be shared with the SEZ Management in lieu of civic amenities provided by them. By such an arrangement, the autonomy of SEZ is protected, the local government's authority is preserved without a drain on the revenues, and resources are mobilised to supplement local government revenues for building additional infrastructure required.

Urban Local Bodies and the State Government

The Commission is of the view that since local bodies (both urban and rural) constitute the third tier of governance, they must have full autonomy in the areas assigned to them. At the same time, it should also be the responsibility of the State Government to ensure that the local governments carry out their activities in accordance with law. But this should not translate into State Government exercising day-to-day control over the functioning of local governments. The powers of the State Government should be confined to a few items like suspension or cancellation of any resolution and dissolution or supercession, of the local body under special circumstances. But even such powers should be used sparingly and only after a report from the local body Ombudsman. In case of resolutions passed by the ULBs which are considered by the respective State Government to be beyond their purview or where the State Government is of the opinion that on grounds of absolute breakdown of the administrative machinery or financial bankruptcy or entrenched corruption etc. the ULB(s) needs to be dissolved or superseded, it should place the records before the local body Ombudsman concerned for investigation and appropriate recommendation.

Index